W9-CNC-669

THE PRINCETON REVIEW

Cracking the SSAT/ISEE

THE PRINCETON REVIEW

Cracking the SSAT/ISEE

by Liz Buffa, Elizabeth Silas, and Reed Talada

1999 EDITION

RANDOM HOUSE, INC.
NEW YORK 1998

www.randomhouse.com

Princeton Review Publishing, L.L.C.
2315 Broadway
New York, NY   10024
E-mail: info@review.com

Copyright © 1998 by Princeton Review Publishing, L.L.C.

All rights reserved under International and Pan-American Copyright Conventions.
Published in the United States by Random House, Inc., New York, and simultaneously in
Canada by Random House of Canada Limited, Toronto.

ISSN   1049–6238

ISBN   0–375–75168–8

Editor: Lesly Atlas
Designer: Illeny Maaza
Production Editor: James Petrozzello
Illustrations by: The Production Department of The Princeton Review

Manufactured in the United States of America on partially recycled paper.

9 8 7 6 5 4 3 2 1

1999 Edition

Contents

How Can I Help? A Parent's Introduction   vii

What Do I Do With This Book? A Student's Introduction   xi

1   **What's So Important About Vocabulary?**   **1**

PART I: THE SSAT   27

2   **Everything You Always Wanted to Know About the SSAT 29**

3   **SSAT Pacing**   **35**

4   **SSAT Math**   **45**

5   **SSAT Verbal**   **99**

6   **Answer Key to SSAT Drills**   **187**

PART II: SSAT PRACTICE TESTS   203

7   **Upper Level Test**   **213**

8   **Lower Level Test**   **239**

9   **Answer Keys**   **283**

10   **Scoring Your Practice SSAT**   **291**

PART III: THE ISEE   299

11   Everything You Always Wanted to Know About the ISEE 301

12:   ISEE Math   305

13   ISEE Verbal   359

14   Answer Key to ISEE Drills   443

PART IV: ISEE PRACTICE TESTS   459

15   Upper Level ISEE PracticeTest   463

16   Middle Level ISEE Practice Test   503

17   Answer Keys   555

18   Scoring Your Practice ISSE   565

     About the Authors   569

How Can I Help?

A PARENT'S INTRODUCTION

Congratulations! Your son or daughter is considering attending a private secondary school and, by virtue of the fact that you hold this book in your hands, you have recognized that either the SSAT or the ISEE is an important part of the admissions process. Providing your son or daughter with the information contained in this book is an excellent first step toward a strong performance on either the SSAT or the ISEE.

As a parent, though, you know well the tenuous line between support and intrusion. To guide you in your efforts to help your son or daughter, we offer a few suggestions:

Have a healthy perspective

Both the SSAT and the ISEE are standardized tests designed to say something about an individual student's chances for success in a private secondary school. Neither is an intelligence test; neither claims to be.

Try not to set your expectations too high, in spite of how well your son or daughter does in school. The skills necessary for strong performance on these tests are very different from those a student uses in school. The additional stress that comes from being "expected" to do well generally serves only to distract a student from taking a test efficiently. At the same time, beware of dismissing disappointing results with a simple "My child doesn't test well." While it is undoubtedly true that some students test better than others, this explanation does little to empower a student to invest time and effort in overcoming obstacles to improved performance.

Know how to interpret performance

Both the SSAT and the ISEE use the same test, for instance, to measure the performance of an eighth- and an eleventh-grade student. It is impossible to interpret scores without regard for the grade level of the student. Percentile rankings have much more value here than do either raw or scaled scores, and percentiles are the numbers schools use to compare students.

Be Informed

The SSAT and the ISEE are neither achievement nor intelligence tests. Your son or daughter needs to understand what is tested and how it is tested in order to score well.

Remember that this is not an English or a math test

There are both verbal and math questions on the SSAT and on the ISEE. However, these questions are often based on skills and concepts that are different from those used on a day-to-day basis in school. For instance, very few English teachers—at any level—spend a lot of time teaching students how to do analogies or sentence completion questions.

This may be frustrating for parents, for students, and for teachers. But in the final judgment, our educational system would take a turn for the worse if it attempted to teach students to do well on the SSAT, the ISEE, or even the SAT. The fact that the valuable skills students learn in school don't directly improve test scores is evidence of a flaw in the testing system, not an indictment of our schools or those who have devoted their professional careers to education.

Realize that all tests are different

Many of the general rules that students are accustomed to applying on tests in school do not apply to either the SSAT or the ISEE. Many students, for instance, actually hurt their scores by trying to answer every question. Although these are timed tests, accuracy is much more important than speed. Once your son or daughter learns the format and structure of these tests, she or he will find it easier to apply his or her knowledge to the test, and the result will be more correct answers.

Provide all the resources you can

This book has been written to provide your son or daughter with a very thorough review of all the math, vocabulary, reading, and writing skills that are necessary for success on the SSAT and ISEE. We have also included practice sections throughout the chapters and practice tests that we have written to simulate actual SSAT or ISEE examinations.

The very best SSAT practice questions, though, are naturally the ones written by SSATB, the organization that writes and administers the SSAT. The best ISEE questions come from the ERB, the folks whose job it is to write real ISEE questions. We encourage you to contact both these organizations (addresses and phone numbers can be found at the end of this section) to obtain any resources containing test questions that can be used for additional practice.

One word of caution: Be wary of other sources of SSAT or ISEE practice material. There are a number of test preparation books available (from companies other than The Princeton Review, of course) that are woefully outdated. The SSAT, for instance, changed in late 1997 when it introduced its writing sample. On top of major structural changes like this, both the SSAT and ISEE change with time in very subtle ways.

Make sure that whatever materials you choose are, to the greatest extent possible, reflective of the test your son or daughter will take, not one that was given years earlier. Also, try to avoid the inevitable confusion that comes from asking a student to follow two different sets of advice. Presumably, you have decided (or are about to decide) to trust The Princeton Review to prepare your son or daughter for this test. In doing so, you have made a wise decision. As we have said, we encourage you to provide any and all sources of additional practice material (as long as it is accurate and reflective of the current test), but providing other test preparation advice tends to muddy the waters and confuse students.

The Rules Have Changed

The SSAT, in particular, has changed dramatically. Make sure that the practice materials your son or daughter uses are up-to-date!

Be patient and be involved

Preparing for the SSAT or the ISEE is not entirely unlike riding a bicycle. You will watch your son or daughter struggle, at first, to develop a level of familiarity and comfort with the test, its format, and its content.

Developing the math, vocabulary, reading, and writing skills that your son or daughter will use on the SSAT or the ISEE is a long-term process. In addition to making certain that he or she is committed to spending the time necessary to work through the chapters of this book, you can also be on the lookout for other opportunities to be supportive. An easy way to do this is to make vocabulary development into a family activity: In the vocabulary chapters, we provide an extensive list of word parts and vocabulary words; learn them as a family, working through flash cards at the breakfast table or during car trips. Not only will you help your son or daughter, you may pick up a new word or two yourself!

A SHORT WORD ON ADMISSIONS

The most important insight into secondary school admissions that we can offer is that a student's score on the SSAT or the ISEE is only one of many components involved in the admissions decision. While many schools will request either SSAT or ISEE scores, all will take a serious look at your son or daughter's academic record. Think about it—which says more about one's nature as a student: a single test, or years of solid (or not so solid) academic performance?

In terms of testing, which is the focus of this book, some schools will specify which test they want applicants to take—the SSAT or the ISEE. Others will allow you to use scores from either test. If you are faced with a decision of whether to focus on the SSAT, the ISEE, or both, we encourage you to be an informed consumer. Call SSATB and ERB, the organizations that administer the tests, and find out as much as you can about the tests-what they measure, how this measurement is made, and how well they achieve their goals.

Another factor that you should consider is the volume of practice material available for each test. All else being equal, a test for which there are extensive practice materials available is easier to prepare for than one for which there are very few practice questions. Of course, if you do have to decide between the tests, this is only one factor to take into account.

Be An Informed Customer

Throughout the process, don't hesitate to call the schools to which your son or daughter may apply for the most accurate information about their admissions policies.

RESOURCES

Secondary School Admissions Testing Board (SSATB)
CN 5339
Princeton, NJ 08543
Phone: (609) 683-4440
Fax: (609) 683-1702
Internet: http://www.ssat.org

Educational Records Bureau (ERB)
345 East 47th Street
New York, NY 10017
Phone: (800) 989-3721
Internet: http://www.erb-test.com/isee.html

What Do I Do With This Book?

A STUDENT'S INTRODUCTION

You've got a hefty amount of paper and information in your hands. How can you work through it thoroughly, without spending eight hours on it the Saturday before the test?

Plan ahead.

We've broken down the contents of this book and suggested a timeline for you to follow in order to work through it all thoroughly. You may want to break the sessions into even smaller chunks of time. You may want to do one, two, or three sessions a week, but we suggest you give yourself at least a day in between each session to absorb the information you've just learned. The one thing you should be doing every day is quizzing yourself on vocabulary and making new index cards.

Also, don't think that you can work through this book during summer vacation, put it aside in September, and then be ready to take the test in December. If you want to start that early, work primarily on vocabulary until about ten weeks before the test. Then you can start on techniques, and they'll be fresh in your mind on the day of the test. If you've finished your preparation too soon and have nothing to practice on in the weeks before the test, you're going to get rusty.

If you know you are significantly weaker in one of the subjects covered by the test, you should begin with that subject so that you can practice it throughout your preparation.

If You Want to Start Early

If you have more than 10 weeks to prepare, start with vocabulary building and essay writing. These skills only get better with time.

AT EACH SESSION

At each session, have sharpened pencils, a pen, blank index cards, and a dictionary. Each chapter is interactive; to understand fully the techniques we present, you need to be ready to try them out.

Get Your Pencil Moving

You'll get the most out of this book by trying techniques out as you read about them.

As you read each chapter, try out the techniques and do all the exercises. Check your answers in the Answer Key as you do each set of problems, and try to figure out what types of errors you made, in order to correct them. Review any techniques that are giving you trouble.

As you begin each session, review the chapter you did at the previous session before moving on to the new chapter.

When You Take a Practice Test

You'll see in the timelines below when to take practice tests. Some guidelines for taking these tests:

◆ Time yourself strictly. Use a timer, watch, or stopwatch that will ring, and do not allow yourself to go overtime for any section. If you try to do so at the real test, your scores will probably be canceled.

◆ Take a practice test in one sitting, allowing yourself breaks of no more than two minutes between sections. You need to build up your endurance for the real test, and you also need an accurate picture of how you will do.

◆ Always take a practice test using an answer sheet with bubbles to fill in, just as you will for the real test. You need to be comfortable transferring answers to the separate sheet, because you will be skipping around a bit.

◆ We won't bore you with the mechanics of how to correctly fill in answer sheet bubbles; suffice it to say that each bubble you choose should be filled in thoroughly, and no other marks should be made in the answer area.

◆ As you fill in the bubble for a question, check to be sure that you are on the right number on the answer sheet. If you fill in the wrong bubble on the answer sheet, it won't matter if you've worked out the problem correctly in your test booklet. All that matters to the machine scoring your test is the Number 2 pencil mark.

If You're Taking the SSAT

SESSION ONE

◆ Read the Vocabulary chapter (chapter 1). Complete the initial exercises and do word webs for Groups 1, 2, and 3. Start working with index cards, and plan out how you're going to work on your vocabulary every day.

◆ Read "Everything You Always Wanted to Know About the SSAT" (chapter 2).

SESSION TWO

◆ Take the practice SSAT in this book (either Lower or Upper Level). Score it and look at the Pacing chapter (chapter 3) to determine your target score for the next practice test.

◆ If you have not done so already, contact SSATB at (609) 683-4440, or http://www.ssat.org, to obtain a practice SSAT to use toward the end of your preparation. If you are unable to get a practice test from SSATB, then save the one in this book to use when you're done with the SSAT chapters, and try to judge your target score by asking the schools you are applying to what their average scores are for incoming students.

SESSION THREE

◆ SSAT Math: Introduction

◆ SSAT Math: Fundamentals

◆ Vocabulary: Group 4 and Hit Parade "Attempting To Be Funny" and "Let's Get Together (UL)"

SESSION FOUR

◆ SSAT Verbal: Introduction

◆ SSAT Verbal: Analogies

◆ Vocabulary: Groups 5 and 6 and Hit Parade "Make It Official"

SESSION FIVE

◆ SSAT Math: Algebra

◆ Vocabulary: Group 7 and Hit Parade "Hard to Handle" and "Hard to Handle (UL)"

SESSION SIX

◆ SSAT Verbal: Synonyms

◆ Vocabulary: Groups 8 and 9 and Hit Parade "The Perfect Mate" and "The Perfect Mate (UL)"

SESSION SEVEN

◆ SSAT Math: Geometry

◆ Vocabulary: Group 10 and Hit Parade "You Don't Want to Know This Guy"

SESSION EIGHT

◆ SSAT Reading

◆ Vocabulary: Group 11 and Hit Parade "You Don't Want to Know This Guy (UL)"

SESSION NINE

- ◆ SSAT Math: Charts & Graphs
- ◆ Vocabulary: Group 12 and Hit Parade "A Bad Scene"

SESSION TEN

- ◆ SSAT Writing Sample
- ◆ Vocabulary: Group 13 and Hit Parade "A Bad Scene (UL)"

SESSION ELEVEN

- ◆ Take another practice SSAT, preferably an actual released test that you've obtained from the SSAT Board. If you are working from their booklet, "Preparing and Applying," take Practice Test I timed, and score it. (Use Practice Test II as additional untimed practice questions, if you have extra time.)

- ◆ If there are questions still giving you trouble, review the appropriate chapters.

If You're Taking the ISEE

SESSION ONE

- ◆ Read the Vocabulary chapter (chapter 1). Complete the initial exercises and do word webs for Groups 1, 2, and 3. Start working with index cards, and plan out how you're going to work on your vocabulary every day.

- ◆ Read "Everything You Always Wanted to Know About the ISEE" (chapter 11).

- ◆ If you have not done so already, contact the Educational Records Bureau at (800) 989-3721, or http://www.erb-test.com, to obtain any practice materials available to supplement your preparation.

SESSION TWO

- ◆ ISEE Math: Introduction
- ◆ ISEE Math: Fundamentals
- ◆ Vocabulary: Group 4 and Hit Parade "Attempting To Be Funny" and "Let's Get Together (UL)"

SESSION THREE

- ◆ ISEE Verbal: Introduction
- ◆ ISEE Verbal: Synonyms
- ◆ Vocabulary: Groups 5 and 6 and Hit Parade "Make It Official"

SESSION FOUR

- ISEE Math: Algebra

- Vocabulary: Group 7 and Hit Parade "Hard to Handle" and "Hard to Handle (UL)"

SESSION FIVE

- ISEE Verbal: Sentence Completions

- Vocabulary: Groups 8 and 9 and Hit Parade "The Perfect Mate" and "The Perfect Mate (UL)"

SESSION SIX

- ISEE Math: Geometry

- Vocabulary: Group 10 and Hit Parade "You Don't Want to Know This Guy"

SESSION SEVEN

- ISEE Reading

- Vocabulary: Group 11 and Hit Parade "You Don't Want to Know This Guy (UL)"

SESSION EIGHT

- ISEE Math: Charts & Graphs

- Vocabulary: Group 12 and Hit Parade "A Bad Scene"

SESSION NINE

- ISEE Essay

- Vocabulary: Group 13 and Hit Parade "A Bad Scene (UL)"

SESSION TEN

- ISEE Math: Quantitative Comparison

SESSION ELEVEN

- Take the practice ISEE contained in this book (Middle or Upper Level).

- If there are questions still giving you trouble, review the appropriate chapters.

THE DAY OF THE EXAM

◆ Wake up refreshed from at least eight hours' sleep the night before.

◆ Eat a good breakfast.

◆ Arrive at the test center about a half-hour early.

◆ Have with you all the necessary paperwork that shows you have registered for the test, four No. 2 pencils with erasers, and a working black pen. You may also want to bring juice or water, and a quick snack like a granola bar. The test center may not allow you to bring food or beverages into the room, but you can leave them in the hall, and you may have a chance to get to them during a short break. Do not bring any books, papers, or calculators.

◆ Remind yourself that you do not have to finish the test to get a good score. Don't let yourself become rushed. Pace yourself.

1

What's So Important About Vocabulary?

Isn't This Book Supposed to Teach me How to Crack the Test?

You're going to learn lots of ways to get verbal questions right when you don't know the exact definitions of the words involved. However, the fastest and most accurate way to answer questions is still to know the words from the start! So while you need to use the techniques you'll be learning to answer questions (especially the difficult ones), your goal in working through vocabulary is to increase the number of questions that seem easy to you.

Take It Easy

The easiest way to get any question right is to know all the words in it!

Learning new words along with the techniques to answer questions will increase your SSAT or ISEE scores much more than just learning the techniques alone. Vocabulary is very important to your verbal score, and it also affects your reading score.

And hey, you'll even be able to argue and speak more persuasively with your parents and friends. Many parts of your SSAT or ISEE preparation will help you with future standardized tests (the PSAT and SAT, for instance), but only the vocabulary is actually useful in everyday life!

Where do I Find New Words?

Your SSAT and ISEE preparation materials

The **Hit Parade**, in this chapter, is a list of words that are at the level of vocabulary tested on the SSAT and ISEE. The words are found on released SSATs, and they're a good place to start your vocabulary work. Make sure you know all these words—test writers are not terribly original, so they often recycle words from old tests.

The section on **Word Parts** (prefixes, roots, and suffixes) in this chapter is excellent for learning the pieces of words that show up again and again in difficult vocabulary. The best way to learn the meaning of a word part is by thinking of the words that you already know that contain it. Then you can stretch this group of words to include new ones. If you learn words this way, you're more likely to remember them, since you've linked them to stuff you already know.

The **Verbal and Reading chapters** have practice questions, many of which contain difficult words. Do the problems without looking anything up, circling the words you're not sure of. Write the circled words on cards, and look them up after you're done.

Everywhere else

Newspapers, magazines, books, people, even television—all are sources of new words for you. Once you become aware of how many new words are right around you, you'll quickly be able to pick them out and make them your own.

You hear and read words you don't know all the time. How do you keep from running to the dictionary every hour? You figure out what the word means from *context*—the other words around it.

Steve had nervous tics that exposed his anxiety at inconvenient times—during an oral report, one or another of his appendages might start twitching uncontrollably.

What do you think an "appendage" is? _body part_____

How about a "tic"? _____

Now look these words up in a dictionary:

appendage: _____

tic: _____

How close were you? If you figured the author meant "parts of the body" when she wrote "appendages," you were right, and you understood the sentence. But notice that the main dictionary definition of "appendage" is different. Next time you see this word, it may refer to something else—not just a body part.

The SSAT and ISEE test dictionary definitions of words, so assuming that you know a word's definition just because you've seen a word before can be danger-ous. Get a dictionary, put it on your desk, and use it. If you're reading something at school and you see a new word, write it down, along with what you think it means from context, and look it up when you get home.

Choose a newspaper or magazine that your parents or older siblings read, or just pick one up yourself. Read a few articles from it each week, keeping the dictionary nearby. If you didn't have to use the dictionary the first week, change your periodical! The Op-Ed pages of major newspapers, as well as science and humanities journals, are also good places to start.

If you're starting way ahead of your scheduled test date, or if you want to continue learning new words and making it easier to do so, you may want to look at these **other books**:

Word Power Made Easy by Norman Lewis
Word Smart and *Word Smart II* by Adam Robinson and the Staff of The Princeton Review

You can also check out some of the **web sites** below for word games and good new vocabulary:

◆ http://www.m-w.com/info/vocab/vocab.htm

◆ http://www.m-w.com/game

◆ http://english.glendale.cc.ca.us/roots.html

◆ http://www.syndicate.com and http://www.vocabulary.com

(These are provided for reference only, and neither they nor any products advertised therein are endorsed by The Princeton Review or the authors of this book.)

How Do I Remember What They Actually Mean?

Looking up a new word is only your first step. The next step is even more important: writing it down.

If you write down words and definitions in a list and then read them over periodically, you'll remember a few of them. But why go to all that trouble looking them up if you're not able to remember most of them afterwards? You need a better way to be sure your vocabulary time isn't wasted.

Here it is: **Make a separate index card for each word**. Yes, flashcards are old news—you've probably used them to study for a test, or to learn a foreign language. Here's how to make them really useful:

- **Have blank cards nearby** whenever you read. Stash some in your bookbag so they're always handy. When you see a word you don't know very well, write it down on one side of the card. Scribble down the sentence or phrase in which you read it or heard it. You can also make a guess at what it means.

- When you get to your dictionary, **write down the definition(s)** you find on the other side of the card.

- Now you need to **associate the word with what you already know**. There are several ways you can do this, and you can use whichever ones work best for you and for the particular word you're learning. You can:

  - **Make up a sentence using the word that connects it** to someone or something you know. If you're trying to remember "banal" and your friend Jeff seems never to have anything original to say, make a sentence for "banal" that stars Jeff.

  - **Draw a picture** to show the meaning. If you're trying to remember "mosaic," sketch tiles laid out in a pattern or picture. To make it more memorable, make the picture funny.

  - **Make up a sentence or phrase that is a mnemonic.** A mnemonic uses the way the word sounds along with its definition to jog your memory. If you want to be sure that you remember that "laud" means "to praise and acclaim," you can imagine a whole congregation proclaiming, "Praise the Laud!" The funnier your mnemonic, the faster you'll remember it when you see the word again.

  - **Write down the word parts that make up the word** you want to remember. In good dictionaries, the roots and prefixes that are found in a word are right in its entry, after the pronunciation and part of speech. If you're making a card for "benevolent," write down "bene—good," and write down other "bene" words you know well—"benefit" and "beneficial." Then group those cards together, and add to them any other "bene" words you come across.

- **Group your cards** by their general definitions—if you've got many cards with words that are bad character traits on them, put those together.

- **Go through your cards weekly** to make sure you remember the meanings. Once you've gotten a card right several times in a row, you may want to put it aside in a separate pile that contains "Words I Definitely Know." You can also take a small stack with you to test yourself whenever you're in the car or on the bus.

- **Have your parents quiz you** with the flashcards.

- **Try this new lexicon out** on your parents and friends! You'll be able to get your point across faster and more accurately with precise verbiage.

- **Be sure to have blank cards handy to write down new words you come across when working in this book.**

cogent
'a cogent argument'

convincing
relevant
having power to compel or constrain

co- together
agere- to drive or act (like in 'agent')

The poet <u>convinced</u> me when he said
'Do not <u>cogent</u>-ly into that good night.'

VOCABULARY-BUILDING PLAN:

List all the types of places we've mentioned so far where you're going to be on the lookout for new vocabulary words, and add any that you think of. Get as specific as you can.

_____   _____   _____

_____   _____   _____

_____   _____   _____

_____   _____   _____

As you come upon each new word (in any of the places you've listed), you're going to do more than just write it down and look at it every now and then. You're going to grab it, hold it up to the light, examine it, chew on it for a while, and digest it, making sure that it becomes part of what you know. How are you going to do this? How are you going to make these words your own? Write down all the ways we've suggested in this section, and add any methods that have helped you learn new things in the past.

_____

_____

_____

_____

_____

_____

WORD PARTS

Suffixes

The suffix (the end part of a word) can often tell you what part of speech a word is. Let's quickly review the most basic parts of speech, or look them up in a good dictionary:

What is a noun? _____

What is a verb? _____

What is an adjective? _____

What is an adverb? _____

Look at the following suffixes and examples, and add some words of your own that end in each suffix. Then look at all the words that end in that suffix—which parts of speech are they? Check your answers in the Word Parts Index at the end of this chapter.

-ness: happiness, friendliness _____

-able: perishable, amiable _____

-ous: androgynous, fibrous _____

-ity: animosity, charity _____

-ology: psychology, sociology _____

-ical: tyrannical, hypothetical _____

-archy: monarchy, anarchy, matriarchy _____

-less: fearless, artless _____

Prefixes and roots

Prefixes come at the beginning of a word, and roots can be anywhere in a word. Both types of word parts are very helpful in trying to remember words that are new to you. For example, say you come upon the word "vociferous" (voh-SIF-uh-rus). You make a card for it, and then you try to think of other words that have that same root, "voc." "Vocal" is a word you know has to do with speaking, and so now when you see "vociferous" again, you'll remember it has to do with speaking. If you always imagine "vociferous" being shouted, you'll remember the rest of its meaning: *loud and insistent* in speaking."

Notice that the sound of "voc" is not the same in "vociferous" as it is in "vocal." Word parts change their sound over time, and most of the words you'll be learning have been around for hundreds of years. Not only do the sounds change, but the meanings also mutate over time, so today's meaning of a word is sometimes far different from the sum of its word parts. Thus, these word parts are to be used to help you remember and group new vocabulary (there's that "voc" again, in a word that has to do with speaking), and not as a substitute for looking up words.

The word parts on each page of this section can be linked together by means of the words that contain them. This is a great way to think about words in general—they're linked by their word parts, and there are so many links crisscrossing that the connections build a web:

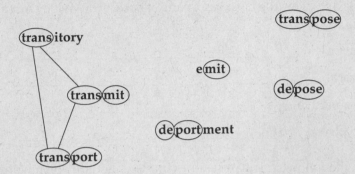

And that's only seven words!

Using the Word Web Pages

On each page in this section, you'll find word parts on the top, and words on the bottom. Here's how to use the pages:

1. Start with one of the words from the bottom of the page. Write it in the center. Circle the word parts it contains.

2. Now choose another word from the list that contains a matching word part. Write that word out, circling any word parts it contains, and draw a line between the parts that match in each word.

3. Repeat this step until you have linked all the words that were on the bottom of the page, making a web like the one we just saw.

4. As you come across a word you don't know, look it up and make an index card for it. There will be lots of words you don't know on these pages. When you look up these words, remember that the word parts and their meanings are at the beginning of the dictionary entries.

5. Now look at the word parts at the top of the page. On the first line under each word part, write down what you think it means, from the words you've seen. Check this in the root index. The index has abbreviated versions of what each root means. Don't be discouraged if you don't guess correctly at the meaning every time; you may be closer than you think, since some word parts have wider meanings than just those we've included.

5. On the second line under each word part, write a word of your own that contains it. You may also want to add your word to the web you drew.

Group 1

ROOT	chron	a	morph	path
meaning				
your word				
ROOT	anti	par	dis	dign/dain
meaning				
your word				

synchronize	chronicle	anachronism	amoral
apathy	apartheid	amorphous	metamorphosis
sympathy	empathy	pathos	antipathy
parity	disparate	dissociate	disparity
disperse	dissuade	dissipate	dignify
deign	disdain		

Group 2

ROOT	mis	gyn	phobe
meaning			
your word			
ROOT	phil	techn	anthr/andr
meaning			
your word			

miscreant	misanthrope	mistake	anthropology
philanthropy	androgynous	misogyny	philosophy
technophile	technophobe	technology	technique

Group 3

ROOT	sub	terr	vers/vert
meaning			
your word			
ROOT	extr	super	sed
meaning			
your word			

substantiate	subterranean	subordinate	terrestrial
terrarium	subvert	advertise	extrovert
traverse	extraterrestrial	extrapolate	supervise
superimpose	supersede	sediment	sedate
subside	subservient	introvert	

Group 4

ROOT	vor	carn	in/en/im/em	tract
meaning				
your word				
ROOT	ante	bell	am	nat/nas/nai
meaning				
your word				
ROOT	omni	pot	scient/scienc	pre
meaning				
your word				

voracious	devour	carnivorous	carnage
incarnation	infiltrate	input	inject
ingratiate	incarnate	intractable	protract
tractor	antecedent	antebellum	rebel
belligerent	bellicose	enamored	amorous
amity	amicable	innate	nascent
naï ve	natal	native	renaissance
omnivorous	omniscient	omnipotent	potential
potent	potentate	prescience	preface
prefix	predestine		

Group 5

ROOT	amb	re	spec/spic	post
meaning				
your word				
ROOT	circ/circum	ven/vent	scrib/script	man
meaning				
your word				

ambitious	amble	circumambulate	circumscribe
circumvent	circumspect	redo	repudiate
recirculate	convene	intervene	inspect
auspicious	transcribe	manuscript	postpone
postscript	manual	manufacture	manifest

Group 6

ROOT	uni	anim	equi/equ	ad/at
meaning				
your word				
ROOT	voc	magna	loc/loq/log	neo/nov
meaning				
your word				

unified	unanimous	animosity	magnanimous
equitable	equilibrium	iniquity	equanimity
equivocate	attract	adhere	advocate
vociferous	vocal	convoke	magnificent
magniloquent	eloquent	loquacious	circumlocution
neologism	novice	innovate	neophyte

Group 7

ROOT	epi	hyper	hypo	derm
meaning				
your word				
ROOT	dem	tens/ten	pan	
meaning				
your word				

epilogue	epithet	hypertension	hypodermic
epidermis	dermatologist	tensile	tenuous
epidemic	democracy	demographics	pandemic
panorama			

Group 8

ROOT	eu	phon	dys	bene
meaning				
your word				
ROOT	dic	mal	fac	fic/fig
meaning				
your word				

euphoria	euphemism	eulogy	euphony
utopia	megaphone	cacophony	dystopia
dyslexia	benefit	beneficent	benevolent
benediction	benign	dictionary	dictation
contradict	malediction	malevolent	malicious
malign	maleficent	malodorous	facile
factory	malefactor	manufacture	deficient
proficient	prolific	effigy	soporific

Group 9

ROOT	ex/ej	clu/clo/cla	cis
meaning			
your word			
ROOT	culp	ten	ac/acr
meaning			
your word			

exit	eject	exculpate	excise
exclusive	preclude	cloister	foreclose
recluse	scissors	incisive	concise
culprit	culpable	extenuate	tenable
tentative	tenacious	acrid	acerbic
acumen	exacerbate	acrimonious	

Group 10

ROOT	co/com/con	cur/cour	her/hes	sequ/secu
meaning				
your word				
ROOT	tact	gen	homo	nom/nym
meaning				
your word				
ROOT	hetero	fid	vi/viv	vid/vis
meaning				
your word				

confide	convivial	cogent	concurrent
convoke	cursory	current	precursor
incur	coherent	cohesive	inherent
consequently	consecutive	tactile	contact
genesis	congenial	progeny	homogenous
homonym	synonym	anonymous	pseudonym
misnomer	ignominy	heterogenous	heterodox
fidelity	infidel	bona fide	diffident
perfidy	fiduciary	vivacious	viable
vivid	vivisection	vista	evident
video	visage	supervise	

Group 11

ROOT	bi	di	ab/abs
meaning			
your word			
ROOT	ad/at	us/ut	ob
meaning			
your word			

bipartisan	bicycle	bisect	dichotomy
digress	diaphanous	divide	dissect
abhor	abdicate	abscond	abstain
attract	adjacent	advocate	abuse
utilitarian	utilize	obstinate	obviate
obscure			

Group 12

ROOT	in/il/im/ir	un/non	cred	mut
meaning				
your word				
ROOT	pun/pen	apt/ept	plac	
meaning				
your word				

illegible	incredible	irresponsible	improper
unusual	nonsense	credible	credence
immutable	permutation	impunity	penalty
punitive	penance	adapt	apt
inept	adept	implacable	placid
placate			

Group 13

ROOT	pro	cli	inter	intra
meaning				
your word				
ROOT	pon/pos	de	port	trans
meaning				
your word				
ROOT	mit/mis	luc/lum	esce	
meaning				
your word				

propose	produce	recline	proclivity
disinclination	interject	interpose	interlude
intervene	intravenous	transpose	deposit
depose	deport	decipher	defame
deportment	purport	portfolio	transitory
transport	translucent	transmit	emissary
missive	remission	demise	emit
luminescent	illustrious	lucid	lackluster
elucidate	obsolescent	coalesce	quiescent
acquiescent			

HIT PARADE

The following vocabulary is from released SSATs. These words give you an idea of the level of difficulty of SSAT and ISEE words, and they're likely to appear on future tests, as well. The definitions included with them are the ones tested on the SSAT; for additional nuances and secondary meanings, consult a dictionary. Unfortunately, the ISEE has not released any practice tests, so these words are all from SSATs, but the level of vocabulary is similar on both tests.

Some words are followed by relevant roots, prefixes, and/or suffixes, or a more familiar variant of the word. These are provided in parentheses for you to use on your index cards.

Index Cards

Go back to the first part of this chapter for ways to use index cards creatively and effectively.

Go through the Hit Parade with one hand covering the definitions, trying to define each word. If you can't get one, it goes on an index card. Lower Level and Middle Level students do not have to know the words marked UL, but they may want to learn them anyway. Upper Level students must know all the words on the list.

Attempting to be funny

irony	the use of words to express the opposite of their literal meaning, *or* a situation that is not what is expected
jest	to joke (court jester)
skit	a short comic scene

Let's get together (UL)

rendezvous	a meeting, usually secret
contiguous	lying side-by-side (con)
fusion	a joining together
fission	a splitting apart
coalesce	to come together (esce)
adjunct	an accessory, something added on (ad+junc/join)
akin	related to *or* just like

Make it official

decree	to command
ratify	to approve, usually a law
assess	to size up, determine the value
procure	to obtain, get (pro)
counsel	to advise
debunk	to prove false

Hard to handle

amorphous	without shape (a+morph+ous)
alleged	supposedly true
writhe	to twist
kinetic	moving
itinerant	nomadic, constantly moving
intangible	not able to be touched or sensed (in+ten+able)

Hard to handle (UL)

polymorphous   having many shapes (poly+morph+ous)
variegated   having many parts or colors
epoch   a period of time
egress   exit

The perfect mate

ingenuity   inventiveness (gen)
congenial   agreeable (con+gen)
adept   skillful
jubilant   joyful
sustain   to keep alive
equivalent   equal (equi)

The perfect mate (UL)

altruistic   doing good for others
benevolence   goodness (bene)
astute   sharp, shrewd
aspirant   someone reaching for something (aspirations)
placate   to quiet down, appease (plac)

You don't want to know this guy

deficient   lacking
brash   bold
irate   enraged
warlock   male witch
abdicate   to give up authority or power (ab)
recalcitrant   disobedient
insolent   disrespectful, rude
brusque   short in speech, to the point of rudeness
debilitating   weakening, harmful (de)
jeer   to make fun of
conventional   traditional, ordinary (con+vent)
animosity   hostility (anim+ity)

You don't want to know this guy (UL)

sanctimonious   acting morally superior, holier-than-thou
incompetent   not able to do something properly (in)
pedantic   overly scholarly, boring
pugnacious   hostile
choleric   irritable
belligerent   hostile, warlike (bell)
browbeat   to intimidate
garrulous   overly talkative
ravenous   extremely hungry
aloof   keeping a distance
corpulent   excessively overweight (corp)

ostentatious	showy
banal	unoriginal and boring
insipid	lacking flavor or interest (in)

A bad scene

hovel	a shack
brig	the prison of a ship
barrage	a flood
plight	a predicament, a bad situation
abyss	a deep narrow pit
quiver	a portable container for arrows
rue	to regret
indictment	the situation of having been charged with a crime (dic)

A bad scene (UL)

founder	to sink ("A boat *founders*")
mar	to spoil, to mark
null	zero value ("*null* and void")
repudiate	to renounce, put down
adverse	unfavorable, opposed, going against (ad+vers)
insinuation	a sneaky suggestion of something bad
assailable	vulnerable (able)
impasse	a deadlock, a point at which one can go no further

WORD PARTS INDEX

The meaning of each word part listed below is a much-abbreviated version of a long historical chain of meanings. For more information about any of these roots, consult a Latin and Greek Root Dictionary.

Suffixes

X-able	adjective "able to be Xed"
X-archy	noun "rulership by X"
X-ical	adjective "characterized by X"
X-ity	noun "condition or state of being X"
X-less	adjective "without X"
X-ness	noun "quality of being X"
X-ology	noun "doctrine or theory of X" (originally "word of X")
X-ous	adjective "having the quality of X"

Prefixes and roots

a	without
ab/abs	away from
ac/acr	sharp
ad/at	to, toward
am	to love
amb	to go, to walk
anim	life, spirit
ante	after

anthr/andr	man
anti	against
apt/ept	skill, ability
bell	war
bene	good
bi	two
carn	flesh
chron	time
circ/circum	around
cis	to cut
cli	to lean
clu/clo/cla	to close, shut
co/com/con	with, together
cred	believe
culp	blame
cur/cour	to run (a course)
de	away from, the opposite of
dem	people
di	apart, through
dic	to say, to tell
dign/dain	worth
dis	apart, away from, not
dys	faulty, bad
epi	upon
equi/equ	equal
esce	to become
eu	good, pleasing
ex/ej	out, put out
extr	outside, beyond
fac	to make, to do
fic/fig	to make, to do
fid	faith, trust
gen	birth, creation, kind
gyn	woman
her/hes	to stick
hetero	different
homo	same
hyper	over
hypo	under
in/il/im/ir	not
in/en/im/em	into
inter	between, among
intra	within
loc/loq/log	to speak
luc/lum	light
magna	great, big
mal	bad

man	hand
mis	wrong, bad
mit/mis	to send
morph	shape
mut	change
nat/nas/nai	to be born
neo/nov	new
nom/nym	name
ob	against, in front of
omni	all, every
pan	all, everywhere
par	equal
path	feeling
phil	love of
phobe	fear of
phon	sound
plac	to please
pon/pos	place, put
port	to carry
post	after
pot	power
pre	before
pro	forward, supporting
pun/pen	to pay, compensate
re	again, back
scient/scienc	knowledge
scrib/script	to write
sed/sid	to sit, be still
sequ/secu	to follow
spec	to look, appear
sub	under, less than
super	over, greater than
tact	touch
techn	tools
ten	to hold
tens/ten	to stretch
terr	earth
trans	across
tract	to drag, pull, draw
un/non	not
uni	one
us/ut	to use
ven/vent	come
vers/vert	to turn
vi/viv	life
vid/vis	to see
voc	to call
vor	to eat

PART I

The SSAT

2

Everything You Always Wanted to Know About the SSAT

THE FIRST STEP

Before you begin to think about preparing for the SSAT, you must complete one essential first step: *Sign up for the SSAT*. The test is administered seven times every year—generally in November, December, January, February, March, April, and June. Once you decide which test date you prefer, we encourage you to register as soon as possible. Testing sites can fill up; and by registering early, you will avoid the possibility of having to take the test at an inconvenient or unfamiliar second-choice location. To receive a registration form, call the Secondary School Admission Test Board (SSATB) at (609) 683-4440.

Plan Ahead

Early registration will not only give you one fewer thing to worry about as the test approaches, but it will also help you get your first choice test center.

The regular registration deadline for the test (at U.S. testing centers) is usually three weeks before the test date. You may return the registration form by mail along with the $60 registration fee for test centers in the United States and Canada (or $110 for international test centers), or for an extra $5, you may submit your registration form by fax or over the Internet (http://www.ssat.org).

If you forget to register for the test or decide to take the SSAT at the last minute, there is a late registration deadline, usually two weeks before the test date (for U.S. testing centers). If you still have at least two weeks, you can register late by either fax or Internet and pay a $20 late registration fee.

Even if you miss the late registration deadline, you can be a "walk-in" for the test. To do this, call SSATB to find the specific location of the test center and go there on the test day. Make sure you arrive early, as walk-ins are accepted on a space-available basis. If you have your completed registration form and all the necessary fees, including the $40 walk-in fee, you will be allowed to take the test. Remember, though, that there is no guarantee that you will be able to walk in to the test, so register in advance if you can. Not only is it less stressful to have a guarantee that you'll be allowed to take the test, but it will save you all those extra fees, too!

WHAT IS THE SSAT?

The Secondary School Admission Test (SSAT) is a standardized test made up of a writing sample, which is not scored, but rather sent along with each score report, and a series of multiple-choice questions divided into quantitative (math), verbal, and reading comprehension sections. The entire test lasts about 150 minutes, during which you will work on six different sections:

Quantitative	25 Questions	25 Minutes
Verbal	60 Questions	25 Minutes
Reading Comprehension	40 Questions	25 Minutes
Quantitative (a second section)	25 Questions	25 Minutes
Experimental (ungraded)	25-60 Questions	25 Minutes
Writing Sample (ungraded)	1 Essay Topic	25 Minutes

Keep in mind that the sections will not necessarily appear in this order. The Writing Sample can come either before or after the multiple-choice sections, and within the multiple-choice portion of the test, the sections can appear in any order.

There are three different types of sections on the SSAT: verbal, reading, and quantitative (or math). You will receive four scores on the test, though. Not only will you get a score for each of these three sections, but your score report will also show an overall score, which is a combination of your verbal and quantitative scores. Reading Comprehension is not included in the computation of your "overall" score.

UPPER VS. LOWER LEVEL

There are two different versions of the SSAT. The Lower Level test is taken by students who are, at the time of testing, in the fifth, sixth, and seventh grades. The Upper Level test is for students who take the test during the eighth, ninth, tenth, and eleventh grades.

The primary difference between the Upper and Lower Level tests is their scale. The Upper Level test gives a student four scaled scores ranging from 250 on the low end to 350 at the top. Scores on the Lower Level test range from 230 to 320. There are also some small differences in content; for instance, vocabulary on the Lower Level test is less challenging than it is on the Upper Level test. In math, you will see similar general concepts tested (arithmetic, algebra, geometry, charts, and graphs) on both tests, but naturally the Lower Level test will ask slightly easier questions than the Upper Level test.

As you work through this book, you will notice that sets of practice problems do not distinguish between Upper and Lower questions. Instead you will find practice sets that generally increase in difficulty as you move from earlier to later questions. Therefore, if you are taking the Lower Level test, don't worry if you have trouble with some of the later questions.

WHAT IS AN EXPERIMENTAL SECTION?

The SSAT's experimental section will look just like one of the other sections—quantitative, verbal, or reading comprehension. You will not know which section of your test is experimental. The only difference between this and a real section of the test is that the experimental section will not count toward your final score. The data from the experimental section is used by SSATB to test new questions to determine how they will be used on future administrations of the SSAT. Is this fair to you? No, it probably isn't. It is a fact, though, so when you take the SSAT, you should always keep in mind that one section doesn't count. If you find yourself struggling with a part of the test, you should always do the best you can, but when you finish, put your pencil down and say, "OK, that one was experimental." Don't ever let one rough section get you down.

PACING

Most people believe that in order to do well on a test, it is important to answer every question. While this is true of most of the tests you take in school, it is not true of many standardized tests, including the SSAT. On this test, it is very possible to score well without answering all of the questions; in fact, many students can improve their scores by answering fewer questions.

Don't Try to Finish

Depending on your goals, you may not need to finish each section. Trying to do too many questions can hurt your score. Be sure to use the pacing chapter.

Wait a second. I can get a better score by doing less work? Yes. The reason for this is that in their effort to answer all the questions, many students spend very little time on easy questions and make careless errors. They then spend more of their time on harder questions that they are likely to answer incorrectly anyway. An easy question is worth just as many points as a hard one, so slow down. Answer fewer questions, but get more of the questions that you do answer right. If you don't finish the test, that's fine, because by working slowly and carefully you get more points than you would have by rushing to answer more questions.

PROCESS OF ELIMINATION

What is the capital of Malawi?

(A) New York   (B) Paris
(C) London   (D) Lilongwe
(E) Washington, DC

There are two ways to get this question right. First, you can know that the capital of Malawi is Lilongwe. If you do, good for you! The second is to know that the capital of Malawi is not New York, Paris, London, or Washington, DC. You don't get more points for knowing the right answer from the start, so one way is just as good as the other. Try to get in the habit of looking at a question and asking, "What are the wrong answers?" instead of "What is the right answer?"

By using the Process of Elimination (or P.O.E.) this way, you will eliminate wrong answers and then have fewer answers from which to pick. The result is that you will pick right answers more often.

GUESSING

The SSAT has a component in its scoring called a guessing penalty—the $\frac{1}{4}$ point that is deducted from your raw score for each wrong answer. This so-called penalty is really not a penalty at all. Each question on the test has five possible answers. It follows that if a student guessed randomly, she would guess the correct answer one time out of five. Think about the math—plus one point for the one right answer, minus four times $\frac{1}{4}$ for the four wrong answers. In the end

Should I Guess?

Random guessing will not improve your SSAT score. Educated guessing, though, is always a good idea.

you break even. The guessing penalty is there for one simple reason: to minimize the effect of random guessing.

Educated guessing, however, is something very different. If you encounter a verbal question, for instance, to which you do not know the right answer, don't just give up and leave it blank. Instead look at the answer choices and try to identify wrong answers so you can eliminate them. Using P.O.E. turns guessing into a way to improve your score. If you can eliminate even one out of five answer choices, the odds are then in your favor to take a guess. Will you always guess correctly? No, but by eliminating just one answer choice on each question, you will then answer one out of four questions correctly. Let's do the math: Add one point for the right answer, then subtract $\frac{1}{4}$, subtract $\frac{1}{4}$, and subtract $\frac{1}{4}$, for the three wrong answers. You end up ahead by $\frac{1}{4}$ point because you made educated guesses. The odds of guessing correctly only get better with each answer choice you eliminate, so P.O.E. is a technique you should use often. Give it a try:

> Which of the following cities is the capital of
> Western Samoa?
> (A) Vila   (B) Boston
> (C) Apia   (D) Chicago
> (E) Los Angeles

You may not know the right answer off the top of your head. But which cities are not the capitals of Western Samoa? You probably know enough about the locations of (B), (D), and (E) to know that neither Boston, Chicago, nor Los Angeles is the capital of Western Samoa.

So what's a good answer to this question? (A) or (C).

What's the right answer? It isn't important. You took a good guess and that's all that matters.

A Quick Summary

These points are important enough that we want to mention them again. Make sure you understand these points about the SSAT before you go any farther in this book.

- ◆ You do not have to answer every question on the test. Slow down!

- ◆ You will not immediately know the correct answer to every question. Instead, use P.O.E. and look for wrong answers that you can eliminate.

- ◆ Random guessing will not improve your score on SSAT. It is a waste of time.

Educated guessing, which means that you eliminate even just one out of the five choices, is a good thing and it will improve your score. As a general rule of thumb, if you invest enough time to read and think about the answer to a question, you should be able to eliminate at least one choice and take a good guess!

3

SSAT Pacing

How To Use This Chapter

What follows is a number of slightly complicated charts that will be helpful in interpreting your SSAT scores, and also in planning to increase them. For each grade level and gender, we provide a chart showing scaled scores, and for each scaled score, a percentile ranking and a proposed number of questions you should attempt to achieve that scaled score. If you have a particular SSAT score goal in mind now, that's great. This chart will help you figure out exactly what you need to do in order to reach your goal.

If you have taken a practice test already, you can use your score on that test to determine your starting point. A good rule of thumb is to add twenty points to your verbal, quantitative, and reading scaled scores and make those higher scores your goal.

If you haven't had a chance to take a practice test, that's no problem. You may want to call some of the schools to which you will apply and ask them for a general sense of the scores they are looking for. You can take those target scores and make them your goal, at least until you have had a chance to take a practice test and see how you are doing.

If you haven't yet taken a practice test and none of the schools will tell you anything about what kind of scores you'll need, that's still fine. We suggest that in this case you skip this chapter for now, and go straight into the math, verbal, and reading chapters to start reviewing. Once you've had a chance to take a practice test, you can come back here and use this information to not only see how you did, but also make a plan to help you improve your performance even further.

What Is A Percentile?

Everything is Relative

Percentile scores compare your performance with the performance of other students of your gender and grade level.

Percentiles are numbers, ranging from 1 to 99, which tell you how your score compares with other students' scores. A score at the 50th percentile indicates that you did better than 50 percent of the students from your grade and gender who took the test. A score at the 80th percentile means that you did better than 80 percent of students like yourself.

On the SSAT, percentiles are very important. The reason for this is that students from all different grade levels take the same test and are scored on the same scale. For instance, on the Lower Level test, imagine that a boy gets a 290 overall score. Is this good or bad? It depends entirely on that particular boy's grade level. If he were in the fifth grade, a 290 overall would say that he was in the 81st percentile, or that he did better than 81 percent of the other fifth-grade boys. Not bad at all! If he were in the seventh grade, though, that same 290 Overall score would be in the 35th percentile, meaning that the boy did better than only 35 percent of other seventh-grade boys.

If you have any questions about these charts and what they mean, don't hesitate to ask your parents, your teacher, or anyone else to help you. Believe it or not, figuring out what your SSAT scores mean can sometimes be more difficult than most of the math questions on the test!

How to Use the Pacing Charts

First, find the appropriate chart for your current grade and your gender. You will see that we've created separate sections for verbal, quantitative, reading, and overall scores. In each section of the chart, you can look up any scaled score and see the percentile—the percent of students just like you who scored below that particular scaled score. Finally, and most importantly, for verbal, quantitative, and reading, we have also included the number of questions you should answer to reach any particular scaled score. In coming up with these numbers, we have allowed for the fact that no matter how carefully you will work, you may still make some errors. If you do the number of questions we suggest and get every one of them right, you will beat your goal—generally by quite a bit!

An Important Note

In all of these pacing charts, the "# of questions to do" number for quantitative (math) refers to *both* sections. So if the pacing chart tells you to answer 30 quantitative questions, that means that you should answer roughly 15 questions in each of the two sections.

GRADE 5

Girls

VERBAL			QUANTITATIVE			READING			OVERALL	
Scaled Score	Percentile	# of Questions to Answer	Scaled Score	Percentile	Total # of Questions to Answer in Both Sections	Scaled Score	Percentile	# of Questions to Answer	Scaled Score	Percentile
320	99	58	320	99	50	320	99	40	320	99
315	99	52	315	99	50	315	99	40	315	99
310	98	49	310	99	50	310	99	40	310	99
305	97	46	305	99	49	305	98	39	305	99
300	95	43	300	98	45	300	96	37	300	97
295	92	40	295	94	42	295	93	35	295	94
290	85	37	290	89	38	290	89	32	290	89
285	76	34	285	83	32	285	81	30	285	80
280	64	31	280	73	28	280	72	28	280	70
275	50	27	275	62	25	275	58	27	275	56
270	37	25	270	49	21	270	46	24	270	39
265	22	21	265	34	16	265	30	22	265	25
260	11	20	260	21	13	260	19	19	260	12
255	4	15	255	12	12	255	10	17	255	5
250	1	15	250	4	12	250	4	15	250	1
245	1	15	245	1	12	245	1	15	245	1
230-240	1	15	230-240	1	12	230-240	1	15	230-240	1

Boys

VERBAL			QUANTITATIVE			READING			OVERALL	
Scaled Score	Percentile	# of Questions to Answer	Scaled Score	Percentile	Total # of Questions to Answer in Both Sections	Scaled Score	Percentile	# of Questions to Answer	Scaled Score	Percentile
320	99	58	320	99	50	320	99	40	320	99
315	99	52	315	99	50	315	99	40	315	99
310	98	49	310	99	50	310	99	40	310	99
305	96	46	305	96	49	305	98	39	305	97
300	92	43	300	93	45	300	95	97	300	93
295	87	40	295	87	42	295	92	35	295	87
290	81	37	290	80	38	290	87	32	290	81
285	70	34	285	72	32	285	79	30	285	70
280	58	31	280	60	28	280	69	28	280	59
275	44	27	275	49	25	275	56	27	275	45
270	32	25	270	37	21	270	44	24	270	31
265	19	21	265	25	16	265	31	22	265	18
260	10	20	260	15	13	260	19	19	260	11
255	4	15	255	8	12	255	10	17	255	4
250	1	15	250	3	12	250	5	15	250	1
245	1	15	245	1	12	245	2	15	245	1
230-240	1	15	230-240	1	12	230-240	1	15	230-240	1

GRADE 6

Girls

VERBAL			QUANTITATIVE			READING			OVERALL	
Scaled Score	Percentile	# of Questions to Answer	Scaled Score	Percentile	Total # of Questions to Answer in Both Sections	Scaled Score	Percentile	# of Questions to Answer	Scaled Score	Percentile
320	99	58	320	99	50	320	99	40	320	99
315	96	52	315	99	50	315	99	40	315	99
310	92	49	310	98	50	310	97	40	310	96
305	87	46	305	94	49	305	94	39	305	92
300	80	43	300	89	45	300	89	37	300	86
295	72	40	295	81	42	295	82	35	295	76
290	61	37	290	71	38	290	72	32	290	66
285	50	34	285	60	32	285	62	30	285	53
280	38	31	280	47	28	280	49	28	280	40
275	26	27	275	35	25	275	37	27	275	28
270	17	25	270	25	21	270	25	24	270	17
265	9	21	265	15	16	265	15	22	265	9
260	4	20	260	9	13	260	9	19	260	4
255	1	15	255	4	12	255	4	17	255	1
250	1	15	250	1	12	250	2	15	250	1
245	1	15	245	1	12	245	1	15	245	1
230-240	1	15	230-240	1	12	230-240	1	15	230-240	1

Boys

VERBAL			QUANTITATIVE			READING			OVERALL	
Scaled Score	Percentile	# of Questions to Answer	Scaled Score	Percentile	Total # of Questions to Answer in Both Sections	Scaled Score	Percentile	# of Questions to Answer	Scaled Score	Percentile
320	99	58	320	99	50	320	99	40	320	99
315	95	52	315	99	50	315	99	40	315	97
310	91	49	310	95	50	310	97	40	310	94
305	86	46	305	88	49	305	94	39	305	88
300	78	43	300	79	45	300	90	37	300	80
295	70	40	295	70	42	295	83	35	295	69
290	59	37	290	60	38	290	75	32	290	58
285	47	34	285	49	32	285	65	30	285	45
280	35	31	280	37	28	280	53	28	280	33
275	24	27	275	28	25	275	40	27	275	23
270	14	25	270	19	21	270	29	24	270	14
265	8	21	265	11	16	265	18	22	265	7
260	4	20	260	6	13	260	11	19	260	3
255	2	15	255	3	12	255	5	17	255	1
250	1	15	250	1	12	250	2	15	250	1
245	1	15	245	1	12	245	1	15	245	1
230-240	1	15	230-240	1	12	230-240	1	15	230-240	1

Grade 7

Girls

VERBAL			QUANTITATIVE			READING			OVERALL	
Scaled Score	Percentile	# of Questions to Answer	Scaled Score	Percentile	Total # of Questions to Answer in Both Sections	Scaled Score	Percentile	# of Questions to Answer	Scaled Score	Percentile
320	99	58	320	99	50	320	99	40	320	99
315	89	52	315	97	50	315	97	40	315	95
310	82	49	310	92	50	310	93	40	310	88
305	73	46	305	83	49	305	86	39	305	78
300	61	43	300	72	45	300	79	37	300	65
295	51	40	295	60	42	295	68	35	295	53
290	40	37	290	48	38	290	57	32	290	41
285	28	34	285	37	32	285	43	30	285	29
280	19	31	280	26	28	280	32	28	280	19
275	12	27	275	17	25	275	21	27	275	12
270	7	25	270	11	21	270	12	24	270	7
265	4	21	265	7	16	265	7	22	365	3
260	2	20	260	4	13	260	4	19	260	1
255	1	15	255	2	12	255	2	17	255	1
250	1	15	250	1	12	250	1	15	250	1
245	1	15	245	1	12	245	1	15	245	1
230-240	1	15	230-240	1	12	230-240	1	15	230-240	1

Boys

VERBAL			QUANTITATIVE			READING			OVERALL	
Scaled Score	Percentile	# of Questions to Answer	Scaled Score	Percentile	Total # of Questions to Answer in Both Sections	Scaled Score	Percentile	# of Questions to Answer	Scaled Score	Percentile
320	99	58	320	99	50	320	99	40	320	99
315	86	52	315	96	50	315	97	40	315	92
310	79	49	310	89	50	310	93	40	310	83
305	68	46	305	77	49	305	85	39	305	71
300	57	43	300	64	45	300	77	37	300	59
295	45	40	295	51	42	295	67	35	295	46
290	35	37	290	40	38	290	57	32	290	35
285	25	34	285	31	32	285	45	30	285	25
280	18	31	280	21	28	280	34	28	280	17
275	12	27	275	15	25	275	23	27	275	10
270	8	25	270	9	21	270	15	24	270	6
265	4	21	265	5	16	265	9	22	265	3
260	2	20	260	3	13	260	5	19	260	1
255	1	15	255	1	12	255	3	17	255	1
250	1	15	250	1	12	250	1	15	250	1
245	1	15	245	1	12	245	1	15	245	1
230-240	1	15	230-240	1	12	230-240	1	15	230-240	1

GRADE 8

Girls

VERBAL			QUANTITATIVE			READING			OVERALL	
Scaled Score	Percentile	# of Questions to Answer	Scaled Score	Percentile	Total # of Questions to Answer in Both Sections	Scaled Score	Percentile	# of Questions to Answer	Scaled Score	Percentile
350	99	60	350	99	50	350	99	40	350	99
345	98	60	345	99	50	345	99	40	345	99
340	97	56	340	98	49	340	99	40	340	98
335	95	54	335	97	46	335	99	40	335	97
330	92	51	330	94	43	330	99	40	330	94
325	88	48	325	90	40	325	97	40	325	90
320	83	46	320	85	36	320	94	39	320	85
315	77	42	315	79	33	315	91	38	315	78
310	69	40	310	70	31	310	85	36	310	69
305	61	37	305	62	27	305	78	34	305	60
300	51	34	300	53	26	300	71	31	300	50
295	40	32	295	43	23	295	59	29	295	39
290	31	29	290	34	20	290	49	26	290	29
285	21	26	285	25	19	285	37	25	285	20
280	15	23	280	17	16	280	25	23	280	13
275	9	21	275	11	14	275	17	21	275	7
270	5	20	270	10	13	270	14	18	270	4
265	3	17	265	10	12	265	14	16	265	1
250-260	1	15	250-260	6	12	250-260	9	15	250-260	1

Boys

VERBAL			QUANTITATIVE			READING			OVERALL	
Scaled Score	Percentile	# of Questions to Answer	Scaled Score	Percentile	Total # of Questions to Answer in Both Sections	Scaled Score	Percentile	# of Questions to Answer	Scaled Score	Percentile
350	99	60	350	99	50	350	99	40	350	99
345	98	60	345	98	50	345	99	40	345	99
340	96	56	640	95	49	640	99	40	340	97
335	94	54	335	92	46	335	99	40	335	94
330	90	51	330	87	43	330	99	40	330	90
325	85	48	325	82	40	325	97	40	325	85
320	80	46	320	74	36	320	94	39	320	78
315	73	42	315	68	33	315	81	38	315	70
310	65	40	310	58	31	310	86	36	310	61
305	56	37	305	51	27	305	79	34	305	51
300	46	34	300	42	26	300	73	31	300	42
295	37	32	295	33	23	295	61	29	295	32
290	28	29	290	26	20	290	51	26	290	23
285	20	26	285	19	19	285	39	25	285	16
280	14	23	280	13	16	280	27	23	280	10
275	9	21	275	8	14	275	19	21	275	6
270	6	20	270	7	13	270	16	18	270	3
265	3	17	265	7	12	265	16	16	265	1
250-260	1	15	250-260	4	12	250-260	11	15	250-260	1

GRADE 9

Girls

VERBAL			QUANTITATIVE			READING			OVERALL	
Scaled Score	Percentile	# of Questions to Answer	Scaled Score	Percentile	Total # of Questions to Answer in Both Sections	Scaled Score	Percentile	# of Questions to Answer	Scaled Score	Percentile
350	99	60	350	99	50	350	99	40	350	99
345	96	60	345	98	50	345	99	40	345	98
340	93	56	340	95	49	340	99	40	340	96
335	90	54	335	92	46	335	98	40	335	93
330	85	51	330	87	43	330	97	40	330	88
325	79	48	325	81	40	325	95	40	325	82
320	73	46	320	74	36	320	90	39	320	74
315	66	42	315	67	33	315	85	38	315	66
310	57	40	310	57	31	310	78	36	310	56
305	48	37	305	49	27	305	68	34	305	46
300	39	34	300	39	26	300	60	31	300	36
295	30	32	295	30	23	295	48	29	295	28
290	24	29	290	23	20	290	40	26	290	20
285	18	26	285	15	19	285	29	25	285	13
280	14	23	280	10	16	280	20	23	280	8
275	9	21	275	6	14	275	14	21	275	4
270	6	20	270	5	13	270	12	18	270	2
265	4	17	265	5	12	265	12	16	265	1
250-260	2	15	250-260	3	12	250-260	9	15	250-260	1

Boys

VERBAL			QUANTITATIVE			READING			OVERALL	
Scaled Score	Percentile	# of Questions to Answer	Scaled Score	Percentile	Total # of Questions to Answer in Both Sections	Scaled Score	Percentile	# of Questions to Answer	Scaled Score	Percentile
350	99	60	350	99	50	350	99	40	350	99
345	96	60	345	96	50	345	99	40	345	97
340	94	56	340	91	49	640	99	40	340	94
335	90	54	335	87	46	335	99	40	335	90
330	85	51	330	80	43	330	98	40	330	84
325	78	48	325	73	40	325	96	40	325	78
320	72	46	320	64	36	320	92	39	320	69
315	64	42	315	56	33	315	87	38	315	61
310	56	40	310	48	31	310	81	36	310	52
305	48	37	305	40	27	305	73	34	305	43
300	41	34	300	32	26	300	66	31	300	34
295	33	32	295	24	23	295	53	29	295	26
290	27	29	290	18	20	290	44	26	290	18
285	21	26	286	13	19	285	35	25	285	12
280	16	23	280	9	16	280	25	23	280	7
275	12	21	275	5	14	275	19	21	275	4
270	8	20	270	5	13	270	17	18	270	2
265	5	17	265	4	12	265	16	16	265	1
250-260	2	15	250-260	3	12	250-260	12	15	250-260	1

GRADE 10

Girls

VERBAL			QUANTITATIVE			READING			OVERALL	
Scaled Score	Percentile	# of Questions to Answer	Scaled Score	Percentile	Total # of Questions to Answer in Both Sections	Scaled Score	Percentile	# of Questions to Answer	Scaled Score	Percentile
350	99	60	350	99	50	350	99	40	350	99
345	94	60	345	98	50	345	99	40	345	97
340	90	56	340	94	49	340	98	40	340	95
335	86	54	335	89	46	335	98	40	335	90
330	81	51	330	82	43	330	97	40	330	84
325	75	48	325	75	40	325	93	40	325	77
320	69	46	320	66	36	320	87	39	320	70
315	61	42	315	58	33	315	81	38	315	60
310	52	40	310	49	31	310	74	36	310	51
305	45	37	305	41	27	305	63	34	305	42
300	37	34	300	32	26	300	55	31	300	33
295	30	32	295	24	23	295	43	29	295	23
290	24	29	290	18	20	290	35	26	290	16
285	19	26	285	13	19	285	26	25	285	10
280	15	23	280	8	16	280	19	23	280	6
275	11	21	275	5	14	275	14	21	275	3
270	8	20	270	4	13	270	12	18	270	1
265	5	17	265	4	12	265	12	16	265	1
250-260	2	15	250-260	2	12	250-260	10	15	250-260	1

Boys

VERBAL			QUANTITATIVE			READING			OVERALL	
Scaled Score	Percentile	# of Questions to Answer	Scaled Score	Percentile	Total # of Questions to Answer in Both Sections	Scaled Score	Percentile	# of Questions to Answer	Scaled Score	Percentile
350	99	60	350	99	50	350	99	40	350	99
345	94	60	345	95	50	345	99	40	345	96
340	90	56	340	88	49	340	99	40	340	92
335	87	54	335	83	46	335	98	40	335	87
330	81	51	330	73	43	330	98	40	330	81
325	75	48	325	66	40	325	95	40	325	73
320	69	46	320	56	36	320	90	39	320	66
315	62	42	315	48	33	315	85	38	315	57
310	54	40	310	38	31	310	78	36	310	47
305	48	37	305	30	27	305	69	34	305	39
300	41	34	300	24	26	300	62	31	300	30
295	34	32	295	17	23	295	51	29	295	22
290	29	29	290	13	20	290	42	26	290	15
285	24	26	285	9	19	285	34	25	285	10
280	19	23	280	6	16	280	25	23	280	6
275	14	21	275	3	14	275	19	21	275	3
270	10	20	270	3	13	270	17	18	270	1
265	5	17	265	3	12	265	17	16	265	1
250-260	2	15	250-260	2	12	250-260	13	15	250-260	1

GRADE 11

Girls

VERBAL			QUANTITATIVE			READING			OVERALL	
Scaled Score	Percentile	# of Questions to Answer	Scaled Score	Percentile	Total # of Questions to Answer in Both Sections	Scaled Score	Percentile	# of Questions to Answer	Scaled Score	Percentile
350	99	60	350	99	50	350	99	40	350	99
345	97	60	345	99	50	345	99	40	345	98
340	93	56	340	95	49	340	99	40	340	96
335	90	54	335	90	46	335	99	40	335	94
330	85	51	330	84	43	330	97	40	330	88
325	81	48	325	79	40	325	95	40	325	84
320	77	46	320	71	36	320	90	39	320	77
315	70	42	315	63	33	315	86	38	315	71
310	62	40	310	53	31	310	80	36	310	61
305	54	37	305	44	27	305	74	34	305	49
300	49	34	300	35	26	300	68	31	300	42
295	43	32	295	27	23	295	59	29	295	31
290	35	29	290	20	20	290	46	26	290	23
285	32	26	285	14	19	285	38	25	285	17
280	23	23	280	10	16	280	29	23	280	11
275	20	21	275	6	14	275	24	21	275	7
270	15	20	270	6	13	270	21	18	270	3
265	11	17	265	5	12	265	20	16	265	2
250-260	7	15	250-260	3	12	250-260	16	15	250-260	1

Boys

VERBAL			QUANTITATIVE			READING			OVERALL	
Scaled Score	Percentile	# of Questions to Answer	Scaled Score	Percentile	Total # of Questions to Answer in Both Sections	Scaled Score	Percentile	# of Questions to Answer	Scaled Score	Percentile
350	99	60	350	100	50	350	99	40	350	99
345	93	60	345	94	50	345	99	40	345	95
340	91	56	340	86	49	340	99	40	340	91
335	87	54	335	82	46	335	98	40	335	88
330	84	51	330	73	43	330	97	40	330	82
325	78	48	325	65	40	325	93	40	325	75
320	73	46	320	58	36	320	89	39	320	70
315	67	42	315	50	33	315	86	38	315	62
310	61	40	310	42	31	310	80	36	310	53
305	53	37	305	35	27	305	73	34	305	44
300	44	34	300	27	26	300	68	31	300	37
295	39	32	295	22	23	295	59	29	295	28
290	33	29	290	15	20	290	50	26	290	20
285	28	26	285	11	19	285	39	25	285	12
280	24	23	280	8	16	280	29	23	280	7
275	19	21	275	5	14	275	24	21	275	5
270	13	20	270	4	13	270	21	18	270	3
265	10	17	265	4	12	265	20	16	265	1
250-260	4	15	250-260	2	12	250-260	16	15	250-260	1

4

SSAT Math

INTRODUCTION

This section will provide you with a review of all the math that you need to take the SSAT. When you get started, you may feel that the material is too easy. Don't worry. The SSAT measures your basic math skills, so although you might feel a little frustrated reviewing things you have already learned, that is undoubtedly the best way to improve your score.

We recommend that you work straight through this math review chapter, first reviewing each concept and then doing each set of drills. If you have trouble with one section, mark the page so you can come back later to go over it again. Keep in mind, though, that you shouldn't breeze over pages or sections just because they look familiar. Take the time to read over the entire chapter so you'll be sure to know all the math you'll need!

Lose Your Calculator

You will not be allowed to use a calculator on the SSAT. If you have developed a habit of reaching for your calculator whenever you need to add or multiply a couple of numbers, follow our advice: Put your calculator away now and take it out again after the test is behind you. Trust us, you'll be glad you did.

Write It Down

Do not try to do math in your head. You are allowed to write in your test booklet. You should write in your test booklet. Even when you are just adding a few numbers together, write them down and do the work on paper. Not only will writing things down help eliminate careless errors, it will also give you something to refer to if you need to check over your work.

One Pass, Two Pass

Don't Get Stuck

Make sure you don't spend too much time working on one tough question, when there might be easier questions left in the section.

Within any math section, you will find three types of questions:

- ◆ those you can answer easily without spending too much time
- ◆ those which, if you had all the time in the world, you could do
- ◆ some questions that you have absolutely no idea how to tackle

When you work on a math section, start out with the first question. If you think you can do it without too much trouble, go ahead. If not, save it for later. Move on to the second question and decide whether to do that one. In general, the questions in each math section are in a very rough order of difficulty. This means that earlier questions tend to be somewhat easier than later ones. This means that you will likely find yourself answering more questions toward the beginning of the section and leaving more questions blank toward the end.

Once you've made it all the way through the section, working slowly and carefully to do all the questions that come easily for you, then go back and try some of the ones that you think you can do, but that it will take a little longer. Hopefully you will pace yourself so that while you're working on the second pass through the section, time will run out. You won't be frustrated, though, because you'll know that you answered all the questions that were easy for you. Using a two-pass system and knowing that you can do the questions in whatever order you like is good, smart test-taking.

GUESSTIMATING

Sometimes accuracy is important. Sometimes it isn't.

Which of the following fractions is less than

$$\frac{1}{4}?$$

(A) $\frac{4}{18}$ $\frac{1}{9}$

(B) $\frac{4}{12}$

(C) $\frac{7}{7}$

(D) $\frac{10}{9}$

(E) $\frac{12}{5}$

Some Things are Easier Than They Seem

Guesstimating, or finding approximate answers, can help you eliminate wrong answers and save lots of time.

Without doing a bit of calculation, think about this question. It asks you to find a fraction smaller than $\frac{1}{4}$. Even if you're not sure which one is actually smaller, you can certainly use P.O.E. to eliminate some wrong answers.

Start simple $\frac{1}{4}$ is less than 1, right? Are there any fractions in the answer choices that are greater than 1? Get rid of (D) and (E).

Look at answer choice (C). $\frac{7}{7}$ equals 1. Can it be less than $\frac{1}{4}$? Eliminate (C). Already without doing a bit of math, you have a 50 percent chance of guessing the right answer.

Here's another good example:

> A group of three men buys a one-dollar lottery ticket that wins $400. If the one dollar that they paid for the ticket is subtracted and the remainder of the prize money is divided equally among the men, how much will each man receive?
>
> (A) $62.50
> (B) $75.00
> (C) $100.00
> (D) $133.00
> (E) $200.00

This isn't a terribly difficult question. To solve it mathematically, you would take $400, subtract $1, and then divide the remainder by three. But by using a little bit of logic, you don't have to do any of that.

The lottery ticket won $400. If there were four men, each one would have won about $100 (actually slightly less because the problem tells you to subtract the $1 price of the ticket, but you get the idea). So far so good?

There weren't four men, though; there were only three. This means fewer men among whom to divide the winnings, so each one should get more than $100, right? Look at the answer choices. Eliminate (A), (B), and (C).

Two choices left. Answer choice (E) is $200.00, half of the amount of the winning ticket? If there were three men, could each one get half? Unfortunately not. Eliminate (E). What's left? The right answer!

Guesstimating also works very well with some geometry questions, but just to give you something you can look forward to, we'll save that for the geometry chapter.

FUNDAMENTALS

MATH VOCABULARY

Many of the questions on the SSAT are word problems. If you're going to do well, you need to make sure you know what the words mean! This table lists some of the most popular math vocabulary words used on these tests. Make sure you know all of them!

TERM	DEFINITION	EXAMPLES
Integer	Any number which does not contain either a fraction or a decimal.	14, 3, 0, −3
Positive Number	Any number greater than zero.	$\frac{1}{2}$, 1, 104
Negitive Number	Any number less than zero.	$\frac{1}{2}$, −1, −104
Even Number	Any number which is evenly divisible by two.	104, 16, 2, 0, −104
Odd Number	Any number which is not evenly divisible by two.	115, 11, 1, −1, −11, −115
Prime Number	Any number which is only divisible by 1 and itself. **NOTE**: One is not a prime number.	2, 3, 5, 7, 13, 131
Digit	The numbers from 0 through 9.	0, 2, 3, 7
Consecutive Number	Any series of numbers listed in the order they appear on the number line.	3, 4, 5, or −1, 0, 1, 2
Distinct Numbers	Numbers that are different from one another.	2, 7, 19 are three distinct numbers. 4 and 4 are not distinct because they are the same number
Sum	The result of addition.	The sum of 6 and 2 is 8 because 6 + 2 − 8.
Difference	The result of subtraction.	The difference between 6 and 2 is 4 because 6 − 2 = 4.
Product	The result of multiplaction.	The product of 6 and 2 is 12 because 6 × 2 = 12.
Quotient	The result of division	The quotient when 6 is divided by 2 is 3 because 6 ÷ 2 = 3.

Practice — Math vocabulary test

1. How many integers are there between –1 and 6?_____

2. List three consecutive even integers:_____

3. How many odd integers are there between 1 and 9? _____

4. What is the tens digit in the number 182.09?_____

5. The product of any number and the smallest positive integer is: _____

6. What is the product of 5, 6, and 3?_____

7. What is the sum of 3, 11, and 16?_____

8. What is the difference between your answer to #6 and your answer to #7?_____

9. List three consecutive positive even numbers:_____

10. Is 11 a prime number?_____

11. What is the sum of the digits in the number 5,647? _____

12. The sum of five consecutive positive integers is 30. What is the square of the largest of the five positive integers?
    (A) 25
    (B) 36
    (C) 49
    (D) 64
    (E) 81

ORDER OF OPERATIONS

How would you attack this problem?

$$16 - 45 \div (2 + 1)^2 \bullet 4 + 5 =$$

To solve a problem like this, use PEMDAS. The order of operations is:

Done together
from left to right
$\left\{\begin{array}{l}\text{Parentheses} \\ \text{Exponents} \\ \text{Multiplication} \\ \text{Division} \\ \text{Addition} \\ \text{Subtraction}\end{array}\right.$

$\left.\begin{array}{l}\text{Addition} \\ \text{Subtraction}\end{array}\right\}$ Done together
from left to right

You can remember the order of operations using this phrase:

"Please Excuse My Dear Aunt Sally."

Now, let's give it a try:

$$16 - 45 \div (2 + 1)^2 \bullet 4 + 5 =$$

1. PARENTHESES:

$$16 - 45 \div \underline{(2 + 1)}^2 \bullet 4 + 5 =$$

$$16 - 45 \div (3)^2 \bullet 4 + 5 =$$

2. EXPONENTS:

$$16 - 45 \div (3)^2 \bullet 4 + 5 =$$

$$16 - 45 \div 9 \bullet 4 + 5 =$$

3. MULTIPLICATION AND DIVISION (from left to right):

$$16 - \underline{45 \div 9} \bullet 4 + 5 =$$

$$16 - \underline{5 \bullet 4} + 5 =$$

$$16 - 20 + 5 =$$

4. ADDITION AND SUBTRACTION (from left to right):

$$\underline{16 - 20} + 5 =$$

$$-4 + 5 = \boxed{1}$$

Just take it one step at a time and the math is easy!

First Things First

Make sure you remember PEMDAS whenever you see a question with more than one operation.

PRACTICE — Order of operations

1. $10 - 3 + 2 =$

2. $15 + (7 - 3) - 3 =$

3. $3 \times 2 + 3 \div 3 =$

4. $2 \times (4 + 6) \div 4 =$

5. $420 \div (5 \times 12 + 10) =$

6. $20 \times 5 \div 10 + 20 =$

7. $(3 + 5) \times 10 \times 7 \div 8 =$

8. $10 \times (8 + 1) \times (3 + 1) \div (8 - 2) =$

9. $12 \div 2 \div 2 \times 5 + 5 =$

10. $200 - 150 \div 3 \times 2 =$

FACTORS

Factors are all the numbers that divide evenly into your original number. For example, two is a factor of ten; it goes in five times. Three is not a factor of ten because ten divided by three does not produce an integer quotient (and therefore does not "go in evenly"). When asked to find the factors of a number, just make a list.

The factors of 16 are:
    1 and 16   (always start with 1 and the original number)
    2 and 8
    4 and 4
    Is 3 a factor of 16? _____

The factors of 18 are:
    1 and 18
    2 and 9
    3 and 6

Knowing some rules of divisibility can save you some time.

A NUMBER IS DIVISIBLE BY	IF...
2	If it ends in 0, 2, 4, 6, or, 8.
3	If the sum of the digits is divisible by 3.
5	If it ends in 0 or 5.
9	If the sum of the digits is divisible by 9.
10	If it ends in 0.

Practice — Factors

1. How many factors does the number 24 have?

    (A) 2
    (B) 4
    (C) 6
    (D) 8
    (E) 10

2. If 12 is a factor of a certain number, what must also be factors of that number?

    (A) 2 and 6 only
    (B) 3 and 4 only
    (C) 12 only
    (D) 1, 2, 3, 4, and 6
    (E) 1, 2, 3, 4, 6, and 24

3. What is the smallest number that can be added to the number 1,024 to produce a result divisible by 9?

    (A) 1
    (B) 2
    (C) 3
    (D) 4
    (E) 6

MULTIPLES

Multiples are the results when you multiply your number by any integer. Fifteen is a multiple of five because five times three equals fifteen. Eighteen is a multiple of three, but not a multiple of five. Another way to think about multiples is to consider them "counting by a number."

Factors are Small; Multiples are Big

The factors of a number are always equal to or less than that number. The multiples of a number are always equal to or greater than that number. Be sure not to confuse the two!

The first seven positive multiples of 7 are:

7	(7×1)
14	(7×2)
21	(7×3)
28	(7×4)
35	(7×5)
42	(7×6)
49	(7×7)

Practice — Multiples

1. Which of the following is a multiple of 3?

   (A) 2
   (B) 6
   (C) 10
   (D) 14
   (E) 16

2. Which of the following is NOT a multiple of 6?

   (A) 12
   (B) 18
   (C) 24
   (D) 23
   (E) 42

3. Which of the following is a multiple of both 3 and 5?

   (A) 10
   (B) 20
   (C) 25
   (D) 45
   (E) 50

4. A company's profit was $75,000 in 1972. In 1992, its profit was $450,000. The profit in 1992 was how many times as great as the profit in 1972?

   (A) 2
   (B) 4
   (C) 6
   (D) 10
   (E) 60

FRACTIONS

A fraction really just tells you to divide. For instance, $\frac{5}{8}$ actually means five divided by eight (which equals 0.625 as a decimal).

Another way to think of this is to imagine a pie cut into eight pieces, $\frac{5}{8}$ tells you something about five of those eight pieces of pie.

The parts of a fraction are called the numerator and the denominator. The numerator is the number on top of the fraction, that refers to the part of the pie. The denominator is on the bottom of the fraction and tells you how many pieces there are in the entire pie.

$$\frac{\text{numerator}}{\text{denominator}}$$

Reducing fractions

Imagine a pie cut into two big pieces. You eat one of the pieces. That means that you have eaten $\frac{1}{2}$ of the pie. Now imagine the same pie cut into four pieces; you eat two. That's $\frac{2}{4}$ this time. But look: The two fractions are equivalent!

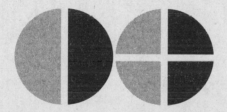

To reduce fractions, just divide the top number and the bottom number by the same amount. Start out with small numbers like 2, 3, 5, or 10 and reduce again if you need to.

$$\frac{12}{24} \begin{matrix} \div 2 \\ \div 2 \end{matrix} = \frac{6}{12} \begin{matrix} \div 2 \\ \div 2 \end{matrix} = \frac{3}{6} \begin{matrix} \div 3 \\ \div 3 \end{matrix} = \frac{1}{2}$$

In this example if you happened to see that both 12 and 24 were divisible by 12, then you could have saved two quick steps. Don't spend very much time, though, looking for the biggest number possible by which to reduce a fraction. Starting out with a small number and doing one extra set of reducing doesn't take very much time and will definitely help prevent careless errors.

Practice — Reducing fractions

1. $\dfrac{6}{8} =$

2. $\dfrac{12}{60} =$

3. $\dfrac{20}{30} =$

4. $\dfrac{36}{96} =$

5. $\dfrac{24}{32} =$

6. $\dfrac{16}{56} =$

7. $\dfrac{1056}{1056} =$

8. $\dfrac{154}{126} =$

9. What does it mean when the number on top is bigger than the one on the bottom?

Adding & subtracting fractions with a common denominator

To add or subtract fractions with a common denominator, just add or subtract the top numbers and leave the bottom number alone.

$$\frac{5}{7} + \frac{1}{7} = \frac{6}{7}$$

$$\frac{5}{7} - \frac{1}{7} = \frac{4}{7}$$

Adding & subtracting fractions when the denominators are different

In the past, you have probably tried to find common denominators so that you could just add or subtract straight across. There is an easier way; it is called the bowtie.

$$\frac{A}{B} + \frac{C}{D} =$$

This diagram may make the bowtie look complicated. It's not. There are three simple steps to adding and subtracting fractions.

Step 1: Multiply diagonally going up.
First **B** × **C**. Write the product next to **C**.
Then **D** × **A**. Write the product next to **A**.

Step 2: Multiply straight across the bottom. **B** × **D**.
Write the product as the denominator in your answer.

Step 3: To add, add the numbers written next to **A** and **C**.
Write the sum as the numerator in your answer.

To subtract, subtract the numbers written next to **A** and **C**.
Write the difference as the numerator in your answer.

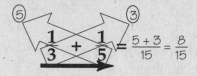

**No More
"Smallest Common
Denominators"**

Using the bowtie to add and
subtract fractions eliminates
the need for a smallest
common denominator.

Practice — Adding & subtracting fractions

1. $\dfrac{3}{8} + \dfrac{2}{3} =$

2. $\dfrac{1}{3} + \dfrac{3}{8} =$

3. $\dfrac{4}{7} + \dfrac{2}{7} =$

4. $\dfrac{3}{4} - \dfrac{2}{3} =$

5. $\dfrac{7}{9} + \dfrac{5}{4} =$

6. $\dfrac{2}{5} - \dfrac{3}{4} =$

7. $\dfrac{10}{12} + \dfrac{7}{2} =$

8. $\dfrac{17}{27} - \dfrac{11}{27} =$

9. $\dfrac{3}{20} + \dfrac{2}{3} =$

10. $\dfrac{x}{3} + \dfrac{4x}{6} =$

Multiplying fractions

Multiplying is the easiest thing to do with fractions. All you need to do is multiply straight across the top and bottom.

$$\frac{3}{7} \times \frac{4}{5} = \frac{3 \times 4}{7 \times 5} = \frac{12}{35}$$

Dividing fractions

Dividing fractions is almost as simple as multiplying. You just have to flip the second fraction and then multiply.

$$\frac{3}{8} \div \frac{2}{5} = \frac{3}{8} \times \frac{5}{2} = \frac{15}{16}$$

When dividing, don't ask why; just flip the second fraction and multiply!

Practice — Multiplying & dividing fractions

1. $\frac{2}{3} \times \frac{1}{2} =$

2. $\frac{5}{8} \div \frac{1}{2} =$

3. $\frac{4}{5} \times \frac{3}{10} =$

4. $\frac{24}{15} \times \frac{10}{16} =$

5. $\frac{16}{25} \div \frac{4}{5} =$

Practice — Fraction problems

1. Joanna owns one-third of the pieces of furniture in the apartment she shares with her friends. If there are a total of twelve pieces of furniture in the apartment, how many pieces does Joanna own?

   (A) 2
   (B) 4
   (C) 6
   (D) 8
   (E) 12

2. A tank of oil is one-third full. When full, the tank holds 90 gallons. How many gallons of oil are in the tank now?

(A) 10
(B) 20
(C) 30
(D) 40
(E) 50

3. Tigger the Cat sleeps three-fourths of every day. In a four-day period, he sleeps the equivalent of how many full days?

(A) $\dfrac{1}{4}$

(B) $\dfrac{3}{4}$

(C) 1
(D) 3
(E) 4

4. Which of the following is the greatest?

(A) $\dfrac{1}{4} + \dfrac{2}{3}$

(B) $\dfrac{3}{4} - \dfrac{1}{3}$

(C) $\dfrac{1}{12} \div \dfrac{1}{3}$

(D) $\dfrac{3}{4} \times \dfrac{1}{3}$

(E) $\dfrac{1}{12} \times 2$

5. $\dfrac{1}{2} + \dfrac{2}{3} + \dfrac{3}{4} + \dfrac{1}{2} + \dfrac{1}{3} + \dfrac{1}{4} =$

(A) $\dfrac{3}{4}$

(B) 1
(C) 6
(D) 3
(E) 12

DECIMALS

Remember, decimals and fractions are just two different ways of writing the same thing. To change a fraction into a decimal, you just divide the bottom number into the top number.

Be sure you know the names of all the decimal places. Here's a quick reminder:

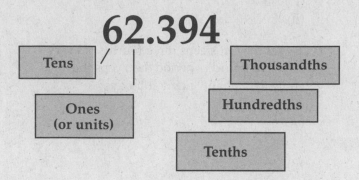

Adding decimals

To add decimals, just line up the decimal places and add.

$$
\begin{array}{r}
48.02 \\
+ \quad 19.12 \\
\hline
67.14
\end{array}
$$

Subtracting decimals

To subtract, do the same thing. Line up the decimal places and subtract.

$$
\begin{array}{r}
67.14 \\
- \quad 48.02 \\
\hline
19.12
\end{array}
$$

Multiplying decimals

To multiply decimals, first count the number of digits to the right of the decimal point in the numbers you are multiplying. Then just multiply and move the decimal point in your answer from right to left by the same number of spaces.

$$
\begin{array}{r}
0.5 \\
\times \quad 4.2 \\
\hline
2.10
\end{array}
$$
(two digits to the right of the decimal point)

Dividing decimals

To divide, move the decimal points in both numbers the same number of spaces to the right until you are working only with integers.

$$12.5 \div .25 = .25\,\overline{)12.5}$$

Now move both decimals over two places and solve the problem.

$$25\,\overline{)1250} \quad \begin{array}{c} 50 \end{array}$$

Practice — Decimals

1. $1.43 + 17.27 =$

2. $2.49 + 1.7 =$

3. $7.08 - 2.3 =$

4. $4.25 \times 2.5 =$

5. $.02 \times .90 =$

6. $180 \div .03 =$

7. $.10 \div .02 =$

8. The product of .34 and 1000 is approximately
   (A) 3.50
   (B) 35
   (C) 65
   (D) 350
   (E) 650

9. $2.398 =$

   (A) $2 \times \dfrac{9}{100} \times \dfrac{3}{10} \times \dfrac{8}{1000}$

   (B) $2 + \dfrac{3}{10} + \dfrac{9}{1000} + \dfrac{8}{100}$

   (C) $2 + \dfrac{9}{100} + \dfrac{8}{1000} + \dfrac{3}{10}$

   (D) $\dfrac{3}{10} + \dfrac{9}{100} + \dfrac{8}{1000}$

   (E) None of the above

Exponents

Exponents are just another way to indicate multiplication. For instance, 3^2 simply means to multiply 3 by itself 2 times, so $3^2 = 3 \times 3 = 9$. Even higher exponents aren't very complicated.

For example: $2^5 = 2 \times 2 \times 2 \times 2 \times 2 = 32$.

The questions on the SSAT and the ISEE don't generally use exponents higher than four or five, so this is likely to be as complicated as it gets.

The rule for exponents is simple: When in doubt, write it out! Don't try to figure out two times two times two times two times two in your head (just look at how silly it looks written down using words!). Instead, write it as a math problem and just work through it one step at a time.

When in Doubt, Write it Out!

Don't try to compute exponents in your head. Write them out and multiply!

What would you do if you were asked to solve this problem?

$$Q^3 \times Q^2 =$$

Let's look at this one carefully. Q^3 means $Q \times Q \times Q$ and Q^2 means $Q \times Q$. Put them together and you've got:

$$(Q \times Q \times Q) \times (Q \times Q) =$$

How many Qs is that? Count them. Five! Be careful when multiplying exponents like this that you don't get confused and multiply the actual exponents, which would give you Q^6. If you are ever unsure, don't spend a second worrying; just write out the exponent and count the number of things you are multiplying.

Practice — Exponents

1. $2^3 =$

2. $2^4 =$

3. $3^3 =$

4. $4^3 =$

5. $2^3 \times 2^3 \times 2^2 =$
   (A) 64
   (B) 2^8
   (C) 2^{10}
   (D) 2^{16}
   (E) 2^{18}

6. For what integer value of m does $2m + 4 = m^3$?
   (A) 1
   (B) 2
   (C) 3
   (D) 4
   (E) 5

ALGEBRA

Manipulating an equation

To solve an equation, your goal is to isolate the variable, meaning that you want to get the variable on one side of the equation and everything else on the other side.

$$3x + 5 = 17$$

To do this, follow these two steps:

Step 1: Move elements around using addition and subtraction. Get variables on one side and numbers on the other. Simplify.

Step 2: Divide both sides of the equation by the *coefficient*, the number in front of the variable. If that number is a fraction, multiply everything by the denominator.

For example:

$3x + 5 = 17$

$\quad -5 \quad -5$ Subtract 5 to get rid of the numbers on the left side.

$3x \quad\quad = 12$

$\div 3 \quad\quad = \div 3$ Divide by 3 to get rid of the 3 on the left side.

$x \quad\quad = 4$ Done!

Always remember:

Whatever you do to one side, you must also do to the other.

Practice — Manipulate!

1. If $6 + 2 = 11 - x$, then $x =$

2. If $4x = 20$, then $x =$

3. If $5x - 20 = 10$, then $x =$

4. If $4x + 3 = 31$, then $x =$

5. If $m + 5 = 3m - 3$, then $m =$

6. If $2.5x = 20$, then $x =$

7. If $0.2x + 2 = 3.6$, then $x =$

8. If $6 = 8x + 4$, then $x =$

9. If $3(x + y) = 21$, then $x + y =$

10. If $3x + 3y = 21$, then $x + y =$

11. If $2.5 \times 3\ 40 - 5y = 65$, then $y =$

Equal Rights for Equations!

You can do anything you want to one side of the equation, as long as you make sure to do exactly the same thing to the other side.

12. One fifth of the students in a class chose recycling as the topic for their science projects. If four students chose recycling, how many students are in the class?

(A) 4
(B) 10
(C) 16
(D) 20
(E) 24

13. If $6x - 4 = 38$, then $x + 10 =$

(A) 7
(B) 10
(C) 16
(D) 17
(E) 19

14. If $3x - 6 = 21$, then what is $x \div 9$?

(A) 0
(B) 1
(C) 3
(D) 6
(E) 9

15. Only one-fifth of the chairs in a classroom are in working order. If three extra chairs are brought in, there are 19 working seats available. How many chairs were originally in the room?

(A) 16
(B) 19
(C) 22
(D) 80
(E) 95

FUNCTIONS

A function is just a set of instructions written in a strange way.

$$\# x = 3x(x + 1)$$

On the left: there is usually a variable with a strange symbol next to or around it.

In the middle: an equal sign

On the right: are the instructions. These tell you what to do with the variable.

$\# x = 3x(x + 1)$ *What does # 5 equal?*

$\# 5 = 3 \bullet 5(5 + 1)$ *Just replace each x with a 5!*

Here the function (indicated by the # sign) simply tells you to substitute a 5 wherever there was an x in the original set of instructions. Functions look confusing because of the strange symbols, but once you know what to do with them, they are just like manipulating an equation.

Sometimes more than one question will refer to the same function. The following drill, for example, contains two questions about one function. In cases such as this, the first question tends to be easier than the second.

Practice — Functions

Questions 1–2 refer to the following definition.

For all real numbers n, $\$n = 10n - 10$

1. $\$7 =$

    (A) 70
    (B) 60
    (C) 17
    (D) 7
    (E) 0

2. If $\$n = 120$, then $n =$

    (A) 11
    (B) 12
    (C) 13
    (D) 120
    (E) 130

Questions 3–5 refer to the following definition.

For all real numbers d and y, $d \; ¿ \; y = (d \bullet y) - (d + y)$.
[Example: $3 \; ¿ \; 2 = (3 \bullet 2) - (3 + 2) = 6 - 5 = 1$]

3. $10 \; ¿ \; 2 =$

    (A) 20
    (B) 16
    (C) 12
    (D) 8
    (E) 4

4. If $K (4 \; ¿ \; 3) = 30$, then $K =$

    (A) 3
    (B) 4
    (C) 5
    (D) 6
    (E) 7

5. $(2 \; ¿ \; 4) \bullet (3 \; ¿ \; 6) =$

    (A) $(9 \; ¿ \; 3) + 3$
    (B) $(6 \; ¿ \; 4) + 1$
    (C) $(5 \; ¿ \; 3) + 4$
    (D) $(8 \; ¿ \; 4) + 2$
    (E) $(9 \; ¿ \; 4) + 3$

PERCENTAGES

Learn a Foreign Language

"Percent language" is easy to learn because there are only four words you need to remember!

Solving percent problems is easy when you know how to translate them from "percent language" into "math language." Once you've done the translation, you guessed it—just manipulate the equation!

What is 40% of 72?

PERCENT LANGUAGE	MATH LANGUAGE
% or "percent"	Out of 100 ($\frac{}{100}$)
Of	Times (as in Multiplication) (×)
What	Your favorite variable (p)
Is, are, were	Equals (=)

Whenever you see words from this table, just translate them into math language and go to work on the equation!

For example:

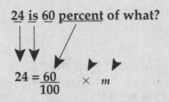

$$\underline{24} \text{ } \underline{is} \text{ } \underline{60} \text{ } \underline{percent} \text{ of what?}$$

$$24 = \frac{60}{100} \times m$$

Practice — Translating & solving percent questions

1. 30 is what percent of 250?

2. What is 12% of 200?

3. What is 25% of 10% of 200?

4. 75% of 20% of what is 12?

Practice — Word Problems Involving Percentages

1. If a harvest yielded 60 bushels of corn, 20 bushels of wheat, and 40 bushels of soybeans, what percent of the total harvest was corn?

   (A) 25%
   (B) 30%
   (C) 33%
   (D) 40%
   (E) 50%

2. At a local store, an item that usually sells for $45 is currently on sale for $30. What discount does that represent?

(A) 10%
(B) 25%
(C) 33%
(D) 50%
(E) 66%

3. Which of the following is most nearly 35% of $19.95?

(A) $13.50
(B) $9.95
(C) $7.00
(D) $5.75
(E) $3.50

4. Of the fifty hotels in the Hilltop Hotels chain, five have indoor swimming pools and fifteen have outdoor swimming pools. What percent of all Hilltop Hotels have either an indoor or an outdoor swimming pool?

(A) 5%
(B) 15%
(C) 20%
(D) 30%
(E) 40%

5. For what price item does 40% off equal a $20 discount?

(A) $50.00
(B) $100.00
(C) $400.00
(D) $800.00
(E) None of the above.

6. A pair of shoes is offered on a special blowout sale. The original price of the shoes is reduced from $50 to $20. What is the percent change in the price of the shoes?

(A) 20%
(B) 25%
(C) 40%
(D) 50%
(E) 60%

7. Lisa buys a silk dress regularly priced at $60, a cotton sweater regularly priced at $40, and four pairs of socks regularly priced at $5 each. If the dress and the socks are on sale for 20% off the regular price and the sweater is on sale for 10% off the regular price, what is the total amount of her purchase?

(A) $90.00
(B) $96.00
(C) $100.00
(D) $102.00
(E) $108.00

8. Thirty percent of $17.95 is closest to

(A) $2.00
(B) $3.00
(C) $6.00
(D) $9.00
(E) $12.00

9. Fifty percent of the 20 students in Mrs. Schweizer's third grade class are boys. If 90 percent of these boys ride the bus to school, which of the following is the number of boys in Mrs. Schweizer's class who ride the bus to school?

(A) 9
(B) 10
(C) 12
(D) 16
(E) 18

10. On a test with 25 questions, Marc scored an 88%. How many questions did Marc answer correctly?

(A) 22
(B) 16
(C) 12
(D) 4
(E) 3

RATIOS

A ratio is like a recipe since it tells you how much of different ingredients go into a mixture.

For example:

To make punch, mix two parts grape juice with three parts orange juice.

This ratio tells you that for every two units of grape juice, you will need to add three units of orange juice. It doesn't matter what the units are; if you were working with ounces, you would mix two ounces of grape juice with three ounces of orange juice to get five ounces of punch. If you were working with gallons, you would mix two gallons of grape juice with three gallons of orange juice. How much punch would you have? Five gallons.

To work through a ratio question, first you need to organize the information you are given. Do this using the ratio box.

In a club with 35 members, the ratio of boys to girls is 3 : 2.

BOYS	GIRLS	TOTAL
3	2	5
× 7	× 7	× 7
21	14	35

To complete your ratio box, fill in the ratio at the top and the "real world" at the bottom. Then look for a "magic number" which you can multiply by the ratio to get to the real world. That's all there is to it!

Practice — Ratios

1. In a jar of lollipops, the ratio of red lollipops to blue lollipops is 3:5. If only red lollipops and blue lollipops are in the jar and if the total number of lollipops in the jar is 56, how many blue lollipops are in the jar?

   (A) 5
   (B) 8
   (C) 21
   (D) 28
   (E) 35

2. At Jed's Country Hotel, there are three types of rooms: singles, doubles, and triples. If the ratio of singles to doubles to triples is 3 : 4 : 5, and the total number of rooms is 36, how many doubles are there?

   (A) 4
   (B) 9
   (C) 12
   (D) 24
   (E) 36

3. Matt's Oak Superstore has exactly three times as many large oak desks as small oak desks in its inventory. If the store only sells these two types of desks, which could be the total number of desks in stock?

(A) 10
(B) 13
(C) 16
(D) 18
(E) 25

4. In Janice's tennis club, 8 of the 12 players are right-handed. What is the ratio of right-handed to left-handed players in Janice's club?

(A) 1 : 2
(B) 2 : 1
(C) 1 : 6
(D) 2 : 3
(E) 3 : 4

5. One-half of the 400 students at Booth Junior High School are girls. Of the girls at the school, the ratio of those who ride a school bus to those who walk is 7 : 3. What is the total number of girls who walk to school?

(A) 10
(B) 30
(C) 60
(D) 120
(E) 140

6. A pet goat eats two pounds of goat food and one pound of grass each day. When the goat has eaten a total of fifteen pounds, how many pounds of grass will it have eaten?

(A) 3
(B) 4
(C) 5
(D) 15
(E) 30

AVERAGES

There are three parts of every average problem: total, number, and average. Most SSAT problems will give you two of the three pieces and ask you to find the third. To help organize the information you are given, use the average pie.

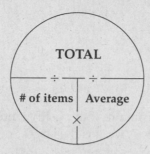

The average pie organizes all of your information visually. It is easy to see all of the relationships between pieces of the pie:

- ◆ TOTAL = (# of items) × (Average)

- ◆ # of items = $\dfrac{Total}{Average}$

- ◆ Average = $\dfrac{Total}{\# \, of \, items}$

For example, if your friend went bowling and bowled three games, scoring 71, 90, and 100, here's how you would compute her average score using the average pie:

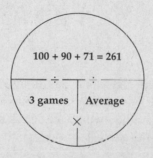

To find the average, you would simply write a fraction that represents $\dfrac{TOTAL}{\# \, of \, items}$, in this case $\dfrac{261}{3}$.

The math becomes simple. $261 \div 3 = 87$. Your friend bowled an average of 87.

Get used to working with the average pie by using it to solve these problems:

Practice — Average problems

1. The average of three numbers is eighteen. What is two times the sum of the three numbers?

   (A) 108
   (B) 54
   (C) 36
   (D) 18
   (E) 6

2. If Set M contains four positive integers whose average is 7, what is the largest number that Set M could contain?

   (A) 6
   (B) 7
   (C) 18
   (D) 25
   (E) 28

3. An art club of 4 boys and 5 girls makes craft projects. If the boys average 2 projects each and the girls average 3 projects each, what is the total number of projects produced by the club?

   (A) 14
   (B) 23
   (C) 26
   (D) 54
   (E) 100

4. If a class of 6 students has an average grade of 72 before a seventh student joins the class, what must the seventh student's grade be in order to raise the class average to 76?

   (A) 76
   (B) 80
   (C) 88
   (D) 92
   (E) 100

5. Catherine scores an 84, 85, and 88 on her first three exams. What must she score on her fourth exam to raise her average to an 89?

   (A) 89
   (B) 91
   (C) 93
   (D) 97
   (E) 99

Plugging In

The SSAT will often ask you questions about real-life situations where the numbers have been replaced with variables. One of the easiest ways to tackle these questions is with a powerful technique called plugging in.

> Mark is two inches taller than John, who is four inches shorter than Evan. If e represents Evan's height in inches, then in terms of j, an expression for Mark's height is:
> (A) $e + 6$
> (B) $e + 4$
> (C) $e + 2$
> (D) e
> (E) $e - 2$

The problem with this question is that we're not used to thinking of people's heights in terms of variables. Have you ever met someone who was j inches tall?

Whenever you see variables used in the question and in the answer choices, just plug in a number to replace the variable.

1. Choose a number for e.

2. Using that number, figure out Mark's and John's heights.

3. Put a box around Mark's height, since that's what the question asked you for.

4. Plug your number for e into the answer choices and choose the one that represents Mark's height.

Take the Algebra Away, and Arithmetic is All That's Left

When you plug in for variables, you won't need to write equations and won't have to solve algebra problems. Doing simple arithmetic is always easier than doing algebra.

Here's how it works:

Mark is two inches taller than John, who is four inches shorter than Evan is. If e represents Evan's height in inches, then <u>in terms of j</u>, an expression for Mark's height is:
(A) $e + 6$
(B) $e + 4$
(C) $e + 2$
(D) e
(E) $e - 2$

> *Ignore this! Because you are plugging in, you don't need to pay any attention to "in terms of" any variable . . .*

For Evan's height, let's pick 60 inches. This means that $e = 60$.

Remember, there is no right or wrong number to pick. 50 would work just as well as 100.

But given that Evan is 60 inches tall, now we can figure out that since John is four inches shorter than Evan, John's height must be $(60 - 4)$ or 56 inches.

The other piece of information we learn from the problem is that Mark is two inches taller than John. If John's height is 56 inches, that means Mark must be 58 inches tall.

So here's what we've got:

Evan	60 inches = e
John	56 inches
Mark	58 inches

Now, the question asks for Mark's height, which is 58 inches. The last step is to go through the answer choices substituting 60 for e, and choose the one that equals 58.

(A)	$e + 6$	$60 + 6 = 66$	ELIMINATE
(B)	$e + 4$	$60 + 4 = 64$	ELIMINATE
(C)	$e + 2$	$60 + 2 = 62$	ELIMINATE
(D)	e	60	ELIMINATE
(E)	$e - 2$	$60 - 2 = 58$	PICK THIS ONE!

This is a very long explanation of all the steps involved when you plug in. Don't be tempted to say, "Plugging in takes too long. I can do the problem just as fast if I write equations for each person's age." Writing equations is a fine way to do algebra in school, but on the SSAT it is a great way to make mistakes. Remember that the people who write these tests expect you to write equations, and anytime you can do things differently than the way you are expected, you should.

Practice — Plugging in

1. At a charity fund-raiser, 200 people each donated x dollars. In terms of x, what was the total number of dollars donated?

   (A) $\dfrac{x}{200}$

   (B) 200

   (C) $\dfrac{200}{x}$

   (D) $200 + x$

   (E) $200x$

2. If 10 magazines cost d dollars, how many magazines can be purchased for 3 dollars?

   (A) $\dfrac{3d}{10}$

   (B) $30d$

   (C) $\dfrac{d}{30}$

   (D) $\dfrac{30}{d}$

   (E) $\dfrac{10d}{3}$

3. The zoo has four times as many monkeys as lions. There are four more lions than there are zebras at the zoo. If z represents the number of zebras in the zoo, then in terms of z, how many monkeys are there in the zoo?

(A) 4z
(B) z + 4
(C) z + 8
(D) 4z + 4
(E) 4z + 16

Occasionally you may run into a plugging-in question that doesn't contain variables. These questions usually ask about a percentage or a fraction of some unknown number or price. This is the one time that you should plug in, even when you don't see variables in the answer!

Also, be sure you plug in good numbers. Good doesn't mean right, because there's no such thing as a right or wrong number to plug in. A good number is one that makes the problem easier to work with. If a question asks about minutes and hours, try plugging in 30 or 60, not 128. Also, whenever you see the word percent, you guessed it, plug in 100!

4. The price of a suit is reduced by half, and then the resulting price is reduced by 10%. The final price is what percent of the original price?

(A) 5%
(B) 10%
(C) 25%
(D) 40%
(E) 45%

5. On Wednesday, Miguel ate one-fourth of a pumpkin pie. On Thursday, he ate one-half of what was left of the pie. What fraction of the entire pie did Miguel eat on Wednesday and Thursday?

(A) $\dfrac{3}{8}$

(B) $\dfrac{1}{2}$

(C) $\dfrac{5}{8}$

(D) $\dfrac{3}{4}$

(E) $\dfrac{7}{8}$

6. If p pieces of candy costs c cents, 10 pieces of candy will cost

(A) $\dfrac{pc}{10}$ cents

(B) $\dfrac{10c}{p}$ cents

(C) $10pc$ cents

(D) $\dfrac{10p}{c}$ cents

(E) $10 + p + c$ cents

7. If J is an odd integer, which of the following must be true?

(A) $(J \div 3) > 1$
(B) $(J - 2)$ is a positive integer.
(C) $2 \bullet J$ is an even integer.
(D) $J^2 > J$
(E) $J > 0$

8. If m is an even integer, n is an odd integer, and p is the product of m and n, which of the following is always true?

(A) p is a fraction.
(B) p is an odd integer.
(C) p is divisible by 2.
(D) p is between m and n.
(E) p is greater than zero.

BACKSOLVING

Backsolving is similar to plugging in. When you have *variables* in the answer choices, you plug in. When you have *numbers* in the answer choices, you will generally backsolve. The only time this may get tricky is when you have a question like the one above that asks for a percent or a fraction of some unknown number.

Backsolving works because on a multiple-choice test, the right answer is always one of the answer choices. On this type of question, you can't plug in any number you want because only one number will work. Instead, you can plug in numbers from the answer choices, one of which must be correct. Here's an example:

Nicole baked a batch of cookies. She gave half to her friend Lisa and six to her mother. If she now has eight cookies left, how many did Nicole bake originally?

(A) 8
(B) 12
(C) 20
(D) 28
(E) 32

See what we mean? It would be hard to just start making up numbers of cookies and hoping that eventually you guessed correctly. However, the number of cookies that Nicole baked originally must be either 8, 12, 20, 28, or 32 (the five answer choices). So pick one—always start with (C)—and then work backward to determine whether or not you have the right choice.

Let's start with (C): Nicole baked 20 cookies. Now work through the events listed in the question.

She had 20 cookies—from answer choice (C)—and she gave half to Lisa. That leaves Nicole with 10 cookies.

What next? She gives 6 to her mom. Now she's got 4 left.

Keep going. The problem says that Nicole now has 8 cookies left. But if she started with 20—answer choice (C)—she would only have 4 left. So is (C) the right answer? No.

No problem. Choose another answer choice and try again. Be smart, though, about which answer choice you pick. When we used the number in (C), Nicole ended up with fewer cookies than we wanted her to have, didn't she? So the right answer must be a number larger than 20, the number we took from (C).

The good news is that the answer choices in most backsolving questions go in order, so it is easy to pick the next larger number—you just pick either (B) or (D), depending on which direction you've decided to go.

Back to Nicole and her cookies. We need a number larger than 20. So let's go to answer choice (D)—28.

Nicole started out with 28 cookies. The first thing she did was give half, or 14, to Lisa. That left Nicole with 14 cookies left.

Then she gave 6 cookies to her mother. $14 - 6 = 8$. Nicole has 8 cookies left over. Keep going with the question. It says "If Nicole now has eight cookies left..." She has eight cookies left and, *voila*—she's supposed to have eight cookies left.

What does this mean? It means you've got the right answer! Pick (D) and move on.

If answer choice (D) had not worked, and you were still certain that you needed a number larger than answer choice (C), you also would be finished. Because you started with the middle answer choice (C), and that didn't work, and then you tried the next larger choice, (D), and that didn't work either, you could pick the only answer bigger than (C) that was left, in this case (E), and be done.

This diagram helps illustrate the way you should move through the answer choices and why you should always start out with answer choice (C).

(A)

(B)

(C) ← Start Here

(D)

(E)

Practice — Backsolving

1. Ted can read 60 pages per hour. Naomi can read 45 pages per hour. If both Ted and Naomi read at the same time, how many minutes will it take them to read a total of 210 pages?

   (A) 36
   (B) 72
   (C) 120
   (D) 145
   (E) 180

2. If the sum of y and $y + 1$ is greater than 18, which of the following is one possible value for y?

   (A) −10
   (B) −8
   (C) 2
   (D) 8
   (E) 10

3. Kenny is 5 years older than Greg is. In 5 years, Kenny will be twice as old as Greg is now. How old is Kenny now?

   (A) 5
   (B) 10
   (C) 15
   (D) 25
   (E) 35

4. Three people—Paul, Sara, and John—want to put their money together in order to buy a $90 radio. If Sara agrees to pay twice as much as John, and Paul agrees to pay three times as much as Sara, how much must Sara pay?

   (A) $10
   (B) $20
   (C) $30
   (D) $45
   (E) $65

5. Four less than a certain number is two-thirds of that number. What is the number?

   (A) 1
   (B) 6
   (C) 8
   (D) 12
   (E) 16

Geometry

Guesstimating: A second look

Guesstimating worked well back in the introduction when we were just using it to estimate or "ballpark" the size of a number, but geometry problems are undoubtedly the best place to guesstimate whenever you can.

Unless a particular question tells you that a figure is not drawn to scale, you can safely assume that the figure *is* drawn to scale.

Don't Forget to Guesstimate!

Guesstimating works best on geometry questions. Make sure you use your common sense, combined with P.O.E. to save time and energy.

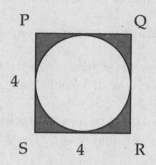

A circle is inscribed in square PQRS. What is the area of the shaded region?

(A) $16 - 6\pi$
(B) $16 - 4\pi$
(C) $16 - 3\pi$
(D) $16 - 2\pi$
(E) 16π

Wow, a circle inscribed in a square—that sounds tough!

It isn't. Look at the picture. What fraction of the square looks like it is shaded? Half? Three-quarters? Less than half? In fact, about one-quarter of the area of the square is shaded. You've just done most of the work necessary to solve this problem.

Now, let's do a tiny bit of math. The length of one side of the square is 4, so the area of the square is 4×4 or 16. Don't worry if you feel a little lost; in the next few pages, we'll discuss area in much more detail.

So the area of the square is 16 and we said that the shaded region was about one-fourth of the square. One-fourth of 16 is 4, right? So we're looking for an answer choice which equals about (not necessarily exactly) 4. Let's look at the choices:

(A) $16 - 6\pi$
(B) $16 - 4\pi$
(C) $16 - 3\pi$
(D) $16 - 2\pi$
(E) 16π

This becomes a tiny bit complicated because the answers include π. For the purposes of guesstimating, and in fact for almost any purpose on either the SSAT or the ISEE, you should just remember that π is a little more than 3.

Let's look back at those answers:

(A) $16 - 6\pi$ is roughly equal to $16 - (6 \times 3) = -2$
(B) $16 - 4\pi$ is roughly equal to $16 - (4 \times 3) = 4$
(C) $16 - 3\pi$ is roughly equal to $16 - (3 \times 3) = 7$
(D) $16 - 2\pi$ is roughly equal to $16 - (2 \times 3) = 10$
(E) 16π is roughly equal to $(16 \times 3) = 48$

Now let's think about what these answers mean.

Answer choice (A) is geometrically impossible. A figure *cannot* have a negative area. Eliminate it.

Answer choice (B) means that the shaded region has an area of about 4. Sounds pretty good.

Answer choice (C) means that the shaded region has an area of about 7. The area of the entire square was 16, so that would mean that the shaded region was almost half the square. Possible, but doubtful.

Answer choice (D) means that the shaded region has an area of about 10. That's more than half the square and in fact, almost three-quarters of the entire square. No way, cross it out.

Finally, answer choice (E) means that the shaded region has an area of about 48. What? The whole square had an area of 16. Is the shaded region three times as big as the square itself? No shot. Eliminate (E).

At this point you are left with only (B), which we feel pretty good about, and (C), which seems a little big. What should you do?

Pick (B) and pat yourself on the back because you chose the right answer without doing a lot of unnecessary work. Also, remember how useful it was to guesstimate and make sure you do it whenever you see a geometry problem, unless the problem tells you that the figure is not drawn to scale!

PERIMETER

The perimeter is the distance around the outside of any figure. To find the perimeter of a figure, just add up the length of all the sides.

What are the perimeters of these figures?

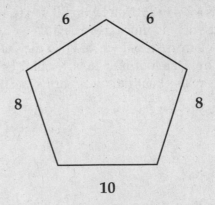

Perimeter = 6 + 6 + 8 + 8 + 10 = 38

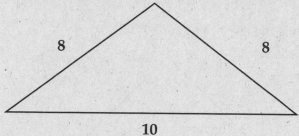

Perimeter = 8 + 8 + 12 = 28

Practice — Perimeter

1. A stop sign has 8 equal sides of length 4. What is its perimeter?

   (A) 4
   (B) 8
   (C) 12
   (D) 32
   (E) It cannot be determined from the information given.

2. If the perimeter of a square is 56, what is the length of each side?

   (A) 4
   (B) 7
   (C) 14
   (D) 28
   (E) 112

3. The perimeter of a square with a side of length 4 is how much less than the perimeter of a rectangle with sides of length 4 and width 6?

   (A) 0
   (B) 2
   (C) 4
   (D) 6
   (E) 8

ANGLES

Straight lines

Angles that form a straight line always total 180°.

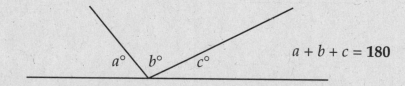

$a + b + c = 180$

Triangles

The Rule of 180

There are 180 degrees in a straight line and in a triangle.

All the angles in a triangle add up to 180°.

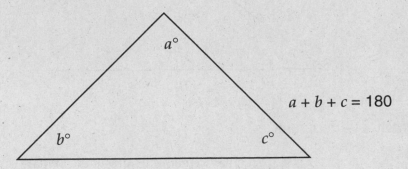

$$a + b + c = 180$$

Four-sided figures

The angles in a square, rectangle, or any other four-sided figure always add up to 360°.

The Rule of 360

There are 360 degrees in a four-sided figure and in a circle.

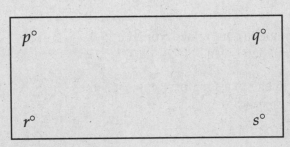

$$p + q + r + s = 360$$

TRIANGLES

Isosceles triangles

Any triangle with two equal sides is an isosceles triangle.

If two sides of a triangle are equal, the angles opposite those sides are always equal.

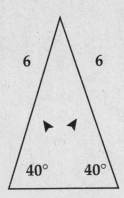

This particular isosceles triangle has two equal sides (of length 6) and therefore two equal angles (40° in this case).

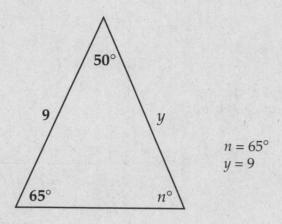

$n = 65°$
$y = 9$

Equilateral triangles

An equilateral triangle is a triangle with three equal sides. If all the sides are equal, then all the angles must be equal. Each angle in an equilateral triangle equals 60°.

Right triangles

A right triangle is a triangle with one 90° angle.

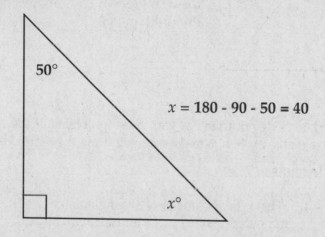

$x = 180 - 90 - 50 = 40$

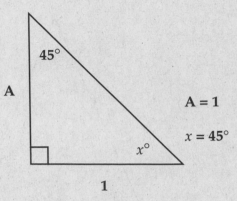

This is as right triangle.
It is also an isosceles triangle.

What does that tell you?

A

A = 1

x = 45°

The Pythagorean theorem

For all right triangles, $a^2 + b^2 = c^2$.

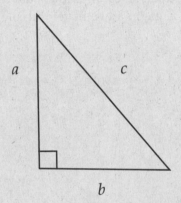

Always remember that c represents the *hypotenuse*, the longest side of the triangle, which is always opposite the right angle.

Test your knowledge of triangles with these problems. If the question describes a figure that isn't shown, make sure you draw the figure yourself!

Practice — Triangles

1. What is the perimeter of an equilateral triangle, one side of which measures 4 inches?

    (A) 12 inches
    (B) 8 inches
    (C) 6 inches
    (D) 4 inches
    (E) It cannot be determined from the information given.

2. $x =$

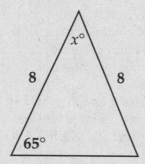

(A) 8
(B) 30
(C) 50
(D) 65
(E) 180

3. If $b=45$, then $v^2 =$

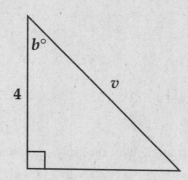

(A) 32
(B) 25
(C) 16
(D) 5
(E) It cannot be determined from the information given.

4. One-half of the difference between the number of degrees in a square and the number of degrees in a triangle is

(A) 45
(B) 90
(C) 180
(D) 240
(E) 360

AREA

The area is the amount of space taken up by a two-dimensional figure. An easy way to think about area is as the amount of paper that a figure covers. The larger the area, the more paper the figure takes up.

In order to determine the area of a square or rectangle, multiply the length by the width.

Remember the formula: **area = length × width**.

What is the area of a rectangle with length 9 and width 4?

In this case the length is 9 and the width is 4, so 9 × 4 = 36.

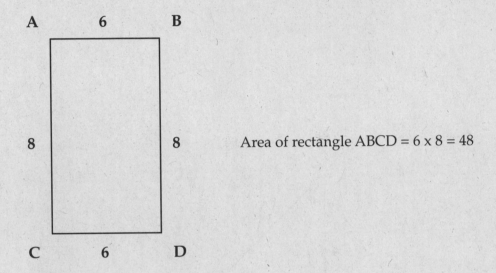

Area of rectangle ABCD = 6 x 8 = 48

To find the area of a triangle, you multiply $\frac{1}{2}$ times the length of the base times the length of the triangle's height, or $\frac{1}{2}$b • h.

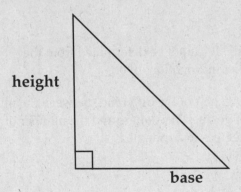

What is the area of a triangle with base 6 and height 3?

(A) 3
(B) 6
(C) 9
(D) 12
(E) 18

Just put the values you are given into the formula and do the math. That's all there is to it!

$$\frac{1}{2}b \cdot h = area$$

$$(\frac{1}{2})(6) \cdot 3 = area$$

$$3 \cdot 3 = 9$$

The only tricky point you may run into when finding the area of a triangle is when the triangle is not a right triangle. In this case, it becomes slightly more difficult to find the height, which is easiest to think of as the distance to the point of the triangle from the base. Here's an illustration to help:

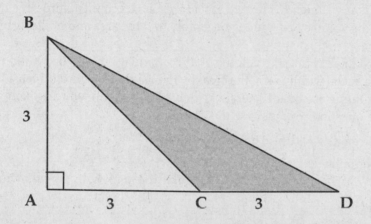

First look at triangle BAC, the unshaded right triangle on the left side. Finding its base and height is simple—they are both 3. So using our formula for the area of a triangle, we can figure out that the area of triangle BAC is $4\frac{1}{2}$.

Now lets think about triangle BCD, the shaded triangle on the right. It isn't a right triangle, so finding the height will involve a little more thought. Remember the question, though: How far up from the base is the point of triangle BCD? Think of the shaded triangle sitting on the floor of your room. How far up would its point stick from the ground? Yes, 3! The height of triangle BCD is exactly the same as the height of triangle BAC. Don't worry about drawing lines inside the shaded triangle or anything like that, just figure out how high its point is from the ground.

Okay, so just to finish up, to find the base of triangle BCD (the shaded one) you will use the same area formula, and just plug in 3 for the base and 3 for the height.

$$\frac{1}{2}b \bullet h = area$$

$$(\frac{1}{2})(3) \bullet 3 = area$$

And once you do the math, you'll see that the area of triangle BCD is $4\frac{1}{2}$.

Not quite convinced? Let's look at the question a little differently. The base of the entire figure (triangle DAB) is 6 and the height is 3. Using your trusty area formula, you can figure out that the area of triangle DAB is 9. You know the area of the unshaded triangle is $4\frac{1}{2}$, so what's left for the shaded part? You guessed it—$4\frac{1}{2}$.

VOLUME

Volume is very similar to area, except it takes into account a third dimension. To compute the volume of a figure, you simply find the area and multiply by a third dimension.

For instance, to find the volume of a rectangular object, you would multiply the length × the width (a.k.a. the area) by the height (the third dimension). So to find the volume of a quadrilateral, the only kind of figure you are likely to see in a volume question, you just use this formula:

length × width × height = volume

For example:

What is the volume of a rectangular fish tank with the following specifications:

length:	6 inches
height:	6 inches
width:	10 inches

There isn't much to it., Just stick the numbers into the formula.

length × width × height = volume

$6 \times 10 \times 6 = 360$

Practice — Area & volume

1. If the area of a square is equal to its perimeter, what is the length of one side?

   (A) 1
   (B) 2
   (C) 4
   (D) 8
   (E) 10

2. The area of a rectangle with width 4 and length 3 is equal to the area of a triangle with a base of 6 and a height of

   (A) 1
   (B) 2
   (C) 3
   (D) 4
   (E) 12

3. Two cardboard boxes have equal volume. The dimensions of one box are $3 \times 4 \times 10$. If the length of the other box is 6 and the width is 4, what is the height of the second box?

   (A) 2
   (B) 5
   (C) 10
   (D) 12
   (E) 24

4. If the area of a square is $64p^2$, what is the length of one side of the square?

   (A) $64p^2$
   (B) $8p^2$
   (C) $64p$
   (D) $8p$
   (E) 8

CHARTS & GRAPHS

Charts

Don't be in too Big a Hurry

When working with charts and graphs, make sure that you take a moment to look at the chart or graph, figure out what it tells you, and then go to the questions.

Chart questions are simple, but you must be careful. Follow these three steps and you'll be well on the way to mastering any chart question.

1. Read any text that accompanies the chart. It is important to know what the chart is showing and what scale the numbers are on.

2. Read the question.

3. Refer to the chart and find the specific information you need.

If there is more than one question about a single chart, the later questions will tend to be more difficult than the earlier ones. Be careful!

Here is a sample chart:

Club membership by state, 1995 and 1996

STATE	1995	1996
California	300	500
Florida	225	250
Illinois	200	180
Massachusetts	150	300
Michigan	150	200
New Jersey	200	250
New York	400	600
Texas	50	100

There are lots of different questions that you can answer based on the information in this chart. For instance:

> What is the difference between the number of members who came from New York in 1995 and the number of members who came from Illinois in 1996?

This question asks you to look up two simple pieces of information and then do a tiny bit of math.

First, the number of members who came from New York in 1995 was 400.

Second, the number of members who came from Illinois in 1996 was 180.

Finally, look back at the question. It asks you to find the difference between these numbers. 400 – 180 = 120. Done.

> What was the percent increase in members
> from New Jersey from 1995 to 1996?

You should definitely know how to do this one! Do you remember how to translate percentage questions? If not, go back to the algebra chapter!

In 1995 there were 200 club members from New Jersey. In 1996 there were 250 members from New Jersey. That represents an increase of 50 members. So to determine the percent increase, you will need to ask yourself "50 (the increase) is what percent of 200 (the original amount)?"

Translated, this becomes:

$$50 = \frac{g}{100} \times 200$$

With a little bit of simple manipulation, this equation becomes:

$$50 = 2g$$

... and ...

$$25 = g$$

So from 1995 to 1996, there was a 25% increase in the number of members from New Jersey. Good work!

> Which state had as many club members in
> 1996 as a combination of Illinois,
> Massachusetts, and Michigan had in 1995?

First, take a second to look up the number of members who came from Illinois, Massachusetts, and Michigan in 1995 and add them together.

$$200 + 150 + 150 = 500.$$

Which state had 500 members in 1996? California. That's all there is to it!

GRAPHS

Some questions will ask you to interpret a graph. You should be familiar with both pie and bar charts. These graphs are generally drawn to scale (meaning that the graphs give an accurate visual impression of the information) so you can always guess based on the figure if you need to.

The way to approach a graph question is exactly the same as the way to approach a chart question. Follow the same three steps:

1. Read any text that accompanies the graph. It is important to know what the graph is showing and what scale the numbers are on.

2. Read the question.

3. Refer back to the graph and find the specific information you need.

This is how it works:

Figure 1

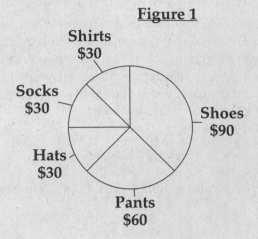

The graph in Figure 1 shows Emily's clothing expenditures for the month of October. On which type of clothing did she spend the most money?

(A) Shoes
(B) Shirts
(C) Socks
(D) Hats
(E) Pants

This one is easy. You can look at the pieces of the pie and identify the largest, or you can look at the amounts shown in the graph and choose the largest one. Either way, the answer is (A), because Emily spent more money on shoes than on any other clothing items in October.

Emily spent half of her clothing money on which two items?

(A) Shoes and pants
(B) Shoes and shirts
(C) Hats and socks
(D) Socks and shirts
(E) Shirts and pants

Again, you can find the answer to this question two different ways. You can look for which two items together make up half the chart, or you can add up the total amount of money Emily spent ($240) and then figure out which two items made up half (or $120) of that amount. Either way is just fine, and either way the right answer is (B) Shoes and shirts.

Practice — Chart and graph problems

Questions 1–3 refer to the following summary of energy costs by district

DISTRICT	1990	1991
A	400	600
B	500	700
C	200	350
D	100	150
E	600	800

(all numbers are in thousands of dollars)

1. In 1991, which district spent twice as much on energy as district A spent in 1990?

   (A) A
   (B) B
   (C) C
   (D) D
   (E) E

2. Which district spent the most on electricity in 1990 and 1991 combined?

   (A) A
   (B) B
   (C) D
   (D) E
   (E) It cannot be determined from the information given.

3. The total increase in energy expenditure in these districts, from 1990 to 1991, is how many dollars?

   (A) $800
   (B) $1,800
   (C) $2,400
   (D) $2,600
   (E) $800,000

Questions 4–5 refer to Figure 2, which shows the number of compact discs owned by five students.

Figure 2

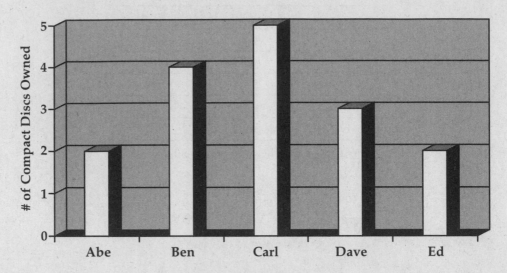

4. Carl owns as many CDs as which two other students combined?

   (A) Abe and Ben
   (B) Ben and Dave
   (C) Abe and Ed
   (D) Abe and Dave
   (E) Ben and Ed

5. Which one student owns one-fourth of the CDs accounted for in Figure 2?

   (A) Abe
   (B) Ben
   (C) Carl
   (D) Dave
   (E) Ed

Questions 6–8 refer to Matt's weekly time card, shown below.

DAY	IN	OUT	HOURS WORKED
Monday	2:00pm	5:30pm	3.5
Tuesday			
Wednesday	2:00pm	6:00pm	4
Thursday	2:00pm	5:30pm	3.5
Friday	2:00pm	5:00pm	3
Saturday			
Sunday			

6. If Matt's hourly salary is $6, what were his earnings for the week?

   (A) $6
   (B) $14
   (C) $21
   (D) $54
   (E) $84

7. What is the average number of hours Matt worked on the days he worked during this particular week?

   (A) 3
   (B) 3.5
   (C) 4
   (D) 7
   (E) 14

8. The hours that Matt worked on Monday accounted for what percent of the total number of hours he worked during this week?

   (A) 3.5
   (B) 20
   (C) 25
   (D) 35
   (E) 50

MATH REVIEW

Make sure you can confidently answer all of the following questions before you take the SSAT.

1. Is zero an integer? _____

2. Is zero positive or negative? _____

3. What operation do you perform to find a sum? _____

4. What operation do you perform to find a product?
   _____

5. What is the result called when you divide?_____

6. Is 312 divisible by 3?_____
   Is 312 divisible by 9? _____
   (Actually dividing isn't fair—use your divisibility rules!)

7. What does the "E" in PEMDAS stand for?_____

8. Is 3 a factor of 12?_____
   _____ Is 12 a factor of 3?_____

9. Is 3 a multiple of 12?_____
   _____ Is 12 a multiple of 3?_____

10. What is the tens digit in the number 304.275?_____

11. What is the tenths digit in the number 304.275? _____

12. $2^3 =$_____

13. In "math language" the word "percent" means: _____

14. In "math language" the word "of'" means:_____

15. In a ratio box, the last column on the right is always the
    _____.

16. Whenever you see a problem involving averages, draw the
    _____.

17. When a problem contains variables in the question and in the
    answers, I will _____.

18. To find the perimeter of a square, I _____ the length(s)
    of _____ side(s).

19. To find the area of a square, I _____ the length(s) of
    _____ sides(s).

20. There are _____ degrees in a straight line.

21. A triangle has _____ angles which total
    _____ degrees.

22. A four-sided figure contains _____ degrees.

23. An isosceles triangle has _____ equal sides; an _____ triangle has three equal sides.

24. The longest side of a right triangle is called the _____ and is located opposite the _____ .

25. To find the area of a triangle, I use the formula: _____.

5

SSAT Verbal

INTRODUCTION

Take a look at the verbal section of one of the practice SSATs in this book. The verbal section on the SSAT consists of:

- ◆ 30 synonym questions (questions 1–30)
- ◆ 30 analogy questions (questions 31–60)

That's 60 questions—but you only have 25 minutes! Should you try to spend 25 seconds on each question to get them all done? NO!

You mean I don't have to do all the questions?

Nope. You'll actually improve your score by answering fewer questions, as long as you're still using all of the allotted time.

"Allotted time"?

If you can't define "allotted," make an index card for it! Look in the Vocabulary chapter for ideas on how to use index cards to learn new words.

Remember, this test is designed for students in three or four different grade levels. There will be vocabulary in some of these questions that is aimed at students older than you, and almost no one in your grade will get those questions right. On the SSAT score report, you will only be compared to students in your own grade. The younger you are in your test level, the fewer questions you are expected to complete. Thus, fifth-graders and eighth-graders are expected to do the least number of questions on the Lower Level and Upper Level Tests, respectively.

Here's an example: An eighth-grade girl takes the Upper Level test. She does better than 92% of all eighth-graders on the Verbal section. How many questions do you think she got right out of 60? 55 questions? 50 questions? Nope. Not even close. She only got 43 Verbal questions right. She's in the top 8 percent of students! Look at the Pacing Chart and figure out how many questions you need to do to hit your target score.

Why rush through the questions you can get right to get to the really tough ones that almost nobody gets? That approach only ensures that you will make hasty, careless errors. Work slowly on the questions that have vocabulary that you know, to make sure you get them right. Then try the ones that have some harder words in them.

Slow and Steady

Working slowly and getting questions right is how you score well. If you haven't already, look at chapter 3 to figure out how many questions you really need to complete.

Look at the Pacing chapter to see how many analogies and synonyms you need to complete in order to reach your target score. Pace yourself—you've got so much more time for each question than the student who thinks she has to get them all done.

Which questions should I do?

The questions are arranged in a rough order of difficulty—the harder synonyms tend to come toward the end of the synonym section, and the harder analogies tend to come at the end of the analogy section.

However, everyone is different. You know some words that your friends don't, and vice versa. What makes some verbal questions difficult is that you don't know the dictionary definitions of the words involved.

You get as many points for an easy question as you do for a hard one. So here's the plan: Do all the questions that are easy for you first. Then go back through and do the ones with words you "sorta" know. You'll probably be staying mostly in the beginning and middle of each section, but don't be afraid to glance ahead—there may be some words you know towards the end. Remember to skip a number on the answer sheet when you skip a question.

Knowing your own vocabulary is the key to quickly deciding if you can answer a question easily.

Know yourself

Categorize the words you see in SSAT questions into:

- words you know
- words you "sorta" know
- words you really don't know

The easiest way to get a verbal question right is by making sure all the words in it fall into the first category—words you know. The best way to do this is by learning new vocabulary **every day**. Check out the Vocabulary chapter (chapter 1) for the best ways to do this.

You can raise your verbal score moderately with the verbal techniques alone. If you want to see a substantial rise, you need to build up your vocabulary, too.

The process of elimination

P.O.E. is the key to getting verbal questions right. With math questions, there's always a "correct" answer; the other answers are simply wrong. In a verbal question, however, things are not that simple. Words are a lot more slippery than numbers are. So verbal questions have "best" answers, not "correct" answers. The other answers aren't necessarily wrong, but the SSAT thinks they're not as good as the "best" one. This means that your goal is to eliminate "worse" answer choices in the verbal and reading sections, even more than on the quantitative sections..

Get used to looking for "worse" answers. There are a lot more of them than there are "best" answers, so "worse" answers are easier to find! When you find them, cross them out in the question booklet to make sure you don't spend any more time looking at them. No matter which other techniques you use to answer a question, you're always eliminating wrong answers, instead of trying to magi cally pick out the best answer.

One thing to remember for the verbal section: You cannot eliminate answer choices that contain words you don't know. It doesn't matter if you don't know what a word means—it could still be the answer.

What if I can't narrow it down to one answer?

Should you guess? Yes. If you can eliminate even just one answer choice, you should guess from the remaining.

Where do I start?

In the verbal section, do analogies first —they're easier to get right when you don't know all the words in the question.

You'll be taking two passes over each section, in this order:

- Analogies with words you know
- Analogies with words you "sorta" know

Bubble Practice

Whenever you do a practice test, use the sample answer sheet so you get used to skipping around when you're filling in bubbles.

P.O.E. and You

Process of Elimination is your best friend on this test. Even when none of the answers looks particularly right, you can usually eliminate at least one.

- ◆ Synonyms with words you know
- ◆ Synonyms with words you "sorta" know
- ◆ Analogies with words you really don't know

THE VERBAL PLAN

Pacing and verbal strategy

Take a look at the Pacing chapter (chapter 3) to answer the next two questions.

How many analogies do I need to do? _____

How many synonyms do I need to do? _____

When I start the verbal section, what question number do I start on? _____

What's the order in which I do questions in the verbal section?

1. _____

2. _____

3. _____

4. _____

5. _____

What's the technique I'll be using all the time, regardless of whatever else I'm using to answer a question? _____

How many answer choices must I have eliminated in order to guess productively? _____

Can I eliminate answer choices that contain words I don't know?_____

    If you have trouble answering any of the questions above, reread this chapter!

Knowing My Vocabulary

Look at each of the following words and decide if it's a word that you know, "sorta" know, or really don't know. If you know it, write down its definition.

insecticide (noun) _____

trifle (verb) _____

repugnant (adjective) _____

mollify (verb) _____

camouflage (verb) _____

historic (adjective) _____

Check the ones you thought you knew or "sorta" knew, and make index cards for the ones you didn't know.

ANALOGIES

What is an analogy?

An analogy, on the SSAT, asks you to:

- ◆ decide how two words are related
- ◆ choose another set of words that has the same relationship

It looks like this:

> A is to B as
>
> (A) C is to D
> (B) C is to D
> (C) C is to D
> (D) C is to D
> (E) C is to D

Or like this:

> A is to B as C is to:
>
> (A) D
> (B) D
> (C) D
> (D) D
> (E) D

A, B, C, and D stand for words. We will call any words that are in the question part of the analogy the "stem words." To figure out the relationship, ignore the "A is to B as C is to D" sentence that they've given you. It doesn't tell you what you need to know. Cross out "is to" and "as."

Instead, use the techniques that follow, depending on the words in the question. Get your pencil ready, because you need to try this stuff out as we go along.

WHEN YOU KNOW THE WORDS

Make a sentence

Here's an analogy in which you'll know all the words:

> Kitten is to cat as
>
> (A) bull is to cow
> (B) snake is to frog
> (C) squirrel is to raccoon
> (D) puppy is to dog
> (E) spider is to fly

You want to be sure you get an easy question like this one right, because it's worth just as much as a hard one. Here's how to be sure you don't make a careless mistake.

Visualize the first two words ("A" and "B") and how they are related.

Kitten i~~s~~ ~~to~~ cat ~~as~~ (Cross out "is to" and "as."
Just picture a kitten and a cat.)

Make a sentence to describe what you see. A good sentence will:

◆ define one of the words using the other one

◆ stay short and simple

A kitten _____ cat.
(Make a sentence.)

Now look at the answer choices and eliminate any that cannot have the same relationship as you've got in your sentence.

(A) bull is to cow
(B) snake is to frog
(C) squirrel is to raccoon
(D) puppy is to dog
(E) spider is to fly

Shop Around

Try every answer choice in a verbal question to be sure you're picking the *best* answer there.

If your sentence was something like "A kitten is a young cat," you can eliminate all but (D). If you had a different sentence, think about how you would define a kitten. Stay away from sentences that use the word "you," as in "You see kittens with female cats." Also avoid sentences like "A kitten is a cat." These sentences don't give you a definition or description of one of the words. Get specific. Yes, a kitten is a cat, but what *else* do you know about it?

As you go through the answer choices, cross out answer choices as you eliminate them. In the "kitten" analogy, you probably knew that (D) was a good fit for your sentence, but don't stop there! Always check all the answers. On the SSAT, often a so-so answer will appear before the "best" answer in the choices, and you don't want to get sidetracked by it. Try *all* the answers so you can be sure to get all the easy analogies right.

In making your sentence, you can start with either of the first two words. Try to start your sentence by defining the first word, but if that doesn't work, start by defining the second word.

House is to tent as (Cross out. Visualize.)

A house _____ tent. (Can you
make a definitional sentence? Not really.)

A tent _____ house. (Make a
sentence.) (Now eliminate.)

House is to tent as bed is to
(A) table
(B) stool
(C) floor
(D) blanket
(E) hammock

Draw an arrow to remind yourself that you started with the second word instead of the first, like we have here. If you reverse the words in your sentence, you need to reverse them when you're trying out the answer choices, too. If you have a sentence like "A tent is a temporary house," then you can eliminate all but (E).

Write your sentence above the question, between the two words. It's a good idea to do this as you start practicing analogies, and most students find it helpful to write out their sentences all the time. If you have a tendency to change your sentence as you go through the answers, you should always write it down.

Notice that in the "house" analogy, they've *given* you the first word of the answer pair. Some of the analogies will be like this, but they're really no different from the others. You'll still be using the same techniques for them, and you may find them a little easier.

Make another sentence

Why would you ever need to change your sentence? Let's see:

Motor is to car as
(Cross out. Visualize. Write a sentence.
Eliminate.)

(A) knob is to door
(B) shovel is to earth
(C) bulb is to lamp
(D) sail is to ship
(E) pond is to ocean

Did you get it down to one? If not, make your sentence more specific. You may have said "A car has a motor," in which case you can only eliminate (B) and (E). The best words to use are active verbs and descriptive adjectives. What does a motor *do* for a car? Make a more specific sentence. (Remember to draw an arrow if you start with the word "car.")

A motor makes a car move. You could also say that a car is powered by a motor. Either sentence will help you eliminate all but (D). When your sentence eliminates some but not all of the choices, make it more specific.

If you have trouble picturing the relationship or making a more specific sentence, ask yourself questions that will help you get at how the two words are related.

Below are some questions to ask yourself that will help you make sentences. ("A" and "B" are the first two words in the analogy. Remember, you can start with either one.) Refer back to these questions if you get stuck when trying to make a sentence.

Rev It Up

Use the most specific, descriptive words you can when you make a sentence. You want the sentence to define one of the words.

If at First You Don't Succeed...

then try the other word! You can start your sentence with the first word ('A'), or the second word ('B').

Help!

These questions will help you come up with a sentence that defines one of the words in an analogy. Refer to them as much as you need to, until you are asking yourself these questions automatically.

- What does A/B do?
- What does A/B mean?
- How does A/B work?
- What does A/B look like?
- How is A/B used?
- Where is A/B found?
- How do A and B compare?
- How are A and B associated?

Practice — Making sentences

Try making a sentence for each of these analogies. Use the questions above if you have trouble. Avoid using "A is B" or "A is the opposite of B." Instead, try using "has" or "lacks," or you can use "with" or "without." Use active verbs. Check your sentences in the Answer Key before you move on to the next practice set.

1. Chapter is to book as _____

2. Scale is to weight as _____

3. Striped is to lines as _____

4. Anger is to rage as _____

5. Rehearsal is to performance as _____

6. Mechanic is to car as _____

7. Traitor is to country as _____

8. Aggravate is to problem as _____

9. Trout is to fish as _____

10. General is to army as _____

11. Law is to crime as _____

12. Buckle is to belt as _____

13. Truculent is to fight as _____

14. Cure is to illness as _____

15. Toxic is to poison as _____

16. Mountain is to pinnacle as _____

17. Perilous is to safety as _____

18. Humanitarian is to philanthropy as _____

19. Notorious is to reputation as _____

20. Miser is to generosity as _____

Practice — Easy analogy techniques

For each analogy that has words you know:

- Make a sentence.

- Try out your sentence on the answer choices.

- Eliminate the ones that don't fit.

- If you need to, make your sentence more specific and eliminate again.

- If there are words you don't know or just "sorta" know in a question, skip it.

- If there are words you don't know or just "sorta" know in an answer choice, do not eliminate it. Just narrow it down as far as you can.

- As always, look up the words you can't define and put them on index cards.

1. Chapter is to book as

    (A) glass is to water
    (B) lamp is to light
    (C) scene is to play
    (D) stew is to meat
    (E) elevator is to building

2. Refrigerator is to cool as furnace is to

    (A) radiator
    (B) house
    (C) oil
    (D) heat
    (E) furniture

3. Fish is to fin as

    (A) fruit is to stem
    (B) bird is to wing
    (C) insect is to shell
    (D) cod is to school
    (E) dog is to tail

4. Driver is to car as

    (A) pilot is to airplane
    (B) police officer is to highway
    (C) secretary is to letter
    (D) baker is to cake
    (E) carpenter is to house

5. Clock is to time as thermometer is to

   (A) air
   (B) pressure
   (C) wind
   (D) ice
   (E) temperature

6. Envelope is to letter as

   (A) suitcase is to clothes
   (B) pen is to paper
   (C) box is to cardboard
   (D) table is to wood
   (E) frame is to picture

7. Librarian is to library as curator is to

   (A) museum
   (B) studio
   (C) gallery
   (D) workshop
   (E) garden

8. Pen is to write as

   (A) pencil is to point
   (B) actor is to perform
   (C) knife is to cut
   (D) desk is to sit
   (E) ink is to stain

9. Hurricane is to breeze as

   (A) storm is to tempest
   (B) fire is to flame
   (C) tidal wave is to ripple
   (D) cloud is to sunlight
   (E) temperature is to weather

10. Circle is to ball as

    (A) square is to cube
    (B) pyramid is to triangle
    (C) point is to line
    (D) side is to rectangle
    (E) hexagon is to polygon

11. Egg is to shell as banana is to

    (A) fruit
    (B) tree
    (C) bunch
    (D) peel
    (E) seed

12. Cup is to quart as

   (A) week is to time
   (B) minute is to hour
   (C) liter is to metric
   (D) coin is to dollar
   (E) spoon is to measure

13. Coach is to team as

   (A) captain is to platoon
   (B) singer is to chorus
   (C) batter is to baseball
   (D) teacher is to homework
   (E) king is to queen

14. Bat is to mammal as

   (A) boar is to hog
   (B) porpoise is to shark
   (C) butterfly is to insect
   (D) whale is to fish
   (E) reptile is to lizard

15. Famished is to hungry as

   (A) clean is to dirty
   (B) destitute is to poor
   (C) abandoned is to lonely
   (D) misdirected is to lost
   (E) worried is to scared

16. Sterilize is to germ as

   (A) cut is to surgeon
   (B) sneeze is to dust
   (C) scour is to grime
   (D) inject is to virus
   (E) rinse is to mouth

17. Director is to actors as conductor is to

   (A) writers
   (B) dancers
   (C) painters
   (D) musicians
   (E) playwrights

18. Applicant is to hire as

   (A) judge is to jury
   (B) candidate is to elect
   (C) cashier is to work
   (D) student is to study
   (E) writer is to research

19. Stale is to bread as

   (A) pungent is to cheese
   (B) rancid is to meat
   (C) thick is to milk
   (D) dry is to rice
   (E) pulpy is to juice

20. Prejudice is to unbiased as worry is to

   (A) adamant
   (B) active
   (C) carefree
   (D) concerned
   (E) occupied

When a sentence doesn't work

There are some really weird analogies on the SSAT, and they usually contain words you know. The problem with the weird analogies is that the words don't have a nice, normal, definitional relationship. Most analogies will have a definitional relationship between A and B (the first two words in the analogy), and the same relationship between C and D (the best answer pair). The weird analogies don't work that way.

If you really do know the words in an analogy, but you can't make a sentence that defines one of them, then try asking yourself these questions, to see if it's a weird one:

Weird Ones

Only if you can't make a sentence that defines the first or the second word should you look for the weird relationships. Ask yourself the questions here.

   ◆ Are A and B synonyms?

   ◆ Do A and B have something in common?

   ◆ Are A and B members of the same group?

   ◆ What kind of sequence or pattern are A and B in?

   ◆ Do A and B rhyme?

   ◆ Do A and B have rearranged letters?

If these questions don't work for A and B, then there's one more weird way the analogy could be built.

   ◆ Can I make a definitional sentence with A and C?

Try visualizing and making a sentence with A and C on this weird one:

Racket is to bat as

   (A) puck is to hockey
   (B) rifle is to duck
   (C) hammer is to nail
   (D) ball is to soccer
   (E) tennis is to baseball

You definitely know these words, "racket" and "bat." So you try making a sentence. You can't make a definitional sentence with these two words, even though you know them. Your next step is to look for a weird relationship, but "racket" and "bat" are not synonyms, and they don't form a pattern, rhyme, or rearrangement of letters. However, they are both instruments used to hit balls in games. That alone might let you eliminate some answers, but it is easier to go one step further—see if "racket" is related to any of the words that are in the "C" position. Is "racket" related to "puck"? No. "Rifle"? No. "Hammer"? No. "Ball"? No. "Tennis"? Yes. A racket is used to hit the ball in tennis. Does that sentence work for "bat" and "baseball"? Sure. Bingo.

Don't worry—there won't be many weird ones. Most analogies will be normal. Just try some more so you'll be ready if you get a few:

Practice — Weird analogy techniques

Refer to the questions you can ask yourself about weird analogies if you need help figuring these out.

1. August is to November as

   (A) February is to April
   (B) March is to June
   (C) July is to May
   (D) January is to December
   (E) September is to November

2. Rough is to cough as

   (A) chapped is to sore
   (B) flight is to fright
   (C) sight is to fight
   (D) seated is to sated
   (E) lair is to liar

3. Swift is to fast as

   (A) slow is to stopped
   (B) beneficial is to detrimental
   (C) athletic is to lithe
   (D) bellicose is to warlike
   (E) grumpy is to frowning

4. Sad is to interested as

   (A) friendly is to ebullient
   (B) pleased is to unhappy
   (C) despair is to obsession
   (D) angry is to neutral
   (E) talkative is to anxious

5. Possible is to required as can is to

   (A) might
   (B) should
   (C) ought
   (D) may
   (E) must

6. Grape is to tree as

    (A) water is to pesticide
    (B) wine is to paper
    (C) fruit is to vegetable
    (D) olive is to oil
    (E) spruce is to pine

WHEN YOU KNOW ONLY ONE OF THE WORDS

Work backwards

Go straight to the answer choices. Make a sentence with each answer choice. Keep your sentences as definitional as possible. If your sentence uses "can" or "might" or "could," or if you find yourself really reaching to try to make a sentence up, then the relationship is not a strong definitional one, and that answer is probably not right. Eliminate it. With each answer choice for which you can create a good sentence, try the sentence with the words on top—the stem words. If you don't know a word in the answer choices, do not eliminate it.

Cygnet is to swan as
  (A) Chicken is to egg   _a chicken lays eggs–a cygnet lays swans?_
  (B) frog is to snake   _a snake can eat a frog–not strong_
  (C) turtle is to raccoon   _no sentence–not strong_
  (D) puppy is to dog   _a puppy is a young dog–a cygnet is a young swan?_
  (E) spider is to fly   _some spiders eat flies–not strong_

Pick the "best" or most likely relationship for "cygnet" and "swan." Which relationship is most like a definition?

Cross out (C), since we couldn't make a sentence at all. (B) and (E) are not great, because snakes and spiders eat other things, too, and their definitions are not based on what they eat, anyway. Eliminate 'em. Now look at (A) and (D). Try their sentences on the stem words. Could something lay a swan? Probably not! Could something be a young swan? Sure, there could be a word that means "baby swan." Sure enough, "cygnet" is exactly that.

Try working backwards with these analogies:

Kinesiology is to motion as
  (A) numerology is to progress   _____
  (B) navigation is to ocean   _____
  (C) astronomy is to weather   _____
  (D) criminology is to perversion   _____
  (E) psychology is to mind   _____

Apiary is to bees as
  (A) stable is to horses   _____
  (B) jar is to honey   _____
  (C) florist is to flowers   _____
  (D) dirt is to ants   _____
  (E) leash is to dog   _____

For the first one, only (B) and (E) allow you to make strong sentences. So try those sentences: Could kinesiology be how you get around on the motion? No. Could kinesiology be the study of human motion? Yep. We got it down to (E).

For the second one, eliminate (B), (D), and (E), because the words' relationships are not strong. Now, do you think that an apiary is a place where bees are kept? Possibly. Do you think an apiary is someone who works with bees? Also possible. Take a guess between (A) and (C). Look up "apiary" and make an index card for it.

Remember that the answer will probably be a relationship based on a definitional sentence that can be made with A and B, but keep in mind that it could also be a relationship between A and C.

Practice—Working backwards

We've hidden one of the words in the stem pair, so you can't know it. Work backwards:

- ◆ Make sentences with the answer choices.

- ◆ Eliminate the sentences that don't show a strong, definitional relationship.

- ◆ Try out each definitional sentence on the stem words.

- ◆ If it helps, say "something" when you have to insert the unknown word.

- ◆ Does it seem possible that the unknown word has that definition? If not, eliminate it.

- ◆ Don't eliminate any answer choices that contain words you don't know.

- ◆ Get as far as you can, and then guess.

    1. Island is to ??????????? as

        (A) castle is to moat
        (B) star is to galaxy
        (C) river is to delta
        (D) bay is to peninsula
        (E) earth is to hemisphere

    2. ??????? is to woman as

        (A) legality is to lawyer
        (B) monarchy is to sovereign
        (C) hierarchy is to heir
        (D) feudalism is to farmer
        (E) duplicity is to thief

    3. ?????????? is to enthusiasm as submissive is to

        (A) solitude
        (B) defiance
        (C) conviction
        (D) admiration
        (E) withdrawn

4. ????????? is to jury as

    (A) eradicate is to problem
    (B) quarantine is to patient
    (C) elect is to politician
    (D) liquidate is to opponent
    (E) evacuate is to city

5. ????????? is to shape as

    (A) amorous is to trust
    (B) temporal is to patience
    (C) enticing is to guile
    (D) bland is to zest
    (E) classical is to harmony

WHEN YOU "SORTA" KNOW THE WORDS

Use "side of the fence"

If you can't make a definitional sentence because you're not sure what the words mean, but you've got some idea from having seen them before, determine whether the words are on the same side of the fence, or different sides. That is, are they similar enough to be grouped together, or are they different enough that you'd say they're on different sides of a fence? If they are similar in meaning, write "S" next to the pair. If their meanings are more like opposites, write "D."

Since the answer pair has to have the same relationship, you can eliminate any that don't match. If your words are similar, you can eliminate any answers that are different. If your words are different, you can eliminate any answers that are similar.

Practice — Judging side of the fence

Mark the following pairs of words as "S" (similar) or "D" (different).

1. healthy is to ailing   ____   7. apathetic is to passion   ____
2. limitless is to end   ____   8. boast is to vain   ____
3. rapture is to happiness   ____   9. tactful is to diplomacy   ____
4. humane is to brutality   ____   10. innocent is to guile   ____
5. obscure is to sight   ____   11. miser is to greedy   ____
6. incendiary is to flame   ____   12. frivolous is to serious   ____

Now we can try a whole analogy:

Lurid is to horror as

    (A) comical is to amusement
    (B) illegal is to law
    (C) cowardly is to fear
    (D) ghastly is to serenity
    (E) humane is to treatment

Don't try to make a sentence—just decide if "lurid" and "horror" are similar or different. Then make the same decision for all the answer choices. You should wind up with a question that looks like this:

Lurid is to horror as   S
(A) comical is to amusement   S
(B) illegal is to law   D
(C) cowardly is to fear   S
(D) ghastly is to serenity   D
(E) humane is to treatment   neither

Now you can guess from just two answers—you've increased your odds considerably! Remember to mark up your test booklet as you eliminate, and guess even if you've only eliminated one choice. If you're not sure of the definition of "lurid," or any other word on this page, make an index card for it!

Practice — Using "side of the fence"

In these analogies, we've taken out the stem words, but told you whether they're similar or different. Eliminate the answers that you know are definitely wrong because you've written a letter next to them that doesn't match the letter next to the stem words. Remember, you can't eliminate answers that contain words you don't know!

1. (SIMILAR WORDS)

    (A) miserly is to greed
    (B) gentle is to harm
    (C) famous is to privacy
    (D) objective is to opinion
    (E) fanciful is to theory

2. (SIMILAR WORDS)

    (A) athletic is to shapely
    (B) darkened is to light
    (C) free is to liberated
    (D) brave is to cowardly
    (E) normal is to unusual

3. (DIFFERENT WORDS)

    (A) refurbish is to worn
    (B) repaint is to beautiful
    (C) reconstruct is to new
    (D) revive is to tired
    (E) cultivate is to fertile

4. (SIMILAR WORDS)

    (A) humid is to moisture
    (B) displeased is to anger
    (C) silent is to discourse
    (D) pointless is to relevance
    (E) guilty is to neutral

5. (DIFFERENT WORDS)

   (A) flourish is to revive
   (B) wilt is to deaden
   (C) protect is to harm
   (D) heal is to injure
   (E) discuss is to debate

6. (DIFFERENT WORDS)

   (A) modify is to vary
   (B) mutter is to speak
   (C) vacillate is to stand
   (D) rectify is to fix
   (E) verify is to discover

7. (DIFFERENT WORDS)

   (A) charitable is to selfish
   (B) favorable is to despised
   (C) productive is to arid
   (D) predictable is to ordinary
   (E) verbose is to tacit

8. (SIMILAR WORDS)

   (A) anticipate is to hope
   (B) alleviate is to lessen
   (C) innovate is to predict
   (D) disseminate is to gather
   (E) elucidate is to muddle

9. (SIMILAR WORDS)

   (A) slander is to libel
   (B) avenge is to forgive
   (C) provoke is to calm
   (D) quibble is to argue
   (E) satiate is to fill

10. (SIMILAR WORDS)

    (A) supreme is to zenith
    (B) infallible is to certain
    (C) prevalent is to vacant
    (D) listless is to energetic
    (E) pessimistic is to negative

Work backwards

You can use this technique for words you just "sorta" know, too, in addition to using it on analogies where you just know one of the words. Try it on this one. "Patent" is a word we all "sorta" know.

Patent is to inventor as

    (A) advertisement is to merchant _____
    (B) money is to consumer _____
    (C) monopoly is to customer _____
    (D) copyright is to author _____
    (E) novelty is to journalist _____

    (C) and (E) should be crossed out for sure—the words are not strongly related. With the other answer choices, you've made sentences. Which sentence works best with "patent" and "inventor"? (D).

WHEN YOU REALLY DON'T KNOW EITHER OF THE WORDS

If you have never seen the stem words before, you're better off putting a circle around the question number in the test booklet and skipping the question. If you have time to go back to the ones you've circled and skipped, then try this:

Work backwards as much as you can

Go straight to the answer choices, and make sentences with them. Now, you can't try the sentences with the stem words, because you don't know the stem words, right? So just look at the sentences you have. Which ones are not likely to be correct? The ones that are not like definitions. Eliminate those answer choices—the ones in which the words are not related in such a way that you need one to define the other.

    Look at these possible answer choices and decide if they're definitional, or if you should eliminate them on a question for which you do not know the words. Write a sentence for the answers you'd keep.

Practice — Working backwards as much as you can

1. tooth is to chewing   _____

2. hammer is to wood   _____

3. archipelago is to islands _____

4. engine is to smoke   _____

5. angry is to violence   _____

6. jest is to humorous   _____

7. wind is to season   _____

    Remember, though, that you're not trying to answer all the questions. There are bound to be words on the test that you do not know. Don't sweat it. Check your Pacing Chart to see how many analogies you need to do. Most students don't need to do analogies with words they don't know at all, even to reach their target scores.

THE ANALOGIES PLAN
If I know the words

If I know the words, then I:

_____

_____

_____

A sentence is good if it's _____ and _____.

If my sentence eliminates some but not all answer choices, I can:

_____

A specific, definitional sentence uses words that are _____

Some questions that can help me make a sentence are:

_____   _____

_____   _____

_____   _____

_____   _____

If I know the words but can't make a sentence, then I ask myself:

_____

_____

_____

_____

_____

And finally, if none of those questions worked with A and B (the first two words in the analogy), then I ask myself:

_____

If I know one of the words

If I know one of the words, then I _____

which means that I _____

and then I _____

If I "sorta" know the words

If I "sorta" know the words, then I use _____

I can also use _____

If I don't know the words

If I don't know the words, I _____

If I have time left, then I go back and _____

If you have trouble with any of the questions above, go back and reread the appropriate part of this chapter.

Practice — All analogies techniques

1. Chocolate is to candy as

   (A) fish is to mammal
   (B) meat is to animal
   (C) broccoli is to vegetable
   (D) brick is to house
   (E) fire is to forest

2. Pound is to weight as

   (A) decibel is to sound
   (B) inch is to foot
   (C) quart is to liter
   (D) fathom is to distance
   (E) length is to height

3. Class is to student as

   (A) cast is to actor
   (B) teacher is to staff
   (C) conductor is to band
   (D) director is to play
   (E) musician is to band

4. Leak is to peak as

   (A) tumble is to rumble
   (B) money is to runny
   (C) lark is to park
   (D) went is to sent
   (E) nimble is to knuckle

5. Composer is to symphony as

   (A) mechanic is to auto
   (B) major is to troops
   (C) architect is to building
   (D) tycoon is to wealth
   (E) writer is to paragraph

6. Link is to chain as

   (A) obstacle is to course
   (B) group is to member
   (C) sidewalk is to path
   (D) mural is to museum
   (E) word is to sentence

7. Tadpole is to frog as caterpillar is to

   (A) worm
   (B) cocoon
   (C) crawl
   (D) larvae
   (E) butterfly

8. Cuff is to wrist as

   (A) string is to hood
   (B) buckle is to waist
   (C) cap is to hat
   (D) vest is to body
   (E) collar is to neck

9. Congregation is to worshippers as

   (A) galaxy is to stars
   (B) party is to politics
   (C) mine is to gems
   (D) job is to employers
   (E) pottery is to shards

10. Tactile is to touch as

    (A) delectable is to drink
    (B) audible is to sound
    (C) potable is to food
    (D) servile is to obey
    (E) nutritious is to meal

11. Conviction is to opinion as

(A) report is to story
(B) reverence is to admiration
(C) debate is to argument
(D) appeal is to affectation
(E) ascend is to precipice

12. Caricature is to drawing as

(A) joke is to punch line
(B) watercolor is to painting
(C) hyperbole is to statement
(D) star is to feature
(E) dynamite is to blast

13. Clap is to stomp as

(A) snap is to shout
(B) hand is to foot
(C) map is to ramp
(D) door is to wall
(E) finger is to chicken

14. Deceleration is to speed as

(A) adulation is to praise
(B) descent is to altitude
(C) tyranny is to leader
(D) hydration is to water
(E) fear is to hatred

15. Melon is to lemon as

(A) cantaloupe is to fruit
(B) star is to rats
(C) trunk is to torso
(D) tames is to mates
(E) tree is to human

16. Dull is to insipid as diverting is to

(A) expecting
(B) feeling
(C) astounding
(D) entertaining
(E) tantalizing

17. Voracious is to food as

(A) greedy is to money
(B) gluttonous is to obesity
(C) clarity is to water
(D) generosity is to object
(E) veracity is to truth

18. Adroit is to motion as

    (A) bridled is to emotion
    (B) unfettered is to restraint
    (C) superior is to skill
    (D) ubiquitous is to presence
    (E) articulate is to speech

19. Anesthetic is to pain as

    (A) lamp is to light
    (B) mnemonic is to memory
    (C) exercise is to diet
    (D) understanding is to comprehension
    (E) muffler is to noise

20. Oven is to kiln as baker is to

    (A) potter
    (B) ceramics
    (C) bread
    (D) miner
    (E) shepherd

21. Impeccable is to adequate as

    (A) impressionable is to eager
    (B) inexhaustible is to sufficient
    (C) impossible is to prepared
    (D) intangible is to popular
    (E) impractical is to sensible

22. Symmetrical is to amorphous as

    (A) metric is to moronic
    (B) shapely is to muscled
    (C) balanced is to unshaped
    (D) flowing is to lined
    (E) external is to internal

SYNONYMS

What is a synonym?

On the SSAT, a synonym question asks you to choose the answer choice that comes closest in meaning to the stem word (the word in capitals). Often the best answer won't mean the exact same thing as the stem word, but it will be closer than any of the other choices.

Just like with analogies, you need to decide which vocabulary category the synonym stem word falls into for you, so you know which technique to use. Do all the synonyms for which you know the stem word first, and then go back and do the ones you "sorta" know.

When You Know The Stem Word

Write down your own definition

Come up with a simple definition—a word or a phrase. Write it next to the stem word. Then look at the answers, eliminate the ones that are farthest from your definition, and choose the closest one.

It's very simple. Don't let the test writers put words in your mouth. Make sure you're armed with your own definition before you look at their answer choices. They often like to put in a word that is a close second to the "best" answer, and if you've got your own synonym ready, you'll be able to make the distinction.

If you need to, cover the answers with your hand, so you can think of your definition before looking. Eventually you may not have to write down your definitions, but you should start out that way.

As you compare the choices to your definition, cross out the ones that are definitely not right. Crossing out answer choices is something you should *always* do—it saves you time because you don't go back to choices you've already decided were not the "best."

As always, don't eliminate words you don't know.

Try this one:

Be Honest

Do you really know the definition of the word? The SSAT uses dictionary definitions, and these may differ from your own sometimes. If you're not positive, you may want to use the techniques for when you 'sorta' know the word.

WITHER: _____ (definition)

(A) play
(B) spoil
(C) greatly improve
(D) wilt
(E) give freely

The stem word means "shrivel" or "dry up." Which answer is closest? (D). You may have been considering (B), but (D) is closer.

Practice — Write your own definition

Just write your definition—a word or two—for each of these stem words.

1. BIZARRE: _____
2. PREFACE: _____
3. GENEROUS: _____
4. MORAL: _____
5. ALTER: _____
6. REVOLVE: _____
7. HOPEFUL: _____
8. LINGER: _____
9. ASSIST: _____
10. CONSTRUCT: _____

11. STOOP: _____

12. CANDID: _____

13. TAUNT: _____

14. COARSE: _____

15. VAIN: _____

16. SERENE: _____

17. UTILIZE: _____

18. VIGOROUS: _____

19. PROLONG: _____

20. BENEFIT: _____

Write another definition

Why would you ever need to change your definition? Let's see:

MANEUVER:

(A) avoidance
(B) deviation
(C) find
(D) contrivance
(E) invent

Your definition might be something like "move" or "control," if you know the word from hearing it applied to cars. You're thinking about "maneuver" as a verb, and that definition isn't in the answer choices. "Maneuver" can also be a noun. It means "a plan, scheme, or trick." Now go back and eliminate.

The SSAT sometimes uses secondary definitions, which can be the same part of speech or a different part of speech from the primary definition. Just stay flexible in your definitions, and you'll be fine.

Parts of Speech?

If you need to, go back and review parts of speech in the 'Word Parts' section of chapter 1.

Practice — Write another definition

Write down as many definitions as you can think of for the following words. Your definitions may be the same part of speech or different. If you have a hard time thinking of different meanings, look the word up.

1. POINT: _____

2. INDUSTRY: _____

3. FLAG: _____

4. FLUID: _____

5. CHAMPION: _____

6. TABLE: _____

7. SERVICE: _____

Practice — Easy synonym techniques

Try these synonyms.

- ◆ Use the definition for the stem word that you wrote down before.

- ◆ Look at the answer choices and eliminate the ones that are farthest from your definition.

- ◆ If there are stem words you don't know well enough to define, just skip them and come back after you've learned techniques for stem words you "sorta" know.

1. BIZARRE:

    (A) lonely
    (B) unable
    (C) odd
    (D) found
    (E) able

2. PREFACE:

    (A) introduce
    (B) state
    (C) propose
    (D) jumble
    (E) make able

3. GENEROUS:

    (A) skimpy
    (B) faulty
    (C) ample
    (D) unusual
    (E) cold

4. MORAL:

    (A) imitation
    (B) full
    (C) genuine
    (D) upright
    (E) sure

5. ALTER:

    (A) sew
    (B) make up
    (C) react
    (D) total
    (E) change

6. REVOLVE:

(A) push against
(B) go forward
(C) leave behind
(D) turn around
(E) move past

7. HOPEFUL:

(A) discouraging
(B) promising
(C) fulfilling
(D) deceiving
(E) frustrating

8. LINGER:

(A) hurry
(B) abate
(C) dawdle
(D) attempt
(E) enter

9. ASSIST:

(A) work
(B) discourage
(C) appeal
(D) hinder
(E) help

10. CONSTRUCT:

(A) build
(B) type
(C) live in
(D) engage
(E) enable

11. STOOP:

(A) raise
(B) elevate
(C) condescend
(D) realize
(E) imagine

12. CANDID:

(A) picture
(B) honest
(C) prepared
(D) unfocused
(E) rehearsed

13. TAUNT:

   (A) delay
   (B) stand
   (C) show
   (D) horrify
   (E) tease

14. COARSE:

   (A) smooth
   (B) crude
   (C) polite
   (D) furious
   (E) emotional

15. VAIN :

   (A) conceited
   (B) beautiful
   (C) talented
   (D) unattractive
   (E) helpless

16. SERENE:

   (A) helpful
   (B) normal
   (C) calm
   (D) disastrous
   (E) floating

17. UTILIZE:

   (A) pass on
   (B) break down
   (C) resort to
   (D) rely on
   (E) make use of

18. VIGOROUS:

   (A) slothful
   (B) aimless
   (C) energetic
   (D) glorious
   (E) victorious

19. PROLONG:

   (A) delay
   (B) lengthen
   (C) exceed
   (D) assert
   (E) resolve

20. BENEFIT:

    (A) cooperate
    (B) struggle
    (C) assist
    (D) deny
    (E) appeal

WHEN YOU "SORTA" KNOW THE STEM WORD

Why should you do synonyms last?
Why are they harder than analogies?

Synonyms are harder to beat than analogies because the SSAT gives you no context with which to figure out words that you "sorta" know. But that doesn't mean you're done after the easy synonyms. You can get the medium ones, too. You just need to create your own context to figure out words you don't know very well.

Keep in mind, also, that your goal is to eliminate the worst answers, in order to make an educated guess. You'll be able to do this for every synonym that you "sorta" know, and even if you just eliminate one choice, **guess**. You'll gain points, overall.

Make your own context

You can create your own context for the word by figuring out how you've heard it used before. Think of the other words you've heard used with the stem word. Is there a certain phrase that comes to mind? What does that phrase mean?

If you still can't come up with a definition for the stem word, just use the context in which you've heard the word to eliminate answers that wouldn't fit at all in that same context.

How about this stem word:

ABOMINABLE:

Where have you heard "abominable"? The Abominable Snowman, of course. Think about it—you know it's a monster-like creature. Which answer choices can you eliminate?

ABOMINABLE:

(A) terrifying		the terrifying snowman? maybe
(B) detestable		the detestable snowman? sure
(C) rude		the rude snowman? probably not
(D) showy		the showy snowman? nope
(E) talkative		The talkative snowman? no way

You can throw out everything but (A) and (B). You can guess, with a much better shot at getting the answer right than guessing from five choices. Or you can think about where else you've heard the stem word. Have you ever heard something called an "abomination"? Was it something that terrified people or was it something people hated? (B) is the answer.

Try this one. Where have you heard this stem word? Try the answers in that context.

SURROGATE:

(A) friendly
(B) requested
(C) paranoid
(D) numerous
(E) substitute

Have you heard the stem word in "surrogate mother"? If you have, you can definitely eliminate (B), (C), and (D), and (A) isn't great either. A surrogate mother is a substitute mother.

Try one more:

ENDANGER:

(A) rescue
(B) frighten
(C) confuse
(D) threaten
(E) isolate

Everyone's associations are different, but you've probably heard of "endangered species" or "endangered lives." Use either of those phrases to eliminate answer choices that can't fit into it. Rescued species? Frightened species? Confused species? Threatened species? Isolated species? (D) works best.

Practice — Making your own context

Write down the phrase in which you've heard each word.

1. Common _____

2. Competent _____

3. Abridge _____

4. Untimely _____

5. Homogenize _____

6. Delinquent _____

7. Inalienable _____

8. Paltry _____

9. Auspicious _____

10. Prodigal _____

Practice — Using your own context

1. COMMON:

   (A) beautiful
   (B) novel
   (C) typical
   (D) constant
   (E) similar

2. COMPETENT:

   (A) angry
   (B) peaceful
   (C) well-written
   (D) capable
   (E) possible

3. ABRIDGE:

   (A) complete
   (B) span
   (C) reach
   (D) shorten
   (E) retain

4. UNTIMELY:

   (A) late
   (B) punctual
   (C) dependent
   (D) inappropriate
   (E) continuous

5. HOMOGENIZE:

   (A) group together
   (B) send
   (C) isolate
   (D) enfold
   (E) purify

6. DELINQUENT:

   (A) underage
   (B) negligent
   (C) superior
   (D) advanced
   (E) independent

7. INALIENABLE:

   (A) misplaced
   (B) universal
   (C) assured
   (D) democratic
   (E) changeable

8. PALTRY:

(A) meager
(B) colored
(C) thick
(D) abundant
(E) indistinguishable

9. AUSPICIOUS:

(A) supple
(B) minor
(C) doubtful
(D) favorable
(E) ominous

10. PRODIGAL:

(A) wasteful
(B) amusing
(C) disadvantaged
(D) lazy
(E) virtuous

Use word parts to piece together a definition

Prefixes, roots, and suffixes can help you figure out what a word means. You should use this technique in addition to (not instead of) word association, since not all word parts retain their original meanings.

You may have never seen this stem word before, but if you've been working on your Vocabulary chapter, you know that the root "pac" or "peac" means peace. You can see the same root in "Pacific," "pacifier," and the word "peace" itself. So what's the answer to this synonym?

PACIFIST:

(A) innocent person
(B) person opposed to war
(C) warmonger
(D) wanderer
(E) journeyman

The answer is (B).

In the following stem word, we see "cred," a word part that means "belief" or "faith." You can see this word part in "incredible," "credit," and "credibility." The answer is now simple.

CREDIBLE:

(A) obsolete
(B) believable
(C) fabulous
(D) mundane
(E) superficial

(B) again. What are the word parts in the
following stem word?

MONOTONOUS:

(A) lively
(B) educational
(C) nutritious
(D) repetitious
(E) helpful

"Mono" means "one." "Tone" has to do with sound. If something keeps striking one sound, how would you describe it? (D) is the answer.

The only way you'll be able to use word parts is if you know them. Get cracking on the Vocabulary chapter!

Use "positive/negative"

Another way to use what you "sorta" know about a stem word is by asking yourself if it is positive or negative. Then decide if each of the answers is positive or negative. Eliminate any answers that do not match. If the stem word is positive, then the answer must be positive. If the stem word is negative, then so must be the answer. Write "+" or "–" or "neither" next to each word as you make your decisions.

If someone said you were belligerent, would you be complimented? No, because "belligerent" is a negative word. You might know that from hearing the word, but you might also know what the word part "bell" means. Now decide whether each answer choice is positive or negative.

BELLIGERENT:

(A) frisky   +
(B) messy   –
(C) friendly +
(D) antagonistic   –
(E) persuasive   +

You can eliminate (A), (C), and (E), because you're looking for a synonym, so if the stem is negative, then the answer must also be negative. "Bell" has to do with war, so the answer is (D).

Try this one:

ZENITH:

(A) distance
(B) failure
(C) high-point
(D) complaint
(E) proximity

How do you know "zenith" is positive? Probably because it's the brand name of a television set, and brand names will generally be positive words. The only really positive answer choice here is (C), and that's the answer.

Practice — Decide positive/negative

1. LUGUBRIOUS: ___
2. DISDAIN: ___
3. CACOPHONOUS: ___
4. COMPASSIONATE: ___
5. SLANDER: ___

6. HARMONIC: ___
7. INCORRIGIBLE ___
8. ELOQUENT: ___
9. AGILE: ___
10. TOIL: ___

Practice — Use positive/negative

In these synonyms, you know only that the stem word is positive or negative. Eliminate as many answers as you can, based on what you know.

1. GOOD WORD:

   (A) harmful
   (B) helpful
   (C) unusual
   (D) horrid
   (E) therapeutic

2. GOOD WORD:

   (A) useful
   (B) handy
   (C) difficult
   (D) regular
   (E) vigorous

3. BAD WORD:

   (A) disgusting
   (B) reliable
   (C) furious
   (D) sturdy
   (E) stabilized

4. BAD WORD:

   (A) beneficial
   (B) placid
   (C) coarse
   (D) noisy
   (E) sluggish

5. BAD WORD:

   (A) faulty
   (B) vague
   (C) grateful
   (D) angry
   (E) indolent

6. GOOD WORD:

   (A) malignant
   (B) unhealthy
   (C) friendly
   (D) forward thinking
   (E) negligent

7. GOOD WORD:

   (A) incapable
   (B) useful
   (C) ferocious
   (D) flavorful
   (E) overzealous

8. BAD WORD:

   (A) assistant
   (B) culprit
   (C) patron
   (D) rival
   (E) acolyte

9. GOOD WORD:

   (A) diverse
   (B) winning
   (C) ruined
   (D) infrequent
   (E) meticulous

10. GOOD WORD:

    (A) honorable
    (B) despicable
    (C) elite
    (D) unsurpassed
    (E) dormant

11. BAD WORD:

    (A) dangerous
    (B) illegal
    (C) sophisticated
    (D) delicious
    (E) venerated

12. BAD WORD:

    (A) rascal
    (B) vermin
    (C) benefactor
    (D) addict
    (E) ally

13. GOOD WORD:

(A) slovenly
(B) gluttonous
(C) envious
(D) beatific
(E) mercenary

14. GOOD WORD:

(A) visionary
(B) despot
(C) malefactor
(D) ingrate
(E) jingoist

15. GOOD WORD:

(A) significant
(B) mediocre
(C) provincial
(D) opulent
(E) vehement

16. BAD WORD:

(A) apathetic
(B) assertive
(C) committed
(D) insipid
(E) robust

17. BAD WORD:

(A) banal
(B) unrealistic
(C) vague
(D) decisive
(E) impartial

18. BAD WORD:

(A) tyrant
(B) rebel
(C) leader
(D) participant
(E) misanthrope

19. GOOD WORD:

(A) quack
(B) expert
(C) narrator
(D) reporter
(E) skeptic

20. GOOD WORD:
  (A) turmoil
  (B) amity
  (C) benign
  (D) virulent
  (E) supercilious

Eliminate wrong parts of speech

Eliminate answers that cannot be the same part of speech as the stem word, even if they're close in meaning. You should keep in mind that many words can be more than one part of speech. As a model, we've written in the parts of speech instead of the actual words:

ADJECTIVE:
  (A) adjective
  (B) noun
  (C) adjective or verb
  (D) adjective
  (E) verb or noun

In the synonym above, you can eliminate (B) and (E) because they cannot be adjectives, and you know that the "best" answer is an adjective here, because that's what the stem word is.

Remember, suffixes can be very helpful in telling you what part of speech a word is. Look in the Vocabulary chapter (chapter 1) for some helpful suffixes.

Practice — Identifying parts of speech

What parts of speech are the following words? (Some of them can be more than one.)

  1. mirror _____

  2. flattery _____

  3. cover _____

  4. emaciated _____

  5. adversity _____

  6. malleable _____

WORDS YOU REALLY DON'T KNOW

Don't spend time on words you've never seen, if you don't know any of their word parts. Check the Pacing chapter to see how many synonyms you need to do.

THE SYNONYMS PLAN

Words I know

When I know the stem word, I _____

If I don't see a definition close to mine, I _____

Words I "sorta" know

When I "sorta" know the stem word, I can use the following techniques:

_____

_____

_____

_____

Words I really don't know

If I've never seen the stem word before, I _____

Can I eliminate answers that contain words I don't know? _____

If you have trouble with any of these questions, reread the Synonyms chapter.

Practice — All synonyms techniques

1. PRINCIPLE:

   (A) leader
   (B) standard
   (C) theory
   (D) game
   (E) chief

2. CAPTURE:

   (A) secure
   (B) lose
   (C) steal
   (D) halt
   (E) release

3. BEFRIEND:

   (A) sever ties
   (B) close down
   (C) approach
   (D) enjoy
   (E) ignore

4. AUTOMATIC:

   (A) involuntary
   (B) enjoyable
   (C) forceful
   (D) hapless
   (E) independent

5. APTITUDE:
   (A) difficulty
   (B) reason
   (C) mistake
   (D) ability
   (E) demeanor

6. CAPITAL:
   (A) primary
   (B) regressive
   (C) capable
   (D) false
   (E) building

7. REPRESS:
   (A) defy
   (B) faithful
   (C) ruling
   (D) outside
   (E) prevent

8. ENDURE:
   (A) take in
   (B) stick with
   (C) add to
   (D) run from
   (E) push out

9. TRANSMIT:
   (A) eliminate
   (B) watch
   (C) send
   (D) symbol
   (E) retrieve

10. DIALOGUE:
    (A) speech
    (B) conversation
    (C) monologue
    (D) sermon
    (E) reading

11. EULOGY:

   (A) attack
   (B) tribute
   (C) complement
   (D) criticism
   (E) encouragement

12. BAN:

   (A) remove
   (B) imposing
   (C) forbid
   (D) specify
   (E) resign

13. APATHY:

   (A) involvement
   (B) compassion
   (C) contempt
   (D) indifference
   (E) honesty

14. OMNISCIENT:

   (A) agile
   (B) logical
   (C) knowledgeable
   (D) capable
   (E) invulnerable

15. TRANSGRESS:

   (A) offend
   (B) eradicate
   (C) include
   (D) attend
   (E) violate

16. VIVACIOUS:

   (A) nimble
   (B) lively
   (C) easily amused
   (D) direct
   (E) constantly aware

17. HYPERBOLE:
    (A) isolation
    (B) identification
    (C) exaggeration
    (D) sharp curve
    (E) qualification

18. CONGENITAL:
    (A) innocent
    (B) inborn
    (C) graceful
    (D) credible
    (E) acquired

19. SUCCINCT:
    (A) subterranean
    (B) confusing
    (C) blatant
    (D) direct
    (E) common

20. CRAFTY:
    (A) apt
    (B) sly
    (C) agile
    (D) wicked
    (E) wayward

21. FLUENT:
    (A) spoken
    (B) quiet
    (C) flowing
    (D) illness
    (E) real

22. IDENTICAL:
    (A) broken
    (B) duplicate
    (C) foolish
    (D) related
    (E) major

23. POPULAR:

    (A) rude
    (B) accepted
    (C) understood
    (D) ultimate
    (E) respected

24. WHARF:

    (A) beach
    (B) raft
    (C) flat ship
    (D) carrier
    (E) dock

25. FAITHFUL:

    (A) hopeful
    (B) unrealistic
    (C) truthful
    (D) pleasant
    (E) devoted

26. OBSTACLE:

    (A) path
    (B) great distance
    (C) ditch
    (D) impediment
    (E) ravine

27. CONVOLUTED:

    (A) interesting
    (B) expensive
    (C) twisted
    (D) forged
    (E) cheap

28. ALIGN:

    (A) repair
    (B) command
    (C) straighten
    (D) replace
    (E) intervene

29. VETO:

    (A) shorten
    (B) discuss
    (C) define
    (D) reject
    (E) submit

30. MANGLE:

    (A) shine
    (B) wear
    (C) torture
    (D) disarm
    (E) mutilate

31. FEEBLE:

    (A) fair
    (B) ineffective
    (C) tough
    (D) hardened
    (E) sickness

32. SLUGGISH:

    (A) aggressive
    (B) slow
    (C) inconsiderate
    (D) wicked
    (E) needy

33. REDUNDANT:

    (A) poor
    (B) superfluous
    (C) abundant
    (D) fancy
    (E) austere

34. LAMPOON:

    (A) article
    (B) biography
    (C) journey
    (D) satire
    (E) presentation

35. TREPIDATION:

   (A) boldness
   (B) irony
   (C) rashness
   (D) comfort
   (E) fear

36. ASSESS:

   (A) deny
   (B) accept
   (C) size up
   (D) dismiss
   (E) portray

37. GHASTLY:

   (A) responsible
   (B) erroneous
   (C) horrible
   (D) favorable
   (E) plausible

38. CENSURE:

   (A) edit
   (B) understanding
   (C) approval
   (D) disapproval
   (E) hate-mongering

39. DISMANTLE:

   (A) discourse with
   (B) break down
   (C) yield to
   (D) drive away
   (E) strip from

40. CACOPHONY:

   (A) melody
   (B) harmony
   (C) musical
   (D) rhythm
   (E) dissonance

READING

WHAT'S READING ALL ABOUT ON THE SSAT?

You have to read the SSAT reading passages differently from the way you read anything else. The passages the test writers use are dense with information.

Generally, when you read a textbook or any other book, you notice one or two phrases you want to remember in each paragraph. You can underline those phrases to show that they seem important, so you can easily find them later.

On the SSAT, however, the passages are chosen precisely because there is a lot of information in only a few paragraphs. It's all packed in together. So if you read your normal way, here's what happens: You read the first sentence and you try to remember it. You read the second sentence and try to remember it. You read the third sentence and, as you try to remember it, you forget the first two.

You have to read with a different goal in mind for the SSAT. This may sound crazy, but *don't* try to learn or remember anything. **You don't get any points for reading the passage well!**

What do you get points for? Answering questions correctly. On the questions and answers, you need to slow down and make sure you're checking each answer carefully before eliminating it. Don't worry about finishing the section, especially if you're in one of the lower grades taking that test. Let's take our example from before: An eighth grade girl takes the Upper Level Test and does better than 91 percent of the eighth-graders in reading. How many reading questions has she gotten right out of 40? 31. She probably never even read the last passage, and she's in the top 9 percent of the students she's being compared to. Even fewer students finish the reading section than finish the verbal or quantitative sections, and those that do are hurting their scores with careless errors. Don't try to finish!

Read Quickly, Answer Slowly

Your goal is to spend more time answering questions (and less time reading the passage).

THE PASSAGES

What are the passages like?

There are 7 or 8 passages in a reading section. The first two passages are the easiest—definitely do them.

After the first two, you can choose which to do. The reading section purposely has far more passages and questions than most students can complete in 25 minutes—7 or 8 passages and 40 questions. Look at the Pacing chapter (chapter 3) to see how many reading questions you need to complete. Don't let the test writers choose which ones you'll get to. Choose for yourself by flipping through them and going with the types you do best. You'll do better on topics that interest you.

Which types of passages do you do better on? Investigate this as you do practice questions and the practice SSAT.

Passage types

Actual historical document • Speech • Newspaper article • Eyewitness account	These are called 'primary sources' because they are written during the time they describe. The SSAT doesn't usually tell you when or where they're from.
History • of a Person • of a Group • of an Event • of a Scientific idea, discovery, or invention	These are 'secondary sources' because they are written after the events they describe, usually based on primary sources. Your history textbook is a secondary source.
Science	These are not historical. Instead, they talk about current scientific explanations.
Opinion • Comparing • Contrasting • Judging	These are written by an author stating his or her opinion. You can practice reading these in the Op-Ed pages of a newspaper.
Story • Entire Story • Part of a Story	Sometimes you get the whole story; sometimes you are dropped down in the middle of one.
Poem	See if you do well on poems in practice tests.

History and Science passages are like parts of textbooks—they tend to be unemotional and objective. An actual historical document or a part of a story can be disorienting, because often you will get no warning as to who is speaking or writing, or what time or place you've been dropped into. You need to get as much of that information as possible from the clues in the passage. Of course, poems are open to even more interpretation than the other types—make sure you do well on practice poem passages if you plan on doing them on the test.

How Do I Read the Passages?

Quickly! Don't try to remember the details in the passage. Your goal is to read the passage quickly to get the main idea.

The SSAT reading section is an open-book test—you can look back at the passage to answer questions about the details.

Label the paragraphs

After you read each paragraph, ask yourself what you just read. Put it in your own words—just a couple of words—and label the side of the paragraph with your summary. This way you'll have something to guide you back to the relevant part of the passage when you answer a question.

Imagine your grandparents are coming to visit, and they're staying in your room. Your parents tell you to clean up your room, and get all that junk off the floor. Now, that junk is important to you. Okay, so maybe you don't need your rollerblades every day, or all those old notes from your best friend, but you do need to be able to get to them. So you get a bunch of boxes, and you throw your rollerblades, ballet slippers, dress shoes, and ice skates in one box. In another, you throw all your old notes, letters, cards, and schoolwork. In another, you throw all your hand-held videogames, CDs, computer software, and floppy disks. Before you put the boxes in the closet, what must you do to be sure you don't have to go through every one of them the next time you want to play Tetris? You need to label them. "Shoes," "papers," and "computer/CDs" should do it.

The same thing is true of the paragraphs you read on the SSAT. You need to be able to go back to the passage and find the answer to a question quickly—you don't want to have to look through every paragraph to find it! The key to labeling the paragraphs is practice—you need to do it quickly, coming up with one or two words that accurately remind you of what's in the paragraph.

If the passage has only one paragraph, try stopping every few sentences to label them with a word or two. Poems do not need to be labeled.

State the main idea

After you have read the entire passage, ask yourself two questions:

- ◆ **What?** What is the passage about?

- ◆ **So what?** What's the author's point about this topic?

The answers to these questions will show you the main idea of the passage. Scribble down this main idea in just a few words. The answer to **What?** is the thing that was being talked about—"Bees" or "weather forecasting." The answer to **So what?** gives you the rest of the sentence—"bees do little dances that tell other bees where to go for pollen," or "Weather forecasting is complicated by many problems."

Don't assume you will find the main idea in the first paragraph. While often the main idea is in the beginning of the passage, it is not *always* in the first sentence or even the first paragraph. The beginning may just be a lead-in to the main point.

Practice — Getting through the passage

As you quickly read each paragraph, label it. When you finish the passage, answer **What?** and **So what?** to get the main idea.

> Contrary to popular belief, the first European known to lay eyes on America was not Christopher Columbus or Amerigo Vespucci but a little-known Viking by the name of Bjarni Herjolfsson. In the summer of 986, Bjarni sailed from Norway to Iceland, heading for the Viking settlement where his father Heriulf resided.
>
> When he arrived in Iceland, Bjarni discovered that his father had already sold his land and estates and set out for the latest Viking settlement on the subarctic island called Greenland. Discovered by a notorious murderer and criminal named Eric the Red, Greenland lay at the limit of the known world. Dismayed, Bjarni set out for this new colony.
>
> Since the Vikings traveled without chart or compass, it was not uncommon for them to lose their way in the unpredictable northern seas. Beset by fog, the crew lost their bearings. When the fog finally cleared, they found themselves before a land that was level and covered with woods.
>
> They traveled farther up the coast, finding more flat, wooded country. Farther north, the landscape revealed glaciers and rocky mountains. Though Bjarni realized this was an unknown land, he was no intrepid explorer. Rather, he was a practical man who had simply set out to find his father. Refusing his crew's request to go ashore, he promptly turned his bow back out to sea. After four days' sailing, Bjarni landed at Herjolfsnes on the southwestern tip of Greenland, the exact place he had been seeking all along.

What is this passage about? _____

So what? What's the author's point? _____

What type of passage is this? _____

Check your answers to be sure you're on the right track.

THE QUESTIONS

Now we're getting to the important part of the Reading section. This is where you need to spend time, in order to avoid careless errors. After reading a passage, you'll have a group of questions that is in no particular order. The first thing you need to decide is whether the question you're answering is general or specific.

General questions

General questions are about the passage as a whole. There are five types:

main idea

- ◆ Which of the following best expresses the main point?
- ◆ The passage is primarily about
- ◆ The main idea of the passage is
- ◆ The best title for this passage would be

tone/attitude

- ◆ The author's tone is
- ◆ The attitude of the author is one of

general interpretation

- ◆ The author's tone/attitude indicates
- ◆ The author would most likely agree with
- ◆ This passage deals with X by
- ◆ The passage implies that
- ◆ Which of the following words best describes the passage?
- ◆ It can be inferred from the passage that
- ◆ The style of the passage is most like
- ◆ Where would you be likely to find this passage?
- ◆ What is the author's opinion of X?
- ◆ The passage is best described as a

purpose

- ◆ The purpose of the passage is
- ◆ The author wrote this passage in order to

prediction

- ◆ Which is likely to happen next?
- ◆ The author will most likely discuss next

Notice that these questions all require you to know the main idea, but the ones at the beginning of the list don't require anything else, and the ones toward the end require you to interpret a little more.

Answering a general question

Keep your answers to "What? So What?" in mind. The answer to a general question will concern the main idea. If you need more, go back to your paragraph labels. The labels will allow you to look at the passage again without getting bogged down in the details.

- For a straight **main idea** question, just ask yourself, "What was the "What? So what?" for this passage?"

- For a **tone/attitude question**, ask yourself, "How did the author feel about the subject?"

- For a **general interpretation** question, ask yourself, "Which answer stays closest to what the author said and how he said it?"

- For a **general purpose** question, ask yourself, "Why did the author write this?"

- For a **prediction** question, ask yourself, "How was the passage arranged?" Take a look at your paragraph labels, and reread the last sentence.

Answer the question in your own words before looking at the answer choices. As always, you want to arm yourself with your own answer before looking at the SSAT's tricky answers.

Practice — Answering a general question

Use the passage about Vikings that you just read and labeled. Reread your main idea and answer the following questions. Use the questions above to help you paraphrase your own answer before looking at the choices.

1. This passage is primarily about
   (A) the Vikings and their civilization
   (B) the waves of Viking immigration
   (C) sailing techniques of Bjarni Herjolfsson
   (D) one Viking's glimpse of the new world
   (E) the hazards of Viking travel

What was the answer to "What? So what?" for this passage?

2. With which of the following statements about Viking explorers would the author most probably agree?
   (A) Greenland and Iceland were the Vikings' final discoveries.
   (B) Viking explorers were cruel and savage.
   (C) The Vikings' most startling discovery was an accidental one.
   (D) Bjarni Herjolfsson was the first settler of America.
   (E) All Viking explorers were fearless.

Which answer is closest to what the author said, overall?

3. What was the author's purpose in writing this passage?
   (A) To turn the reader against Italian adventurers
   (B) To show his disdain for Eric the Red
   (C) To demonstrate the Vikings' nautical skills
   (D) To correct a common misconception about the European discovery of America
   (E) To prove the Vikings were far more advanced than previously thought

Specific questions

Specific questions are about a detail or a section of the passage. There are four main types:

fact

- According to the passage/author
- The author states that
- Which of these questions is answered by the passage?
- All of the following are mentioned EXCEPT

definition in context

- What does the passage mean by X?
- X probably represents/means
- Which word best replaces the word X without changing the meaning?

specific interpretation

- The author implies in line X
- It can be inferred from paragraph X
- The most likely interpretation of X is

purpose

- The author uses X in order to
- Why does the author say X?

Again, the questions above range from flat-out requests for information found in the passage (just like the straight "main idea" general questions) to questions that require some interpretation of what you find in the passage (like the general questions that ask what the author is "likely to agree with").

Answering a specific question

For specific questions, always reread the part of the passage concerned. Remember, this is an open-book test!

Of course, you don't want to have to reread the entire passage. What part are they focusing on? To find the relevant part:

- Use your paragraph labels to go straight to the information you need.

- Use the line or paragraph reference, if there is one, but be careful. With a line reference ("In line 10 . . ."), be sure to read the whole surrounding paragraph, not just the line. If the question says "In line 10 . . ." then you need to read lines 5 through 15 to actually find the answer.

- Use words that stand out in the question and passage. Names, places, and long words will be easy to find back in the passage. We call these *lead words* because they lead you back to the right place in the passage.

Once you're in the right area, answer the question in your own words. Then look at the answer choices and eliminate any that aren't like yours.

Answering special specific questions

Definition-in-context questions

Creating your own answer before looking at the choices makes definition-in-context questions especially easy. Remember, they want to know how the word or phrase is being used *in context*, so come up with your own word that fits in the sentence before looking at the answer choices. Try one:

> In line 15, the word "spot" most closely means

Cross out the word they're asking about, and replace it with your own.

> A raptor must also have a sharp, often hooked
> beak so that it may tear the flesh of its prey. Because
> they hunt from the sky, these birds must have
> extremely sharp eyesight, which allows them to *spot*
> potential prey from a great distance.

Now look at the answer choices and eliminate the ones that are not at all like yours.

> (A) taint
> (B) mark
> (C) hunt
> (D) detect
> (E) circle

You probably came up with something like "see." The closest answer to "see" is (D). Notice that "taint" and "mark" are possible meanings of "spot," but they don't work in this context. Those answer choices are there to catch students who do not go back to the passage to see how the word is used and to replace it with their own.

Definition-in-context questions are so quick that if you only have a few minutes left, you should definitely do them first.

I, II, III Questions

The questions that have three roman numerals are confusing and time-consuming. They look like this:

According to the passage, which of the following is true?

    I.   The sky is blue.

    II.   Nothing rhymes with "orange."

    III.   Smoking cigarettes increases lung capacity.

        (A)   I only
        (B)   II only
        (C)   III only
        (D)   I and II only
        (E)   I, II, and III

On the SSAT, you will need to look up each of the three statements in the passage. This will always be time-consuming, but you can make them less confusing by making sure that you look up just one statement at a time.

For instance, in the question above, say you look back at the passage and see that the passage says "I" is true. Write a big "T" next to it. What can you eliminate? (B) and (C). Now you check out "II," and you find that sure enough, they've said that, too. "II" gets a big "T" and you cross off (A). Next, looking in the paragraph you labeled "Smoking is bad," you find that the passage actually says that smoking decreases lung capacity. What can you eliminate? (E).

You may want to skip a I, II, III question because it will be time-consuming, especially if you're on your last passage and there are other questions you can do instead.

EXCEPT/LEAST/NOT Questions

This is another confusing type of question. The test writers are reversing what you need to look for, asking you which answer is false.

All of the following can be inferred from the
passage EXCEPT:

Before you go any further, cross out the "EXCEPT." Now you have a much more positive question to answer. Of course, as always, you will go through *all* the answer choices, but for this type of question you will put a little "T" or "F" next to the answers as you check them out. Let's say we've checked out these answers:

        (A) Americans are patriotic.   **T**
        (B) Americans have great ingenuity.   **T**
        (C) Americans love war.   **F**
        (D) Americans do what they can to help
             one another.   **T**
        (E) Americans are brave in times of war.   **T**

Which one stands out? The one with the "F." That's your answer. You made a confusing question much simpler than the test writers wanted it to be. If you don't go through all the choices and mark them, you run the risk of accidentally picking one of the choices that you know is true, because that's what you usually look for on reading questions.

You should skip an EXCEPT/LEAST/NOT question if you're on your last passage and there are other questions you can do instead.

Practice — Answering a specific question

Use the passage about Vikings that you just read and labeled. Use your paragraph labels and the lead words in each question to get to the part of the passage you need, and then put the answer in your own words before going back to the answer choices.

1. According to the passage, Bjarni Herjolfsson left Norway to

   (A) found a new colony
   (B) open trading lanes
   (C) visit his relations
   (D) map the North Sea
   (E) settle in Greenland

   What's the lead word here? Norway. 'Norway' should also be in one of your labels.

2. Bjarni's reaction upon landing in Iceland can best be described as

   (A) disappointed
   (B) satisfied
   (C) amused
   (D) indifferent
   (E) fascinated

   What's the lead word here?_____ Again, this should be in one of your labels.

3. "The crew lost their bearings," in the third paragraph, probably means that

   (A) the ship was damaged beyond repair
   (B) the crew became disoriented
   (C) the crew decided to mutiny
   (D) the crew went insane
   (E) the ship's compass broke

   For a paragraph reference, just go back and read that paragraph. Replace the words they've quoted with your own.

4. It can be inferred from the passage that prior to Bjarni Herjolfsson's voyage, Greenland

   (A) was covered in grass and shrubs
   (B) was overrun with Vikings
   (C) was rich in fish and game
   (D) was populated by criminals
   (E) was as far west as the Vikings had traveled

   What's the lead word here?_____ Is it in one of your labels? What does that part of the passage say about Greenland? Paraphrase before looking at the answers!

THE ANSWERS

Before you ever look at an answer choice, you've come up with your own answer, in your own words. What do you do next?

Well, you're looking for the closest answer to yours, but it's a lot easier to eliminate answers than to try to magically zone in on the "best" one. Work through the answers using process of elimination. As soon as you eliminate an answer, cross off the letter in your test booklet so that you no longer think of that choice as a possibility.

How do I eliminate answer choices?

On a general question:
Eliminate an answer that is:

- too small. The passage may mention it, but it's only a detail—not a main idea.

- not mentioned in the passage.

- in contradiction to the passage—It says the opposite of what you read.

- too big. The answer tries to say that more was discussed than really was.

- too extreme. An extreme answer is too negative or too positive, or it uses absolute words like "all," "every," "never," "always." Eliminating extreme answers makes tone/attitude questions especially easy and quick.

- going against common sense. The passage is not likely to back up answers that just don't make sense at all.

On a specific question:
Eliminate an answer that is:

- too extreme

- contradicting passage details

- not mentioned in the passage

- against common sense

If you look back at the questions you did for the Viking passage, you'll see that many of the wrong answer choices fit into the categories above.

What kinds of answers do I keep?
"Best" answers are likely to be:

- paraphrases of the words in the passage.
- traditional and conservative in their outlook.
- moderate, using words like "may," "can," and "often."

Practice — Eliminating answers

The following phrases are answer choices. You haven't read the passage, or even the question, that goes with each of them. However, you *can* decide if each one is a *possible* correct answer or if you can eliminate it, based on the criteria we just listed. Cross out any that you can eliminate.

Index Card Alert
What's the definition of 'criteria'?

For a general question:

(A) The author refutes each argument exhaustively.

(B) The author admires the courage of most Americans.

(C) Creativity finds full expression in a state of anarchy.

(D) The passage criticizes Western society for not allowing freedom of expression to artists.

(E) The ancient Egyptians were barbaric.

(F) The author proves that Native American writing does not have a multicultural perspective.

(G) The author emphasizes the significance of diversity in the United States.

(H) The passage reports the record cold temperatures in Boston in 1816.

For a general tone/attitude question:

(I) respectful

(J) confused

(K) angry condemnation

(L) admiring

(M) mournful

(N) objective

(O) thrilled optimism

(P) exaggeration

(Q) disgusted

(R) neutral

(S) condescending

(T) indifferent

For a specific question:

(U) They were always in danger of being deprived of their power.

(V) Voters were easily misled by mud-slinging campaigns.

(W) One-celled organisms could be expected to act in fairly predictable ways.

(X) Only a show of athletic ability can excite an audience.

(Y) Economic events can have political repercussions.

When you've got it down to two:

If you've eliminated all but two answers, don't get stuck and waste time. Keep the main idea in the back of your mind and step back.

- Reread the question.
- Look at what makes the two answers different.
- Go back to the passage.
- Which answer is worse? Eliminate it.

THE READING PLAN

The passages

After I read each paragraph, I _____ it.

After I read an entire passage, I ask myself _____ ? _____ ?

I am better at doing these types of passages:

_____

_____

_____

_____

The questions

The five main types of general questions, and the questions I can ask myself in order to answer them, are:

_____   _____

_____   _____

_____   _____

_____   _____

_____   _____

To find the answer to a specific question, I can use three clues:

_____

_____

_____

If the question says "In line 22," where do I begin reading for the answer?_____

The answers

On a general question, I eliminate answers that are:

_____

_____

_____

_____

_____

_____

On a specific question, I eliminate answers that are:

_____

_____

_____

_____

When I've got it down to two possible answers, I:

_____

_____

_____

_____

If you have trouble with any of these questions, be sure to reread this chapter before moving on.

Practice — All reading techniques

The term "tides" has come to represent the cyclical rising and falling of ocean waters, most notably evident along the shoreline as the border between land and sea moves in and out with the passing of the day. The primary reason for this constant redefinition of the boundaries of the sea is the gravitational force of the moon.

This force of lunar gravity is not as strong as earth's own gravitational pull, which keeps our bodies and our homes from being pulled off the ground, through the sky, and into space toward the moon. It is a strong enough force, however, to exert a certain gravitational pull as the moon passes over the earth's surface. This pull causes the water level to rise (as the water is literally pulled ever-so-slightly toward the moon) in those parts of the ocean that are exposed to the moon and its gravitational forces. When the water level in one part of the ocean rises, it must naturally fall in another, and this is what causes water level to change, dramatically at times, along any given piece of coastline.

1. Which one of the following is the most obvious effect of the tides?

   (A) A part of the beach that was once dry is now underwater.
   (B) Floods cause great damage during heavy rainstorms.
   (C) The moon is not visible.
   (D) Water falls.
   (E) The ocean rises.

2. The word "lunar" in the beginning of the second paragraph most nearly means

   (A) weak
   (B) strong
   (C) destructive
   (D) related to the moon
   (E) foolish

3. It can be inferred from the passage that if one were to travel to the moon

   (A) that water would be found on its surface
   (B) that an object, if dropped, would float away from the surface of the moon
   (C) that other planets besides the moon have an influence on the tides of the earth's oceans
   (D) that tides are more dramatic during the day than during the night
   (E) that an object, if dropped, would fall to the moon's surface

4. The author's primary purpose in writing this passage is to

(A) prove the existence of water on the moon
(B) refute claims that tides are caused by the moon
(C) explain the main cause of the ocean's tides
(D) argue that humans should not interfere with the processes of nature
(E) convince students to study astrophysics

Additional practice

Read the opinion and editorial pages and the science section of a major newspaper to get practice reading short passages with lots of information in them. Also complete all reading practice exercises you can get from the SSAT Board. For even more Reading passages and questions (some of which will be harder than SSAT passages), check out a book with practice SAT questions from the College Board.

WRITING SAMPLE

WHAT'S THE WRITING SAMPLE?

The SSAT's newest section is the writing sample essay. It's quite new, actually; it was introduced in November 1997. How important is your essay to your SSAT scores? It doesn't affect them one bit. The SSAT Board does not score your writing sample.

They do, however, copy it and send it to schools along with each of your score reports. Keep in mind that though it does not matter what the SSAT people think of the essay that you write, you are writing it for the admissions officers at the schools to which you are applying.

The SSAT gives you 25 minutes to write an essay on an assigned topic.

Index Card Alert

What exactly is a 'proverb'?

The topic

The topic is usually some sort of proverb or saying, and you need to either agree or disagree with it. Here are some examples of SSAT topics:

No pain, no gain.

Actions speak louder than words.

The greatest sorrows are those we cause ourselves.

As you can see, the saying can be interpreted in many ways—it's very vague. The test writers leave the topic open to interpretation on purpose. Don't worry about interpreting it the "correct" way. Go with whatever you think it means. If you have trouble, try putting it in your own words. With the example above, "No pain, no gain," how would you explain what it means to someone else?

—————————————————————

You might explain "no pain, no gain" by saying, "In order to accomplish something worthwhile, you often have to make sacrifices."

The assignment

Here's the assignment that you'll see along with the essay topic:

> Do you agree or disagree with the topic statement? Support your position with one or two specific examples from personal experience, the experience of others, current events, history, or literature.

You **must** decide if you agree or disagree. No straddling the fence here, even if you could really care less about the topic. You have to muster an opinion.

In the assignment, besides specifying that you need to agree or disagree, the SSAT has also told you that you need to support your opinion with examples. They've listed different types that you can use. However, all examples are not equal. You want to form the strongest possible argument, and for that you need the strongest examples you can think of. How can you be sure you'll have some at hand? Prepare them in advance!

Any of the types of examples mentioned in the assignment—history, current events, literature, or personal experience—can be strong support for your opinion. You may think that personal experience is the way to go, since it's what you know best, so you'll always be able to think of something, right? Well, you may have had many meaningful things happen to you, or you may even think you'll be able to pretend you have. However, sometimes an essay can be made much stronger with the addition of a more scholarly example from history, current events, or literature.

If creativity strikes on the day of the test, and you come up with the perfect story to support your opinion, then go for it. But what if nothing comes to you? If you're prepared with some examples you can use, you'll be less anxious on the day of the test, because you'll have something to write, no matter what the topic is.

Index Card Alert

What does 'muster' mean?

PREPARE YOUR EXAMPLES

Brainstorm some examples that you can use on any essay topic the SSAT throws at you. The essay topics are always vague, and if you have a bunch of solid examples you've thought about and reviewed in advance, you'll save a lot of time at the test. Your potential examples will be in the forefront of your mind, and you can choose one or two that are supportive of your opinion on whatever your topic may be.

Prepare history and current event examples

For history and current event examples, stay away from potentially controversial issues and events. Also avoid those that have recently been turned into movies or TV shows.

- ◆ What have you studied in school?

- ◆ What have you heard people talking about in the news?

- ◆ Get specific. Come up with as many details as you can—names, dates, general order of events, issues involved. Go back to your school notes, if you need to, for details you've forgotten. Details will make your example stronger and help you to explain exactly *how* it supports your opinion.

CURRENT EVENTS	HISTORY
_____	_____
_____	_____
_____	_____
_____	_____
_____	_____
_____	_____

If you're having trouble thinking of events and issues, see if any of these are something you know about:

homelessness	the Salem Witch Trials
censorship	the Civil War
smoking in public	the American Revolution
environmental issues	the breakup of the USSR
drunk driving	slavery
gun control	World War I or World War II
underage drinking	any historical event or war

If you want to start from our list above, you must remember that you need to flesh out the details on these issues and events. For example, you *don't* want to say "Environmental issues are a good example of . . ." because "environmental issues" can cover a whole host of concerns and viewpoints. Break it down. What do you know about the issues? There's the greenhouse effect (what does that mean?), endangered species (why do they matter?), air pollution (what is being done about it?), water pollution (how does it happen?), nuclear power (what are the pros and cons?). In the same way, you need to think about "slavery." What were the conditions under slavery? Who rebelled or helped runaway slaves? When was slavery in practice in the United States? Who and what led to its demise?

Index Card Alert

What is a 'demise'?

For any big issue or event, break down what is involved—get specific! It may help to talk it out with your parents while jotting down notes on what you're saying. If you just studied the Salem Witch Trials, for instance, try explaining to your parents what happened (even if they already know), and the significance of the events. You'll get deeper into the example so you can be sure to have a paragraph or two to write about it. Doing all the practice writing samples we've included will help, also.

Prepare literature examples

Books, short stories, poems, and plays you've read for school (and perhaps some you've read on your own) provide you with events and characters that can support your opinion. The key is, the work must be "literature," a work that most educators would consider a classic. Movies and television shows do not count. It's very difficult to use a work that isn't well known, because the reader will probably be unfamiliar with it, and you'll need to spend precious minutes explaining plot.

Think back now (instead of during the test!) to recall those works of literature you have read and can use in your SSAT writing sample. Write down the author of each, and the characters and main events in the work. Again, refer to your old school notes or the book itself to refresh your memory.

LITERATURE

_____

_____

_____

_____

_____

_____

_____

_____

If you've read anything by Homer, Shakespeare, Dickens, Steinbeck, Hemingway, Conrad—those are classics you can use. There are many, many more; ask your English teacher if you're in doubt about a particular work you've read.

In your essay:

- Stick to the classics.

- Name the author.

- Underline the titles of books, plays, and epic poems.

- Put quotation marks around short stories, essays, articles, and poems.

- You probably know these words from school: *plot*, *protagonist*, *antagonist*, *climax*, *theme*. Use them!

Prepare personal experience examples

Use personal experiences that are "deep." Academic and athletic achievements, family history, and personal aspirations work well. Avoid boyfriend/girlfriend stories. Use experiences that have taught you something.

PERSONAL EXPERIENCE

_____

_____

_____

_____

_____

_____

_____

These are sometimes the hardest examples to make strong, because what is meaningful to you may not be to someone else. Ask your parents what they think of the ones you've written down.

PLAN YOUR ESSAY

When the writing sample section begins, in order to form an opinion and organize your essay, take three minutes to note some examples you could use to agree or disagree with the topic. Do this on the test booklet or on scratch paper—not on the lined essay answer sheet. Don't take too long, and don't worry about being original; just come up with examples that really support either opinion.

Try this with our topics from before:

No pain, no gain.

Agree	Disagree
_____	_____
_____	_____
_____	_____

Actions speak louder than words.

Agree	Disagree
_____	_____
_____	_____
_____	_____

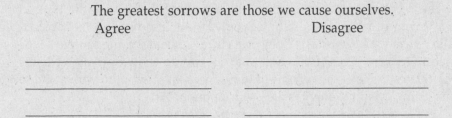

The greatest sorrows are those we cause ourselves.

Agree   Disagree

_____   _____

_____   _____

_____   _____

For which side do you have stronger examples? Remember, you just need **one** or **two** good ones that you can write a few paragraphs about. Cross out the other side. You now have your outline!

How do you flesh out your outline and make it into an essay in the next 22 minutes? Stick to basic essay structure.

ORGANIZE YOUR ESSAY

> Opening Paragraph: Introduction
> ◆ Put the topic in your own words—show them you understand it.
> ◆ State your opinion.
> ◆ Introduce your examples.

> Body Paragraph: First Example
> ◆ State your first example and explain how it supports your opinion.

> Body Paragraph: Second Example
> ◆ State your second example and explain how it supports your opinion *or* state another way in which your first example supports your opinion.

> Final Paragraph: Conclusion
> ◆ Paraphrase your opinion.
> ◆ End with "The Kicker," a final sentence that shows the wider significance of your opinion.

This looks very familiar, right? You've probably been writing the "five paragraph essay" or some variant thereof for many years. You may be way beyond it now, but for this timed essay, it's the best way to be sure you've got a structure to rely on. If you practice getting all of the above elements into your essay, and you also have examples planned, then you've left very little to chance. You know everything you're going to write, except the topic.

You can, of course, have more body paragraphs than are laid out above. However, no matter how much more you want to write, be sure to leave yourself at least three minutes to write a conclusion. It's better to have just one example with a conclusion than two examples without a conclusion!

The "Kicker" in your conclusion is something that relates the topic of the essay to more than just the examples you've used. It shows how the topic applies to life, society, the world—the bigger picture. Look at writing sample #2 to see a typical "Kicker." Even if you don't have a way to show how the position you took relates to the grand scheme of things, you *must* wrap up with some sort of conclusion, even if it only restates your opinion.

Let's practice writing some of these paragraphs.

INTRODUCTIONS

Write a quick opening paragraph for each of the essays you just outlined. Show that you understand the topic, state your opinion, and introduce your examples. Spend five minutes on each. Remember, the introduction is where the reader gets his first impression of you, so be extra careful in spelling, punctuation, and grammar here.

Some words you can use if you're agreeing with the topic: *sustain, support, advocate, uphold, endorse, espouse, maintain, bolster, strengthen, fortify, align with.*

Some words you can use if you're disagreeing with the topic: *refute, counter, oppose, controvert, contest, dispute, differ.*

If you want to use one of these words but it is unfamiliar to you, look it up, try using it, and then ask a parent or teacher to read your sentence or paragraph and tell you if you've used it correctly.

No pain, no gain.

_____

_____

_____

_____

Actions speak louder than words.

_____

_____

_____

_____

The greatest sorrows are those we cause ourselves.

_____

_____

_____

_____

BODY

The body of your essay will consist of paragraphs that explain how your examples support your opinion. As we've said, details help you make a strong case. They allow you to give the reader concrete information and description, and that helps the reader understand what it is in your example that bolsters your case.

For example, the issue of air pollution supports my agreement with "The greatest sorrows are those we cause ourselves." When you read that sentence, you probably made some connection in your mind between "air pollution" and "humans causing their own problems." But you've made a very vague connection. You only sort of know what I mean. My job, as the writer, is to convince you that the two are intimately connected. Thus, I tell you about the hundreds of millions of tons of particles that are pumped into the air every day from factories—the very factories from which we demand products that we think will make our lives easier. And I also have to tell you how those particles are causing us pain, by describing the prevalence of asthma and allergies in children and adults, and the rising incidence of cancers in metropolitan areas.

There are lots of other details I could have used instead of the ones I did, but I needed to use some sort of description and explanation to make it perfectly clear that air pollution is something that humans do to themselves, and how great a danger it is.

Explaining your examples is the most important thing you must do while writing the body paragraphs. Assume the burden of responsibility for making your points clear to the reader.

Something else to think about while writing these paragraphs is how you and your reader get from one paragraph to another. You want the reader to see a smooth transition from one paragraph to the next, so she knows she's still reading the same essay. Thus, if your first example for "The greatest sorrows are those we cause ourselves," is historical, and your second example is the air pollution one, you'll want to smoothly switch from one to the other. The beginning of the air pollution paragraph could be something like, "Humans continue to harm themselves, into the present day. One of the ways they do this is by poisoning their own air . . ."

In order to make the transition from one paragraph to another, you can point out similarities or differences that the two examples have, or in some way show that they are related. You don't want to spend time thinking about this at the test, though. If nothing comes to mind, you can fall back on "Another example of . . .is . . ." You can also take a peek in most basic writing, grammar, and style handbooks, if you want to see some more transition words and phrases in action.

For now, reread your introductions and choose one to continue. Spend 15 minutes developing your examples in body paragraphs.

Get a Second Opinion

Get as many people as possible to read your practice essays and tell you if there are parts that are not clear, or points that could be developed better. Make sure they know you only have 25 minutes to write.

CONCLUSIONS

Write a quick closing paragraph for each of the three topics we've been using. Remember to paraphrase (don't use the same words you used in your introduction) and try writing a "kicker" that broadens the essay outward, and makes it more meaningful. If you can't come up with a "kicker," don't worry—just write something that wraps up. Try to spend just 3-5 minutes on each conclusion.

Some words you can use to show you're concluding your essay: *therefore, in sum, clearly, consequently, thus, in conclusion.*

_____

_____

_____

_____

_____

_____

_____

_____

_____

_____

_____

_____

_____

_____

_____

_____

_____

_____

The basics

Basic things to keep in mind:

- Write legibly. The test center should provide you with a black pen to write your essay, so practice hand-writing essays in pen. Nothing turns a reader off more quickly than an essay that's messy and difficult to decipher. Think about how many essays a school admissions officer has to read!

- If you need to delete words, draw one neat line through them.

- Indent your paragraphs substantially, so the reader can see at a glance that you've organized your essay.

- Stay within the lines and margins.

- Stick to the assigned topic.

- Keep your sentences easy to understand. If you see you've written a long, complicated sentence, think about breaking it up. You want the reader to be able to understand your points.

- Use some big vocabulary words, if you're sure you really know them.

- If you're not sure how to spell a word, think of another one you can use.

- Watch for the punctuation and grammar mistakes that you've made in the past, and still tend to make. (Ask your English teacher if you're not sure which you make!)

Index Card Alert

What does 'prolific' mean?

- Write as much as you can. If an admissions officer sees a half-page essay instead of two pages, he'll think you don't have much to say. Even though you'll be writing this essay after two hours of multiple-choice questions, try to gear up to be prolific.

- Try to leave a minute or two to read over your essay when you're done. Catch any careless errors, and neatly correct them.

Now let's look at some sample essays. As you read them, decide which one follows the assignment and our guidelines better.

Writing Sample 1

Topic: No pain, no gain.

Assignment: Do you agree or disagree with the topic statement? Support your position with one or two specific examples from personal experience, the experience of others, current events, history, or literature.

I agree with the statement "No pain, no gain." In this competetive society, an individual cannot expect to accomplish all of his goals without suffering first. This suffering provides a person with the incentive to learn from his or her mistakes and try harder to obtain what he or she desires. The following examples will help to make this idea clearer.

An athlete must always keep his body in ~~shape~~ top form. If the person doesn't, then his competitors will knock him out of the sport with ease. The athlete must practice many hours per day by pushing himself beyond his limits. For example, the weightlifter must lift weights that start out light and get heavier as he progresses. When the weightlifter can lift a certain amount with ease, he is forced to try a heavier amount, which may hurt at first. However, in the long run the weightlifter will be stronger than before.

In American Colonial days, colonists were in some ways tortured by the mother country, England. The Stamp Acts, tea taxes, Quartering Acts, etc., imposed by England angered the ~~people~~ colonists because they hurt their trade, causing the colonists to become more dependent on England. In the long run, however, these actions by England helped the colonists to win their independance. Each time England imposed another law, the colonists grew more angry. Finally, the people got up the courage to rebel. Thus, they gained their independence.

What Do You Think Of Sample 1?

Use these questions to evaluate sample 1:

- Is the essay legible?
- Does the essay have an introduction that is a separate paragraph?
- Does the author understand the topic?
- Is the author's opinion stated clearly?
- Does the author use examples to support his opinion?
- How many examples? What kind? How convincing are they?
- Does the author explain *how* the examples support the opinion?
- Has the author moved smoothly from one paragraph to the next?
- Is the essay organized? Does each example have a paragraph?
- Are the paragraphs well indented?

For Those Who Can Help You

You can show these questions to people who read your practice essays, and ask them to answer the questions as they apply to your essays, too.

- Has the author stayed neatly within the lines?

- Has the author used impressive vocabulary correctly?

- Does the essay have a conclusion that is a separate paragraph?

- Does the conclusion summarize the points in the essay without being just a word-for-word repeat of the intro?

WRITING SAMPLE 2

It is absolutely true that one cannot accomplish anything without bearing some sort of pain, whether it is physical or emotional. This has been true throughout history, and remains true in our world today. One example of this is drug testing, during which animals must be hurt or killed so that new, lifesaving drugs may be developed. Another example is the Civil Rights movement, during which many people had to sacrifice a great deal for the greater good.

Before a new medicine or drug can be used on human beings, it must undergo a tremendous amount of testing on animals, to ensure that it is safe and effective. During this process, most of the animals die or are hurt so badly that they must be killed. Many people protest that it is not fair to harm all these animals, but I think this is a very good example of "no pain, no gain." Animals' pain is an unfortunate but necessary step in our making medical gains.

During the American Civil Rights movement, such people as Rosa Parks and Martin Luther King, Jr. had to undergo tremendous physical and emotional pain in order to move the country toward racial equality. Rosa Parks knew that she would be arrested for sitting in the "whites only" part of the bus, but she did it anyway, knowing that it was necessary to pay the price for advancing civil rights. She was not only arrested, but she and her whole family were harassed, recieving death threats for a long time. She did not let these dangers stop her from continuing to protest, boycott, and speak for the movement. Martin Luther King, Jr. also made many sacrifices to work for racial equality, and he died striving to further the cause, but his life and death resulted in great gains.

In summary, nothing positive can happen without some pain. We must learn to take the good with the bad, and realize that we can not gain the former without accepting the latter. It is only through this realization that we can continue to advance as individuals, citizens, and human beings.

WHAT DO YOU THINK OF SAMPLE 2?

Use these questions to evaluate sample 2:

- Is the essay legible?

- Does the essay have an introduction that is a separate paragraph?

- Does the author understand the topic?

- Is the author's opinion stated clearly?
- Does the author use examples to support her opinion?
- How many examples? What kind? How convincing are they?
- Does the author explain *how* the examples support the opinion?
- Has the author moved smoothly from one paragraph to the next?
- Is the essay organized? Does each example have a paragraph?
- Are the paragraphs well indented?
- Has the author stayed neatly within the lines?
- Has the author used impressive vocabulary correctly?
- Does the essay have a conclusion that is a separate paragraph?
- Does the conclusion summarize the points in the essay without being just a word-for-word repeat of the intro?

Which writing sample was better?

Take a look at the answer key for our evaluations of these essays.

THE WRITING SKILLS PLAN

The first 3 minutes

How do I spend the first three minutes?

_____

_____

_____

Writing the essay

Opening Paragraph: _____

What do I include here?

_____

_____

_____

Body Paragraphs: _____

What do I include here?

_____

_____

_____

Final Paragraph: _____

What do I include here?

_____

_____

When I've only got three minutes left, what must I be sure to do?

_____

If you're not sure of the answer to any of these questions, review this chapter before moving on.

Practice — Prepare examples

Create index cards for the examples you've already written down on the previous pages, and any other examples you think of. Index cards will allow you to flip through your examples the morning of the test so they're really fresh in your mind.

- ◆ On each card, write down details that you can use in your essay. Go through your old school notes to jog your memory. You'll be glad you did.

- ◆ For a current event or historical example, write down names, dates, chronology, and the issues involved.

- ◆ For a literature example, write down titles, authors, character names, and a summary of the plot.

Practice — Coming up with examples

It's not what you do, but how well you do it.

Agree   Disagree

_____   _____

_____   _____

_____   _____

Simple pleasures are the best pleasures.

Agree   Disagree

_____   _____

_____   _____

_____   _____

Neither a borrower nor a lender be.

Agree   Disagree

_____   _____

_____   _____

_____   _____

Winning isn't everything.

Agree   Disagree

_____   _____

_____   _____

_____   _____

It is better to give than to receive.

Agree   Disagree

_____   _____

_____   _____

_____   _____

Look before you leap.

Agree   Disagree

_____   _____

_____   _____

_____   _____

Practice — Writing essays

Time yourself for each of the following essays. When you're done with each, ask yourself the same questions you used to evaluate the sample "No pain, no gain" essay.

Ask a parent or teacher to read it, also, but be sure to let them know that what they're reading is a timed 25-minute essay, so they should read primarily for content and organization. Ask them not to grade it, but to tell you what you did well and what you could do better.

If your grammar, spelling, or punctuation is such that your reader has a hard time understanding the essay, you should pick up a basic handbook so you can identify your weak points and work on them. However, don't be concerned about a few minor errors. If you have solid examples that support your main idea, and you've organized them well and written clearly and legibly, then you've covered the most important areas. Developing your writing style by learning to vary the length of your sentences, and reviewing the basics of grammar, usage, spelling, and punctuation can be useful, also, and will add to the polish of your essay. However, only if you have plenty of preparation time should you check out handbooks of style and usage.

If you'd like to do more essays than those that follow, then use the topics that you developed examples for above.

Topic: Haste makes waste.

Assignment: Do you agree or disagree with the topic statement? Support your position with one or two specific examples from personal experience, the experience of others, current events, history, or literature.

Topic: Be careful what you ask for, because you may get it.

Assignment: Do you agree or disagree with the topic statement? Support your position with one or two specific examples from personal experience, the experience of others, current events, history, or literature.

Topic: People rarely stand up for what they believe.

Assignment: Do you agree or disagree with the topic statement? Support your position with one or two specific examples from personal experience, the experience of others, current events, history, or literature.

_____

_____

_____

_____

_____

_____

_____

_____

_____

_____

_____

_____

_____

_____

_____

_____

_____

_____

_____

_____

_____

_____

_____

_____

_____

_____

Topic: The ends justify the means.

Assignment: Do you agree or disagree with the topic statement? Support your position with one or two specific examples from personal experience, the experience of others, current events, history, or literature.

Topic: You get what you pay for.

Assignment: Do you agree or disagree with the topic statement? Support your position with one or two specific examples from personal experience, the experience of others, current events, history, or literature.

_____
_____
_____
_____
_____
_____
_____
_____
_____
_____
_____
_____
_____
_____
_____
_____
_____
_____
_____
_____
_____
_____
_____
_____
_____
_____
_____
_____

6

Answer Key to SSAT Drills

FUNDAMENTALS

MATH VOCABULARY TEST

1. 6   0, 1, 2, 3, 4, and 5
2. 2, 4, 6 Many sets of integers would answer this question correctly.
3. 3   3, 5, and 7
4. 8
5. That number. The smallest positive integer is 1, and any number times 1 is itself.
6. 90 $5 \times 6 \times 3 = 90$
7. 30 $3 + 11 + 16 = 30$
8. 60 $90 - 30 = 60$
9. 2, 4, 6. Your answer to #2, as long as your integers are positive, answers this one too!
10. Yes
11. 22 $5 + 6 + 4 + 7 = 22$
12. D

Order of operations

1. 9
2. 16
3. 7
4. 5
5. 6
6. 30
7. 70
8. 60
9. 20
10. 100

Factors

1. D
2. D
3. B

Multiples

1. B
2. D
3. D
4. C

Reducing fractions

1. $\dfrac{3}{4}$

2. $\dfrac{1}{5}$

3. $\dfrac{2}{3}$

4. $\dfrac{3}{8}$

5. $\dfrac{3}{4}$

6. $\dfrac{2}{7}$

7. 1

8. $\dfrac{11}{9}$

9. If the number on top is bigger than the number on the bottom, the fraction is greater than 1.

Adding & subtracting fractions

1. $\dfrac{25}{24}$

2. $\dfrac{17}{24}$

3. $\dfrac{6}{7}$ Did you use the bowtie here? There was a common denominator already!

4. $\dfrac{1}{12}$

5. $\dfrac{73}{36}$ or $2\dfrac{1}{36}$

6. $-\dfrac{7}{20}$

7. $\dfrac{13}{3}$

8. $\dfrac{2}{9}$

9. $\dfrac{49}{60}$

10. $\dfrac{18x}{18} = x$

Multiplying & dividing fractions

1. $\dfrac{1}{3}$

2. $\dfrac{5}{4}$ or $1\dfrac{1}{4}$

3. $\dfrac{6}{25}$

4. 1

5. $\dfrac{4}{5}$

Fraction problems

1. B
2. C
3. D
4. A
5. D   Did you use the bowtie to add all those fractions? If so, look for an easier way to combine things: $\dfrac{1}{2}$ + $\dfrac{1}{2}$ = 1 and $\dfrac{2}{3}$ + $\dfrac{1}{3}$ = 1, etc.

Decimals

1. 18.7
2. 4.19
3. 4.78
4. 10.625
5. .018
6. 6000
7. 5
8. D
9. C

Exponents

1. 8
2. 16
3. 27
4. 64
5. B
6. B

ALGEBRA

Manipulate

1. 3
2. 5
3. 6
4. 7
5. 4
6. 8
7. 8
8. $\dfrac{1}{4}$
9. 7

10. 7   Number 9 and number 10 are really the same question. Did you see it?
11. 7
12. D
13. D   Be careful! If you chose (A), you did all the work, but didn't answer the right question!
14. B   Be careful of answer choice (E)!
15. D

Functions

1. B
2. C
3. D
4. D
5. A

Translating & solving percent questions

1. 12
2. 24
3. 5
4. 80

Word problems involving percentages

1. E
2. C
3. C
4. E
5. A
6. E
7. C
8. C
9. A
10. A

Ratios

1. E
2. C
3. C
4. B
5. C
6. C

Average problems

1. A   Be careful of (B)—what does the question ask for?
2. D
3. B
4. E
5. E

Plugging in

1. E
2. D
3. E
4. E
5. C If you had trouble, try plugging in 8 for the number of pieces in the pie, drawing a pie with eight pieces, and crossing pieces off as Miguel eats them.
6. B
7. C
8. C

Backsolving

1. C
2. E
3. C
4. B
5. D

GEOMETRY

Perimeter

1. D
2. C
3. C

Triangles

1. A
2. C
3. A
4. B

Area & volume

1. C Backsolve!
2. D
3. B
4. D

CHARTS & GRAPHS

Chart and graph problems

1. E
2. D
3. E Be careful of (A)—look at the little note underneath the chart!
4. D
5. B
6. E
7. B
8. C

MATH REVIEW

1. Yes.
2. It is neither positive nor negative.
3. Addition
4. Multiplication
5. The quotient
6. Yes; No
7. Exponents
8. Yes; No
9. No; Yes
10. Zero
11. Two
12. $2 \times 2 \times 2 = 8$
13. Over 100 $\dfrac{\quad}{100}$
14. Multiplication—×
15. Total
16. Average pie
17. Plug in a number
18. Add; all four
19. Multiply; two (or one, since all the sides of a square are the same)
20. 180
21. 3; 180
22. 360
23. 2; equilateral
24. Hypotenuse; right angle
25. Area (of a triangle) $= \dfrac{1}{2} \times$ base $\times$ height

ANALOGIES

Making sentences

1. C is a section of B
2. S is used to measure W
3. S means having L
4. R is a very strong A
5. R is practice for P
6. M fixes C
7. T betrays C
8. A means to make a P worse
9. T is a type of F
10. G leads an A
11. C is when someone breaks the L
12. B fastens a B
13. T means prone to F
14. C gets rid of I

15. P is something T
16. P is the top of an M
17. P means lacking S
18. H practices P
19. N means having a bad R
20. M is a person without G

Easy analogy techniques

1. C   C is a section of a B
2. D   R is used to C
3. B   F uses an F to move itself
4. A   D propels/moves a C (Visualize!)
5. E   C is used to measure T
6. A   E encloses/transports/encases/protects L (Visualize!)
7. A   L is the person in charge of the L
8. C   P is used primarily to W
9. C   H is a very, very strong B
10. A   B is a three-dimensional C (answer B is wrong because the words are reversed)
11. D   S is on the outside of E
12. B   a C is a smaller unit of measure than a Q is
13. A   C leads a T
14. C   B is a type of flying M (Get specific!)
15. B   F means very H
16. C   S means to get rid of G
17. D   D directs A
18. B   A wants to be Hed/ wants someone to H him (Think about who's doing what!)
19. B   S is how B is when it gets old
20. C   U means without P

Weird analogy techniques

1. B   There are two months between A and N (pattern)
2. C   R and C are spelled the same except for the first letter (letters)
3. D   S and F mean the same thing (synonyms)
4. C   D is when someone is very S, and O is when someone is very I (A:C/B:D definitional relationship)
5. E   C means something is P, and M means something is R (C:A/D:B definitional relationship)
6. B   W is made from G, and P is made from T (C:A/D:B definitional relationship)

Working backwards

1. A or B   C is surrounded by M, or G is a group of S
2. B   M is ruled by an S (E is okay, but do thieves always practice duplicity? not really—just thievery)

3. B   S is lacking D
4. B or C Q means to isolate a J, or E means to choose a P
5. D   B means lacking Z

Judging side of the fence

1. D
2. D
3. S
4. D
5. D
6. S
7. D
8. S
9. S
10. D
11. S
12. D

Using side of the fence

1. A
2. A or C
3. A or D
4. A or B
5. C or D
6. B, C, or E
7. A, B, C, or E
8. A or B
9. A, D, or E
10. A, B, or E

Working backwards as much as you can

1. T is used for C
2. Eliminate
3. A is a group of I
4. Eliminate
5. Eliminate
6. To J means to try to be H
7. Eliminate

All analogies techniques

1. C   C is a type of C
2. A   P is a unit that measures W
3. A   C is made up of Ss
4. C   L and P rhyme and start with L and P (rhyme with same first letters)
5. C   C creates an S (answer E is not as good because a W creates a P, but a P is not a large, complete work)
6. E   Many Ls make up a C
7. E   T is a young form of an F

8. E   C is the part of a shirt that is at the W (Get specific!)
9. A   C consists of W
10. B   T is sensed by T
11. B   C means to be strong in one's O
12. C   C is an exaggerated D
13. C   C is a sound made by an H, and S is a sound made by an F (A:C/B:D definitional relationship)
14. B   D means S is decreasing
15. D   The first and third letters of the words are switched (rearranged letters)
16. D   D and I mean the same thing, and D and E mean the same thing (synonyms)
17. A   V means wanting a lot of F
18. E   A is deft of/skilled in M (answer C is close, but answer E is better)
19. E   A dulls P
20. A   O is used by B, and K is used by P (A:C/B:D definitional relationship)
21. B   I means far beyond A
22. C   S means B, and A means U (A:C/B:D synonyms)

SYNONYMS

Write your own definition
Possible definitions:
1. weird
2. introduction
3. giving
4. doing the right thing
5. change
6. spin
7. optimistic
8. stick around
9. help
10. build
11. bend
12. honest
13. tease
14. rough
15. self-centered
16. quiet
17. use
18. full of life
19. stretch out
20. positive result

Easy synonym techniques

1. C
2. A
3. C
4. D
5. E
6. D
7. B
8. C
9. E
10. A
11. C
12. B
13. E
14. B
15. A
16. C
17. E
18. C
19. B
20. C

Making your own context

Possible contexts:

1. common cold; common man
2. competent to stand trial
3. abridged dictionary
4. untimely demise; untimely remark
5. homogenized milk
6. juvenile delinquent; delinquent payments
7. inalienable rights
8. paltry sum
9. auspicious beginning; auspicious occasion
10. prodigal son

Using Your Own Context

1. C
2. D
3. D
4. D
5. A
6. B
7. C
8. A
9. D
10. A

Decide Positive/Negative

1. –
2. –
3. –
4. +
5. –
6. +
7. –
8. +
9. +
10. –

Use Positive/Negative

Answers remaining should be:

1. B C E
2. A B D E
3. A C
4. C D E
5. A B D E
6. C D
7. B D
8. B D
9. A B E
10. A C D
11. A B
12. A B D
13. C D
14. A
15. A D E
16. A D
17. A B C
18. A B E
19. B C D
20. B C

Identifying Parts of Speech

1. Noun or verb
2. Noun
3. Noun or verb
4. Adjective
5. Noun
6. Adjective

All Synonyms Techniques

1. B
2. A
3. C
4. A
5. D
6. A
7. E
8. B
9. C
10. B
11. B
12. C
13. D
14. C
15. E
16. B
17. C
18. B
19. D
20. B
21. C
22. B
23. B
24. E
25. E
26. D
27. C
28. C
29. D
30. E
31. B
32. B
33. B
34. D
35. E
36. C
37. C
38. D
39. B
40. E

READING

Getting through the passage

You should have brief labels like the following:

Label for 1st paragraph: Norway—>Iceland

Label for 2nd paragraph: Iceland—>Greenland

Label for 3rd paragraph: lost

Label for 4th paragraph: saw America; landed Greenland

What? a Viking

So What? found America early

Passage type? history of an event

Answering a general question

1. D
2. C
3. D

Answering a specific question

1. C
2. A   Lead word: Iceland
3. B
4. E   Lead word: Greenland

Eliminating answers

Eliminate on a general question:

A   Too big—she or he can't do that in a few paragraphs

C   Extreme

D   Extreme

E   Extreme

F   Extreme

H   Too small—this is only a detail

Eliminate on a tone/attitude question:

J

K

M

O   Still too extreme, even though it's positive!

P

Q

S

T   Why would anyone write about something she/he doesn't care about?

Eliminate on a specific question:

U   Extreme

V   Extreme

X   Extreme and against common sense

All reading techniques

What? Tides
So What? are caused by the moon.

1. A
2. D
3. E
4. C

WRITING SAMPLE

Writing sample #1 evaluation

Sample 1 has several good points: It is legible, it has a separate introduction that clearly states the author's opinion and shows that he understands the topic, and has two examples to support his opinion. However, the examples are weak and not fully developed. The first example is a generalized statement of which the author does not even claim to have personal experience, and the second example needs to be explained a bit further. There are separate paragraphs, showing that the author has organized his ideas, but there are no transitions from paragraph to paragraph. There are a few spelling errors and strikeouts, but this essay's biggest problem is its lack of any conclusion for the essay as a whole. Sample 1 is an essay that is a little below average.

Writing sample #2 evaluation

Sample 2 is a slightly longer essay that is also legible, with only a few spelling errors. It has a separate introduction that states the author's opinion, shows that she understands the topic, and introduces the examples that will support her opinion. In this essay, the author used two strong examples. One is a current event, and the other is historical. They are both explained so that the reader knows some details about each, and gains some understanding of the "pains" and "gains" involved in each. Transitions between sections could be smoother, but the essay is organized and the reader can quickly see that by looking at the indentations. Finally, the reader is left with a conclusion that both summarizes the author's opinion, and also broadens the essay outward, showing the importance of the topic. Sample 2 is a slightly above average essay.

PART II

SSAT Practice Tests

7

Upper Level
SSAT Practice Test

Upper Level Practice Test

Upper Level SSAT
Section 1
Time-25 minutes
60 Questions

This section consists of two different types of questions. There are directions and a sample question for each type.

Each of the following questions consists of one word followed by five words or phrases. You are to select the one word or phrase whose meaning is closest to the word in capital letters.

Sample Question:

CHILLY:
(A) lazy
(B) nice
(C) dry
(D) cold
(E) sunny ⓐ ⓑ ⓒ ● Ⓔ

---

1. CONTORT:
   (A) bend
   (B) deform
   (C) color
   (D) amuse
   (E) occupy

2. GRIM:
   (A) clean
   (B) relaxing
   (C) frown
   (D) harsh
   (E) irresponsible

3. WOEFUL:
   (A) wretched
   (B) bloated
   (C) dim
   (D) animated
   (E) reasonable

4. VACANT:
   (A) stark
   (B) varied
   (C) dreary
   (D) rented
   (E) huge

5. AUSTERE:
   (A) plentiful
   (B) ornate
   (C) miserly
   (D) severe
   (E) empty

6. QUELL:
   (A) stifle
   (B) dissemble
   (C) articulate
   (D) rock gently
   (E) praise highly

7. FORTIFY:
   (A) emphasize
   (B) strengthen
   (C) revere
   (D) diffuse
   (E) surround

8. PROCLIVITY:
   (A) efficiency
   (B) tend
   (C) authenticity
   (D) propensity
   (E) proprietary

GO ON TO THE NEXT PAGE.

1

9. FORMIDABLE:
   (A) malleable
   (B) menacing
   (C) talented
   (D) fear
   (E) trainable

10. STYMIE:
    (A) construct
    (B) swindle
    (C) depress
    (D) frustrate
    (E) reason

11. ERRATIC:
    (A) constant
    (B) amiable
    (C) innate
    (D) inconsistent
    (E) caustic

12. CONCILIATE:
    (A) pacify
    (B) replace
    (C) inform
    (D) expose
    (E) surpass

13. REFRACTORY:
    (A) stubborn
    (B) excessive
    (C) ironic
    (D) inhumane
    (E) improper

14. TRUNCATE:
    (A) packed
    (B) shorten
    (C) grow
    (D) remind
    (E) reproach

15. MEAGER:
    (A) gullible
    (B) novel
    (C) sparse
    (D) vulnerable
    (E) providential

16. CREDIBLE:
    (A) obsolete
    (B) plausible
    (C) fabulous
    (D) mundane
    (E) superficial

17. CULPABLE:
    (A) elusive
    (B) unheralded
    (C) esoteric
    (D) worthy of blame
    (E) sanctioned

18. DEPLORE:
    (A) rejoice
    (B) mitigate
    (C) lament
    (D) imply
    (E) prevent

19. ACCLAIM:
    (A) compliment
    (B) feast
    (C) assert
    (D) blame
    (E) compose

20. GUILE:
    (A) vengeance
    (B) fear
    (C) trust
    (D) loathing
    (E) cunning

GO ON TO THE NEXT PAGE.

21. FALLOW:
    - (A) prompt
    - (B) unused
    - (C) deep
    - (D) secondary
    - (E) recessive

22. CHAMPION:
    - (A) deter
    - (B) force
    - (C) fight
    - (D) side with
    - (E) change

23. IMBUE:
    - (A) renew
    - (B) suffuse
    - (C) dawdle
    - (D) compete
    - (E) impress

24. POSTHUMOUS:
    - (A) in the future
    - (B) post war
    - (C) after death
    - (D) during the age of
    - (E) promptly

25. PROHIBIT:
    - (A) attempt
    - (B) recount
    - (C) diminish
    - (D) conserve
    - (E) forbid

26. RENAISSANCE:
    - (A) carnival
    - (B) fortune
    - (C) burial
    - (D) revival
    - (E) earlier time

27. DECOMPOSITION:
    - (A) combustion
    - (B) infiltration
    - (C) perturbation
    - (D) equalization
    - (E) disintegration

28. AGGRANDIZEMENT:
    - (A) assessment
    - (B) leniency
    - (C) restitution
    - (D) annulment
    - (E) glorification

29. GULLIBLE:
    - (A) stranded
    - (B) easily deceived
    - (C) distant
    - (D) assailable
    - (E) scheduled

30. REFUTATION:
    - (A) attraction
    - (B) disproof
    - (C) legal activity
    - (D) deny
    - (E) enthusiastic response

GO ON TO THE NEXT PAGE.

The following questions ask you to find relationships between words. For each question, select the answer choice that best completes the meaning of the sentence.

Sample Question:

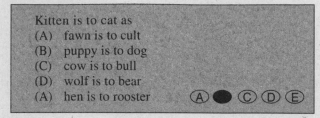

Kitten is to cat as
(A) fawn is to cult
(B) puppy is to dog
(C) cow is to bull
(D) wolf is to bear
(A) hen is to rooster

Choice (B) is the best answer because a kitten is a young cat, just as a puppy is a young dog. Of all the answer choices, (B) states a relationship that is most like the relationship between <u>kitten</u> and <u>cat</u>.

---

31. Composer is to score as
    (A) conductor is to orchestra
    (B) operator is to telephone
    (C) teacher is to classroom
    (D) attorney is to trial
    (E) author is to book

32. Stoic is to emotion as
    (A) serious is to concern
    (B) soothe is to injury
    (C) amorphous is to shape
    (D) choke is to morsel
    (E) breathe is to life

33. Sovereign is to monarchy as principal is to
    (A) school
    (B) administrators
    (C) workers
    (D) crew
    (E) town

34. Cylinder is to can as
    (A) circle is to square
    (B) perimeter is to area
    (C) cube is to dice
    (D) line is to angle
    (E) arc is to sphere

35. Laughter is to joke as
    (A) read is to story
    (B) question is to answer
    (C) wince is to pain
    (D) talk is to conversation
    (E) cramp is to swim

36. Massive is to size as
    (A) archaic is to age
    (B) acute is to hearing
    (C) tender is to feeling
    (D) simple is to thought
    (E) foolish is to idea

37. Pint is to quart as
    (A) cup is to teaspoon
    (B) mile is to road
    (C) measure is to recipe
    (D) week is to year
    (E) temperature is to thermometer

38. Scrawl is to writing as
    (A) decipher is to code
    (B) babble is to speaking
    (C) carve is to stone
    (D) tango is to dancing
    (E) direct is to acting

GO ON TO THE NEXT PAGE.

39. Stanza is to poem as
    (A) sonnet is to play
    (B) drama is to theater
    (C) paragraph is to prose
    (D) teacher is to class
    (E) chapter is to book

40. Frugal is to spending as unruly is to
    (A) fractious
    (B) impossible
    (C) obedient
    (D) warmth
    (E) pride

41. Integrity is to honesty as
    (A) comprehension is to instruction
    (B) fame is to celebrity
    (C) resolution is to determination
    (D) severity is to compassion
    (E) quotation is to report

42. Lily is to flower as pine is to
    (A) oak
    (B) needle
    (C) forest
    (D) winter
    (E) wood

43. Kitchen is to house as
    (A) wheel is to car
    (B) fireplace is to heat
    (C) lobby is to apartment
    (D) galley is to ship
    (E) exhibit is to museum

44. Blooming is to rose as
    (A) withered is to vine
    (B) prolific is to weed
    (C) fertile is to field
    (D) edible is to corn
    (E) ripe is to tomato

45. Mask is to face as
    (A) coat is to fabric
    (B) shoe is to foot
    (C) belt is to leather
    (D) hem is to skirt
    (A) invitation is to party

46. Agenda is to meeting as
    (A) clipboard is to paper
    (B) rule is to order
    (C) map is to car
    (D) blueprint is to building
    (E) gavel is to podium

47. Pathology is to disease as psychology is to
    (A) mind
    (B) science
    (C) doctor
    (D) anguish
    (E) hospital

48. Autobiography is to author as
    (A) autograph is to signature
    (B) self-sufficiency is to provision
    (C) automation is to worker
    (D) self-portrait is to artist
    (E) autopsy is to doctor

49. Bird is to migration as
    (A) parrot is to imitation
    (B) ranger is to conservation
    (C) bear is to hibernation
    (D) lawyer is to accusation
    (E) traveler is to location

50. Border is to country as
    (A) perimeter is to object
    (B) land is to owner
    (C) road is to street
    (D) area is to volume
    (E) capital is to state

GO ON TO THE NEXT PAGE.

51. Patter is to rain as
    (A) rainbow is to storm
    (B) call is to telephone
    (C) clank is to chain
    (D) volume is to radio
    (E) eruption is to volcano

52. Brazen is to tact as
    (A) lethargic is to energy
    (B) agile is to strength
    (C) humongous is to size
    (D) ancient is to time
    (E) fallen is to grace

53. Taciturn is to words as
    (A) thrifty is to money
    (B) petty is to concern
    (C) silly is to extras
    (D) startled is to surprise
    (E) trusting is to care

54. Scalpel is to razor as surgeon is to
    (A) barber
    (B) gardener
    (C) chef
    (D) patient
    (E) engineer

55. Storyteller is to listener as
    (A) accompanist is to composer
    (B) critique is to commentator
    (C) banter is to humorist
    (D) anthologist is to editor
    (E) pantomime is to viewer

56. Gully is to erosion as
    (A) drought is to precipitation
    (B) mine is to excavation
    (C) clot is to dispersion
    (D) forest is to cultivation
    (E) water is to inundation

57. Drip is to deluge as
    (A) shine is to polish
    (B) warm is to heat
    (C) yearn is to wish
    (D) smolder is to blaze
    (E) bend is to straight

58. Lax is to resolution
    (A) hapless is to circumstance
    (B) detrimental is to destruction
    (C) deceitful is to sincerity
    (D) vulnerable is to wound
    (E) accessible is to rewarded

59. Hammer is to pound as
    (A) vase is to flowers
    (B) briefcase is to papers
    (C) nail is to wood
    (D) screwdriver is to tool
    (E) jack is to raise

60. Lexicon is to words as anthology is to
    (A) reading
    (B) library
    (C) books
    (D) works
    (E) illustrations

1

STOP

IF YOU FINISH BEFORE TIME IS CALLED,
YOU MAY CHECK YOUR WORK ON THIS SECTION ONLY.
DO NOT TURN TO ANY OTHER SECTION IN THE TEST.

Upper Level SSAT
Section 2
Time-25 Minutes
25 Questions

Following each problem in this section, there are five suggested answers. Work each problem in your head or in the blank space provided at the right of the page. Then look at the five suggested answers and decide which one is best.

<u>Note:</u> Figures that accompany problems in this section are drawn as accurately as possible EXCEPT when it is stated in a specific problem that its figure is not drawn to scale.

Sample Problem:

$$\begin{array}{r} 5,413 \\ -4,827 \end{array}$$

(A) 586
(B) 596
(C) 696
(D) 1,586
(E) 1,686   ● (B) (C) (D) (E)

USE THIS SPACE FOR FIGURING.

1. If $h = 2$, and h, i, and j are consecutive even integers and $h < i < j$, what is $h + i + j$?

(A) 3
(B) 5
(C) 9
(D) 10
(E) 12

---

2. If $x = \dfrac{1}{2} + \dfrac{1}{3} + \dfrac{1}{4}$ and $y = \dfrac{1}{2} + \dfrac{2}{3} + \dfrac{3}{4}$, then

$x + y =$

(A) 3

(B) 1

(C) $\dfrac{2}{3}$

(D) $\dfrac{1}{24}$

(E)

GO ON TO THE NEXT PAGE.

3. If the product of 412.7 and 100 is rounded to the nearest hundred, the answer will be

   (A) 400
   (B) 4,100
   (C) 4,127
   (D) 41,270
   (E) 41,300

USE THIS SPACE FOR FIGURING.

2

4. If $\frac{4}{5}$ of a number is 28, then $\frac{1}{5}$ of that number is

   (A) 4
   (B) 7
   (C) 21
   (D) 35
   (E) 112

5. $14 + 3 \times 7 + (12 \div 2) =$

   (A) 140
   (B) 125
   (C) $65\frac{1}{2}$
   (D) 41
   (E) 20

6. The perimeter of a square with area 100 is

   (A) 10
   (B) 25
   (C) 40
   (D) 100
   (E) 1000

GO ON TO THE NEXT PAGE.

Questions 7-8 refer to the following chart.

USE THIS SPACE FOR FIGURING.

2

Money Raised at Candy Sale

Cost of Candy	$1.00	$5.00	$10.00	$15.00
# Sold	100	25	20	5

7. How much more money was raised by the $10.00 candy than by the $5.00 candy?

 (A) $50
 (B) $75
 (C) $125
 (D) $200
 (E) $32

8. The money raised by the $15.00 candy is approximately what percent of the total money raised at the candy sale?

 (A) 15%
 (B) 20%
 (C) 30%
 (D) 45%
 (E) 50%

9. An art gallery has three collections: modern art, sculpture, and photography. If the 24 items which make up the modern art collection represent 25% of the total number of items in the gallery, then the average number of items in each collection is

 (A) 8
 (B) 24
 (C) 32
 (D) 96
 (E) 288

GO ON TO THE NEXT PAGE.

10. At Calvin U. Smith Elementary School, the ratio of students to teachers is 9 : 1. What fractional part of the entire population at the school is teachers?

   (A) $\dfrac{1}{10}$

   (B) $\dfrac{1}{9}$

   (C) $\dfrac{1}{8}$

   (D) $\dfrac{8}{1}$

   (E) $\dfrac{9}{1}$

USE THIS SPACE FOR FIGURING.

2

11. The Ace Delivery Company employs two drivers to make deliveries on a certain Saturday. If Driver A makes d deliveries and Driver B makes $d + 2$ deliveries, then in terms of d, the average number of deliveries made by each driver is

   (A) d
   (B) $d + 1$
   (C) $d + 2$

   (D) $\dfrac{1}{2}\,d + 2$

   (E) $\dfrac{3}{2}d$

12. Which of the following is equal to w?

   (A) $180 - v$
   (B) $180 + v$
   (C) $2v$
   (D) 105
   (E) 115

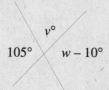

GO ON TO THE NEXT PAGE.

13. Tracy goes to the store and buys only candy bars and cans of soda. She buys 3 times as many candy bars as cans of soda. If she buys a total of 24 items, how many of those items are candy bars?

   (A) 3
   (B) 12
   (C) 18
   (D) 21
   (E) 24

USE THIS SPACE FOR FIGURING.

2

Questions 14–16 refer to the following definition.

For all integers x and y, $x \sim y = \dfrac{xy}{3}$

14. $10 \sim 6 =$

   (A) 4
   (B) 10
   (C) 15
   (D) 18
   (E) 20

15. If $x \sim 4$ is an integer, what is one possible value of x?

   (A) 6
   (B) 7
   (C) 8
   (D) 11
   (E) 13

16. Which of the following produces the greatest value?

   (A) $6 \sim 4$
   (B) $8 \sim 3$
   (C) $9 \sim 2$
   (D) $-9 \sim -3$
   (E) $-9 \sim -6$

GO ON TO THE NEXT PAGE.

17. The average measure of the angles that make up the shaded figures is

    (A) 60
    (B) 72
    (C) 120
    (D) 240
    (E) 360

USE THIS SPACE FOR FIGURING.

2

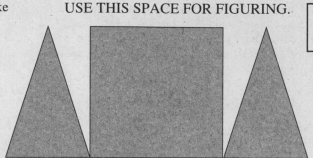

18. There are twelve homes on a certain street. If four homes are painted blue, three are painted red, and the remaining homes are green, what fractional part of the homes on the street are green?

    (A) 7
    (B) 5
    (C) $\dfrac{7}{12}$
    (D) $\dfrac{5}{12}$
    (E) $\dfrac{1}{12}$

19. Christina is twice as old as Amy, and Amy is five years younger than Kimberly. If Christina is 12, how old will Kimberly be in 15 years?

    (A) 6
    (B) 11
    (C) 15
    (D) 26
    (E) 27

GO ON TO THE NEXT PAGE.

20. If, at a fund raising dinner, x guests each donate \$200 and y guests each donate \$300, in terms of x and y, what is the total number of dollars raised?

    (A) $250(x + y)$
    (B) $200x + 300y$
    (C) $250xy$
    (D) $\dfrac{xy}{250}$
    (E) $500xy$

USE THIS SPACE FOR FIGURING.

2

21. A rectangular fish tank with dimensions 2 feet x 3 feet x 4 feet is being filled by a hose which produces 6 cubic feet of water per minute. At this rate, how many minutes will it take to fill the tank?

    (A) 24
    (B) 6
    (C) 4
    (D) 3
    (E) 2

22. With 4 days left in the Mountain Lake Critter Collection Contest, Mary has caught 15 fewer critters than Natalie. If Mary is to win the contest by collecting more critters than Natalie, at least how many critters per day must Mary catch?

    (A) 4
    (B) 5
    (C) 16
    (D) 30
    (E) 46

23. If $3x - y = 23$ and x is an integer greater than 0, which of the following is NOT a possible value for y?

   (A) 9
   (B) 7
   (C) 4
   (D) 1
   (E) −2

24. Rectangle PQRS has an area of 12. What is its perimeter?

   (A) 12
   (B) 14
   (C) 16
   (D) 24
   (E) It cannot be determined from the information given.

25. $30.00 is taken off the price of a dress. If the new price is now 60% of the original price, what was the original price of the dress?

   (A) $75.00
   (B) $60.00
   (C) $50.00
   (D) $45.00
   (E) $30.00

STOP

IF YOU FINISH BEFORE TIME IS CALLED,
YOU MAY CHECK YOUR WORK ON THIS SECTION ONLY.
DO NOT TURN TO ANY OTHER SECTION IN THE TEST.

Upper Level SSAT
Section 3
Time-25 minutes
40 Questions

Read each passage carefully and then answer the questions about it. For each question, decide on the basis of the passage which one of the choices best answers the questions.

The reading passages in this test are brief excerpts or adaptations of excerpts from published material. To make the text suitable for testing purposes, we may have, in some cases, altered the style, contents, or point of view of the original.

Florence Nightingale was a woman ahead of her time. Before the 19th century, the profession of nursing was largely untrained. Midwives were the only practitioners who had any training at all. For the most part, sick people were looked after by the women of the house in their own home.

Florence Nightingale began a school in London, England, to set the standards for nursing. She was able to do this because she had already established a reputation for her work with soldiers during the Crimean War. She carried a lamp above her head as she walked among the wounded men, thereby earning the nickname "the lady with the lamp." It was this great lady who lit the way for nursing to become the respected profession it is today.

---

1. The passage is mainly about

(A) the impact of nursing on the soldiers of the Crimean War
(B) Florence Nightingale and her influence on the profession of nursing
(C) the difference between nurses and midwives
(D) how Florence Nightingale earned the nickname "the lady with the lamp"
(E) why only females entered the profession of nursing

2. Which of the following was a method for people to receive care before Florence Nightingale's time?

(A) They would be cared for only by doctors.
(B) They would be cared for by their children.
(C) They were largely left uncared for.
(D) They were cared for by midwives.
(E) They were cared for by female relatives.

3. The style of the passage is most like that found in a

(A) personal letter to a trusted friend
(B) anthology of short biographies of famous women

(C) history of 19th-century England
(D) textbook on medicine
(E) editorial written for a daily paper

4. According to the author, the primary reason that Florence Nightingale was able to open a school for nursing was that

(A) she was already famous for her work in the war
(B) her family was willing to finance her work
(C) she had gained notoriety as a difficult woman to challenge
(D) she had cared for many wealthy sick people herself
(E) she worked endless hours every night

5. According to the passage, all of the following could be said of nurses EXCEPT

(A) prior to Florence Nightingale, only midwives were trained
(B) Florence Nightingale raised the standards of their profession
(C) they are well-respected professionals today
(D) they are exceedingly well paid for their work
(E) prior to Florence Nightingale, their work was done often by female relatives

GO ON TO THE NEXT PAGE.

3

William Dean Howells once referred to Mark Twain, one of the great American authors, as "the Lincoln of our literature." He was born Samuel L. Clemens in 1865, and before he became famous for his writing, he worked as a pilot on the Mississippi River, a newspaperman, and even a silver miner.

Mark Twain was said to be in many ways like some of his characters. He made fun of Tom Sawyer's love of tricks, yet he himself sought out any new gadget. Like Huckleberry Finn, he yearned for freedom and yet felt great responsibility for the injustice in the world. His books were humorous but included deep social satire as well. His great masterpiece, *Huckleberry Finn,* showed the promise of America while at the same time showing the evils of slavery. Unfortunately, Twain died unhappy with the progress the country had made.

6. The passage is mainly about

(A) the great men of letters of the 19th and 20th centuries
(B) the works of William Dean Howells
(C) the inhumanity of slavery
(D) the writings of Mark Twain and the man himself
(E) Mark Twain and William Dean Howells' friendship

7. Which of the following explains how Mark Twain was like his characters?

(A) He was very young.
(B) He felt great contradictions in what he wanted and how things were.
(C) He was ridiculed for his sentiment.
(D) He was fond of the water.
(E) He had many different jobs.

8. It can be inferred from the passage that the author felt what for Mark Twain?

(A) Admiration for his talent
(B) Disgust at his inability to resolve his problems
(C) Pity for the way he died
(D) Pride for his great heritage
(E) Remorse for the way his country treated him

9. The quote from Howells at the beginning of the passage is meant to imply which of the following about Twain?

(A) He was tall and thin.
(B) He made great speeches.
(C) He was a president of the United States.
(D) He was assassinated.
(E) He was as great an author as Lincoln was a president.

10. The word "deep" in line 7 most closely means

(A) buried
(B) rich
(C) profound
(D) tired
(E) low

GO ON TO THE NEXT PAGE.

3

Flax has been raised for many thousands of years, for many different reasons. Probably the two most important reasons are for the fabric it makes and the oil it produces. The woody stem of the flax plant contains the long, strong fibers that are used to make linen. The seeds are rich in an oil important for its industrial uses.

The people of ancient Egypt, Assyria, and Mesopotamia raised flax for cloth; Egyptian mummies were wrapped in linen. Since the discovery of its drying ability, the oil from flaxseed, called linseed oil, has been used as a drying agent in paints and varnishes.

The best fiber and the best seed cannot be obtained from the same kinds of plant. Fiber flax grows tall and has few branches. It needs a short, cool growing season with plenty of rainfall evenly distributed, otherwise, the plants become woody and the fiber is rough and dry. On the other hand, seed flax grows well in places that are too dry for fiber flax. The plants are lower to the ground and have more branches.

11. Which of the following would be the best title for the passage?

(A) How Mummies Were Preserved
(B) The Many Uses of the Flax Plant
(C) The Difference Between Seeds and Fibers
(D) The Types of Plant Life Around the World
(E) Ancient Sources of Oil and Linen

12. The author suggests that ancient people raised flax primarily for

(A) its oil, used to preserve wood
(B) its oil, used as a rich source of nutrient
(C) its fabric, used for their clothes
(D) its fabric, used to wrap their dead
(E) its fabric and oil, for industrial uses

13. This passage sounds as if it were an excerpt from

(A) a letter to the Egyptians
(B) a book on plant life
(C) a scientific treatise
(D) a persuasive essay from an ecologist
(E) a friendly reminder to a politician

14. Which of the following questions is answered by the passage?

(A) Can the same plant be grown for the best fabric and the best oil?
(B) How did the Egyptians wrap their mummies?
(C) What temperature is optimal for growing flax?
(D) How is flax harvested?
(E) Is it possible to produce a new type of flax for fabric and oil production?

15. Which of the following is the author most likely to discuss next?

(A) How flax is used around the world today
(B) Other types of useful plants
(C) Other sources of oil
(D) The usefulness of synthetic fabrics
(E) The advantages of pesticides and crop rotation

GO ON TO THE NEXT PAGE.

3

William, duke of Normandy, conquered England in 1066. One of the first tasks he undertook as king was the building of a fortress in the city of London. Begun in 1066 and completed several years later by William's son, William Rufus, this structure was called the White Tower.

The Tower of London is not just one building, but an 18-acre complex of buildings. In addition to the White Tower, there are 19 other towers. The Thames River flows by one side of the complex and a large moat, or shallow ditch, surrounds it. Once filled with water, the moat was drained in 1843 and is now covered with grass.

The Tower of London is the city's most popular tourist attraction. A great deal of fascinating history has taken place within its walls. The tower has served as a fortress, a royal residence, a prison, the royal mint, public records office, observatory, military barracks, place of execution, and city zoo.

As recently as 1941 the tower was used as a prison for Adolf Hitler's associate Rudolf Hess. Although it is no longer used as a prison, it still houses the crown jewels and a great deal of English history.

16. The primary purpose of this passage is to

    (A) discuss the future of the Tower of London
    (B) discuss the ramifications of using the Tower as a prison
    (C) argue that the Tower is an improper place for crown jewels
    (D) discuss the history of the Tower of London
    (E) debate the relative merits of the uses of the Tower in the past to the present

17. All of the following were uses for the Tower of London EXCEPT

    (A) a place where money was made
    (B) a palace for the royals
    (C) a place where executions were held
    (D) a place of religious pilgrimage
    (E) a place where records were stored

18. Which of the following questions is answered by the passage?

    (A) What controversy has surrounded the Tower of London?
    (B) How much revenue does the Tower generate for England?
    (C) In what year did construction on the Tower of London begin?
    (D) What is the type of stone used in the Tower of London?
    (E) Who was the most famous prisoner in the Tower?

19. When discussing the Tower of London the author's tone could best be described as

    (A) bewildered
    (B) objective
    (C) overly emotional
    (D) envious
    (E) disdainful

20. Which of the following does the author imply about Rudolph Hess?

    (A) He was executed at the Tower of London.
    (B) He was one of the last prisoners in the Tower of London.
    (C) He died an untimely death.
    (D) He was a tourist attraction.
    (E) He was respectful of the great Tower of London.

21. The author would most probably agree that

    (A) the Tower of London is only useful as a tourist attraction
    (B) the Tower of London could never be built today
    (C) the Tower of London cannot generate enough revenue to justify its expenses
    (D) the Tower of London has a complex history
    (E) the prisoners at the Tower were relatively well treated

GO ON TO THE NEXT PAGE.

3

When I was eighteen I wanted something to do. I had tried teaching for two years and hated it; I had tried sewing and could not earn my bread that way, at the cost of health; I tried storywriting and got five dollars for stories that now bring a hundred; I had thought seriously of going up on the stage, but certain highly respectable relatives were so shocked at the mere idea that I relinquished my dramatic aspirations.

"What *shall* I do?" was still the question that perplexed me. I was ready to work, eager to be independent, and too proud to endure patronage. But the right task seemed hard to find, and my bottled energies were fermenting in a way that threatened an explosion.

22. Which of the following best expresses the author's attitude toward work?

   (A) Work is to be avoided at all costs.
   (B) It is better to work at any job than not to work at all.
   (C) It is difficult to find a job that pays well and is rewarding.
   (D) Jobs are plentiful if you know where to look.
   (E) Patronage is as humiliating as work.

23. The author implies that writing is a job that is

   (A) profitable
   (B) rewarding
   (C) miserable
   (D) unprofitable
   (E) stimulating

24. The author uses the example of her relatives to explain

   (A) why she gave up her dream of a career as an actress
   (B) why she did not want to be an actress
   (C) why she felt that acting was not a respectable profession
   (D) why she wanted to become a writer
   (E) why she was unable to find any jobs

25. According to the author her energy was like

   (A) a carbonated drink
   (B) a bomb that might go off
   (C) an amusing book
   (D) a sewing job
   (E) a stew that is cooking

GO ON TO THE NEXT PAGE.

The first old "horseless carriages" of the 1880s may have been worthy of a snicker or two, but not the cars of today. The progress that has been made over the last one hundred years has been phenomenal. In fact, much progress was made even in the first twenty years—in 1903 cars could travel at 70 mph. The major change from the old cars to today is the expense. Whereas cars were once a luxury that only the very wealthy could afford, today, people of all income levels own cars.

In fact, there are so many cars that if they were to line up end to end, they would touch the moon. Cars are used for everyday transportation for millions of people, for recreation, and for work. Many people's jobs depend on cars—policemen, healthcare workers, and taxi drivers all rely on automobiles.

One thing that hasn't changed is how cars are powered. The first cars ran on gas and diesel fuel just as the most modern ones do. The newer cars, however, are much more fuel efficient and much research is devoted to saving fuel and finding new sources of energy for cars.

26. The "progress" mentioned in line 2 most likely refers to

(A) the ability of a car to move forward
(B) technological advancement
(C) research
(D) the new types of fuels available
(E) the cost of the car

27. Which of the following is answered by the passage?

(A) What are some ways people use cars?
(B) Why did people laugh at the "horseless carriage"?
(C) Where will the fuels of the future come from?
(D) When will cars become even more efficient?
(E) How much money is spent on cars today?

28. The passage is primarily concerned with

(A) the problem of fuel consumption
(B) the difficulty of driving
(C) the invention of the car
(D) the development of the car from the past to now
(E) the future of automobiles

29. Scientist devote much of their research today to

(A) making cars faster
(B) making more cars
(C) making cars more affordable
(D) making cars more fuel efficient
(E) making cars that hold more people

30. When discussing the technological advances of the early car, the author's tone could best be described as

(A) proud
(B) hesitant
(C) informative
(D) pedantic
(E) sarcastic

31. The author would most likely agree that

(A) cars are incredibly useful to many different sorts of people
(B) the problems we face in the future are very important
(C) cars are more trouble than they are worth
(D) early car owners were all snobs
(E) we will never make the same technological advances as we did in the past

GO ON TO THE NEXT PAGE.

3

By the rude bridge that arched the flood,
Their flag to April's breeze unfurled,
Here once the embattled farmers stood
And fired the shot heard round the world.
The foe long since in silence slept;
Alike the conqueror silent sleeps;
And Time the ruined bridge has swept
Down the dark stream which seaward creeps.
On this green bank, by this soft stream,
We set to-day a votive stone;
That memory may their deed redeem,
When, like our sires, our sons are gone.
Spirit, that made those heroes dare
To die, and leave their children free,
Bid Time and Nature gently spare
The shaft we raise to them and thee.

—"Concord Hymn" by Ralph Waldo Emerson

32. The statements in lines 3-4 most likely mean

   (A) the narrator is a farmer
   (B) the place described is a battle site
   (C) a crime took place at that site
   (D) the farmers described were all killed
   (A) it is a cold day

33. In the poem, the speaker claims which of the reasons for writing this poem?

   I.   To warn future generation about the horrors of war
   II. To keep the memory of the great deeds of soldiers alive
   III. To gain courage to fight himself

   (A) I only
   (B) II only
   (C) II and III only
   (D) I and III only
   (E) I, II, and III

34. The "votive stone" referred to in line 10 probably refers to

   (A) a candle
   (B) a weapon
   (C) an old stone fence
   (D) a war memorial
   (E) a natural landmark

35. With which statement would the author most strongly agree?

   (A) All war is in vain.
   (B) Farming is a difficult life.
   (C) It is important to remember the brave soldiers.
   (D) How a man fights is as important as how he lives his life.
   (E) A memorial is an insignificant way to remember the past.

GO ON TO THE NEXT PAGE.

> Born as Gertrude Margaret Zelle in the Netherlands in 1876, Mata Hari was probably the most infamous spy of all time. During World War I, she was a beautiful dancer who worked in Paris. Mata Hari was her stage name.
>
> Many believe that Mata Hari was a double agent—that means that she spied for two countries at the same time. It was believed that she spied for the Germans by stealing secrets from the French, and for the French by stealing secrets from the Germans. She charmed military men with her great beauty to find many military secrets. Mata Hari was arrested and executed by the French in 1917.

3

36. Which of the following is the primary purpose of the passage?

   (A) To discuss the moral ramifications of spying
   (B) To help uncover the reasons Mata Hari turned to spying
   (C) To discuss a little about the background of Mata Hari
   (D) To conclude that Mata Hari was a double agent
   (E) To demonstrate Mata Hari's great beauty

37. The word "charmed" in line 6 most closely means

   (A) enchanted
   (B) bejeweled
   (C) enriched
   (D) fooled
   (E) found

38. The author's attitude toward Mata Hari's work can best be described as one of

   (A) disgust
   (B) rage
   (C) neutrality
   (D) admiration
   (E) envy

39. It can be inferred that one of the primary reasons that Mata Hari was a successful spy was that

   (A) she was very secretive
   (B) she was a talented dancer
   (C) she was very attractive
   (D) she loved to talk to people
   (A) she had a special affection for soldiers

40. Which of the following can be inferred from the passage about Mata Hari's status as a double agent?

   (A) It was even more dangerous than regular spying.
   (B) It required great diplomacy.
   (C) She was considered the greatest double agent of all time.
   (D) She was incapable of continuing.
   (E) No one ever knew for sure if she was a double agent.

STOP

IF YOU FINISH BEFORE TIME IS CALLED,
YOU MAY CHECK YOUR WORK ON THIS SECTION ONLY.
DO NOT TURN TO ANY OTHER SECTION IN THE TEST.

Upper Level SSAT
Section 4
Time-25 Minutes
25 Questions

Following each problem in this section, there are five suggested answers. Work each problem in your head or in the blank space provided at the right of the page. Then look at the five suggested answers and decide which one is best.

Note: Figures that accompany problems in this section are drawn as accurately as possible EXCEPT when it is stated in a specific problem that its figure is not drawn to scale.

Sample Problem:

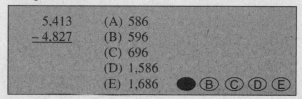

5,413
−4,827

(A) 586
(B) 596
(C) 696
(D) 1,586
(E) 1,686 ●ⒷⒸⒹⒺ

USE THIS SPACE FOR FIGURING.

1. $2^4 =$

   (A) 24
   (B) 16
   (C) 8
   (D) 6
   (E) 4

2. $x =$

   (A) 30
   (B) 60
   (C) 90
   (D) 120
   (E) 300

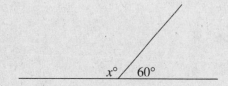

3. If $-4 < x < 2$, how many possible integer values for x are there?

   (A) 6
   (B) 5
   (C) 4
   (D) 3
   (E) 2

GO ON TO THE NEXT PAGE.

Questions 4–6 refer to the following graph.

USE THIS SPACE FOR FIGURING.

Ken's Savings Account Balance, 1994 - 1997

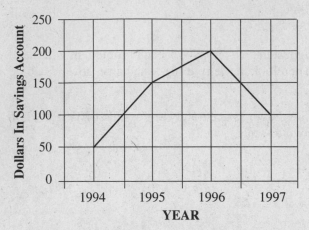

4. By how many dollars did Ken's savings account balance grow from 1994 to 1995?

   (A) $25.00
   (B) $50.00
   (C) $75.00
   (D) $100.00
   (E) $150.00

5. The decrease in Ken's account balance from 1996 to 1997 equals what percent of Ken's account balance at the start of 1995?

   (A) 100%

   (B) 75%

   (C) $66\frac{2}{3}$%

   (D) 50%

   (E) 25%

6. If during 1997, Ken withdrew from his account one-half the amount he withdrew in 1996, how many dollars would be left in his account at the end of 1997?

   (A) $50
   (B) $75
   (C) $100
   (D) $150
   (E) $200

7. If M is an integer that is divisible by both 5 and 4, which of the following is a possible value for M?

    (A) 9
    (B) 12
    (C) 24
    (D) 45
    (E) 60

USE THIS SPACE FOR FIGURING.

4

8. If $3^x = 9^4$, then $x =$

    (A) 2
    (B) 4
    (C) 8
    (D) 12
    (E) 16

9. Which of the following is greatest?

    (A) $\dfrac{3}{4}$

    (B) $\dfrac{5}{8}$

    (C) $\dfrac{1}{2}$

    (D) $\dfrac{3}{7}$

    (E) $\dfrac{5}{9}$

10. If $x + y = z$, then $z =$

    (A) 180
    (B) 90
    (C) 60
    (D) 45
    (E) 30

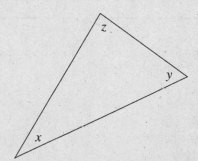

GO ON TO THE NEXT PAGE.

11. Anita bowled a 100, 120, and an 88 on her first three games. What must her score be on the fourth game to raise her average for the day to a 130?

(A) 80
(B) 95
(C) $102\frac{2}{3}$
(D) 145
(E) 212

USE THIS SPACE FOR FIGURING.

12. $\frac{5}{6}$ is closest in value to which of the following?

(A) .20
(B) .30
(C) .60
(D) .80
(E) .90

13. If 10 rolls of film can be purchased for *n* dollars, how many rolls can be purchased for *m* dollars?

(A) $\frac{10n}{m}$

(B) $\frac{nm}{10}$

(C) $\frac{10}{mn}$

(D) $\frac{m}{10n}$

(E) $\frac{10m}{n}$

14. All numbers divisible by both 6 and by 15 are also divisible by

(A) 3
(B) 7
(C) 8
(D) 9
(E) 10

15. The ratio of rhubarb plants to tomato plants in Jim's garden is 4 to 5. If there is a total of 45 rhubarb and tomato plants all together, how many of these plants are rhubarb plants?

    (A) 4
    (B) 5
    (C) 9
    (D) 20
    (E) 25

USE THIS SPACE FOR FIGURING.

4

16. If m is a non-zero integer, and if $3 + 16 \div m$ is an integer less than 19, which of the following must be true of m?

    (A) $m = 19$
    (B) m is even
    (C) $m = 16$
    (D) m is positive
    (E) m is a multiple of four

17. If an item that is discounted by 20% still costs more than $28.00, the original price of the item must be

    (A) less than $3.50
    (B) less than $7.00
    (C) less than $35.00
    (D) equal to $35.00
    (E) more than $35.00

18. What is the perimeter of triangle MNO?

    (A) 3
    (B) 9
    (C) 18
    (D) 27
    (E) It cannot be determined from the information given.

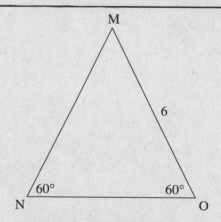

GO ON TO THE NEXT PAGE.

Questions 19–20 refer to the following definition.

For all integers x, £$x = (\dfrac{x}{x - 1}) + 1$

19. £3 =

    (A) 4

    (B) $2\dfrac{1}{2}$

    (C) 2

    (D)

    (E)

20. $\dfrac{1}{2}$ (£4) =

    (A) $\dfrac{4}{3}$

    (B) $1\dfrac{1}{6}$

    (C) 2

    (D) $2\dfrac{1}{3}$

    (E) $4\dfrac{2}{3}$

Questions 21–22 refer to the following chart.

USE THIS SPACE FOR FIGURING.

4

Number of patients seen by four doctors during a certain week

	MONDAY	TUESDAY	WEDNESDAY	THURSDAY	FRIDAY	TOTAL
Dr. Adams	6	12	10	0	0	28
Dr. Chou	8	8	0	8	8	32
Dr. Davis	4	0	5	3	4	16
Dr. Rosenthal	0	8	10	6	0	24
TOTAL	18	28	25	17	12	100

21. The number of patients that Dr. Davis saw on Friday represents what percent of the total number of patients she saw during the entire week?

(A) $33\frac{1}{3}$ %
(B) 25%
(C) 10%
(D) 4%
(E) It cannot be determined from the information given.

22. Over the entire week, Dr. Adams and Dr. Davis together saw what percent of the total number of patients seen by all four doctors?

(A) 16%
(B) 28%
(C) 44%
(D) 50%
(E) 88%

GO ON TO THE NEXT PAGE.

23. A store sells mints for 50¢ each or $4.80 for a case of twelve mints. The cost per mint is what percent greater when the mints are purchased separately than when purchased in a case?

(A) 10%
(B) 20%
(C) 22%
(D) 25%
(E) 30%

USE THIS SPACE FOR FIGURING.

4

24. A certain hen house contains x hens. A farmer puts 1x2 new hens into the house, and later that day moves one-quarter of the hens out of the hen house. If no other hens are put into or taken from the house, then in terms of x, how many hens are left in the hen house?

(A) $\dfrac{3x}{4} + 9$

(B) $x + 4$

(C) $4x + 12$

(D) $\dfrac{x + 12}{4}$

(E) $4x + 48$

25. If the length of one of the legs of a right triangle is decreased by 10%, and the length of the other leg is increased by 20%, then what is the approximate percent change in the area of the triangle?

(A) 2%
(B) 8%
(C) 10%
(D) 15%
(E) 18%

STOP

IF YOU FINISH BEFORE TIME IS CALLED,
YOU MAY CHECK YOUR WORK ON THIS SECTION ONLY.
DO NOT TURN TO ANY OTHER SECTION IN THE TEST.

Upper Level SSAT
Section 5
Time-25 minutes
1 Topic

You have 25 minutes to complete a brief writing sample. This writing exercise will not be scored but is used by admission officers to assess your writing skills.

Directions: Read the following topic carefully. Take a few minutes to think about the topic and organize your thoughts before you begin writing. Be sure that your handwriting is legible and that you stay within the lines and margins.

| **Topic:** Imagination is more important than knowledge. | **Assignment:** Do you agree or disagree with the topic statement? Support your position with one or two specific examples from personal experience, the experience of others, current events, history, or literature. |

8

Lower Level
SSAT Practice Test

Lower Level Practice Test

Lower Level SSAT
Section 1
Time-25 minutes
60 Questions

This section consists of two different types of questions. There are directions and a sample question for each type.

Each of the following questions consists of one word followed by five words or phrases. You are to select the one word or phrase whose meaning is closest to the word in capital letters.

Sample Question:

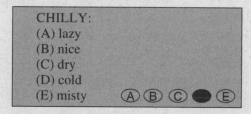

CHILLY:
(A) lazy
(B) nice
(C) dry
(D) cold
(E) misty

1. OBEDIENT:
   (A) amenable
   (B) excessive
   (C) ironic
   (D) inhumane
   (E) improper

2. CONTAMINATE:
   (A) deodorize
   (B) decongest
   (C) deter
   (D) taint
   (E) defoliate

3. INAUSPICIOUS:
   (A) colorless
   (B) prudent
   (C) misplaced
   (D) ominous
   (E) raising intelligent questions

4. PRACTICAL:
   (A) difficult to learn
   (B) inferior in quality
   (C) providing great support
   (D) having great usefulness
   (E) feeling great regret

5. SCRUTINIZE:
   (A) examine carefully
   (B) announce publicly
   (C) infer correctly
   (D) decide promptly
   (E) warn swiftly

6. CONFIDE:
   (A) judge carefully
   (B) entrust
   (C) secret
   (D) decide promptly
   (E) warn

7. INITIATE:
   (A) bring to an end
   (B) sign
   (C) commence
   (D) hinder
   (E) guide

8. FORTUNATE:
   (A) lucky
   (B) wealthy
   (C) intelligent
   (D) poor
   (E) downtrodden

GO ON TO THE NEXT PAGE.

1

9. CORROBORATION:
   - (A) attraction
   - (B) confirmation
   - (C) legal activity
   - (D) unfulfilled expectation
   - (E) enthusiastic response

10. DESPERATE:
   - (A) hungry
   - (B) frantic
   - (C) delicate
   - (D) adaptable
   - (E) contaminated

11. FRET:
   - (A) listen
   - (B) provide
   - (C) worry
   - (D) require
   - (E) stash

12. VERSATILE:
   - (A) peaceful
   - (B) disruptive
   - (C) adaptable
   - (D) truthful
   - (E) charming

13. ASSIST:
   - (A) support
   - (B) bring
   - (C) distrust
   - (D) yearn
   - (E) destroy

14. REPRIMAND:
   - (A) praise
   - (B) insure
   - (C) liberate
   - (D) chide
   - (E) forgive

15. EVADE:
   - (A) take from
   - (B) blind
   - (C) help
   - (D) sidestep
   - (E) successful

16. FATIGUE:
   - (A) grow weary
   - (B) become fluid
   - (C) increase in height
   - (D) recede from view
   - (E) improve

17. ANTIDOTE:
   - (A) foundation
   - (B) vacation
   - (C) poison
   - (D) learning experience
   - (E) antitoxin

18. PROPOSE:
   - (A) speak up
   - (B) marriage
   - (C) fall away
   - (D) suggest
   - (E) lease

19. INCREDIBLE:
   - (A) mundane
   - (B) uncivilized
   - (C) sophisticated
   - (D) believable
   - (E) extraordinary

20. VIGILANT:
   - (A) observant
   - (B) sleepy
   - (C) overly anxious
   - (D) brutal
   - (E) moving

GO ON TO THE NEXT PAGE.

21. TATTERED:
   - (A) unkempt
   - (B) neat
   - (C) exuberant
   - (D) unruly
   - (E) pressed

22. PRECEDE:
   - (A) stand alongside
   - (B) move towards
   - (C) come before
   - (D) hurl
   - (E) beg

23. LAMENT:
   - (A) relish
   - (B) drench
   - (C) moan
   - (D) invent
   - (E) incline

24. ENGAGE:
   - (A) date
   - (B) employ
   - (C) train
   - (D) dismiss
   - (E) fear

25. COMPETENT:
   - (A) disastrous
   - (B) fast
   - (C) cautious
   - (D) able
   - (E) inanimate

26. SINCERE:
   - (A) new
   - (B) passionate
   - (C) expensive
   - (D) genuine
   - (E) untold

27. RICKETY:
   - (A) strong
   - (B) wooden
   - (C) antique
   - (D) beautiful
   - (E) feeble

28. CONSPICUOUS:
   - (A) plain as day
   - (B) identity
   - (C) camouflaged
   - (D) shiny
   - (E) cramped

29. DISGUISE:
   - (A) mystery
   - (B) convict
   - (C) present
   - (D) false front
   - (E) pressure

30. CRUMBLE:
   - (A) eat
   - (B) stumble
   - (C) dry out
   - (D) small
   - (E) deteriorate

1

GO ON TO THE NEXT PAGE.

The following questions ask you to find relationships between words. For each question, select the answer choice that best completes the meaning of the sentence.

Sample Question:

> Kitten is to cat as
> (A)   fawn is to cult
> (B)   puppy is to dog
> (C)   cow is to bull
> (D)   wolf is to bear
> (E)   hen is to rooster   Ⓐ ● Ⓒ Ⓓ Ⓔ

Choice (B) is the best answer because a kitten is a young cat, just as a puppy is a young dog. Of all the answer choices, (B) states a relationship that is most like the relationship between <u>kitten</u> and <u>cat</u>.

1

31. Fish is to water as
(A)   bird is to egg
(B)   roe is to pouch
(C)   lion is to land
(D)   flower is to pollen
(E)   bee is to honey

32. Sick is to healthy as jailed is to
(A)   convicted
(B)   free
(C)   guilty
(D)   trapped
(E)   hurt

33. Dancer is to feet as
(A)   surgeon is to heart
(B)   juggler is to hands
(C)   drummer is to drums
(D)   conductor is to voice
(E)   musician is to eyes

34. Bystander is to event as
(A)   juror is to verdict
(B)   culprit is to crime
(C)   tourist is to journey
(D)   spectator is to game
(E)   model is to portrait

35. Baker is to bread as
(A)   shop is to goods
(B)   butcher is to livestock
(C)   politician is to votes
(D)   sculptor is to statue
(E)   family is to confidence

36. Igneous is to rock as
(A)   stratum is to dig
(B)   fossil is to dinosaur
(C)   computer is to technology
(D)   watercolor is to painting
(E)   calendar is to date

37. Delicious is to taste as melodious is to
(A)   sound
(B)   music
(C)   ears
(D)   eyes
(E)   sight

38. Clog is to shoe as
(A)   sneaker is to run
(B)   lace is to tie
(C)   beret is to hat
(D)   shirt is to torso
(E)   sock is to foot

GO ON TO THE NEXT PAGE.

39. Cube is to square as
    (A) box is to cardboard
    (B) circle is to street
    (C) cylinder is to pen
    (D) line is to angle
    (E) sphere is to circle

40. Jam is to fruit as
    (A) bread is to toast
    (B) butter is to milk
    (C) crayon is to color
    (D) height is to stone
    (E) write is to pencil

41. Mile is to length as
    (A) sky is to height
    (B) coffee is to drink
    (C) pot is to stew
    (D) floor is to ground
    (E) quart is to volume

42. Biologist is to scientist as surgeon is to
    (A) doctor
    (B) scar
    (C) cut
    (D) heart
    (E) scalpel

43. Clay is to potter as
    (A) sea is to captain
    (B) magazine is to reader
    (C) marble is to sculptor
    (D) word is to teacher
    (E) bubble is to child

44. Clip is to movie as
    (A) buckle is to shoe
    (B) excerpt is to novel
    (C) jar is to liquid
    (D) room is to house
    (E) filling is to pie

45. Ruthless is to mercy as naive is to
    (A) thoughtfulness
    (B) illness
    (C) worldliness
    (D) contempt
    (E) purity

46. Glacier is to ice as
    (A) rain is to snow
    (B) bay is to ocean
    (C) cloud is to storm
    (D) river is to water
    (E) pond is to fish

47. Glass is to window as
    (A) wood is to building
    (B) car is to motor
    (C) job is to skills
    (D) fabric is to clothing
    (E) loan is to interest

48. Buttress is to support as scissor is to
    (A) press
    (B) store
    (C) create
    (D) cool
    (E) cut

49. Sneer is to disdain as cringe is to
    (A) loneliness
    (B) bravery
    (C) intelligence
    (D) distrust
    (E) fear

50. Library is to book as
    (A) bank is to money
    (B) museum is to patron
    (C) opera is to audience
    (D) restaurant is to waiter
    (E) concert is to music

51. Famine is to food as
    (A) drought is to water
    (B) paper is to print
    (C) legend is to fantasy
    (D) debate is to issue
    (E) clause is to contract

52. Teacher is to student as
    (A) coach is to player
    (B) assistant is to executive
    (C) nurse is to doctor
    (D) patient is to dentist
    (E) theory is to technician

GO ON TO THE NEXT PAGE.

53. Muffle is to noise as
    (A) engine is to bicycle
    (B) wind is to vane
    (C) dam is to flood
    (D) aroma is to fetid
    (E) nibble is to eat

54. Rest is to exhaustion as
    (A) pack is to vacation
    (B) water is to thirst
    (C) audit is to forms
    (D) jury is to trial
    (E) tide is to ocean

55. Playwright is to script as
    (A) choreographer is to dance
    (B) mathematician is to science
    (C) philosopher is to insight
    (D) enemy is to strategy
    (E) athlete is to prowess

56. Gluttony is to food as
    (A) shear is to wall
    (B) avarice is to money
    (C) enterprise is to earning
    (D) curiosity is to danger
    (A) mystery is to solution

57. Facile is to effort as
    (A) deception is to trick
    (B) helpful is to friend
    (C) inconsiderate is to thought
    (D) pious is to religion
    (E) incompetent is to task

58. Single-handed is to assistance as anonymous is to
    (A) praise
    (B) authorship
    (C) recognition
    (D) sincerity
    (E) ideas

59. Stable is to horse as kennel is to
    (A) farm
    (B) storage
    (C) dog
    (D) groomer
    (E) boarding

60. Coin is to mint as
    (A) janitor is to school
    (B) actor is to studio
    (C) car is to showroom
    (D) snake is to zoo
    (E) wine is to vineyard

STOP

IF YOU FINISH BEFORE TIME IS CALLED,
YOU MAY CHECK YOUR WORK ON THIS SECTION ONLY.
DO NOT TURN TO ANY OTHER SECTION IN THE TEST.

Lower Level SSAT
Section 2
Time-25 minutes
40 Questions

Following each problem in this section, there are five suggested answers. Work each problem in your head or in the blank space provided at the right of the page. Then look at the five suggested answers and decide which one is best.

<u>Note:</u> Figures that accompany problems in this section are drawn as accurately as possible EXCEPT when it is stated in a specific problem that its figure is not drawn to scale.

Sample Problem:

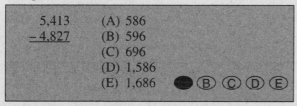

5,413	(A) 586
− 4,827	(B) 596
	(C) 696
	(D) 1,586
	(E) 1,686 ● Ⓑ Ⓒ Ⓓ Ⓔ

1. Which fraction equals $\frac{2}{3}$?

    (A) $\frac{3}{2}$

    (B) $\frac{3}{6}$

    (C) $\frac{9}{12}$

    (D) $\frac{8}{12}$

    (E) $\frac{5}{6}$

USE THIS SPACE FOR FIGURING.

2. Which of the following is an even positive integer that lies between 22 and 27?

    (A) 25
    (B) 24
    (C) 22
    (D) 21
    (E) 20

GO ON TO THE NEXT PAGE.

3. In the number 281, the sum of the digits is how much less than the product of the digits?
   (A) 16
   (B) 11
   (C) 10
   (D) 5
   (E) 4

USE THIS SPACE FOR FIGURING.

2

4. $(109 - 102) \times 3 - 4^2 =$

   (A) 5
   (B) 0
   (C) -5
   (D) -7
   (E) -336

5. A concert is held at a stadium that has 25,000 seats. If exactly $\frac{3}{4}$ of the seats were filled, to the nearest thousand, how many people attended the concert?

   (A) 10,000
   (B) 14,000
   (C) 15,000
   (D) 19,000
   (E) 21,000

6. The perimeter of a square with an area of 81 is

   (A) 81
   (B) 54
   (C) 36
   (D) 18
   (E) 9

7. If the sum of three consecutive positive integers is 9, what is the middle integer?

   (A) 1
   (B) 2
   (C) 3

GO ON TO THE NEXT PAGE.

(D) 4
(E) 5

USE THIS SPACE FOR FIGURING.

2

8. A number greater than 2 that is a factor of both
20 and 16 is also a factor of which number?
(A) 10
(B) 14
(C) 18
(D) 24
(E) 30

9. $(2^3)^2 =$

(A) 2
(B) 2^5
(C) 2^6
(D) 4^5
(E) 4^6

10. If is greater than $\dfrac{M}{16}$, then M could be

(A) 7
(B) 8
(C) 9
(D) 10
(E) 32

11. The sum of the lengths of two sides of an
equilateral triangle is 4. What is the perimeter
of the triangle?

(A) 2
(B) 4
(C) 6
(D) 8
(E) 12

GO ON TO THE NEXT PAGE.

Questions 12–14 refer to the following chart

Stacey's Weekly Mileage

DAY	MILES DRIVEN
MONDAY	35
TUESDAY	70
WEDNESDAY	50
THURSDAY	105
FRIDAY	35
SATURDAY	35
SUNDAY	20
TOTAL	350

12. What percentage of her total weekly mileage did Stacey drive on Monday?
    (A) 10%
    (B) 20%
    (C) 35%
    (D) 60%
    (E) 90%

13. The number of miles Stacey drove on Thursday is equal to the sum of the miles she drove on which days?
    (A) Monday and Wednesday
    (B) Saturday and Sunday
    (C) Tuesday, Wednesday, and Friday
    (D) Friday, Saturday, and Sunday
    (E) Monday, Friday, and Saturday

GO ON TO THE NEXT PAGE.

14. The number of miles Stacey drove on Sunday is equal to what percent of the number of miles she drove on Wednesday?

   (A) 10%
   (B) 20%
   (C) 40%
   (D) 50%
   (E) 80%

USE THIS SPACE FOR FIGURING.

2

15. If $x = \dfrac{3}{2}$, which of the following is equal to $\dfrac{1}{x}$?

   (A) 10%
   (B) 20%
   (C) 40%
   (D) 2
   (E) 3

16. What is 20% of 25% of 80?

   (A) 4
   (B) 5
   (C) 10
   (D) 16
   (E) 20

17. During one week, Roy worked 3 hours on Monday, 5 hours on Tuesday, and 8 hours each day on Saturday and Sunday. The following week Roy worked a total of 40 hours. What was the average number of hours Roy worked each week?

   (A) 32
   (B) 28
   (C) 24
   (D) 12
   (E) 6

18. A box with dimensions $4 \times 8 \times 10$ is equal in volume to a box with dimensions $16 \times g \times 2$. What does g equal?

   (A) 2
   (B) 4
   (C) 8
   (D) 10
   (E) 16

GO ON TO THE NEXT PAGE.

19. Otto wants to buy two tapes that regularly sell for *b* dollars each. The store is having a sale where the second tape costs half price. If he buys the tapes at this store, what is the overall percent he will save on the price of the two tapes?

    (A) 10%
    (B) 25%
    (C) $33\frac{1}{3}\%$
    (D) 50%
    (E) 75%

USE THIS SPACE FOR FIGURING.

2

20. In a certain month Ben eats 8 dinners at Italian restaurants, 4 dinners at Chinese restaurants, and 6 dinners at steakhouses. If these dinners account for all Ben's restaurant visits during the month, what percent of Ben's restaurant meals were at steakhouses?

    (A) 75%
    (B) 66%
    (C) 50%
    (D) 33%
    (E) 10%

21. What is the area of the shaded region?

    (A) 48
    (B) 36
    (C) 24
    (D) 12
    (E) It cannot be determined from the information given.

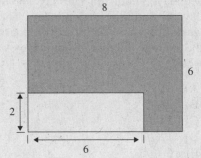

22. In the equation $(2 + \_ + 3)(2) = 16$, what does the _ stand for?

    (A) 3
    (B) 8
    (C) 9
    (D) 10
    (E) 12

GO ON TO THE NEXT PAGE.

23. At Skytop Farm the ratio of cows to pigs is 16 to 1. Which of the following could be the total number of cows and pigs at the farm?

    (A) 15
    (B) 16
    (C) 32
    (D) 68
    (E) 74

USE THIS SPACE FOR FIGURING.

2

24. Sibyl has seen four more films than Linda has seen. Linda has seen twice as many films as Joel has seen. If Sibyl has seen *s* films, then in terms of *s*, which of the following is an expression for the number of films Joel has seen?

    (A) $\dfrac{s}{2} - 2$

    (B) $\dfrac{s}{2} - 4$

    (C) $s - 2$

    (D) $s - 4$

    (E) $\dfrac{8}{s - 2}$

Question 25 refers to the following definition.

For all integers *x*,   @ *x* = 2*x* if *x* is even; and
@ *x* = 2x if *x* is odd

25. @3 - @2 =
    (A) @4
    (B) @2
    (C) @1
    (D) @-2
    (E) @-3

STOP

IF YOU FINISH BEFORE TIME IS CALLED,
YOU MAY CHECK YOUR WORK ON THIS SECTION ONLY.
DO NOT TURN TO ANY OTHER SECTION IN THE TEST.

USE THIS SPACE FOR FIGURING.

2

NO TEST MATERIAL ON THIS PAGE.

Lower Level SSAT
Section 3
Time–25 minutes
40 Questions

Read each passage carefully and then answer the questions about it. For each question, decide on the basis of the passage which one of the choices best answers the questions.

The reading passages in this test are brief excerpts or adaptations of excerpts from published material. To make the text suitable for testing purposes, we may have, in some cases, altered the style, contents, or point of view of the original.

> The native inhabitants of the Americas arrived from Asia more than 20,000 years ago. They belonged to numerous tribes and many were skilled hunters, farmers, and fishers. Some of the most famous of the tribes of Native Americans are the Sioux, the Cheyenne, the Iroquois, and the Apache.
>
> These tribes settled and developed organized societies. The settlers to North America from Europe fought the Native Americans for land. Geronimo was the last great Native American chief to organize rebellions against the settlers. He led raids across the southwest and into Mexico. Although he was eventually captured, he later became a celebrity.
>
> After a long battle, the United States government moved the Native Americans onto reservations—special sections of land set aside for them—where many still reside today.

1. The main purpose of this passage is to

   (A) report on the current status of Native Americans
   (B) offer a solution to the problems of Native Americans
   (C) give a brief history of Native Americans
   (D) discuss ways Native Americans are able to work on reservations
   (E) give a history of different Native American tribes

2. According to the passage, the fate of Geronimo was

   (A) to live out his life in disgrace
   (B) to become a great war hero with no defeats
   (C) to become famous throughout the country
   (D) to die penniless and alone
   (E) to commit suicide

3. The author's tone in regard to the fate of Native Americans is

   (A) passionate
   (B) objective
   (C) disappointed
   (D) ambivalent
   (E) envious

4. Which of the following is the author most likely to discuss next?

   (A) Possible causes of Native American resentment
   (B) The life of the Native American in modern society
   (C) The battle that defeated Geronimo
   (D) The differences among tribes
   (E) A detailed history of the Sioux

5. The passage names all the following as skills possessed by Native Americans EXCEPT

   (A) farming
   (B) hunting
   (C) fishing
   (D) gathering
   (E) fighting

GO ON TO THE NEXT PAGE.

3

Twenty percent of all the land on earth consists of deserts. When most people think of deserts, they think of searing heat, big huge sand dunes, and camels. Not all deserts are huge sand piles—many are strewn with rocks and some, like those at high altitudes, may actually be quite cold.

Desert life is interesting and varied as well. Though the desert is a punishing place—not much plant life to feed on survives there—many animals live there. Because there is so little water, desert animals have adapted. Camels can survive for days without drinking. Other animals get their water from the insects and plants they eat. The extreme temperatures of the desert can make life difficult as well. Many of the mammals have thick fur to keep out the heat and the cold. Many desert animals are nocturnal, sleeping by day and hunting by night when the air is cooler. It may seem that all deserts are the same, but they are as different as the animals that inhabit them.

6. The passage is primarily about

(A) deserts and desert wildlife
(B) nocturnal animals
(C) plant life of the desert
(D) sources of water in the desert
(E) average desert temperatures

7. Which of the following can be inferred as an example of an adaptation to desert life?

(A) The large claws of the lizard
(B) The heavy outer shell of the beetle
(C) The long ears of the hedgehog that give off heat to cool the animal
(D) The large hood of the cobra that scares off predators
(E) The quick speed of the mongoose so that it may catch its prey

8. The style of the passage is most like that found in a

(A) scientific thesis
(B) general book on desert life
(C) advanced text on animal adaptations
(D) diary of a naturalist
(E) notes for a novel on the desert

9. According to the passage, camels are well adapted to desert life because

(A) they have long legs
(B) they have thick fur that keeps them cool
(C) they have large hooded eyes
(D) they are capable of hunting at night
(E) they can store water for many days

10. According to the passage, some deserts

(A) are filled with lush vegetation
(B) are home to large bodies of water
(C) actually get a good deal of rainfall
(D) can be in a cold climate
(E) are home to large, thriving cities

11. The word "punishing" in line 4 most closely means

(A) beating
(B) harsh
(C) unhappy
(D) deadly
(E) fantastic

GO ON TO THE NEXT PAGE.

3

The inspiration for the modern Olympic Games started in Greece more than 2,000 years ago. These games were originally a religious festival, which at their greatest lasted for five days. Only men could compete, and the sports included running, wrestling, and chariot racing.

Today's Olympic Games are quite a bit different. First of all, there are two varieties: Winter Olympics and Summer Olympics. They each boast many men and women competing in a multitude of sports, from skiing to gymnastics. They are each held every four years, but not during the same year. They alternate so that there are Olympic Games every two years. The Olympics are not held only in one country, either. They are hosted by different cities around the world. The opening ceremony is a spectacular display, usually incorporating the traditional dances and culture of the host city.

The highlight of the opening ceremony is the lighting of the Olympic flame. Teams of runners carry the torch from Olympia, the site of the ancient Greek games. Although the games have changed greatly throughout the centuries, the spirit of competition is still alive and the flame represents that.

12. The passage is primarily concerned with

    (A) justifying the existence of the Olympic Games
    (B) explaining all about the games in Ancient Greece
    (C) discussing the differences between Winter Olympics and Summer Olympics
    (D) comparing the modern Olympic Games to those in Ancient Greece
    (E) explaining the process for choosing a host country

13. The author mentions "traditional dances and culture of the host city" in order to

    (A) give an example as to how the opening ceremony is so spectacular
    (B) explain the differences among the different host cities
    (C) show that Ancient Greek games were quite boring by contrast
    (D) make an analogy to the life of the Ancient Greeks
    (E) illustrate the complexity of the modern games

14. The author's tone in the passage can best be described as

    (A) disinterested
    (B) upbeat
    (C) gloating
    (D) depressing
    (E) fatalistic

15. The lighting of the torch is meant to symbolize

    (A) the destruction caused in Ancient Greece
    (B) the spirit of Ancient Greek competition
    (C) the rousing nature of the games
    (D) the heat generated in competition
    (E) an eternal flame so that the games will continue forever

16. Which of the following is the author most likely to discuss next?

    (A) The origin of the Ancient Greek games
    (B) The future of the Winter Olympics
    (C) A discussion of the types of sports that are played at the Olympics
    (D) The reasons that the Ancient Greek games ended
    (E) The history of sports

GO ON TO THE NEXT PAGE.

Like snakes, lizards, and crocodiles, turtles are reptiles. The earliest fossils recognized as turtles are about 200 million years old and date from the time when dinosaurs roamed the Earth. Unbelievably, turtles have changed little in appearance since that time.

There are many different types of turtles in many different climates around the world. In contrast to other reptiles, whose populations are confined largely to the tropics, turtles are most abundant in southeastern North America and southeastern Asia. They live in lakes, ponds, salt marshes, rivers, forests, and even deserts. The sizes of turtles vary. Bog or mud turtles grow no larger than about 4 inches (10 centimeters) long. At the other end of the spectrum is the sea-roving leatherback turtle, which may be more than 6.5 feet (2 meters) in length and weigh more than 1,100 pounds (500 kilograms).

Turtles live longer than most other animals, but reports of turtles living more than a century are questionable. Several kinds, however, have lived more than 50 years in captivity. Even in natural environments, box turtles and slider turtles can reach ages of 20 to 30 years. The ages of some turtles can be estimated by counting the growth rings that form each year on the external bony plates of the shell.

3

17. The author mentions dinosaurs in the first paragraph to

  (A) illustrate the age of the turtle fossils
  (B) uncover the mystery of turtle origins
  (C) show that turtles may become extinct
  (D) give an example of the type of predator that turtles once faced
  (E) bring the life of the turtle into focus

18. The author suggests that turtles are different from other reptiles because they

  (A) date back to dinosaur times
  (B) have not adapted to their environment
  (C) live in different climates
  (D) are desert dwellers
  (E) are good pets

19. When discussing the theory that turtles may live to be more than 100, the author's tone can best be described as

  (A) respectful
  (B) ridiculing
  (C) horrified
  (D) interested
  (E) skeptical

20. One of the ways the author mentions that can be used to verify the age of a turtle is to

  (A) measure the turtle
  (B) count the rings on its shell
  (C) examine the physical deterioration of its shell
  (D) weigh the turtle
  (E) subtract its weight from its length

21. The author would most probably agree that

  (A) turtles are more interesting than other reptiles
  (B) there is a lot to be learned about turtles
  (C) turtles live longer than any other animal
  (D) turtles can be very dangerous
  (E) there are no bad turtles

GO ON TO THE NEXT PAGE.

3

> The summer holidays! Those magic words! The mere mention of them used to send shivers of joy rippling over my skin. All my summer holidays, from when I was four years old to when I was seventeen (1920 to 1932), were idyllic. This, I am certain, was because we always went to the same idyllic place, and that place was Norway.
>
> Except for my ancient half-sister and my not-quite-so-ancient half-brother, the rest of us were all pure Norwegian by blood. We all spoke Norwegian and all our relations lived over there. So in a way, going to Norway every summer was like going home.
>
> Even the journey was an event. Do not forget that there were no commercial aeroplanes in those times, so it took us four whole days to complete the trip out and another four days to get home again.

22. The author's goal in writing was to express

   (A) his affection for Norway
   (B) his dislike of his half-sister and half-brother
   (C) dismay at the drudgery of the journey
   (D) how different life was back then
   (E) his realization that the trip was so long

23. The author uses the word "idyllic" in the second paragraph to mean

   (A) scary
   (B) pleasant
   (C) religious
   (D) cold
   (E) boring

24. The author uses the analogy that "going to Norway every summer was like going home" to illustrate

   (A) how much he dreaded the journey
   (B) how frequently they went to Norway
   (C) why his half-sister and half-brother were going along
   (D) how long they stayed in Norway
   (E) how happy and comfortable he was there

25. The author mentions the length of the trip in order to

   (A) make the reader sympathetic to his plight
   (B) make the reader understand why the trip was an adventure
   (C) help the reader visualize the boredom that he faced
   (D) give the reader some sympathy for the half-sister and half-brother
   (E) help the reader visualize Norway

GO ON TO THE NEXT PAGE.

3

You may love to walk along the seashore and collect beautiful shells, but do you ever think about whose home that shell was before you found it? That's right, sea shells are the home of a whole group of creatures known as shellfish. Some of the most common types of shellfish are the mussel, the clam, and the scallop.

It may surprise you to learn that the shellfish themselves make the shells. They manage to draw calcium carbonate, a mineral, from the water. They use that mineral to build the shell up layer by layer. The shell can grow larger and larger as the shellfish grows in size.

There are two main types of shells. There are those that are one single unit, like a conch's shell, and those that are in two pieces, like a clam's shell. The two-piece shell is called a bivalve, and the two pieces are hinged together, like a door, so that the shell can open and close for feeding.

26. The "home" mentioned in line 2 most likely refers to

   (A) the sea
   (B) the planet
   (C) the places shellfish can be found
   (D) the shell
   (E) a shelter for fish

27. Which of the following questions is answered by the passage?

   (A) How do shellfish reproduce?
   (B) How much does the average shellfish weigh?
   (C) What is the average life span of a shellfish?
   (D) What do shellfish feed on?
   (E) How do shellfish make their shells?

28. This passage is primarily concerned with

   (A) how shellfish differ from other fish
   (B) the life span of shellfish
   (C) shellfish and their habitats
   (D) a general discussion of shells
   (E) the origin of shells

29. The author uses the comparison of the bivalves' hinge to a door in order to

   (A) illustrate how the shell opens and closes
   (B) explain why the shell is so fragile
   (C) give a reason for the shells that are found open
   (D) explain the mechanism for how the shells are made
   (E) illustrate that shellfish are not so different from other fish

30. Which of the following is most likely to come next in the discussion?

   (A) A mention of other fish habitats
   (B) An explanation for the reasons shellfish are so often used for food
   (C) A discussion of the colors of shells
   (D) Reasons that aquatic life is so varied
   (E) Features of plant life in the ocean

31. According to the passage, the primary difference between the conch's shell and the clam's shell is that

   (A) the conch shell is more valuable than the clam's shell
   (B) the conch shell protects better than the clam's shell
   (C) the conch shell is more beautiful than the clam's shell
   (D) the clam's shell is more difficult for the clam to manufacture than the conch shell is for the conch to manufacture
   (E) the conch shell has fewer pieces than the clam shell

GO ON TO THE NEXT PAGE.

3

> By day the bat is cousin to the mouse;
>
> He likes the attic of an aging house.
>
> His fingers make a hat about his head.
>
> His pulse-beat is so slow we think him dead.
>
> He loops in crazy figures half the night
>
> Among the trees that face the corner light.
>
> But when he brushes up against a screen,
>
> We are afraid of what our eyes have seen:
>
> For something is amiss or out of place
>
> When mice with wings can wear a human face.
>
> —Theodore Roethke

32. The "hat" referred to in line 3 is meant to refer to

    (A) the attic of the house
    (B) the bat's head
    (C) the bat's wings
    (D) the death of the bat
    (E) the mouse

33. The author uses which of the following to describe the bat?

    I. The image of a winged mouse
    II. The image of a vampire
    III. The way he flies

    (A) I only
    (B) I and II only
    (C) II and III only
    (D) I and III only
    (E) I, II, and III

34. The author mentions the "crazy figures" in line 5 to refer to

    (A) the comic notion of a mouse with wings.
    (B) the pattern of the bat's flight.
    (C) the shape of the house.
    (D) the reason the bat appears dead.
    (E) the trees in the yard.

35. The author would most probably agree with which of the following statements?

    (A) Bats are useful animals.
    (B) Bats are related to mice.
    (C) Bats are feared by many.
    (D) Most people have bats in their attic.
    (E) Bats are a strange phenomenon.

GO ON TO THE NEXT PAGE.

3

Did you ever watch a sport and admire the player's uniforms? Perhaps you play in a sport and know the thrill of putting on your team's uniform. Uniforms are important for many different reasons, whether you are playing a sport or watching one.

If you are playing a sport, you have many reasons to appreciate your uniform. You may notice how different uniforms are for different sports. That's because they are designed to make participation both safe and easy. If you participate in track and field, your uniform is designed to help you run faster and move more easily. If you participate in a sport like boxing or football, your uniform will protect you as well. You may wear special shoes, like sneakers or cleats, to help you run faster or keep you from slipping.

If you watch sports, you can appreciate uniforms as well. Imagine how difficult it would be to tell the players on a field apart without their uniforms. And of course, as sports fans all over the world do, you can show support for the team you favor by wearing the colors of the team's uniform.

36. The primary purpose of the passage is to

(A) discuss the importance of team spirit
(B) explain why uniforms are important for safety
(C) give a general history of uniforms
(D) help shed light on the controversy surrounding uniforms
(E) give some reasons why uniforms are useful

37. The "support" mentioned in line 11 most probably means

(A) nourishment
(B) salary
(C) endorsement
(D) brace
(E) relief

38. Which of the following best describes the author's attitude toward uniforms?

(A) Most of them are basically the same.
(B) They have many different purposes.
(C) They're most useful as protection against injury.
(D) They are fun to wear.
(E) They don't serve any real purpose.

39. According to the passage, people need special uniforms for track and field sports to

(A) help spectators cheer on the team
(B) distinguish them from other athletes
(C) protect against injury
(D) give them freedom of movement
(E) prevent them from losing

40. According to the passage, the primary reason that spectators like uniforms is that

(A) they help them to distinguish teams
(B) they have such vibrant colors
(C) they make great souvenirs
(D) they are collectable
(E) they are not too expensive

STOP

IF YOU FINISH BEFORE TIME IS CALLED,
YOU MAY CHECK YOUR WORK ON THIS SECTION ONLY.
DO NOT TURN TO ANY OTHER SECTION IN THE TEST.

Lower Level
Section 4
Time-25 Minutes
25 Questions

Following each problem in this section, there are five suggested answers. Work each problem in your head or in the blank space provided at the right of the page. Then look at the five suggested answers and decide which one is best.

<u>Note:</u> Figures that accompany problems in this section are drawn as accurately as possible EXCEPT when it is stated in a specific problem that its figure is not drawn to scale.

Sample Problem:

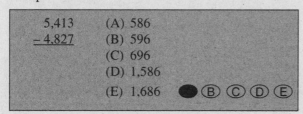

1. Which of the following fractions is greatest?   USE THIS SPACE FOR FIGURING.

   (A) $\dfrac{3}{4}$

   (B) $\dfrac{5}{8}$

   (C) $\dfrac{1}{2}$

   (D) $\dfrac{3}{7}$

   (E) $\dfrac{5}{9}$

2. The sum of the factors of 12 is

   (A) 28
   (B) 21
   (C) 20
   (D) 16
   (E) 15

GO ON TO THE NEXT PAGE.

3. $16 + 2 \times 3 + 2 =$

(A) 90
(B) 56
(C) 24
(D) 23
(E) 18

4. $D + E + F + G =$

(A) 45
(B) 90
(C) 180
(D) 270
(E) 360

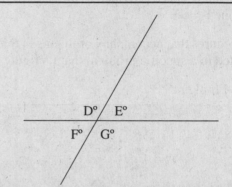

5. What are two different prime factors of 48?

(A) 2 and 3
(B) 3 and 4
(C) 4 and 6
(D) 4 and 12
(E) 6 and 8

6. The difference between 12 and the product of 4 and 6 is

(A) 12
(B) 10
(C) 2
(D) 1
(E) 0

7. The sum of the number of degrees in a straight line and the number of degrees in a triangle equals

(A) 720
(B) 540
(C) 360
(D) 180
(E) 90

Questions 8–10 refer to the following graph.

USE THIS SPACE FOR FIGURING.

4

Joseph's Winter Clothing

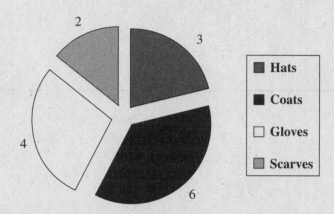

Legend:
- Hats
- Coats
- Gloves
- Scarves

8. The number of scarves Joe owns plus the number of coats he owns equals

    (A) 5
    (B) 7
    (C) 8
    (D) 9
    (E) 10

9. Hats represent what percentage of the total number of garments accounted for in the graph?

    (A) 10%
    (B) 20%
    (C) 30%
    (D) 50%
    (E) 80%

10. Which types of garments represent one-third of the total number of garments accounted for in the graph?

    (A) hats and coats
    (B) gloves and scarves
    (C) hats and scarves
    (D) gloves and coats
    (E) hats, gloves, and scarves

GO ON TO THE NEXT PAGE.

11. George bought five slices of pizza for $1.00. At this rate, how many slices of pizza could he buy with $3.20?

    (A) 16
    (B) 15
    (C) 14
    (D) 12
    (E) 10

USE THIS SPACE FOR FIGURING.

4

12. On a certain English test, the 10 students in Mrs. Bennett's class score an average of 85. On the same test, 15 students in Mrs. Grover's class score an average of 70. What is the combined average score for all the students in Mrs. Bennett's and Mrs. Grover's classes?

    (A) 80
    (B) 77.5
    (C) 76
    (D) 75
    (E) 72

13. If Mary bought e pencils, Jane bought 5 times as many pencils as Mary, and Peggy bought 2 pencils fewer than Mary, then in terms of e, how many pencils did the three girls buy all together?

    (A) $7e - 2$
    (B) $5e - 2$
    (C) 7
    (D) $8e$
    (E) $8e - 2$

14. $\dfrac{4}{1000} + \dfrac{3}{10} + 3 =$
    (A) 4033
    (B) 433
    (C) 334
    (D) 3.34
    (E) 3.304

Questions 15–16 refer to the following definition.

For all real numbers f, $[f] = -2f$

15. $[0] =$

(A) 4
(B) 2
(C) 0
(D) −2
(E) −4

16. $[2] \cdot [3] =$

(A) [12]
(B) [2]
(C) [3]
(D) [−3]
(E) [−12]

17. $2\dfrac{1}{4}\ \% =$

(A) 0.0025
(B) 0.0225
(C) 0.225
(D) 2.025
(E) 2.25

18. The area of triangle UVW is

(A) h^2
(B) h
(C) 3
(D) 2
(E) 1

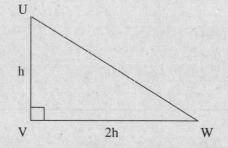

GO ON TO THE NEXT PAGE.

19. 9^4 is equal to which of the following?

(A) $(3) \cdot (3) \cdot (3) \cdot (3)$
(B) $(9) \cdot (3) \cdot (9) \cdot (3)$
(C) $(9) \cdot (4)$
(D) $(3) \cdot (3) \cdot (3) \cdot (3) \cdot (3) \cdot (3) \cdot (3) \cdot (3)$
(E) $(9) \cdot (9) + (9) \cdot (9)$

USE THIS SPACE FOR FIGURING.

20. It costs h cents to make 12 handkerchiefs. At the same rate, how many cents will it cost to make 30 handkerchiefs?

(A) $30h$

(B) $\dfrac{360}{h}$

(C) $\dfrac{2h}{5}$

(D) $\dfrac{2}{5h}$

(E) $5h$

21. A girl collects rocks. If her collection consists of 12 pieces of halite, 16 pieces of sandstone, 8 pieces of mica, and 8 pieces of galaxite, then the average number of pieces of each type of rock in her collection is

(A) 8
(B) 11
(C) 12
(D) 16
(E) 44

22. A recipe calls for 24 ounces of water for every two ounces of sugar. If 12 ounces of sugar are used, how much water should be added?

(A) 6
(B) 12
(C) 24
(D) 36
(E) 144

23. The number of people now employed by a certain company is 240, which is 60% of the number employed five years ago. How many more employees did the company have five years ago than it has now?

   (A) 160
   (B) 360
   (C) 400
   (D) 720
   (E) 960

$$\begin{array}{r} 1B5 \\ \times\ 15 \\ \hline 2025 \end{array}$$

24. In the multiplication problem above, B represents which digit?

   (A) 1
   (B) 2
   (C) 3
   (D) 5
   (E) 7

25. If the area of each of the smaller squares which make up rectangle ABCD is 4, what is the perimeter of rectangle ABCD?

   (A) 220
   (B) 64
   (C) 55
   (D) 32
   (E) 4

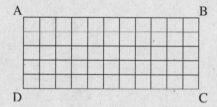

STOP

**IF YOU FINISH BEFORE TIME IS CALLED,
YOU MAY CHECK YOUR WORK ON THIS SECTION ONLY.
DO NOT TURN TO ANY OTHER SECTION IN THE TEST.**

USE THIS SPACE FOR FIGURING.

4

NO TEST MATERIAL ON THIS PAGE.

Lower Level SSAT
Section 5
Time-25 minutes
1 Topic

You have 25 minutes to complete a brief writing sample. This writing exercise will not be scored but is used by admission officers to assess your writing skills.

Directions: Read the following topic carefully. Take a few minutes to think about the topic and organize your thoughts before you begin writing. Be sure that your handwriting is legible and that you stay within the lines and margins.

Topic: Out with the old, in with the new.	Assignment: Do you agree or disagree with the topic statement? Support your position with one or two specific examples from personal experience, the experience of others, current events, history, or literature.

_____

_____

_____

_____

_____

_____

_____

_____

_____

_____

_____

_____

_____

_____

_____

_____

_____

Upper Level Practice Test

Be sure each mark *completely* fills the answer space.
Start with number 1 for each new section of the test. You may find more answer spaces than you need.
If so, please leave them blank.

SECTION 1

1 Ⓐ Ⓑ Ⓒ Ⓓ Ⓔ	13 Ⓐ Ⓑ Ⓒ Ⓓ Ⓔ	25 Ⓐ Ⓑ Ⓒ Ⓓ Ⓔ	37 Ⓐ Ⓑ Ⓒ Ⓓ Ⓔ	49 Ⓐ Ⓑ Ⓒ Ⓓ Ⓔ
2 Ⓐ Ⓑ Ⓒ Ⓓ Ⓔ	14 Ⓐ Ⓑ Ⓒ Ⓓ Ⓔ	26 Ⓐ Ⓑ Ⓒ Ⓓ Ⓔ	38 Ⓐ Ⓑ Ⓒ Ⓓ Ⓔ	50 Ⓐ Ⓑ Ⓒ Ⓓ Ⓔ
3 Ⓐ Ⓑ Ⓒ Ⓓ Ⓔ	15 Ⓐ Ⓑ Ⓒ Ⓓ Ⓔ	27 Ⓐ Ⓑ Ⓒ Ⓓ Ⓔ	39 Ⓐ Ⓑ Ⓒ Ⓓ Ⓔ	51 Ⓐ Ⓑ Ⓒ Ⓓ Ⓔ
4 Ⓐ Ⓑ Ⓒ Ⓓ Ⓔ	16 Ⓐ Ⓑ Ⓒ Ⓓ Ⓔ	28 Ⓐ Ⓑ Ⓒ Ⓓ Ⓔ	40 Ⓐ Ⓑ Ⓒ Ⓓ Ⓔ	52 Ⓐ Ⓑ Ⓒ Ⓓ Ⓔ
5 Ⓐ Ⓑ Ⓒ Ⓓ Ⓔ	17 Ⓐ Ⓑ Ⓒ Ⓓ Ⓔ	29 Ⓐ Ⓑ Ⓒ Ⓓ Ⓔ	41 Ⓐ Ⓑ Ⓒ Ⓓ Ⓔ	53 Ⓐ Ⓑ Ⓒ Ⓓ Ⓔ
6 Ⓐ Ⓑ Ⓒ Ⓓ Ⓔ	18 Ⓐ Ⓑ Ⓒ Ⓓ Ⓔ	30 Ⓐ Ⓑ Ⓒ Ⓓ Ⓔ	42 Ⓐ Ⓑ Ⓒ Ⓓ Ⓔ	54 Ⓐ Ⓑ Ⓒ Ⓓ Ⓔ
7 Ⓐ Ⓑ Ⓒ Ⓓ Ⓔ	19 Ⓐ Ⓑ Ⓒ Ⓓ Ⓔ	31 Ⓐ Ⓑ Ⓒ Ⓓ Ⓔ	43 Ⓐ Ⓑ Ⓒ Ⓓ Ⓔ	55 Ⓐ Ⓑ Ⓒ Ⓓ Ⓔ
8 Ⓐ Ⓑ Ⓒ Ⓓ Ⓔ	20 Ⓐ Ⓑ Ⓒ Ⓓ Ⓔ	32 Ⓐ Ⓑ Ⓒ Ⓓ Ⓔ	44 Ⓐ Ⓑ Ⓒ Ⓓ Ⓔ	56 Ⓐ Ⓑ Ⓒ Ⓓ Ⓔ
9 Ⓐ Ⓑ Ⓒ Ⓓ Ⓔ	21 Ⓐ Ⓑ Ⓒ Ⓓ Ⓔ	33 Ⓐ Ⓑ Ⓒ Ⓓ Ⓔ	45 Ⓐ Ⓑ Ⓒ Ⓓ Ⓔ	57 Ⓐ Ⓑ Ⓒ Ⓓ Ⓔ
10 Ⓐ Ⓑ Ⓒ Ⓓ Ⓔ	22 Ⓐ Ⓑ Ⓒ Ⓓ Ⓔ	34 Ⓐ Ⓑ Ⓒ Ⓓ Ⓔ	46 Ⓐ Ⓑ Ⓒ Ⓓ Ⓔ	58 Ⓐ Ⓑ Ⓒ Ⓓ Ⓔ
11 Ⓐ Ⓑ Ⓒ Ⓓ Ⓔ	23 Ⓐ Ⓑ Ⓒ Ⓓ Ⓔ	35 Ⓐ Ⓑ Ⓒ Ⓓ Ⓔ	47 Ⓐ Ⓑ Ⓒ Ⓓ Ⓔ	59 Ⓐ Ⓑ Ⓒ Ⓓ Ⓔ
12 Ⓐ Ⓑ Ⓒ Ⓓ Ⓔ	24 Ⓐ Ⓑ Ⓒ Ⓓ Ⓔ	36 Ⓐ Ⓑ Ⓒ Ⓓ Ⓔ	48 Ⓐ Ⓑ Ⓒ Ⓓ Ⓔ	60 Ⓐ Ⓑ Ⓒ Ⓓ Ⓔ

SECTION 2

1 Ⓐ Ⓑ Ⓒ Ⓓ Ⓔ	6 Ⓐ Ⓑ Ⓒ Ⓓ Ⓔ	11 Ⓐ Ⓑ Ⓒ Ⓓ Ⓔ	16 Ⓐ Ⓑ Ⓒ Ⓓ Ⓔ	21 Ⓐ Ⓑ Ⓒ Ⓓ Ⓔ
2 Ⓐ Ⓑ Ⓒ Ⓓ Ⓔ	7 Ⓐ Ⓑ Ⓒ Ⓓ Ⓔ	12 Ⓐ Ⓑ Ⓒ Ⓓ Ⓔ	17 Ⓐ Ⓑ Ⓒ Ⓓ Ⓔ	22 Ⓐ Ⓑ Ⓒ Ⓓ Ⓔ
3 Ⓐ Ⓑ Ⓒ Ⓓ Ⓔ	8 Ⓐ Ⓑ Ⓒ Ⓓ Ⓔ	13 Ⓐ Ⓑ Ⓒ Ⓓ Ⓔ	18 Ⓐ Ⓑ Ⓒ Ⓓ Ⓔ	23 Ⓐ Ⓑ Ⓒ Ⓓ Ⓔ
4 Ⓐ Ⓑ Ⓒ Ⓓ Ⓔ	9 Ⓐ Ⓑ Ⓒ Ⓓ Ⓔ	14 Ⓐ Ⓑ Ⓒ Ⓓ Ⓔ	19 Ⓐ Ⓑ Ⓒ Ⓓ Ⓔ	24 Ⓐ Ⓑ Ⓒ Ⓓ Ⓔ
5 Ⓐ Ⓑ Ⓒ Ⓓ Ⓔ	10 Ⓐ Ⓑ Ⓒ Ⓓ Ⓔ	15 Ⓐ Ⓑ Ⓒ Ⓓ Ⓔ	20 Ⓐ Ⓑ Ⓒ Ⓓ Ⓔ	25 Ⓐ Ⓑ Ⓒ Ⓓ Ⓔ

SECTION 3

1 Ⓐ Ⓑ Ⓒ Ⓓ Ⓔ	9 Ⓐ Ⓑ Ⓒ Ⓓ Ⓔ	17 Ⓐ Ⓑ Ⓒ Ⓓ Ⓔ	25 Ⓐ Ⓑ Ⓒ Ⓓ Ⓔ	33 Ⓐ Ⓑ Ⓒ Ⓓ Ⓔ
2 Ⓐ Ⓑ Ⓒ Ⓓ Ⓔ	10 Ⓐ Ⓑ Ⓒ Ⓓ Ⓔ	18 Ⓐ Ⓑ Ⓒ Ⓓ Ⓔ	26 Ⓐ Ⓑ Ⓒ Ⓓ Ⓔ	34 Ⓐ Ⓑ Ⓒ Ⓓ Ⓔ
3 Ⓐ Ⓑ Ⓒ Ⓓ Ⓔ	11 Ⓐ Ⓑ Ⓒ Ⓓ Ⓔ	19 Ⓐ Ⓑ Ⓒ Ⓓ Ⓔ	27 Ⓐ Ⓑ Ⓒ Ⓓ Ⓔ	35 Ⓐ Ⓑ Ⓒ Ⓓ Ⓔ
4 Ⓐ Ⓑ Ⓒ Ⓓ Ⓔ	12 Ⓐ Ⓑ Ⓒ Ⓓ Ⓔ	20 Ⓐ Ⓑ Ⓒ Ⓓ Ⓔ	28 Ⓐ Ⓑ Ⓒ Ⓓ Ⓔ	36 Ⓐ Ⓑ Ⓒ Ⓓ Ⓔ
5 Ⓐ Ⓑ Ⓒ Ⓓ Ⓔ	13 Ⓐ Ⓑ Ⓒ Ⓓ Ⓔ	21 Ⓐ Ⓑ Ⓒ Ⓓ Ⓔ	29 Ⓐ Ⓑ Ⓒ Ⓓ Ⓔ	37 Ⓐ Ⓑ Ⓒ Ⓓ Ⓔ
6 Ⓐ Ⓑ Ⓒ Ⓓ Ⓔ	14 Ⓐ Ⓑ Ⓒ Ⓓ Ⓔ	22 Ⓐ Ⓑ Ⓒ Ⓓ Ⓔ	30 Ⓐ Ⓑ Ⓒ Ⓓ Ⓔ	38 Ⓐ Ⓑ Ⓒ Ⓓ Ⓔ
7 Ⓐ Ⓑ Ⓒ Ⓓ Ⓔ	15 Ⓐ Ⓑ Ⓒ Ⓓ Ⓔ	23 Ⓐ Ⓑ Ⓒ Ⓓ Ⓔ	31 Ⓐ Ⓑ Ⓒ Ⓓ Ⓔ	39 Ⓐ Ⓑ Ⓒ Ⓓ Ⓔ
8 Ⓐ Ⓑ Ⓒ Ⓓ Ⓔ	16 Ⓐ Ⓑ Ⓒ Ⓓ Ⓔ	24 Ⓐ Ⓑ Ⓒ Ⓓ Ⓔ	32 Ⓐ Ⓑ Ⓒ Ⓓ Ⓔ	40 Ⓐ Ⓑ Ⓒ Ⓓ Ⓔ

SECTION 4

1 Ⓐ Ⓑ Ⓒ Ⓓ Ⓔ	6 Ⓐ Ⓑ Ⓒ Ⓓ Ⓔ	11 Ⓐ Ⓑ Ⓒ Ⓓ Ⓔ	16 Ⓐ Ⓑ Ⓒ Ⓓ Ⓔ	21 Ⓐ Ⓑ Ⓒ Ⓓ Ⓔ
2 Ⓐ Ⓑ Ⓒ Ⓓ Ⓔ	7 Ⓐ Ⓑ Ⓒ Ⓓ Ⓔ	12 Ⓐ Ⓑ Ⓒ Ⓓ Ⓔ	17 Ⓐ Ⓑ Ⓒ Ⓓ Ⓔ	22 Ⓐ Ⓑ Ⓒ Ⓓ Ⓔ
3 Ⓐ Ⓑ Ⓒ Ⓓ Ⓔ	8 Ⓐ Ⓑ Ⓒ Ⓓ Ⓔ	13 Ⓐ Ⓑ Ⓒ Ⓓ Ⓔ	18 Ⓐ Ⓑ Ⓒ Ⓓ Ⓔ	23 Ⓐ Ⓑ Ⓒ Ⓓ Ⓔ
4 Ⓐ Ⓑ Ⓒ Ⓓ Ⓔ	9 Ⓐ Ⓑ Ⓒ Ⓓ Ⓔ	14 Ⓐ Ⓑ Ⓒ Ⓓ Ⓔ	19 Ⓐ Ⓑ Ⓒ Ⓓ Ⓔ	24 Ⓐ Ⓑ Ⓒ Ⓓ Ⓔ
5 Ⓐ Ⓑ Ⓒ Ⓓ Ⓔ	10 Ⓐ Ⓑ Ⓒ Ⓓ Ⓔ	15 Ⓐ Ⓑ Ⓒ Ⓓ Ⓔ	20 Ⓐ Ⓑ Ⓒ Ⓓ Ⓔ	25 Ⓐ Ⓑ Ⓒ Ⓓ Ⓔ

Upper Level Practice Test

Be sure each mark *completely* fills the answer space.
Start with number 1 for each new section of the test. You may find more answer spaces than you need.
If so, please leave them blank.

SECTION 1

1 Ⓐ Ⓑ Ⓒ Ⓓ Ⓔ	13 Ⓐ Ⓑ Ⓒ Ⓓ Ⓔ	25 Ⓐ Ⓑ Ⓒ Ⓓ Ⓔ	37 Ⓐ Ⓑ Ⓒ Ⓓ Ⓔ	49 Ⓐ Ⓑ Ⓒ Ⓓ Ⓔ
2 Ⓐ Ⓑ Ⓒ Ⓓ Ⓔ	14 Ⓐ Ⓑ Ⓒ Ⓓ Ⓔ	26 Ⓐ Ⓑ Ⓒ Ⓓ Ⓔ	38 Ⓐ Ⓑ Ⓒ Ⓓ Ⓔ	50 Ⓐ Ⓑ Ⓒ Ⓓ Ⓔ
3 Ⓐ Ⓑ Ⓒ Ⓓ Ⓔ	15 Ⓐ Ⓑ Ⓒ Ⓓ Ⓔ	27 Ⓐ Ⓑ Ⓒ Ⓓ Ⓔ	39 Ⓐ Ⓑ Ⓒ Ⓓ Ⓔ	51 Ⓐ Ⓑ Ⓒ Ⓓ Ⓔ
4 Ⓐ Ⓑ Ⓒ Ⓓ Ⓔ	16 Ⓐ Ⓑ Ⓒ Ⓓ Ⓔ	28 Ⓐ Ⓑ Ⓒ Ⓓ Ⓔ	40 Ⓐ Ⓑ Ⓒ Ⓓ Ⓔ	52 Ⓐ Ⓑ Ⓒ Ⓓ Ⓔ
5 Ⓐ Ⓑ Ⓒ Ⓓ Ⓔ	17 Ⓐ Ⓑ Ⓒ Ⓓ Ⓔ	29 Ⓐ Ⓑ Ⓒ Ⓓ Ⓔ	41 Ⓐ Ⓑ Ⓒ Ⓓ Ⓔ	53 Ⓐ Ⓑ Ⓒ Ⓓ Ⓔ
6 Ⓐ Ⓑ Ⓒ Ⓓ Ⓔ	18 Ⓐ Ⓑ Ⓒ Ⓓ Ⓔ	30 Ⓐ Ⓑ Ⓒ Ⓓ Ⓔ	42 Ⓐ Ⓑ Ⓒ Ⓓ Ⓔ	54 Ⓐ Ⓑ Ⓒ Ⓓ Ⓔ
7 Ⓐ Ⓑ Ⓒ Ⓓ Ⓔ	19 Ⓐ Ⓑ Ⓒ Ⓓ Ⓔ	31 Ⓐ Ⓑ Ⓒ Ⓓ Ⓔ	43 Ⓐ Ⓑ Ⓒ Ⓓ Ⓔ	55 Ⓐ Ⓑ Ⓒ Ⓓ Ⓔ
8 Ⓐ Ⓑ Ⓒ Ⓓ Ⓔ	20 Ⓐ Ⓑ Ⓒ Ⓓ Ⓔ	32 Ⓐ Ⓑ Ⓒ Ⓓ Ⓔ	44 Ⓐ Ⓑ Ⓒ Ⓓ Ⓔ	56 Ⓐ Ⓑ Ⓒ Ⓓ Ⓔ
9 Ⓐ Ⓑ Ⓒ Ⓓ Ⓔ	21 Ⓐ Ⓑ Ⓒ Ⓓ Ⓔ	33 Ⓐ Ⓑ Ⓒ Ⓓ Ⓔ	45 Ⓐ Ⓑ Ⓒ Ⓓ Ⓔ	57 Ⓐ Ⓑ Ⓒ Ⓓ Ⓔ
10 Ⓐ Ⓑ Ⓒ Ⓓ Ⓔ	22 Ⓐ Ⓑ Ⓒ Ⓓ Ⓔ	34 Ⓐ Ⓑ Ⓒ Ⓓ Ⓔ	46 Ⓐ Ⓑ Ⓒ Ⓓ Ⓔ	58 Ⓐ Ⓑ Ⓒ Ⓓ Ⓔ
11 Ⓐ Ⓑ Ⓒ Ⓓ Ⓔ	23 Ⓐ Ⓑ Ⓒ Ⓓ Ⓔ	35 Ⓐ Ⓑ Ⓒ Ⓓ Ⓔ	47 Ⓐ Ⓑ Ⓒ Ⓓ Ⓔ	59 Ⓐ Ⓑ Ⓒ Ⓓ Ⓔ
12 Ⓐ Ⓑ Ⓒ Ⓓ Ⓔ	24 Ⓐ Ⓑ Ⓒ Ⓓ Ⓔ	36 Ⓐ Ⓑ Ⓒ Ⓓ Ⓔ	48 Ⓐ Ⓑ Ⓒ Ⓓ Ⓔ	60 Ⓐ Ⓑ Ⓒ Ⓓ Ⓔ

SECTION 2

1 Ⓐ Ⓑ Ⓒ Ⓓ Ⓔ	6 Ⓐ Ⓑ Ⓒ Ⓓ Ⓔ	11 Ⓐ Ⓑ Ⓒ Ⓓ Ⓔ	16 Ⓐ Ⓑ Ⓒ Ⓓ Ⓔ	21 Ⓐ Ⓑ Ⓒ Ⓓ Ⓔ
2 Ⓐ Ⓑ Ⓒ Ⓓ Ⓔ	7 Ⓐ Ⓑ Ⓒ Ⓓ Ⓔ	12 Ⓐ Ⓑ Ⓒ Ⓓ Ⓔ	17 Ⓐ Ⓑ Ⓒ Ⓓ Ⓔ	22 Ⓐ Ⓑ Ⓒ Ⓓ Ⓔ
3 Ⓐ Ⓑ Ⓒ Ⓓ Ⓔ	8 Ⓐ Ⓑ Ⓒ Ⓓ Ⓔ	13 Ⓐ Ⓑ Ⓒ Ⓓ Ⓔ	18 Ⓐ Ⓑ Ⓒ Ⓓ Ⓔ	23 Ⓐ Ⓑ Ⓒ Ⓓ Ⓔ
4 Ⓐ Ⓑ Ⓒ Ⓓ Ⓔ	9 Ⓐ Ⓑ Ⓒ Ⓓ Ⓔ	14 Ⓐ Ⓑ Ⓒ Ⓓ Ⓔ	19 Ⓐ Ⓑ Ⓒ Ⓓ Ⓔ	24 Ⓐ Ⓑ Ⓒ Ⓓ Ⓔ
5 Ⓐ Ⓑ Ⓒ Ⓓ Ⓔ	10 Ⓐ Ⓑ Ⓒ Ⓓ Ⓔ	15 Ⓐ Ⓑ Ⓒ Ⓓ Ⓔ	20 Ⓐ Ⓑ Ⓒ Ⓓ Ⓔ	25 Ⓐ Ⓑ Ⓒ Ⓓ Ⓔ

SECTION 3

1 Ⓐ Ⓑ Ⓒ Ⓓ Ⓔ	9 Ⓐ Ⓑ Ⓒ Ⓓ Ⓔ	17 Ⓐ Ⓑ Ⓒ Ⓓ Ⓔ	25 Ⓐ Ⓑ Ⓒ Ⓓ Ⓔ	33 Ⓐ Ⓑ Ⓒ Ⓓ Ⓔ
2 Ⓐ Ⓑ Ⓒ Ⓓ Ⓔ	10 Ⓐ Ⓑ Ⓒ Ⓓ Ⓔ	18 Ⓐ Ⓑ Ⓒ Ⓓ Ⓔ	26 Ⓐ Ⓑ Ⓒ Ⓓ Ⓔ	34 Ⓐ Ⓑ Ⓒ Ⓓ Ⓔ
3 Ⓐ Ⓑ Ⓒ Ⓓ Ⓔ	11 Ⓐ Ⓑ Ⓒ Ⓓ Ⓔ	19 Ⓐ Ⓑ Ⓒ Ⓓ Ⓔ	27 Ⓐ Ⓑ Ⓒ Ⓓ Ⓔ	35 Ⓐ Ⓑ Ⓒ Ⓓ Ⓔ
4 Ⓐ Ⓑ Ⓒ Ⓓ Ⓔ	12 Ⓐ Ⓑ Ⓒ Ⓓ Ⓕ	20 Ⓐ Ⓑ Ⓒ Ⓓ Ⓔ	28 Ⓐ Ⓑ Ⓒ Ⓓ Ⓔ	36 Ⓐ Ⓑ Ⓒ Ⓓ Ⓔ
5 Ⓐ Ⓑ Ⓒ Ⓓ Ⓔ	13 Ⓐ Ⓑ Ⓒ Ⓓ Ⓔ	21 Ⓐ Ⓑ Ⓒ Ⓓ Ⓔ	29 Ⓐ Ⓑ Ⓒ Ⓓ Ⓔ	37 Ⓐ Ⓑ Ⓒ Ⓓ Ⓔ
6 Ⓐ Ⓑ Ⓒ Ⓓ Ⓔ	14 Ⓐ Ⓑ Ⓒ Ⓓ Ⓔ	22 Ⓐ Ⓑ Ⓒ Ⓓ Ⓔ	30 Ⓐ Ⓑ Ⓒ Ⓓ Ⓔ	38 Ⓐ Ⓑ Ⓒ Ⓓ Ⓔ
7 Ⓐ Ⓑ Ⓒ Ⓓ Ⓔ	15 Ⓐ Ⓑ Ⓒ Ⓓ Ⓔ	23 Ⓐ Ⓑ Ⓒ Ⓓ Ⓔ	31 Ⓐ Ⓑ Ⓒ Ⓓ Ⓔ	39 Ⓐ Ⓑ Ⓒ Ⓓ Ⓔ
8 Ⓐ Ⓑ Ⓒ Ⓓ Ⓔ	16 Ⓐ Ⓑ Ⓒ Ⓓ Ⓔ	24 Ⓐ Ⓑ Ⓒ Ⓓ Ⓔ	32 Ⓐ Ⓑ Ⓒ Ⓓ Ⓔ	40 Ⓐ Ⓑ Ⓒ Ⓓ Ⓔ

SECTION 4

1 Ⓐ Ⓑ Ⓒ Ⓓ Ⓔ	6 Ⓐ Ⓑ Ⓒ Ⓓ Ⓔ	11 Ⓐ Ⓑ Ⓒ Ⓓ Ⓔ	16 Ⓐ Ⓑ Ⓒ Ⓓ Ⓔ	21 Ⓐ Ⓑ Ⓒ Ⓓ Ⓔ
2 Ⓐ Ⓑ Ⓒ Ⓓ Ⓔ	7 Ⓐ Ⓑ Ⓒ Ⓓ Ⓔ	12 Ⓐ Ⓑ Ⓒ Ⓓ Ⓔ	17 Ⓐ Ⓑ Ⓒ Ⓓ Ⓔ	22 Ⓐ Ⓑ Ⓒ Ⓓ Ⓔ
3 Ⓐ Ⓑ Ⓒ Ⓓ Ⓔ	8 Ⓐ Ⓑ Ⓒ Ⓓ Ⓔ	13 Ⓐ Ⓑ Ⓒ Ⓓ Ⓔ	18 Ⓐ Ⓑ Ⓒ Ⓓ Ⓔ	23 Ⓐ Ⓑ Ⓒ Ⓓ Ⓔ
4 Ⓐ Ⓑ Ⓒ Ⓓ Ⓔ	9 Ⓐ Ⓑ Ⓒ Ⓓ Ⓔ	14 Ⓐ Ⓑ Ⓒ Ⓓ Ⓔ	19 Ⓐ Ⓑ Ⓒ Ⓓ Ⓔ	24 Ⓐ Ⓑ Ⓒ Ⓓ Ⓔ
5 Ⓐ Ⓑ Ⓒ Ⓓ Ⓔ	10 Ⓐ Ⓑ Ⓒ Ⓓ Ⓔ	15 Ⓐ Ⓑ Ⓒ Ⓓ Ⓔ	20 Ⓐ Ⓑ Ⓒ Ⓓ Ⓔ	25 Ⓐ Ⓑ Ⓒ Ⓓ Ⓔ

Upper Level Practice Test

Be sure each mark *completely* fills the answer space.
Start with number 1 for each new section of the test. You may find more answer spaces than you need.
If so, please leave them blank.

SECTION 1

1 Ⓐ Ⓑ Ⓒ Ⓓ Ⓔ	13 Ⓐ Ⓑ Ⓒ Ⓓ Ⓔ	25 Ⓐ Ⓑ Ⓒ Ⓓ Ⓔ	37 Ⓐ Ⓑ Ⓒ Ⓓ Ⓔ	49 Ⓐ Ⓑ Ⓒ Ⓓ Ⓔ
2 Ⓐ Ⓑ Ⓒ Ⓓ Ⓔ	14 Ⓐ Ⓑ Ⓒ Ⓓ Ⓔ	26 Ⓐ Ⓑ Ⓒ Ⓓ Ⓔ	38 Ⓐ Ⓑ Ⓒ Ⓓ Ⓔ	50 Ⓐ Ⓑ Ⓒ Ⓓ Ⓔ
3 Ⓐ Ⓑ Ⓒ Ⓓ Ⓔ	15 Ⓐ Ⓑ Ⓒ Ⓓ Ⓔ	27 Ⓐ Ⓑ Ⓒ Ⓓ Ⓔ	39 Ⓐ Ⓑ Ⓒ Ⓓ Ⓔ	51 Ⓐ Ⓑ Ⓒ Ⓓ Ⓔ
4 Ⓐ Ⓑ Ⓒ Ⓓ Ⓔ	16 Ⓐ Ⓑ Ⓒ Ⓓ Ⓔ	28 Ⓐ Ⓑ Ⓒ Ⓓ Ⓔ	40 Ⓐ Ⓑ Ⓒ Ⓓ Ⓔ	52 Ⓐ Ⓑ Ⓒ Ⓓ Ⓔ
5 Ⓐ Ⓑ Ⓒ Ⓓ Ⓔ	17 Ⓐ Ⓑ Ⓒ Ⓓ Ⓔ	29 Ⓐ Ⓑ Ⓒ Ⓓ Ⓔ	41 Ⓐ Ⓑ Ⓒ Ⓓ Ⓔ	53 Ⓐ Ⓑ Ⓒ Ⓓ Ⓔ
6 Ⓐ Ⓑ Ⓒ Ⓓ Ⓔ	18 Ⓐ Ⓑ Ⓒ Ⓓ Ⓔ	30 Ⓐ Ⓑ Ⓒ Ⓓ Ⓔ	42 Ⓐ Ⓑ Ⓒ Ⓓ Ⓔ	54 Ⓐ Ⓑ Ⓒ Ⓓ Ⓔ
7 Ⓐ Ⓑ Ⓒ Ⓓ Ⓔ	19 Ⓐ Ⓑ Ⓒ Ⓓ Ⓔ	31 Ⓐ Ⓑ Ⓒ Ⓓ Ⓔ	43 Ⓐ Ⓑ Ⓒ Ⓓ Ⓔ	55 Ⓐ Ⓑ Ⓒ Ⓓ Ⓔ
8 Ⓐ Ⓑ Ⓒ Ⓓ Ⓔ	20 Ⓐ Ⓑ Ⓒ Ⓓ Ⓔ	32 Ⓐ Ⓑ Ⓒ Ⓓ Ⓔ	44 Ⓐ Ⓑ Ⓒ Ⓓ Ⓔ	56 Ⓐ Ⓑ Ⓒ Ⓓ Ⓔ
9 Ⓐ Ⓑ Ⓒ Ⓓ Ⓔ	21 Ⓐ Ⓑ Ⓒ Ⓓ Ⓔ	33 Ⓐ Ⓑ Ⓒ Ⓓ Ⓔ	45 Ⓐ Ⓑ Ⓒ Ⓓ Ⓔ	57 Ⓐ Ⓑ Ⓒ Ⓓ Ⓔ
10 Ⓐ Ⓑ Ⓒ Ⓓ Ⓔ	22 Ⓐ Ⓑ Ⓒ Ⓓ Ⓔ	34 Ⓐ Ⓑ Ⓒ Ⓓ Ⓔ	46 Ⓐ Ⓑ Ⓒ Ⓓ Ⓔ	58 Ⓐ Ⓑ Ⓒ Ⓓ Ⓔ
11 Ⓐ Ⓑ Ⓒ Ⓓ Ⓔ	23 Ⓐ Ⓑ Ⓒ Ⓓ Ⓔ	35 Ⓐ Ⓑ Ⓒ Ⓓ Ⓔ	47 Ⓐ Ⓑ Ⓒ Ⓓ Ⓔ	59 Ⓐ Ⓑ Ⓒ Ⓓ Ⓔ
12 Ⓐ Ⓑ Ⓒ Ⓓ Ⓔ	24 Ⓐ Ⓑ Ⓒ Ⓓ Ⓔ	36 Ⓐ Ⓑ Ⓒ Ⓓ Ⓔ	48 Ⓐ Ⓑ Ⓒ Ⓓ Ⓔ	60 Ⓐ Ⓑ Ⓒ Ⓓ Ⓔ

SECTION 2

1 Ⓐ Ⓑ Ⓒ Ⓓ Ⓔ	6 Ⓐ Ⓑ Ⓒ Ⓓ Ⓔ	11 Ⓐ Ⓑ Ⓒ Ⓓ Ⓔ	16 Ⓐ Ⓑ Ⓒ Ⓓ Ⓔ	21 Ⓐ Ⓑ Ⓒ Ⓓ Ⓔ
2 Ⓐ Ⓑ Ⓒ Ⓓ Ⓔ	7 Ⓐ Ⓑ Ⓒ Ⓓ Ⓔ	12 Ⓐ Ⓑ Ⓒ Ⓓ Ⓔ	17 Ⓐ Ⓑ Ⓒ Ⓓ Ⓔ	22 Ⓐ Ⓑ Ⓒ Ⓓ Ⓔ
3 Ⓐ Ⓑ Ⓒ Ⓓ Ⓔ	8 Ⓐ Ⓑ Ⓒ Ⓓ Ⓔ	13 Ⓐ Ⓑ Ⓒ Ⓓ Ⓔ	18 Ⓐ Ⓑ Ⓒ Ⓓ Ⓔ	23 Ⓐ Ⓑ Ⓒ Ⓓ Ⓔ
4 Ⓐ Ⓑ Ⓒ Ⓓ Ⓔ	9 Ⓐ Ⓑ Ⓒ Ⓓ Ⓔ	14 Ⓐ Ⓑ Ⓒ Ⓓ Ⓔ	19 Ⓐ Ⓑ Ⓒ Ⓓ Ⓔ	24 Ⓐ Ⓑ Ⓒ Ⓓ Ⓔ
5 Ⓐ Ⓑ Ⓒ Ⓓ Ⓔ	10 Ⓐ Ⓑ Ⓒ Ⓓ Ⓔ	15 Ⓐ Ⓑ Ⓒ Ⓓ Ⓔ	20 Ⓐ Ⓑ Ⓒ Ⓓ Ⓔ	25 Ⓐ Ⓑ Ⓒ Ⓓ Ⓔ

SECTION 3

1 Ⓐ Ⓑ Ⓒ Ⓓ Ⓔ	9 Ⓐ Ⓑ Ⓒ Ⓓ Ⓔ	17 Ⓐ Ⓑ Ⓒ Ⓓ Ⓔ	25 Ⓐ Ⓑ Ⓒ Ⓓ Ⓔ	33 Ⓐ Ⓑ Ⓒ Ⓓ Ⓔ
2 Ⓐ Ⓑ Ⓒ Ⓓ Ⓔ	10 Ⓐ Ⓑ Ⓒ Ⓓ Ⓔ	18 Ⓐ Ⓑ Ⓒ Ⓓ Ⓔ	26 Ⓐ Ⓑ Ⓒ Ⓓ Ⓔ	34 Ⓐ Ⓑ Ⓒ Ⓓ Ⓔ
3 Ⓐ Ⓑ Ⓒ Ⓓ Ⓔ	11 Ⓐ Ⓑ Ⓒ Ⓓ Ⓔ	19 Ⓐ Ⓑ Ⓒ Ⓓ Ⓔ	27 Ⓐ Ⓑ Ⓒ Ⓓ Ⓔ	35 Ⓐ Ⓑ Ⓒ Ⓓ Ⓔ
4 Ⓐ Ⓑ Ⓒ Ⓓ Ⓔ	12 Ⓐ Ⓑ Ⓒ Ⓓ Ⓔ	20 Ⓐ Ⓑ Ⓒ Ⓓ Ⓔ	28 Ⓐ Ⓑ Ⓒ Ⓓ Ⓔ	36 Ⓐ Ⓑ Ⓒ Ⓓ Ⓔ
5 Ⓐ Ⓑ Ⓒ Ⓓ Ⓔ	13 Ⓐ Ⓑ Ⓒ Ⓓ Ⓔ	21 Ⓐ Ⓑ Ⓒ Ⓓ Ⓔ	29 Ⓐ Ⓑ Ⓒ Ⓓ Ⓔ	37 Ⓐ Ⓑ Ⓒ Ⓓ Ⓔ
6 Ⓐ Ⓑ Ⓒ Ⓓ Ⓔ	14 Ⓐ Ⓑ Ⓒ Ⓓ Ⓔ	22 Ⓐ Ⓑ Ⓒ Ⓓ Ⓔ	30 Ⓐ Ⓑ Ⓒ Ⓓ Ⓔ	38 Ⓐ Ⓑ Ⓒ Ⓓ Ⓔ
7 Ⓐ Ⓑ Ⓒ Ⓓ Ⓔ	15 Ⓐ Ⓑ Ⓒ Ⓓ Ⓔ	23 Ⓐ Ⓑ Ⓒ Ⓓ Ⓔ	31 Ⓐ Ⓑ Ⓒ Ⓓ Ⓔ	39 Ⓐ Ⓑ Ⓒ Ⓓ Ⓔ
8 Ⓐ Ⓑ Ⓒ Ⓓ Ⓔ	16 Ⓐ Ⓑ Ⓒ Ⓓ Ⓔ	24 Ⓐ Ⓑ Ⓒ Ⓓ Ⓔ	32 Ⓐ Ⓑ Ⓒ Ⓓ Ⓔ	40 Ⓐ Ⓑ Ⓒ Ⓓ Ⓔ

SECTION 4

1 Ⓐ Ⓑ Ⓒ Ⓓ Ⓔ	6 Ⓐ Ⓑ Ⓒ Ⓓ Ⓔ	11 Ⓐ Ⓑ Ⓒ Ⓓ Ⓔ	16 Ⓐ Ⓑ Ⓒ Ⓓ Ⓔ	21 Ⓐ Ⓑ Ⓒ Ⓓ Ⓔ
2 Ⓐ Ⓑ Ⓒ Ⓓ Ⓔ	7 Ⓐ Ⓑ Ⓒ Ⓓ Ⓔ	12 Ⓐ Ⓑ Ⓒ Ⓓ Ⓔ	17 Ⓐ Ⓑ Ⓒ Ⓓ Ⓔ	22 Ⓐ Ⓑ Ⓒ Ⓓ Ⓔ
3 Ⓐ Ⓑ Ⓒ Ⓓ Ⓔ	8 Ⓐ Ⓑ Ⓒ Ⓓ Ⓔ	13 Ⓐ Ⓑ Ⓒ Ⓓ Ⓔ	18 Ⓐ Ⓑ Ⓒ Ⓓ Ⓔ	23 Ⓐ Ⓑ Ⓒ Ⓓ Ⓔ
4 Ⓐ Ⓑ Ⓒ Ⓓ Ⓔ	9 Ⓐ Ⓑ Ⓒ Ⓓ Ⓔ	14 Ⓐ Ⓑ Ⓒ Ⓓ Ⓔ	19 Ⓐ Ⓑ Ⓒ Ⓓ Ⓔ	24 Ⓐ Ⓑ Ⓒ Ⓓ Ⓔ
5 Ⓐ Ⓑ Ⓒ Ⓓ Ⓔ	10 Ⓐ Ⓑ Ⓒ Ⓓ Ⓔ	15 Ⓐ Ⓑ Ⓒ Ⓓ Ⓔ	20 Ⓐ Ⓑ Ⓒ Ⓓ Ⓔ	25 Ⓐ Ⓑ Ⓒ Ⓓ Ⓔ

Upper Level Practice Test

Be sure each mark *completely* fills the answer space.
Start with number 1 for each new section of the test. You may find more answer spaces than you need.
If so, please leave them blank.

SECTION 1

1 Ⓐ Ⓑ Ⓒ Ⓓ Ⓔ	13 Ⓐ Ⓑ Ⓒ Ⓓ Ⓔ	25 Ⓐ Ⓑ Ⓒ Ⓓ Ⓔ	37 Ⓐ Ⓑ Ⓒ Ⓓ Ⓔ	49 Ⓐ Ⓑ Ⓒ Ⓓ Ⓔ
2 Ⓐ Ⓑ Ⓒ Ⓓ Ⓔ	14 Ⓐ Ⓑ Ⓒ Ⓓ Ⓔ	26 Ⓐ Ⓑ Ⓒ Ⓓ Ⓔ	38 Ⓐ Ⓑ Ⓒ Ⓓ Ⓔ	50 Ⓐ Ⓑ Ⓒ Ⓓ Ⓔ
3 Ⓐ Ⓑ Ⓒ Ⓓ Ⓔ	15 Ⓐ Ⓑ Ⓒ Ⓓ Ⓔ	27 Ⓐ Ⓑ Ⓒ Ⓓ Ⓔ	39 Ⓐ Ⓑ Ⓒ Ⓓ Ⓔ	51 Ⓐ Ⓑ Ⓒ Ⓓ Ⓔ
4 Ⓐ Ⓑ Ⓒ Ⓓ Ⓔ	16 Ⓐ Ⓑ Ⓒ Ⓓ Ⓔ	28 Ⓐ Ⓑ Ⓒ Ⓓ Ⓔ	40 Ⓐ Ⓑ Ⓒ Ⓓ Ⓔ	52 Ⓐ Ⓑ Ⓒ Ⓓ Ⓔ
5 Ⓐ Ⓑ Ⓒ Ⓓ Ⓔ	17 Ⓐ Ⓑ Ⓒ Ⓓ Ⓔ	29 Ⓐ Ⓑ Ⓒ Ⓓ Ⓔ	41 Ⓐ Ⓑ Ⓒ Ⓓ Ⓔ	53 Ⓐ Ⓑ Ⓒ Ⓓ Ⓔ
6 Ⓐ Ⓑ Ⓒ Ⓓ Ⓔ	18 Ⓐ Ⓑ Ⓒ Ⓓ Ⓔ	30 Ⓐ Ⓑ Ⓒ Ⓓ Ⓔ	42 Ⓐ Ⓑ Ⓒ Ⓓ Ⓔ	54 Ⓐ Ⓑ Ⓒ Ⓓ Ⓔ
7 Ⓐ Ⓑ Ⓒ Ⓓ Ⓔ	19 Ⓐ Ⓑ Ⓒ Ⓓ Ⓔ	31 Ⓐ Ⓑ Ⓒ Ⓓ Ⓔ	43 Ⓐ Ⓑ Ⓒ Ⓓ Ⓔ	55 Ⓐ Ⓑ Ⓒ Ⓓ Ⓔ
8 Ⓐ Ⓑ Ⓒ Ⓓ Ⓔ	20 Ⓐ Ⓑ Ⓒ Ⓓ Ⓔ	32 Ⓐ Ⓑ Ⓒ Ⓓ Ⓔ	44 Ⓐ Ⓑ Ⓒ Ⓓ Ⓔ	56 Ⓐ Ⓑ Ⓒ Ⓓ Ⓔ
9 Ⓐ Ⓑ Ⓒ Ⓓ Ⓔ	21 Ⓐ Ⓑ Ⓒ Ⓓ Ⓔ	33 Ⓐ Ⓑ Ⓒ Ⓓ Ⓔ	45 Ⓐ Ⓑ Ⓒ Ⓓ Ⓔ	57 Ⓐ Ⓑ Ⓒ Ⓓ Ⓔ
10 Ⓐ Ⓑ Ⓒ Ⓓ Ⓔ	22 Ⓐ Ⓑ Ⓒ Ⓓ Ⓔ	34 Ⓐ Ⓑ Ⓒ Ⓓ Ⓔ	46 Ⓐ Ⓑ Ⓒ Ⓓ Ⓔ	58 Ⓐ Ⓑ Ⓒ Ⓓ Ⓔ
11 Ⓐ Ⓑ Ⓒ Ⓓ Ⓔ	23 Ⓐ Ⓑ Ⓒ Ⓓ Ⓔ	35 Ⓐ Ⓑ Ⓒ Ⓓ Ⓔ	47 Ⓐ Ⓑ Ⓒ Ⓓ Ⓔ	59 Ⓐ Ⓑ Ⓒ Ⓓ Ⓔ
12 Ⓐ Ⓑ Ⓒ Ⓓ Ⓔ	24 Ⓐ Ⓑ Ⓒ Ⓓ Ⓔ	36 Ⓐ Ⓑ Ⓒ Ⓓ Ⓔ	48 Ⓐ Ⓑ Ⓒ Ⓓ Ⓔ	60 Ⓐ Ⓑ Ⓒ Ⓓ Ⓔ

SECTION 2

1 Ⓐ Ⓑ Ⓒ Ⓓ Ⓔ	6 Ⓐ Ⓑ Ⓒ Ⓓ Ⓔ	11 Ⓐ Ⓑ Ⓒ Ⓓ Ⓔ	16 Ⓐ Ⓑ Ⓒ Ⓓ Ⓔ	21 Ⓐ Ⓑ Ⓒ Ⓓ Ⓔ
2 Ⓐ Ⓑ Ⓒ Ⓓ Ⓔ	7 Ⓐ Ⓑ Ⓒ Ⓓ Ⓔ	12 Ⓐ Ⓑ Ⓒ Ⓓ Ⓔ	17 Ⓐ Ⓑ Ⓒ Ⓓ Ⓔ	22 Ⓐ Ⓑ Ⓒ Ⓓ Ⓔ
3 Ⓐ Ⓑ Ⓒ Ⓓ Ⓔ	8 Ⓐ Ⓑ Ⓒ Ⓓ Ⓔ	13 Ⓐ Ⓑ Ⓒ Ⓓ Ⓔ	18 Ⓐ Ⓑ Ⓒ Ⓓ Ⓔ	23 Ⓐ Ⓑ Ⓒ Ⓓ Ⓔ
4 Ⓐ Ⓑ Ⓒ Ⓓ Ⓔ	9 Ⓐ Ⓑ Ⓒ Ⓓ Ⓔ	14 Ⓐ Ⓑ Ⓒ Ⓓ Ⓔ	19 Ⓐ Ⓑ Ⓒ Ⓓ Ⓔ	24 Ⓐ Ⓑ Ⓒ Ⓓ Ⓔ
5 Ⓐ Ⓑ Ⓒ Ⓓ Ⓔ	10 Ⓐ Ⓑ Ⓒ Ⓓ Ⓔ	15 Ⓐ Ⓑ Ⓒ Ⓓ Ⓔ	20 Ⓐ Ⓑ Ⓒ Ⓓ Ⓔ	25 Ⓐ Ⓑ Ⓒ Ⓓ Ⓔ

SECTION 3

1 Ⓐ Ⓑ Ⓒ Ⓓ Ⓔ	9 Ⓐ Ⓑ Ⓒ Ⓓ Ⓔ	17 Ⓐ Ⓑ Ⓒ Ⓓ Ⓔ	25 Ⓐ Ⓑ Ⓒ Ⓓ Ⓔ	33 Ⓐ Ⓑ Ⓒ Ⓓ Ⓔ
2 Ⓐ Ⓑ Ⓒ Ⓓ Ⓕ	10 Ⓐ Ⓑ Ⓒ Ⓓ Ⓔ	18 Ⓐ Ⓑ Ⓒ Ⓓ Ⓔ	26 Ⓐ Ⓑ Ⓒ Ⓓ Ⓔ	34 Ⓐ Ⓑ Ⓒ Ⓓ Ⓔ
3 Ⓐ Ⓑ Ⓒ Ⓓ Ⓔ	11 Ⓐ Ⓑ Ⓒ Ⓓ Ⓔ	19 Ⓐ Ⓑ Ⓒ Ⓓ Ⓔ	27 Ⓐ Ⓑ Ⓒ Ⓓ Ⓔ	35 Ⓐ Ⓑ Ⓒ Ⓓ Ⓔ
4 Ⓐ Ⓑ Ⓒ Ⓓ Ⓔ	12 Ⓐ Ⓑ Ⓒ Ⓓ Ⓔ	20 Ⓐ Ⓑ Ⓒ Ⓓ Ⓔ	28 Ⓐ Ⓑ Ⓒ Ⓓ Ⓔ	36 Ⓐ Ⓑ Ⓒ Ⓓ Ⓔ
5 Ⓐ Ⓑ Ⓒ Ⓓ Ⓔ	13 Ⓐ Ⓑ Ⓒ Ⓓ Ⓔ	21 Ⓐ Ⓑ Ⓒ Ⓓ Ⓔ	29 Ⓐ Ⓑ Ⓒ Ⓓ Ⓔ	37 Ⓐ Ⓑ Ⓒ Ⓓ Ⓔ
6 Ⓐ Ⓑ Ⓒ Ⓓ Ⓔ	14 Ⓐ Ⓑ Ⓒ Ⓓ Ⓔ	22 Ⓐ Ⓑ Ⓒ Ⓓ Ⓔ	30 Ⓐ Ⓑ Ⓒ Ⓓ Ⓔ	38 Ⓐ Ⓑ Ⓒ Ⓓ Ⓔ
7 Ⓐ Ⓑ Ⓒ Ⓓ Ⓔ	15 Ⓐ Ⓑ Ⓒ Ⓓ Ⓔ	23 Ⓐ Ⓑ Ⓒ Ⓓ Ⓔ	31 Ⓐ Ⓑ Ⓒ Ⓓ Ⓔ	39 Ⓐ Ⓑ Ⓒ Ⓓ Ⓔ
8 Ⓐ Ⓑ Ⓒ Ⓓ Ⓔ	16 Ⓐ Ⓑ Ⓒ Ⓓ Ⓔ	24 Ⓐ Ⓑ Ⓒ Ⓓ Ⓔ	32 Ⓐ Ⓑ Ⓒ Ⓓ Ⓔ	40 Ⓐ Ⓑ Ⓒ Ⓓ Ⓔ

SECTION 4

1 Ⓐ Ⓑ Ⓒ Ⓓ Ⓔ	6 Ⓐ Ⓑ Ⓒ Ⓓ Ⓔ	11 Ⓐ Ⓑ Ⓒ Ⓓ Ⓔ	16 Ⓐ Ⓑ Ⓒ Ⓓ Ⓔ	21 Ⓐ Ⓑ Ⓒ Ⓓ Ⓔ
2 Ⓐ Ⓑ Ⓒ Ⓓ Ⓔ	7 Ⓐ Ⓑ Ⓒ Ⓓ Ⓔ	12 Ⓐ Ⓑ Ⓒ Ⓓ Ⓔ	17 Ⓐ Ⓑ Ⓒ Ⓓ Ⓔ	22 Ⓐ Ⓑ Ⓒ Ⓓ Ⓔ
3 Ⓐ Ⓑ Ⓒ Ⓓ Ⓔ	8 Ⓐ Ⓑ Ⓒ Ⓓ Ⓔ	13 Ⓐ Ⓑ Ⓒ Ⓓ Ⓔ	18 Ⓐ Ⓑ Ⓒ Ⓓ Ⓔ	23 Ⓐ Ⓑ Ⓒ Ⓓ Ⓔ
4 Ⓐ Ⓑ Ⓒ Ⓓ Ⓔ	9 Ⓐ Ⓑ Ⓒ Ⓓ Ⓔ	14 Ⓐ Ⓑ Ⓒ Ⓓ Ⓔ	19 Ⓐ Ⓑ Ⓒ Ⓓ Ⓔ	24 Ⓐ Ⓑ Ⓒ Ⓓ Ⓔ
5 Ⓐ Ⓑ Ⓒ Ⓓ Ⓔ	10 Ⓐ Ⓑ Ⓒ Ⓓ Ⓔ	15 Ⓐ Ⓑ Ⓒ Ⓓ Ⓔ	20 Ⓐ Ⓑ Ⓒ Ⓓ Ⓔ	25 Ⓐ Ⓑ Ⓒ Ⓓ Ⓔ

Upper Level Practice Test

Be sure each mark *completely* fills the answer space.
Start with number 1 for each new section of the test. You may find more answer spaces than you need.
If so, please leave them blank.

SECTION 1

1 Ⓐ Ⓑ Ⓒ Ⓓ Ⓔ	13 Ⓐ Ⓑ Ⓒ Ⓓ Ⓔ	25 Ⓐ Ⓑ Ⓒ Ⓓ Ⓔ	37 Ⓐ Ⓑ Ⓒ Ⓓ Ⓔ	49 Ⓐ Ⓑ Ⓒ Ⓓ Ⓔ
2 Ⓐ Ⓑ Ⓒ Ⓓ Ⓔ	14 Ⓐ Ⓑ Ⓒ Ⓓ Ⓔ	26 Ⓐ Ⓑ Ⓒ Ⓓ Ⓔ	38 Ⓐ Ⓑ Ⓒ Ⓓ Ⓔ	50 Ⓐ Ⓑ Ⓒ Ⓓ Ⓔ
3 Ⓐ Ⓑ Ⓒ Ⓓ Ⓔ	15 Ⓐ Ⓑ Ⓒ Ⓓ Ⓔ	27 Ⓐ Ⓑ Ⓒ Ⓓ Ⓔ	39 Ⓐ Ⓑ Ⓒ Ⓓ Ⓔ	51 Ⓐ Ⓑ Ⓒ Ⓓ Ⓔ
4 Ⓐ Ⓑ Ⓒ Ⓓ Ⓔ	16 Ⓐ Ⓑ Ⓒ Ⓓ Ⓔ	28 Ⓐ Ⓑ Ⓒ Ⓓ Ⓔ	40 Ⓐ Ⓑ Ⓒ Ⓓ Ⓔ	52 Ⓐ Ⓑ Ⓒ Ⓓ Ⓔ
5 Ⓐ Ⓑ Ⓒ Ⓓ Ⓔ	17 Ⓐ Ⓑ Ⓒ Ⓓ Ⓔ	29 Ⓐ Ⓑ Ⓒ Ⓓ Ⓔ	41 Ⓐ Ⓑ Ⓒ Ⓓ Ⓔ	53 Ⓐ Ⓑ Ⓒ Ⓓ Ⓔ
6 Ⓐ Ⓑ Ⓒ Ⓓ Ⓔ	18 Ⓐ Ⓑ Ⓒ Ⓓ Ⓔ	30 Ⓐ Ⓑ Ⓒ Ⓓ Ⓔ	42 Ⓐ Ⓑ Ⓒ Ⓓ Ⓔ	54 Ⓐ Ⓑ Ⓒ Ⓓ Ⓔ
7 Ⓐ Ⓑ Ⓒ Ⓓ Ⓔ	19 Ⓐ Ⓑ Ⓒ Ⓓ Ⓔ	31 Ⓐ Ⓑ Ⓒ Ⓓ Ⓔ	43 Ⓐ Ⓑ Ⓒ Ⓓ Ⓔ	55 Ⓐ Ⓑ Ⓒ Ⓓ Ⓔ
8 Ⓐ Ⓑ Ⓒ Ⓓ Ⓔ	20 Ⓐ Ⓑ Ⓒ Ⓓ Ⓔ	32 Ⓐ Ⓑ Ⓒ Ⓓ Ⓔ	44 Ⓐ Ⓑ Ⓒ Ⓓ Ⓔ	56 Ⓐ Ⓑ Ⓒ Ⓓ Ⓔ
9 Ⓐ Ⓑ Ⓒ Ⓓ Ⓔ	21 Ⓐ Ⓑ Ⓒ Ⓓ Ⓔ	33 Ⓐ Ⓑ Ⓒ Ⓓ Ⓔ	45 Ⓐ Ⓑ Ⓒ Ⓓ Ⓔ	57 Ⓐ Ⓑ Ⓒ Ⓓ Ⓔ
10 Ⓐ Ⓑ Ⓒ Ⓓ Ⓔ	22 Ⓐ Ⓑ Ⓒ Ⓓ Ⓔ	34 Ⓐ Ⓑ Ⓒ Ⓓ Ⓔ	46 Ⓐ Ⓑ Ⓒ Ⓓ Ⓔ	58 Ⓐ Ⓑ Ⓒ Ⓓ Ⓔ
11 Ⓐ Ⓑ Ⓒ Ⓓ Ⓔ	23 Ⓐ Ⓑ Ⓒ Ⓓ Ⓔ	35 Ⓐ Ⓑ Ⓒ Ⓓ Ⓔ	47 Ⓐ Ⓑ Ⓒ Ⓓ Ⓔ	59 Ⓐ Ⓑ Ⓒ Ⓓ Ⓔ
12 Ⓐ Ⓑ Ⓒ Ⓓ Ⓔ	24 Ⓐ Ⓑ Ⓒ Ⓓ Ⓔ	36 Ⓐ Ⓑ Ⓒ Ⓓ Ⓔ	48 Ⓐ Ⓑ Ⓒ Ⓓ Ⓔ	60 Ⓐ Ⓑ Ⓒ Ⓓ Ⓔ

SECTION 2

1 Ⓐ Ⓑ Ⓒ Ⓓ Ⓔ	6 Ⓐ Ⓑ Ⓒ Ⓓ Ⓔ	11 Ⓐ Ⓑ Ⓒ Ⓓ Ⓔ	16 Ⓐ Ⓑ Ⓒ Ⓓ Ⓔ	21 Ⓐ Ⓑ Ⓒ Ⓓ Ⓔ
2 Ⓐ Ⓑ Ⓒ Ⓓ Ⓔ	7 Ⓐ Ⓑ Ⓒ Ⓓ Ⓔ	12 Ⓐ Ⓑ Ⓒ Ⓓ Ⓔ	17 Ⓐ Ⓑ Ⓒ Ⓓ Ⓔ	22 Ⓐ Ⓑ Ⓒ Ⓓ Ⓔ
3 Ⓐ Ⓑ Ⓒ Ⓓ Ⓔ	8 Ⓐ Ⓑ Ⓒ Ⓓ Ⓔ	13 Ⓐ Ⓑ Ⓒ Ⓓ Ⓔ	18 Ⓐ Ⓑ Ⓒ Ⓓ Ⓔ	23 Ⓐ Ⓑ Ⓒ Ⓓ Ⓔ
4 Ⓐ Ⓑ Ⓒ Ⓓ Ⓔ	9 Ⓐ Ⓑ Ⓒ Ⓓ Ⓔ	14 Ⓐ Ⓑ Ⓒ Ⓓ Ⓔ	19 Ⓐ Ⓑ Ⓒ Ⓓ Ⓔ	24 Ⓐ Ⓑ Ⓒ Ⓓ Ⓔ
5 Ⓐ Ⓑ Ⓒ Ⓓ Ⓔ	10 Ⓐ Ⓑ Ⓒ Ⓓ Ⓔ	15 Ⓐ Ⓑ Ⓒ Ⓓ Ⓔ	20 Ⓐ Ⓑ Ⓒ Ⓓ Ⓔ	25 Ⓐ Ⓑ Ⓒ Ⓓ Ⓔ

SECTION 3

1 Ⓐ Ⓑ Ⓒ Ⓓ Ⓔ	9 Ⓐ Ⓑ Ⓒ Ⓓ Ⓔ	17 Ⓐ Ⓑ Ⓒ Ⓓ Ⓔ	25 Ⓐ Ⓑ Ⓒ Ⓓ Ⓔ	33 Ⓐ Ⓑ Ⓒ Ⓓ Ⓔ
2 Ⓐ Ⓑ Ⓒ Ⓓ Ⓔ	10 Ⓐ Ⓑ Ⓒ Ⓓ Ⓔ	18 Ⓐ Ⓑ Ⓒ Ⓓ Ⓔ	26 Ⓐ Ⓑ Ⓒ Ⓓ Ⓔ	34 Ⓐ Ⓑ Ⓒ Ⓓ Ⓔ
3 Ⓐ Ⓑ Ⓒ Ⓓ Ⓔ	11 Ⓐ Ⓑ Ⓒ Ⓓ Ⓔ	19 Ⓐ Ⓑ Ⓒ Ⓓ Ⓔ	27 Ⓐ Ⓑ Ⓒ Ⓓ Ⓔ	35 Ⓐ Ⓑ Ⓒ Ⓓ Ⓔ
4 Ⓐ Ⓑ Ⓒ Ⓓ Ⓔ	12 Ⓐ Ⓑ Ⓒ Ⓓ Ⓔ	20 Ⓐ Ⓑ Ⓒ Ⓓ Ⓔ	28 Ⓐ Ⓑ Ⓒ Ⓓ Ⓔ	36 Ⓐ Ⓑ Ⓒ Ⓓ Ⓔ
5 Ⓐ Ⓑ Ⓒ Ⓓ Ⓔ	13 Ⓐ Ⓑ Ⓒ Ⓓ Ⓔ	21 Ⓐ Ⓑ Ⓒ Ⓓ Ⓔ	29 Ⓐ Ⓑ Ⓒ Ⓓ Ⓔ	37 Ⓐ Ⓑ Ⓒ Ⓓ Ⓔ
6 Ⓐ Ⓑ Ⓒ Ⓓ Ⓔ	14 Ⓐ Ⓑ Ⓒ Ⓓ Ⓔ	22 Ⓐ Ⓑ Ⓒ Ⓓ Ⓔ	30 Ⓐ Ⓑ Ⓒ Ⓓ Ⓔ	38 Ⓐ Ⓑ Ⓒ Ⓓ Ⓔ
7 Ⓐ Ⓑ Ⓒ Ⓓ Ⓔ	15 Ⓐ Ⓑ Ⓒ Ⓓ Ⓔ	23 Ⓐ Ⓑ Ⓒ Ⓓ Ⓔ	31 Ⓐ Ⓑ Ⓒ Ⓓ Ⓔ	39 Ⓐ Ⓑ Ⓒ Ⓓ Ⓔ
8 Ⓐ Ⓑ Ⓒ Ⓓ Ⓔ	16 Ⓐ Ⓑ Ⓒ Ⓓ Ⓔ	24 Ⓐ Ⓑ Ⓒ Ⓓ Ⓔ	32 Ⓐ Ⓑ Ⓒ Ⓓ Ⓔ	40 Ⓐ Ⓑ Ⓒ Ⓓ Ⓔ

SECTION 4

1 Ⓐ Ⓑ Ⓒ Ⓓ Ⓔ	6 Ⓐ Ⓑ Ⓒ Ⓓ Ⓔ	11 Ⓐ Ⓑ Ⓒ Ⓓ Ⓔ	16 Ⓐ Ⓑ Ⓒ Ⓓ Ⓔ	21 Ⓐ Ⓑ Ⓒ Ⓓ Ⓔ
2 Ⓐ Ⓑ Ⓒ Ⓓ Ⓔ	7 Ⓐ Ⓑ Ⓒ Ⓓ Ⓔ	12 Ⓐ Ⓑ Ⓒ Ⓓ Ⓔ	17 Ⓐ Ⓑ Ⓒ Ⓓ Ⓔ	22 Ⓐ Ⓑ Ⓒ Ⓓ Ⓔ
3 Ⓐ Ⓑ Ⓒ Ⓓ Ⓔ	8 Ⓐ Ⓑ Ⓒ Ⓓ Ⓔ	13 Ⓐ Ⓑ Ⓒ Ⓓ Ⓔ	18 Ⓐ Ⓑ Ⓒ Ⓓ Ⓔ	23 Ⓐ Ⓑ Ⓒ Ⓓ Ⓔ
4 Ⓐ Ⓑ Ⓒ Ⓓ Ⓔ	9 Ⓐ Ⓑ Ⓒ Ⓓ Ⓔ	14 Ⓐ Ⓑ Ⓒ Ⓓ Ⓔ	19 Ⓐ Ⓑ Ⓒ Ⓓ Ⓔ	24 Ⓐ Ⓑ Ⓒ Ⓓ Ⓔ
5 Ⓐ Ⓑ Ⓒ Ⓓ Ⓔ	10 Ⓐ Ⓑ Ⓒ Ⓓ Ⓔ	15 Ⓐ Ⓑ Ⓒ Ⓓ Ⓔ	20 Ⓐ Ⓑ Ⓒ Ⓓ Ⓔ	25 Ⓐ Ⓑ Ⓒ Ⓓ Ⓔ

Lower Level Practice Test

Be sure each mark *completely* fills the answer space.
Start with number 1 for each new section of the test. You may find more answer spaces than you need.
If so, please leave them blank.

SECTION 1

1 Ⓐ Ⓑ Ⓒ Ⓓ Ⓔ	13 Ⓐ Ⓑ Ⓒ Ⓓ Ⓔ	25 Ⓐ Ⓑ Ⓒ Ⓓ Ⓔ	37 Ⓐ Ⓑ Ⓒ Ⓓ Ⓔ	49 Ⓐ Ⓑ Ⓒ Ⓓ Ⓔ
2 Ⓐ Ⓑ Ⓒ Ⓓ Ⓔ	14 Ⓐ Ⓑ Ⓒ Ⓓ Ⓔ	26 Ⓐ Ⓑ Ⓒ Ⓓ Ⓔ	38 Ⓐ Ⓑ Ⓒ Ⓓ Ⓔ	50 Ⓐ Ⓑ Ⓒ Ⓓ Ⓔ
3 Ⓐ Ⓑ Ⓒ Ⓓ Ⓔ	15 Ⓐ Ⓑ Ⓒ Ⓓ Ⓔ	27 Ⓐ Ⓑ Ⓒ Ⓓ Ⓔ	39 Ⓐ Ⓑ Ⓒ Ⓓ Ⓔ	51 Ⓐ Ⓑ Ⓒ Ⓓ Ⓔ
4 Ⓐ Ⓑ Ⓒ Ⓓ Ⓔ	16 Ⓐ Ⓑ Ⓒ Ⓓ Ⓔ	28 Ⓐ Ⓑ Ⓒ Ⓓ Ⓔ	40 Ⓐ Ⓑ Ⓒ Ⓓ Ⓔ	52 Ⓐ Ⓑ Ⓒ Ⓓ Ⓔ
5 Ⓐ Ⓑ Ⓒ Ⓓ Ⓔ	17 Ⓐ Ⓑ Ⓒ Ⓓ Ⓔ	29 Ⓐ Ⓑ Ⓒ Ⓓ Ⓔ	41 Ⓐ Ⓑ Ⓒ Ⓓ Ⓔ	53 Ⓐ Ⓑ Ⓒ Ⓓ Ⓔ
6 Ⓐ Ⓑ Ⓒ Ⓓ Ⓔ	18 Ⓐ Ⓑ Ⓒ Ⓓ Ⓔ	30 Ⓐ Ⓑ Ⓒ Ⓓ Ⓔ	42 Ⓐ Ⓑ Ⓒ Ⓓ Ⓔ	54 Ⓐ Ⓑ Ⓒ Ⓓ Ⓔ
7 Ⓐ Ⓑ Ⓒ Ⓓ Ⓔ	19 Ⓐ Ⓑ Ⓒ Ⓓ Ⓔ	31 Ⓐ Ⓑ Ⓒ Ⓓ Ⓔ	43 Ⓐ Ⓑ Ⓒ Ⓓ Ⓔ	55 Ⓐ Ⓑ Ⓒ Ⓓ Ⓔ
8 Ⓐ Ⓑ Ⓒ Ⓓ Ⓔ	20 Ⓐ Ⓑ Ⓒ Ⓓ Ⓔ	32 Ⓐ Ⓑ Ⓒ Ⓓ Ⓔ	44 Ⓐ Ⓑ Ⓒ Ⓓ Ⓔ	56 Ⓐ Ⓑ Ⓒ Ⓓ Ⓔ
9 Ⓐ Ⓑ Ⓒ Ⓓ Ⓔ	21 Ⓐ Ⓑ Ⓒ Ⓓ Ⓔ	33 Ⓐ Ⓑ Ⓒ Ⓓ Ⓔ	45 Ⓐ Ⓑ Ⓒ Ⓓ Ⓔ	57 Ⓐ Ⓑ Ⓒ Ⓓ Ⓔ
10 Ⓐ Ⓑ Ⓒ Ⓓ Ⓔ	22 Ⓐ Ⓑ Ⓒ Ⓓ Ⓔ	34 Ⓐ Ⓑ Ⓒ Ⓓ Ⓔ	46 Ⓐ Ⓑ Ⓒ Ⓓ Ⓔ	58 Ⓐ Ⓑ Ⓒ Ⓓ Ⓔ
11 Ⓐ Ⓑ Ⓒ Ⓓ Ⓔ	23 Ⓐ Ⓑ Ⓒ Ⓓ Ⓔ	35 Ⓐ Ⓑ Ⓒ Ⓓ Ⓔ	47 Ⓐ Ⓑ Ⓒ Ⓓ Ⓔ	59 Ⓐ Ⓑ Ⓒ Ⓓ Ⓔ
12 Ⓐ Ⓑ Ⓒ Ⓓ Ⓔ	24 Ⓐ Ⓑ Ⓒ Ⓓ Ⓔ	36 Ⓐ Ⓑ Ⓒ Ⓓ Ⓔ	48 Ⓐ Ⓑ Ⓒ Ⓓ Ⓔ	60 Ⓐ Ⓑ Ⓒ Ⓓ Ⓔ

SECTION 2

1 Ⓐ Ⓑ Ⓒ Ⓓ Ⓔ	6 Ⓐ Ⓑ Ⓒ Ⓓ Ⓔ	11 Ⓐ Ⓑ Ⓒ Ⓓ Ⓔ	16 Ⓐ Ⓑ Ⓒ Ⓓ Ⓔ	21 Ⓐ Ⓑ Ⓒ Ⓓ Ⓔ
2 Ⓐ Ⓑ Ⓒ Ⓓ Ⓔ	7 Ⓐ Ⓑ Ⓒ Ⓓ Ⓔ	12 Ⓐ Ⓑ Ⓒ Ⓓ Ⓔ	17 Ⓐ Ⓑ Ⓒ Ⓓ Ⓔ	22 Ⓐ Ⓑ Ⓒ Ⓓ Ⓔ
3 Ⓐ Ⓑ Ⓒ Ⓓ Ⓔ	8 Ⓐ Ⓑ Ⓒ Ⓓ Ⓔ	13 Ⓐ Ⓑ Ⓒ Ⓓ Ⓔ	18 Ⓐ Ⓑ Ⓒ Ⓓ Ⓔ	23 Ⓐ Ⓑ Ⓒ Ⓓ Ⓔ
4 Ⓐ Ⓑ Ⓒ Ⓓ Ⓔ	9 Ⓐ Ⓑ Ⓒ Ⓓ Ⓔ	14 Ⓐ Ⓑ Ⓒ Ⓓ Ⓔ	19 Ⓐ Ⓑ Ⓒ Ⓓ Ⓔ	24 Ⓐ Ⓑ Ⓒ Ⓓ Ⓔ
5 Ⓐ Ⓑ Ⓒ Ⓓ Ⓔ	10 Ⓐ Ⓑ Ⓒ Ⓓ Ⓔ	15 Ⓐ Ⓑ Ⓒ Ⓓ Ⓔ	20 Ⓐ Ⓑ Ⓒ Ⓓ Ⓔ	25 Ⓐ Ⓑ Ⓒ Ⓓ Ⓔ

SECTION 3

1 Ⓐ Ⓑ Ⓒ Ⓓ Ⓔ	9 Ⓐ Ⓑ Ⓒ Ⓓ Ⓔ	17 Ⓐ Ⓑ Ⓒ Ⓓ Ⓔ	25 Ⓐ Ⓑ Ⓒ Ⓓ Ⓔ	33 Ⓐ Ⓑ Ⓒ Ⓓ Ⓔ
2 Ⓐ Ⓑ Ⓒ Ⓓ Ⓔ	10 Ⓐ Ⓑ Ⓒ Ⓓ Ⓔ	18 Ⓐ Ⓑ Ⓒ Ⓓ Ⓔ	26 Ⓐ Ⓑ Ⓒ Ⓓ Ⓔ	34 Ⓐ Ⓑ Ⓒ Ⓓ Ⓔ
3 Ⓐ Ⓑ Ⓒ Ⓓ Ⓔ	11 Ⓐ Ⓑ Ⓒ Ⓓ Ⓔ	19 Ⓐ Ⓑ Ⓒ Ⓓ Ⓔ	27 Ⓐ Ⓑ Ⓒ Ⓓ Ⓔ	35 Ⓐ Ⓑ Ⓒ Ⓓ Ⓔ
4 Ⓐ Ⓑ Ⓒ Ⓓ Ⓔ	12 Ⓐ Ⓑ Ⓒ Ⓓ Ⓔ	20 Ⓐ Ⓑ Ⓒ Ⓓ Ⓔ	28 Ⓐ Ⓑ Ⓒ Ⓓ Ⓔ	36 Ⓐ Ⓑ Ⓒ Ⓓ Ⓔ
5 Ⓐ Ⓑ Ⓒ Ⓓ Ⓔ	13 Ⓐ Ⓑ Ⓒ Ⓓ Ⓔ	21 Ⓐ Ⓑ Ⓒ Ⓓ Ⓔ	29 Ⓐ Ⓑ Ⓒ Ⓓ Ⓔ	37 Ⓐ Ⓑ Ⓒ Ⓓ Ⓔ
6 Ⓐ Ⓑ Ⓒ Ⓓ Ⓔ	14 Ⓐ Ⓑ Ⓒ Ⓓ Ⓔ	22 Ⓐ Ⓑ Ⓒ Ⓓ Ⓔ	30 Ⓐ Ⓑ Ⓒ Ⓓ Ⓔ	38 Ⓐ Ⓑ Ⓒ Ⓓ Ⓔ
7 Ⓐ Ⓑ Ⓒ Ⓓ Ⓔ	15 Ⓐ Ⓑ Ⓒ Ⓓ Ⓔ	23 Ⓐ Ⓑ Ⓒ Ⓓ Ⓔ	31 Ⓐ Ⓑ Ⓒ Ⓓ Ⓔ	39 Ⓐ Ⓑ Ⓒ Ⓓ Ⓔ
8 Ⓐ Ⓑ Ⓒ Ⓓ Ⓔ	16 Ⓐ Ⓑ Ⓒ Ⓓ Ⓔ	24 Ⓐ Ⓑ Ⓒ Ⓓ Ⓔ	32 Ⓐ Ⓑ Ⓒ Ⓓ Ⓔ	40 Ⓐ Ⓑ Ⓒ Ⓓ Ⓔ

SECTION 4

1 Ⓐ Ⓑ Ⓒ Ⓓ Ⓔ	6 Ⓐ Ⓑ Ⓒ Ⓓ Ⓔ	11 Ⓐ Ⓑ Ⓒ Ⓓ Ⓔ	16 Ⓐ Ⓑ Ⓒ Ⓓ Ⓔ	21 Ⓐ Ⓑ Ⓒ Ⓓ Ⓔ
2 Ⓐ Ⓑ Ⓒ Ⓓ Ⓔ	7 Ⓐ Ⓑ Ⓒ Ⓓ Ⓔ	12 Ⓐ Ⓑ Ⓒ Ⓓ Ⓔ	17 Ⓐ Ⓑ Ⓒ Ⓓ Ⓔ	22 Ⓐ Ⓑ Ⓒ Ⓓ Ⓔ
3 Ⓐ Ⓑ Ⓒ Ⓓ Ⓔ	8 Ⓐ Ⓑ Ⓒ Ⓓ Ⓔ	13 Ⓐ Ⓑ Ⓒ Ⓓ Ⓔ	18 Ⓐ Ⓑ Ⓒ Ⓓ Ⓔ	23 Ⓐ Ⓑ Ⓒ Ⓓ Ⓔ
4 Ⓐ Ⓑ Ⓒ Ⓓ Ⓔ	9 Ⓐ Ⓑ Ⓒ Ⓓ Ⓔ	14 Ⓐ Ⓑ Ⓒ Ⓓ Ⓔ	19 Ⓐ Ⓑ Ⓒ Ⓓ Ⓔ	24 Ⓐ Ⓑ Ⓒ Ⓓ Ⓔ
5 Ⓐ Ⓑ Ⓒ Ⓓ Ⓔ	10 Ⓐ Ⓑ Ⓒ Ⓓ Ⓔ	15 Ⓐ Ⓑ Ⓒ Ⓓ Ⓔ	20 Ⓐ Ⓑ Ⓒ Ⓓ Ⓔ	25 Ⓐ Ⓑ Ⓒ Ⓓ Ⓔ

Lower Level Practice Test

Be sure each mark *completely* fills the answer space.
Start with number 1 for each new section of the test. You may find more answer spaces than you need.
If so, please leave them blank.

SECTION 1

1 Ⓐ Ⓑ Ⓒ Ⓓ Ⓔ	13 Ⓐ Ⓑ Ⓒ Ⓓ Ⓔ	25 Ⓐ Ⓑ Ⓒ Ⓓ Ⓔ	37 Ⓐ Ⓑ Ⓒ Ⓓ Ⓔ	49 Ⓐ Ⓑ Ⓒ Ⓓ Ⓔ
2 Ⓐ Ⓑ Ⓒ Ⓓ Ⓔ	14 Ⓐ Ⓑ Ⓒ Ⓓ Ⓔ	26 Ⓐ Ⓑ Ⓒ Ⓓ Ⓔ	38 Ⓐ Ⓑ Ⓒ Ⓓ Ⓔ	50 Ⓐ Ⓑ Ⓒ Ⓓ Ⓔ
3 Ⓐ Ⓑ Ⓒ Ⓓ Ⓔ	15 Ⓐ Ⓑ Ⓒ Ⓓ Ⓔ	27 Ⓐ Ⓑ Ⓒ Ⓓ Ⓔ	39 Ⓐ Ⓑ Ⓒ Ⓓ Ⓔ	51 Ⓐ Ⓑ Ⓒ Ⓓ Ⓔ
4 Ⓐ Ⓑ Ⓒ Ⓓ Ⓔ	16 Ⓐ Ⓑ Ⓒ Ⓓ Ⓔ	28 Ⓐ Ⓑ Ⓒ Ⓓ Ⓔ	40 Ⓐ Ⓑ Ⓒ Ⓓ Ⓔ	52 Ⓐ Ⓑ Ⓒ Ⓓ Ⓔ
5 Ⓐ Ⓑ Ⓒ Ⓓ Ⓔ	17 Ⓐ Ⓑ Ⓒ Ⓓ Ⓔ	29 Ⓐ Ⓑ Ⓒ Ⓓ Ⓔ	41 Ⓐ Ⓑ Ⓒ Ⓓ Ⓔ	53 Ⓐ Ⓑ Ⓒ Ⓓ Ⓔ
6 Ⓐ Ⓑ Ⓒ Ⓓ Ⓔ	18 Ⓐ Ⓑ Ⓒ Ⓓ Ⓔ	30 Ⓐ Ⓑ Ⓒ Ⓓ Ⓔ	42 Ⓐ Ⓑ Ⓒ Ⓓ Ⓔ	54 Ⓐ Ⓑ Ⓒ Ⓓ Ⓔ
7 Ⓐ Ⓑ Ⓒ Ⓓ Ⓔ	19 Ⓐ Ⓑ Ⓒ Ⓓ Ⓔ	31 Ⓐ Ⓑ Ⓒ Ⓓ Ⓔ	43 Ⓐ Ⓑ Ⓒ Ⓓ Ⓔ	55 Ⓐ Ⓑ Ⓒ Ⓓ Ⓔ
8 Ⓐ Ⓑ Ⓒ Ⓓ Ⓔ	20 Ⓐ Ⓑ Ⓒ Ⓓ Ⓔ	32 Ⓐ Ⓑ Ⓒ Ⓓ Ⓔ	44 Ⓐ Ⓑ Ⓒ Ⓓ Ⓔ	56 Ⓐ Ⓑ Ⓒ Ⓓ Ⓔ
9 Ⓐ Ⓑ Ⓒ Ⓓ Ⓔ	21 Ⓐ Ⓑ Ⓒ Ⓓ Ⓔ	33 Ⓐ Ⓑ Ⓒ Ⓓ Ⓔ	45 Ⓐ Ⓑ Ⓒ Ⓓ Ⓔ	57 Ⓐ Ⓑ Ⓒ Ⓓ Ⓔ
10 Ⓐ Ⓑ Ⓒ Ⓓ Ⓔ	22 Ⓐ Ⓑ Ⓒ Ⓓ Ⓔ	34 Ⓐ Ⓑ Ⓒ Ⓓ Ⓔ	46 Ⓐ Ⓑ Ⓒ Ⓓ Ⓔ	58 Ⓐ Ⓑ Ⓒ Ⓓ Ⓔ
11 Ⓐ Ⓑ Ⓒ Ⓓ Ⓔ	23 Ⓐ Ⓑ Ⓒ Ⓓ Ⓔ	35 Ⓐ Ⓑ Ⓒ Ⓓ Ⓔ	47 Ⓐ Ⓑ Ⓒ Ⓓ Ⓔ	59 Ⓐ Ⓑ Ⓒ Ⓓ Ⓔ
12 Ⓐ Ⓑ Ⓒ Ⓓ Ⓔ	24 Ⓐ Ⓑ Ⓒ Ⓓ Ⓔ	36 Ⓐ Ⓑ Ⓒ Ⓓ Ⓔ	48 Ⓐ Ⓑ Ⓒ Ⓓ Ⓔ	60 Ⓐ Ⓑ Ⓒ Ⓓ Ⓔ

SECTION 2

1 Ⓐ Ⓑ Ⓒ Ⓓ Ⓔ	6 Ⓐ Ⓑ Ⓒ Ⓓ Ⓔ	11 Ⓐ Ⓑ Ⓒ Ⓓ Ⓔ	16 Ⓐ Ⓑ Ⓒ Ⓓ Ⓔ	21 Ⓐ Ⓑ Ⓒ Ⓓ Ⓔ
2 Ⓐ Ⓑ Ⓒ Ⓓ Ⓔ	7 Ⓐ Ⓑ Ⓒ Ⓓ Ⓔ	12 Ⓐ Ⓑ Ⓒ Ⓓ Ⓔ	17 Ⓐ Ⓑ Ⓒ Ⓓ Ⓔ	22 Ⓐ Ⓑ Ⓒ Ⓓ Ⓔ
3 Ⓐ Ⓑ Ⓒ Ⓓ Ⓔ	8 Ⓐ Ⓑ Ⓒ Ⓓ Ⓔ	13 Ⓐ Ⓑ Ⓒ Ⓓ Ⓔ	18 Ⓐ Ⓑ Ⓒ Ⓓ Ⓔ	23 Ⓐ Ⓑ Ⓒ Ⓓ Ⓔ
4 Ⓐ Ⓑ Ⓒ Ⓓ Ⓔ	9 Ⓐ Ⓑ Ⓒ Ⓓ Ⓔ	14 Ⓐ Ⓑ Ⓒ Ⓓ Ⓔ	19 Ⓐ Ⓑ Ⓒ Ⓓ Ⓔ	24 Ⓐ Ⓑ Ⓒ Ⓓ Ⓔ
5 Ⓐ Ⓑ Ⓒ Ⓓ Ⓔ	10 Ⓐ Ⓑ Ⓒ Ⓓ Ⓔ	15 Ⓐ Ⓑ Ⓒ Ⓓ Ⓔ	20 Ⓐ Ⓑ Ⓒ Ⓓ Ⓔ	25 Ⓐ Ⓑ Ⓒ Ⓓ Ⓔ

SECTION 3

1 Ⓐ Ⓑ Ⓒ Ⓓ Ⓔ	9 Ⓐ Ⓑ Ⓒ Ⓓ Ⓔ	17 Ⓐ Ⓑ Ⓒ Ⓓ Ⓔ	25 Ⓐ Ⓑ Ⓒ Ⓓ Ⓔ	33 Ⓐ Ⓑ Ⓒ Ⓓ Ⓔ
2 Ⓐ Ⓑ Ⓒ Ⓓ Ⓔ	10 Ⓐ Ⓑ Ⓒ Ⓓ Ⓔ	18 Ⓐ Ⓑ Ⓒ Ⓓ Ⓔ	26 Ⓐ Ⓑ Ⓒ Ⓓ Ⓔ	34 Ⓐ Ⓑ Ⓒ Ⓓ Ⓔ
3 Ⓐ Ⓑ Ⓒ Ⓓ Ⓔ	11 Ⓐ Ⓑ Ⓒ Ⓓ Ⓔ	19 Ⓐ Ⓑ Ⓒ Ⓓ Ⓔ	27 Ⓐ Ⓑ Ⓒ Ⓓ Ⓔ	35 Ⓐ Ⓑ Ⓒ Ⓓ Ⓔ
4 Ⓐ Ⓑ Ⓒ Ⓓ Ⓔ	12 Ⓐ Ⓑ Ⓒ Ⓓ Ⓔ	20 Ⓐ Ⓑ Ⓒ Ⓓ Ⓔ	28 Ⓐ Ⓑ Ⓒ Ⓓ Ⓔ	36 Ⓐ Ⓑ Ⓒ Ⓓ Ⓔ
5 Ⓐ Ⓑ Ⓒ Ⓓ Ⓔ	13 Ⓐ Ⓑ Ⓒ Ⓓ Ⓔ	21 Ⓐ Ⓑ Ⓒ Ⓓ Ⓔ	29 Ⓐ Ⓑ Ⓒ Ⓓ Ⓔ	37 Ⓐ Ⓑ Ⓒ Ⓓ Ⓔ
6 Ⓐ Ⓑ Ⓒ Ⓓ Ⓔ	14 Ⓐ Ⓑ Ⓒ Ⓓ Ⓔ	22 Ⓐ Ⓑ Ⓒ Ⓓ Ⓔ	30 Ⓐ Ⓑ Ⓒ Ⓓ Ⓔ	38 Ⓐ Ⓑ Ⓒ Ⓓ Ⓔ
7 Ⓐ Ⓑ Ⓒ Ⓓ Ⓔ	15 Ⓐ Ⓑ Ⓒ Ⓓ Ⓔ	23 Ⓐ Ⓑ Ⓒ Ⓓ Ⓔ	31 Ⓐ Ⓑ Ⓒ Ⓓ Ⓔ	39 Ⓐ Ⓑ Ⓒ Ⓓ Ⓔ
8 Ⓐ Ⓑ Ⓒ Ⓓ Ⓔ	16 Ⓐ Ⓑ Ⓒ Ⓓ Ⓔ	24 Ⓐ Ⓑ Ⓒ Ⓓ Ⓔ	32 Ⓐ Ⓑ Ⓒ Ⓓ Ⓔ	40 Ⓐ Ⓑ Ⓒ Ⓓ Ⓔ

SECTION 4

1 Ⓐ Ⓑ Ⓒ Ⓓ Ⓔ	6 Ⓐ Ⓑ Ⓒ Ⓓ Ⓔ	11 Ⓐ Ⓑ Ⓒ Ⓓ Ⓔ	16 Ⓐ Ⓑ Ⓒ Ⓓ Ⓔ	21 Ⓐ Ⓑ Ⓒ Ⓓ Ⓔ
2 Ⓐ Ⓑ Ⓒ Ⓓ Ⓔ	7 Ⓐ Ⓑ Ⓒ Ⓓ Ⓔ	12 Ⓐ Ⓑ Ⓒ Ⓓ Ⓔ	17 Ⓐ Ⓑ Ⓒ Ⓓ Ⓔ	22 Ⓐ Ⓑ Ⓒ Ⓓ Ⓔ
3 Ⓐ Ⓑ Ⓒ Ⓓ Ⓔ	8 Ⓐ Ⓑ Ⓒ Ⓓ Ⓔ	13 Ⓐ Ⓑ Ⓒ Ⓓ Ⓔ	18 Ⓐ Ⓑ Ⓒ Ⓓ Ⓔ	23 Ⓐ Ⓑ Ⓒ Ⓓ Ⓔ
4 Ⓐ Ⓑ Ⓒ Ⓓ Ⓔ	9 Ⓐ Ⓑ Ⓒ Ⓓ Ⓔ	14 Ⓐ Ⓑ Ⓒ Ⓓ Ⓔ	19 Ⓐ Ⓑ Ⓒ Ⓓ Ⓔ	24 Ⓐ Ⓑ Ⓒ Ⓓ Ⓔ
5 Ⓐ Ⓑ Ⓒ Ⓓ Ⓔ	10 Ⓐ Ⓑ Ⓒ Ⓓ Ⓔ	15 Ⓐ Ⓑ Ⓒ Ⓓ Ⓔ	20 Ⓐ Ⓑ Ⓒ Ⓓ Ⓔ	25 Ⓐ Ⓑ Ⓒ Ⓓ Ⓔ

Lower Level Practice Test

Be sure each mark *completely* fills the answer space.
Start with number 1 for each new section of the test. You may find more answer spaces than you need.
If so, please leave them blank.

SECTION 1

1 Ⓐ Ⓑ Ⓒ Ⓓ Ⓔ	13 Ⓐ Ⓑ Ⓒ Ⓓ Ⓔ	25 Ⓐ Ⓑ Ⓒ Ⓓ Ⓔ	37 Ⓐ Ⓑ Ⓒ Ⓓ Ⓔ	49 Ⓐ Ⓑ Ⓒ Ⓓ Ⓔ
2 Ⓐ Ⓑ Ⓒ Ⓓ Ⓔ	14 Ⓐ Ⓑ Ⓒ Ⓓ Ⓔ	26 Ⓐ Ⓑ Ⓒ Ⓓ Ⓔ	38 Ⓐ Ⓑ Ⓒ Ⓓ Ⓔ	50 Ⓐ Ⓑ Ⓒ Ⓓ Ⓔ
3 Ⓐ Ⓑ Ⓒ Ⓓ Ⓔ	15 Ⓐ Ⓑ Ⓒ Ⓓ Ⓔ	27 Ⓐ Ⓑ Ⓒ Ⓓ Ⓔ	39 Ⓐ Ⓑ Ⓒ Ⓓ Ⓔ	51 Ⓐ Ⓑ Ⓒ Ⓓ Ⓔ
4 Ⓐ Ⓑ Ⓒ Ⓓ Ⓔ	16 Ⓐ Ⓑ Ⓒ Ⓓ Ⓔ	28 Ⓐ Ⓑ Ⓒ Ⓓ Ⓔ	40 Ⓐ Ⓑ Ⓒ Ⓓ Ⓔ	52 Ⓐ Ⓑ Ⓒ Ⓓ Ⓔ
5 Ⓐ Ⓑ Ⓒ Ⓓ Ⓔ	17 Ⓐ Ⓑ Ⓒ Ⓓ Ⓔ	29 Ⓐ Ⓑ Ⓒ Ⓓ Ⓔ	41 Ⓐ Ⓑ Ⓒ Ⓓ Ⓔ	53 Ⓐ Ⓑ Ⓒ Ⓓ Ⓔ
6 Ⓐ Ⓑ Ⓒ Ⓓ Ⓔ	18 Ⓐ Ⓑ Ⓒ Ⓓ Ⓔ	30 Ⓐ Ⓑ Ⓒ Ⓓ Ⓔ	42 Ⓐ Ⓑ Ⓒ Ⓓ Ⓔ	54 Ⓐ Ⓑ Ⓒ Ⓓ Ⓔ
7 Ⓐ Ⓑ Ⓒ Ⓓ Ⓔ	19 Ⓐ Ⓑ Ⓒ Ⓓ Ⓔ	31 Ⓐ Ⓑ Ⓒ Ⓓ Ⓔ	43 Ⓐ Ⓑ Ⓒ Ⓓ Ⓔ	55 Ⓐ Ⓑ Ⓒ Ⓓ Ⓔ
8 Ⓐ Ⓑ Ⓒ Ⓓ Ⓔ	20 Ⓐ Ⓑ Ⓒ Ⓓ Ⓔ	32 Ⓐ Ⓑ Ⓒ Ⓓ Ⓔ	44 Ⓐ Ⓑ Ⓒ Ⓓ Ⓔ	56 Ⓐ Ⓑ Ⓒ Ⓓ Ⓔ
9 Ⓐ Ⓑ Ⓒ Ⓓ Ⓔ	21 Ⓐ Ⓑ Ⓒ Ⓓ Ⓔ	33 Ⓐ Ⓑ Ⓒ Ⓓ Ⓔ	45 Ⓐ Ⓑ Ⓒ Ⓓ Ⓔ	57 Ⓐ Ⓑ Ⓒ Ⓓ Ⓔ
10 Ⓐ Ⓑ Ⓒ Ⓓ Ⓔ	22 Ⓐ Ⓑ Ⓒ Ⓓ Ⓔ	34 Ⓐ Ⓑ Ⓒ Ⓓ Ⓔ	46 Ⓐ Ⓑ Ⓒ Ⓓ Ⓔ	58 Ⓐ Ⓑ Ⓒ Ⓓ Ⓔ
11 Ⓐ Ⓑ Ⓒ Ⓓ Ⓔ	23 Ⓐ Ⓑ Ⓒ Ⓓ Ⓔ	35 Ⓐ Ⓑ Ⓒ Ⓓ Ⓔ	47 Ⓐ Ⓑ Ⓒ Ⓓ Ⓔ	59 Ⓐ Ⓑ Ⓒ Ⓓ Ⓔ
12 Ⓐ Ⓑ Ⓒ Ⓓ Ⓔ	24 Ⓐ Ⓑ Ⓒ Ⓓ Ⓔ	36 Ⓐ Ⓑ Ⓒ Ⓓ Ⓔ	48 Ⓐ Ⓑ Ⓒ Ⓓ Ⓔ	60 Ⓐ Ⓑ Ⓒ Ⓓ Ⓔ

SECTION 2

1 Ⓐ Ⓑ Ⓒ Ⓓ Ⓔ	6 Ⓐ Ⓑ Ⓒ Ⓓ Ⓔ	11 Ⓐ Ⓑ Ⓒ Ⓓ Ⓔ	16 Ⓐ Ⓑ Ⓒ Ⓓ Ⓔ	21 Ⓐ Ⓑ Ⓒ Ⓓ Ⓔ
2 Ⓐ Ⓑ Ⓒ Ⓓ Ⓔ	7 Ⓐ Ⓑ Ⓒ Ⓓ Ⓔ	12 Ⓐ Ⓑ Ⓒ Ⓓ Ⓔ	17 Ⓐ Ⓑ Ⓒ Ⓓ Ⓔ	22 Ⓐ Ⓑ Ⓒ Ⓓ Ⓔ
3 Ⓐ Ⓑ Ⓒ Ⓓ Ⓔ	8 Ⓐ Ⓑ Ⓒ Ⓓ Ⓔ	13 Ⓐ Ⓑ Ⓒ Ⓓ Ⓔ	18 Ⓐ Ⓑ Ⓒ Ⓓ Ⓔ	23 Ⓐ Ⓑ Ⓒ Ⓓ Ⓔ
4 Ⓐ Ⓑ Ⓒ Ⓓ Ⓔ	9 Ⓐ Ⓑ Ⓒ Ⓓ Ⓔ	14 Ⓐ Ⓑ Ⓒ Ⓓ Ⓔ	19 Ⓐ Ⓑ Ⓒ Ⓓ Ⓔ	24 Ⓐ Ⓑ Ⓒ Ⓓ Ⓔ
5 Ⓐ Ⓑ Ⓒ Ⓓ Ⓔ	10 Ⓐ Ⓑ Ⓒ Ⓓ Ⓔ	15 Ⓐ Ⓑ Ⓒ Ⓓ Ⓔ	20 Ⓐ Ⓑ Ⓒ Ⓓ Ⓔ	25 Ⓐ Ⓑ Ⓒ Ⓓ Ⓔ

SECTION 3

1 Ⓐ Ⓑ Ⓒ Ⓓ Ⓔ	9 Ⓐ Ⓑ Ⓒ Ⓓ Ⓔ	17 Ⓐ Ⓑ Ⓒ Ⓓ Ⓔ	25 Ⓐ Ⓑ Ⓒ Ⓓ Ⓔ	33 Ⓐ Ⓑ Ⓒ Ⓓ Ⓔ
2 Ⓐ Ⓑ Ⓒ Ⓓ Ⓔ	10 Ⓐ Ⓑ Ⓒ Ⓓ Ⓔ	18 Ⓐ Ⓑ Ⓒ Ⓓ Ⓔ	26 Ⓐ Ⓑ Ⓒ Ⓓ Ⓔ	34 Ⓐ Ⓑ Ⓒ Ⓓ Ⓔ
3 Ⓐ Ⓑ Ⓒ Ⓓ Ⓔ	11 Ⓐ Ⓑ Ⓒ Ⓓ Ⓔ	19 Ⓐ Ⓑ Ⓒ Ⓓ Ⓔ	27 Ⓐ Ⓑ Ⓒ Ⓓ Ⓔ	35 Ⓐ Ⓑ Ⓒ Ⓓ Ⓔ
4 Ⓐ Ⓑ Ⓒ Ⓓ Ⓔ	12 Ⓐ Ⓑ Ⓒ Ⓓ Ⓔ	20 Ⓐ Ⓑ Ⓒ Ⓓ Ⓔ	28 Ⓐ Ⓑ Ⓒ Ⓓ Ⓔ	36 Ⓐ Ⓑ Ⓒ Ⓓ Ⓔ
5 Ⓐ Ⓑ Ⓒ Ⓓ Ⓔ	13 Ⓐ Ⓑ Ⓒ Ⓓ Ⓔ	21 Ⓐ Ⓑ Ⓒ Ⓓ Ⓔ	29 Ⓐ Ⓑ Ⓒ Ⓓ Ⓔ	37 Ⓐ Ⓑ Ⓒ Ⓓ Ⓔ
6 Ⓐ Ⓑ Ⓒ Ⓓ Ⓔ	14 Ⓐ Ⓑ Ⓒ Ⓓ Ⓔ	22 Ⓐ Ⓑ Ⓒ Ⓓ Ⓔ	30 Ⓐ Ⓑ Ⓒ Ⓓ Ⓔ	38 Ⓐ Ⓑ Ⓒ Ⓓ Ⓔ
7 Ⓐ Ⓑ Ⓒ Ⓓ Ⓔ	15 Ⓐ Ⓑ Ⓒ Ⓓ Ⓔ	23 Ⓐ Ⓑ Ⓒ Ⓓ Ⓔ	31 Ⓐ Ⓑ Ⓒ Ⓓ Ⓔ	39 Ⓐ Ⓑ Ⓒ Ⓓ Ⓔ
8 Ⓐ Ⓑ Ⓒ Ⓓ Ⓔ	16 Ⓐ Ⓑ Ⓒ Ⓓ Ⓔ	24 Ⓐ Ⓑ Ⓒ Ⓓ Ⓔ	32 Ⓐ Ⓑ Ⓒ Ⓓ Ⓔ	40 Ⓐ Ⓑ Ⓒ Ⓓ Ⓔ

SECTION 4

1 Ⓐ Ⓑ Ⓒ Ⓓ Ⓔ	6 Ⓐ Ⓑ Ⓒ Ⓓ Ⓔ	11 Ⓐ Ⓑ Ⓒ Ⓓ Ⓔ	16 Ⓐ Ⓑ Ⓒ Ⓓ Ⓔ	21 Ⓐ Ⓑ Ⓒ Ⓓ Ⓔ
2 Ⓐ Ⓑ Ⓒ Ⓓ Ⓔ	7 Ⓐ Ⓑ Ⓒ Ⓓ Ⓔ	12 Ⓐ Ⓑ Ⓒ Ⓓ Ⓔ	17 Ⓐ Ⓑ Ⓒ Ⓓ Ⓔ	22 Ⓐ Ⓑ Ⓒ Ⓓ Ⓔ
3 Ⓐ Ⓑ Ⓒ Ⓓ Ⓔ	8 Ⓐ Ⓑ Ⓒ Ⓓ Ⓔ	13 Ⓐ Ⓑ Ⓒ Ⓓ Ⓔ	18 Ⓐ Ⓑ Ⓒ Ⓓ Ⓔ	23 Ⓐ Ⓑ Ⓒ Ⓓ Ⓔ
4 Ⓐ Ⓑ Ⓒ Ⓓ Ⓔ	9 Ⓐ Ⓑ Ⓒ Ⓓ Ⓔ	14 Ⓐ Ⓑ Ⓒ Ⓓ Ⓔ	19 Ⓐ Ⓑ Ⓒ Ⓓ Ⓔ	24 Ⓐ Ⓑ Ⓒ Ⓓ Ⓔ
5 Ⓐ Ⓑ Ⓒ Ⓓ Ⓔ	10 Ⓐ Ⓑ Ⓒ Ⓓ Ⓔ	15 Ⓐ Ⓑ Ⓒ Ⓓ Ⓔ	20 Ⓐ Ⓑ Ⓒ Ⓓ Ⓔ	25 Ⓐ Ⓑ Ⓒ Ⓓ Ⓔ

Lower Level Practice Test

Be sure each mark *completely* fills the answer space.
Start with number 1 for each new section of the test. You may find more answer spaces than you need.
If so, please leave them blank.

SECTION 1

1 Ⓐ Ⓑ Ⓒ Ⓓ Ⓔ	13 Ⓐ Ⓑ Ⓒ Ⓓ Ⓔ	25 Ⓐ Ⓑ Ⓒ Ⓓ Ⓔ	37 Ⓐ Ⓑ Ⓒ Ⓓ Ⓔ	49 Ⓐ Ⓑ Ⓒ Ⓓ Ⓔ
2 Ⓐ Ⓑ Ⓒ Ⓓ Ⓔ	14 Ⓐ Ⓑ Ⓒ Ⓓ Ⓔ	26 Ⓐ Ⓑ Ⓒ Ⓓ Ⓔ	38 Ⓐ Ⓑ Ⓒ Ⓓ Ⓔ	50 Ⓐ Ⓑ Ⓒ Ⓓ Ⓔ
3 Ⓐ Ⓑ Ⓒ Ⓓ Ⓔ	15 Ⓐ Ⓑ Ⓒ Ⓓ Ⓔ	27 Ⓐ Ⓑ Ⓒ Ⓓ Ⓔ	39 Ⓐ Ⓑ Ⓒ Ⓓ Ⓔ	51 Ⓐ Ⓑ Ⓒ Ⓓ Ⓔ
4 Ⓐ Ⓑ Ⓒ Ⓓ Ⓔ	16 Ⓐ Ⓑ Ⓒ Ⓓ Ⓔ	28 Ⓐ Ⓑ Ⓒ Ⓓ Ⓔ	40 Ⓐ Ⓑ Ⓒ Ⓓ Ⓔ	52 Ⓐ Ⓑ Ⓒ Ⓓ Ⓔ
5 Ⓐ Ⓑ Ⓒ Ⓓ Ⓔ	17 Ⓐ Ⓑ Ⓒ Ⓓ Ⓔ	29 Ⓐ Ⓑ Ⓒ Ⓓ Ⓔ	41 Ⓐ Ⓑ Ⓒ Ⓓ Ⓔ	53 Ⓐ Ⓑ Ⓒ Ⓓ Ⓔ
6 Ⓐ Ⓑ Ⓒ Ⓓ Ⓔ	18 Ⓐ Ⓑ Ⓒ Ⓓ Ⓔ	30 Ⓐ Ⓑ Ⓒ Ⓓ Ⓔ	42 Ⓐ Ⓑ Ⓒ Ⓓ Ⓔ	54 Ⓐ Ⓑ Ⓒ Ⓓ Ⓔ
7 Ⓐ Ⓑ Ⓒ Ⓓ Ⓔ	19 Ⓐ Ⓑ Ⓒ Ⓓ Ⓔ	31 Ⓐ Ⓑ Ⓒ Ⓓ Ⓔ	43 Ⓐ Ⓑ Ⓒ Ⓓ Ⓔ	55 Ⓐ Ⓑ Ⓒ Ⓓ Ⓔ
8 Ⓐ Ⓑ Ⓒ Ⓓ Ⓔ	20 Ⓐ Ⓑ Ⓒ Ⓓ Ⓔ	32 Ⓐ Ⓑ Ⓒ Ⓓ Ⓔ	44 Ⓐ Ⓑ Ⓒ Ⓓ Ⓔ	56 Ⓐ Ⓑ Ⓒ Ⓓ Ⓔ
9 Ⓐ Ⓑ Ⓒ Ⓓ Ⓔ	21 Ⓐ Ⓑ Ⓒ Ⓓ Ⓔ	33 Ⓐ Ⓑ Ⓒ Ⓓ Ⓔ	45 Ⓐ Ⓑ Ⓒ Ⓓ Ⓔ	57 Ⓐ Ⓑ Ⓒ Ⓓ Ⓔ
10 Ⓐ Ⓑ Ⓒ Ⓓ Ⓔ	22 Ⓐ Ⓑ Ⓒ Ⓓ Ⓔ	34 Ⓐ Ⓑ Ⓒ Ⓓ Ⓔ	46 Ⓐ Ⓑ Ⓒ Ⓓ Ⓔ	58 Ⓐ Ⓑ Ⓒ Ⓓ Ⓔ
11 Ⓐ Ⓑ Ⓒ Ⓓ Ⓔ	23 Ⓐ Ⓑ Ⓒ Ⓓ Ⓔ	35 Ⓐ Ⓑ Ⓒ Ⓓ Ⓔ	47 Ⓐ Ⓑ Ⓒ Ⓓ Ⓔ	59 Ⓐ Ⓑ Ⓒ Ⓓ Ⓔ
12 Ⓐ Ⓑ Ⓒ Ⓓ Ⓔ	24 Ⓐ Ⓑ Ⓒ Ⓓ Ⓔ	36 Ⓐ Ⓑ Ⓒ Ⓓ Ⓔ	48 Ⓐ Ⓑ Ⓒ Ⓓ Ⓔ	60 Ⓐ Ⓑ Ⓒ Ⓓ Ⓔ

SECTION 2

1 Ⓐ Ⓑ Ⓒ Ⓓ Ⓔ	6 Ⓐ Ⓑ Ⓒ Ⓓ Ⓔ	11 Ⓐ Ⓑ Ⓒ Ⓓ Ⓔ	16 Ⓐ Ⓑ Ⓒ Ⓓ Ⓔ	21 Ⓐ Ⓑ Ⓒ Ⓓ Ⓔ
2 Ⓐ Ⓑ Ⓒ Ⓓ Ⓔ	7 Ⓐ Ⓑ Ⓒ Ⓓ Ⓔ	12 Ⓐ Ⓑ Ⓒ Ⓓ Ⓔ	17 Ⓐ Ⓑ Ⓒ Ⓓ Ⓔ	22 Ⓐ Ⓑ Ⓒ Ⓓ Ⓔ
3 Ⓐ Ⓑ Ⓒ Ⓓ Ⓔ	8 Ⓐ Ⓑ Ⓒ Ⓓ Ⓔ	13 Ⓐ Ⓑ Ⓒ Ⓓ Ⓔ	18 Ⓐ Ⓑ Ⓒ Ⓓ Ⓔ	23 Ⓐ Ⓑ Ⓒ Ⓓ Ⓔ
4 Ⓐ Ⓑ Ⓒ Ⓓ Ⓔ	9 Ⓐ Ⓑ Ⓒ Ⓓ Ⓔ	14 Ⓐ Ⓑ Ⓒ Ⓓ Ⓔ	19 Ⓐ Ⓑ Ⓒ Ⓓ Ⓔ	24 Ⓐ Ⓑ Ⓒ Ⓓ Ⓔ
5 Ⓐ Ⓑ Ⓒ Ⓓ Ⓔ	10 Ⓐ Ⓑ Ⓒ Ⓓ Ⓔ	15 Ⓐ Ⓑ Ⓒ Ⓓ Ⓔ	20 Ⓐ Ⓑ Ⓒ Ⓓ Ⓔ	25 Ⓐ Ⓑ Ⓒ Ⓓ Ⓔ

SECTION 3

1 Ⓐ Ⓑ Ⓒ Ⓓ Ⓔ	9 Ⓐ Ⓑ Ⓒ Ⓓ Ⓔ	17 Ⓐ Ⓑ Ⓒ Ⓓ Ⓔ	25 Ⓐ Ⓑ Ⓒ Ⓓ Ⓔ	33 Ⓐ Ⓑ Ⓒ Ⓓ Ⓔ
2 Ⓐ Ⓑ Ⓒ Ⓓ Ⓔ	10 Ⓐ Ⓑ Ⓒ Ⓓ Ⓔ	18 Ⓐ Ⓑ Ⓒ Ⓓ Ⓔ	26 Ⓐ Ⓑ Ⓒ Ⓓ Ⓔ	34 Ⓐ Ⓑ Ⓒ Ⓓ Ⓔ
3 Ⓐ Ⓑ Ⓒ Ⓓ Ⓔ	11 Ⓐ Ⓑ Ⓒ Ⓓ Ⓔ	19 Ⓐ Ⓑ Ⓒ Ⓓ Ⓔ	27 Ⓐ Ⓑ Ⓒ Ⓓ Ⓔ	35 Ⓐ Ⓑ Ⓒ Ⓓ Ⓔ
4 Ⓐ Ⓑ Ⓒ Ⓓ Ⓔ	12 Ⓐ Ⓑ Ⓒ Ⓓ Ⓔ	20 Ⓐ Ⓑ Ⓒ Ⓓ Ⓔ	28 Ⓐ Ⓑ Ⓒ Ⓓ Ⓔ	36 Ⓐ Ⓑ Ⓒ Ⓓ Ⓔ
5 Ⓐ Ⓑ Ⓒ Ⓓ Ⓔ	13 Ⓐ Ⓑ Ⓒ Ⓓ Ⓔ	21 Ⓐ Ⓑ Ⓒ Ⓓ Ⓔ	29 Ⓐ Ⓑ Ⓒ Ⓓ Ⓔ	37 Ⓐ Ⓑ Ⓒ Ⓓ Ⓔ
6 Ⓐ Ⓑ Ⓒ Ⓓ Ⓔ	14 Ⓐ Ⓑ Ⓒ Ⓓ Ⓔ	22 Ⓐ Ⓑ Ⓒ Ⓓ Ⓔ	30 Ⓐ Ⓑ Ⓒ Ⓓ Ⓔ	38 Ⓐ Ⓑ Ⓒ Ⓓ Ⓔ
7 Ⓐ Ⓑ Ⓒ Ⓓ Ⓔ	15 Ⓐ Ⓑ Ⓒ Ⓓ Ⓔ	23 Ⓐ Ⓑ Ⓒ Ⓓ Ⓔ	31 Ⓐ Ⓑ Ⓒ Ⓓ Ⓔ	39 Ⓐ Ⓑ Ⓒ Ⓓ Ⓔ
8 Ⓐ Ⓑ Ⓒ Ⓓ Ⓔ	16 Ⓐ Ⓑ Ⓒ Ⓓ Ⓔ	24 Ⓐ Ⓑ Ⓒ Ⓓ Ⓔ	32 Ⓐ Ⓑ Ⓒ Ⓓ Ⓔ	40 Ⓐ Ⓑ Ⓒ Ⓓ Ⓔ

SECTION 4

1 Ⓐ Ⓑ Ⓒ Ⓓ Ⓔ	6 Ⓐ Ⓑ Ⓒ Ⓓ Ⓔ	11 Ⓐ Ⓑ Ⓒ Ⓓ Ⓔ	16 Ⓐ Ⓑ Ⓒ Ⓓ Ⓔ	21 Ⓐ Ⓑ Ⓒ Ⓓ Ⓔ
2 Ⓐ Ⓑ Ⓒ Ⓓ Ⓔ	7 Ⓐ Ⓑ Ⓒ Ⓓ Ⓔ	12 Ⓐ Ⓑ Ⓒ Ⓓ Ⓔ	17 Ⓐ Ⓑ Ⓒ Ⓓ Ⓔ	22 Ⓐ Ⓑ Ⓒ Ⓓ Ⓔ
3 Ⓐ Ⓑ Ⓒ Ⓓ Ⓔ	8 Ⓐ Ⓑ Ⓒ Ⓓ Ⓔ	13 Ⓐ Ⓑ Ⓒ Ⓓ Ⓔ	18 Ⓐ Ⓑ Ⓒ Ⓓ Ⓔ	23 Ⓐ Ⓑ Ⓒ Ⓓ Ⓔ
4 Ⓐ Ⓑ Ⓒ Ⓓ Ⓔ	9 Ⓐ Ⓑ Ⓒ Ⓓ Ⓔ	14 Ⓐ Ⓑ Ⓒ Ⓓ Ⓔ	19 Ⓐ Ⓑ Ⓒ Ⓓ Ⓔ	24 Ⓐ Ⓑ Ⓒ Ⓓ Ⓔ
5 Ⓐ Ⓑ Ⓒ Ⓓ Ⓔ	10 Ⓐ Ⓑ Ⓒ Ⓓ Ⓔ	15 Ⓐ Ⓑ Ⓒ Ⓓ Ⓔ	20 Ⓐ Ⓑ Ⓒ Ⓓ Ⓔ	25 Ⓐ Ⓑ Ⓒ Ⓓ Ⓔ

Lower Level Practice Test

Be sure each mark *completely* fills the answer space.
Start with number 1 for each new section of the test. You may find more answer spaces than you need.
If so, please leave them blank.

SECTION 1

1 Ⓐ Ⓑ Ⓒ Ⓓ Ⓔ	13 Ⓐ Ⓑ Ⓒ Ⓓ Ⓔ	25 Ⓐ Ⓑ Ⓒ Ⓓ Ⓔ	37 Ⓐ Ⓑ Ⓒ Ⓓ Ⓔ	49 Ⓐ Ⓑ Ⓒ Ⓓ Ⓔ
2 Ⓐ Ⓑ Ⓒ Ⓓ Ⓔ	14 Ⓐ Ⓑ Ⓒ Ⓓ Ⓔ	26 Ⓐ Ⓑ Ⓒ Ⓓ Ⓔ	38 Ⓐ Ⓑ Ⓒ Ⓓ Ⓔ	50 Ⓐ Ⓑ Ⓒ Ⓓ Ⓔ
3 Ⓐ Ⓑ Ⓒ Ⓓ Ⓔ	15 Ⓐ Ⓑ Ⓒ Ⓓ Ⓔ	27 Ⓐ Ⓑ Ⓒ Ⓓ Ⓔ	39 Ⓐ Ⓑ Ⓒ Ⓓ Ⓔ	51 Ⓐ Ⓑ Ⓒ Ⓓ Ⓔ
4 Ⓐ Ⓑ Ⓒ Ⓓ Ⓔ	16 Ⓐ Ⓑ Ⓒ Ⓓ Ⓔ	28 Ⓐ Ⓑ Ⓒ Ⓓ Ⓔ	40 Ⓐ Ⓑ Ⓒ Ⓓ Ⓔ	52 Ⓐ Ⓑ Ⓒ Ⓓ Ⓔ
5 Ⓐ Ⓑ Ⓒ Ⓓ Ⓔ	17 Ⓐ Ⓑ Ⓒ Ⓓ Ⓔ	29 Ⓐ Ⓑ Ⓒ Ⓓ Ⓔ	41 Ⓐ Ⓑ Ⓒ Ⓓ Ⓔ	53 Ⓐ Ⓑ Ⓒ Ⓓ Ⓔ
6 Ⓐ Ⓑ Ⓒ Ⓓ Ⓔ	18 Ⓐ Ⓑ Ⓒ Ⓓ Ⓔ	30 Ⓐ Ⓑ Ⓒ Ⓓ Ⓔ	42 Ⓐ Ⓑ Ⓒ Ⓓ Ⓔ	54 Ⓐ Ⓑ Ⓒ Ⓓ Ⓔ
7 Ⓐ Ⓑ Ⓒ Ⓓ Ⓔ	19 Ⓐ Ⓑ Ⓒ Ⓓ Ⓔ	31 Ⓐ Ⓑ Ⓒ Ⓓ Ⓔ	43 Ⓐ Ⓑ Ⓒ Ⓓ Ⓔ	55 Ⓐ Ⓑ Ⓒ Ⓓ Ⓔ
8 Ⓐ Ⓑ Ⓒ Ⓓ Ⓔ	20 Ⓐ Ⓑ Ⓒ Ⓓ Ⓔ	32 Ⓐ Ⓑ Ⓒ Ⓓ Ⓔ	44 Ⓐ Ⓑ Ⓒ Ⓓ Ⓔ	56 Ⓐ Ⓑ Ⓒ Ⓓ Ⓔ
9 Ⓐ Ⓑ Ⓒ Ⓓ Ⓔ	21 Ⓐ Ⓑ Ⓒ Ⓓ Ⓔ	33 Ⓐ Ⓑ Ⓒ Ⓓ Ⓔ	45 Ⓐ Ⓑ Ⓒ Ⓓ Ⓔ	57 Ⓐ Ⓑ Ⓒ Ⓓ Ⓔ
10 Ⓐ Ⓑ Ⓒ Ⓓ Ⓔ	22 Ⓐ Ⓑ Ⓒ Ⓓ Ⓔ	34 Ⓐ Ⓑ Ⓒ Ⓓ Ⓔ	46 Ⓐ Ⓑ Ⓒ Ⓓ Ⓔ	58 Ⓐ Ⓑ Ⓒ Ⓓ Ⓔ
11 Ⓐ Ⓑ Ⓒ Ⓓ Ⓔ	23 Ⓐ Ⓑ Ⓒ Ⓓ Ⓔ	35 Ⓐ Ⓑ Ⓒ Ⓓ Ⓔ	47 Ⓐ Ⓑ Ⓒ Ⓓ Ⓔ	59 Ⓐ Ⓑ Ⓒ Ⓓ Ⓔ
12 Ⓐ Ⓑ Ⓒ Ⓓ Ⓔ	24 Ⓐ Ⓑ Ⓒ Ⓓ Ⓔ	36 Ⓐ Ⓑ Ⓒ Ⓓ Ⓔ	48 Ⓐ Ⓑ Ⓒ Ⓓ Ⓔ	60 Ⓐ Ⓑ Ⓒ Ⓓ Ⓔ

SECTION 2

1 Ⓐ Ⓑ Ⓒ Ⓓ Ⓔ	6 Ⓐ Ⓑ Ⓒ Ⓓ Ⓔ	11 Ⓐ Ⓑ Ⓒ Ⓓ Ⓔ	16 Ⓐ Ⓑ Ⓒ Ⓓ Ⓔ	21 Ⓐ Ⓑ Ⓒ Ⓓ Ⓔ
2 Ⓐ Ⓑ Ⓒ Ⓓ Ⓔ	7 Ⓐ Ⓑ Ⓒ Ⓓ Ⓔ	12 Ⓐ Ⓑ Ⓒ Ⓓ Ⓔ	17 Ⓐ Ⓑ Ⓒ Ⓓ Ⓔ	22 Ⓐ Ⓑ Ⓒ Ⓓ Ⓔ
3 Ⓐ Ⓑ Ⓒ Ⓓ Ⓔ	8 Ⓐ Ⓑ Ⓒ Ⓓ Ⓔ	13 Ⓐ Ⓑ Ⓒ Ⓓ Ⓔ	18 Ⓐ Ⓑ Ⓒ Ⓓ Ⓔ	23 Ⓐ Ⓑ Ⓒ Ⓓ Ⓔ
4 Ⓐ Ⓑ Ⓒ Ⓓ Ⓔ	9 Ⓐ Ⓑ Ⓒ Ⓓ Ⓔ	14 Ⓐ Ⓑ Ⓒ Ⓓ Ⓔ	19 Ⓐ Ⓑ Ⓒ Ⓓ Ⓔ	24 Ⓐ Ⓑ Ⓒ Ⓓ Ⓔ
5 Ⓐ Ⓑ Ⓒ Ⓓ Ⓔ	10 Ⓐ Ⓑ Ⓒ Ⓓ Ⓔ	15 Ⓐ Ⓑ Ⓒ Ⓓ Ⓔ	20 Ⓐ Ⓑ Ⓒ Ⓓ Ⓔ	25 Ⓐ Ⓑ Ⓒ Ⓓ Ⓔ

SECTION 3

1 Ⓐ Ⓑ Ⓒ Ⓓ Ⓔ	9 Ⓐ Ⓑ Ⓒ Ⓓ Ⓔ	17 Ⓐ Ⓑ Ⓒ Ⓓ Ⓔ	25 Ⓐ Ⓑ Ⓒ Ⓓ Ⓔ	33 Ⓐ Ⓑ Ⓒ Ⓓ Ⓔ
2 Ⓐ Ⓑ Ⓒ Ⓓ Ⓔ	10 Ⓐ Ⓑ Ⓒ Ⓓ Ⓔ	18 Ⓐ Ⓑ Ⓒ Ⓓ Ⓔ	26 Ⓐ Ⓑ Ⓒ Ⓓ Ⓔ	34 Ⓐ Ⓑ Ⓒ Ⓓ Ⓔ
3 Ⓐ Ⓑ Ⓒ Ⓓ Ⓔ	11 Ⓐ Ⓑ Ⓒ Ⓓ Ⓔ	19 Ⓐ Ⓑ Ⓒ Ⓓ Ⓔ	27 Ⓐ Ⓑ Ⓒ Ⓓ Ⓔ	35 Ⓐ Ⓑ Ⓒ Ⓓ Ⓔ
4 Ⓐ Ⓑ Ⓒ Ⓓ Ⓔ	12 Ⓐ Ⓑ Ⓒ Ⓓ Ⓔ	20 Ⓐ Ⓑ Ⓒ Ⓓ Ⓔ	28 Ⓐ Ⓑ Ⓒ Ⓓ Ⓔ	36 Ⓐ Ⓑ Ⓒ Ⓓ Ⓔ
5 Ⓐ Ⓑ Ⓒ Ⓓ Ⓔ	13 Ⓐ Ⓑ Ⓒ Ⓓ Ⓔ	21 Ⓐ Ⓑ Ⓒ Ⓓ Ⓔ	29 Ⓐ Ⓑ Ⓒ Ⓓ Ⓔ	37 Ⓐ Ⓑ Ⓒ Ⓓ Ⓔ
6 Ⓐ Ⓑ Ⓒ Ⓓ Ⓔ	14 Ⓐ Ⓑ Ⓒ Ⓓ Ⓔ	22 Ⓐ Ⓑ Ⓒ Ⓓ Ⓔ	30 Ⓐ Ⓑ Ⓒ Ⓓ Ⓔ	38 Ⓐ Ⓑ Ⓒ Ⓓ Ⓔ
7 Ⓐ Ⓑ Ⓒ Ⓓ Ⓔ	15 Ⓐ Ⓑ Ⓒ Ⓓ Ⓔ	23 Ⓐ Ⓑ Ⓒ Ⓓ Ⓔ	31 Ⓐ Ⓑ Ⓒ Ⓓ Ⓔ	39 Ⓐ Ⓑ Ⓒ Ⓓ Ⓔ
8 Ⓐ Ⓑ Ⓒ Ⓓ Ⓔ	16 Ⓐ Ⓑ Ⓒ Ⓓ Ⓔ	24 Ⓐ Ⓑ Ⓒ Ⓓ Ⓔ	32 Ⓐ Ⓑ Ⓒ Ⓓ Ⓔ	40 Ⓐ Ⓑ Ⓒ Ⓓ Ⓔ

SECTION 4

1 Ⓐ Ⓑ Ⓒ Ⓓ Ⓔ	6 Ⓐ Ⓑ Ⓒ Ⓓ Ⓔ	11 Ⓐ Ⓑ Ⓒ Ⓓ Ⓔ	16 Ⓐ Ⓑ Ⓒ Ⓓ Ⓔ	21 Ⓐ Ⓑ Ⓒ Ⓓ Ⓔ
2 Ⓐ Ⓑ Ⓒ Ⓓ Ⓔ	7 Ⓐ Ⓑ Ⓒ Ⓓ Ⓔ	12 Ⓐ Ⓑ Ⓒ Ⓓ Ⓔ	17 Ⓐ Ⓑ Ⓒ Ⓓ Ⓔ	22 Ⓐ Ⓑ Ⓒ Ⓓ Ⓔ
3 Ⓐ Ⓑ Ⓒ Ⓓ Ⓔ	8 Ⓐ Ⓑ Ⓒ Ⓓ Ⓔ	13 Ⓐ Ⓑ Ⓒ Ⓓ Ⓔ	18 Ⓐ Ⓑ Ⓒ Ⓓ Ⓔ	23 Ⓐ Ⓑ Ⓒ Ⓓ Ⓔ
4 Ⓐ Ⓑ Ⓒ Ⓓ Ⓔ	9 Ⓐ Ⓑ Ⓒ Ⓓ Ⓔ	14 Ⓐ Ⓑ Ⓒ Ⓓ Ⓔ	19 Ⓐ Ⓑ Ⓒ Ⓓ Ⓔ	24 Ⓐ Ⓑ Ⓒ Ⓓ Ⓔ
5 Ⓐ Ⓑ Ⓒ Ⓓ Ⓔ	10 Ⓐ Ⓑ Ⓒ Ⓓ Ⓔ	15 Ⓐ Ⓑ Ⓒ Ⓓ Ⓔ	20 Ⓐ Ⓑ Ⓒ Ⓓ Ⓔ	25 Ⓐ Ⓑ Ⓒ Ⓓ Ⓔ

9

Answer Key to SSAT
Practice Tests

SSAT UL VERBAL 1

1. A
2. D
3. A
4. A
5. D
6. A
7. B
8. D
9. B
10. D
11. D
12. A
13. A
14. B
15. C
16. B
17. D
18. C
19. A
20. E
21. B
22. D
23. B
24. C
25. E
26. D
27. E
28. E
29. B
30. B
31. E
32. C
33. A
34. C
35. C
36. A
37. D
38. B
39. C
40. C
41. C
42. E
43. D
44. E
45. B
46. D

47. A
48. D
49. C
50. A
51. C
52. A
53. A
54. A
55. E
56. B
57. D
58. C
59. E
60. D

SSAT UL MATH 2

1. E
2. A
3. E
4. B
5. D
6. C
7. B
8. A
9. C
10. A
11. B
12. E
13. C
14. E
15. A
16. E
17. B
18. D
19. D
20. B
21. C
22. A
23. A
24. E
25. A

SSAT UL READING 3

1. B
2. E
3. B

4. A
5. D
6. D
7. B
8. A
9. E
10. C
11. B
12. D
13. B
14. A
15. A
16. D
17. D
18. C
19. B
20. B
21. D
22. C
23. D
24. A
25. A
26. B
27. A
28. D
29. D
30. C
31. A
32. B
33. B
34. D
35. C
36. C
37. A
38. C
39. C
40. E

SSAT UL MATH 4

1. B
2. D
3. B
4. D
5. C
6. A
7. E

8. C
9. A
10. B
11. E
12. D
13. E
14. A
15. D
16. B
17. E
18. C
19. B
20. B
21. B
22. C
23. D
24. A
25. B

SSAT LL VERBAL 1

1. A
2. D
3. D
4. D
5. A
6. B
7. C
8. A
9. B
10. B
11. C
12. C
13. A
14. D
15. D
16. A
17. E
18. D
19. E
20. A
21. A
22. C
23. C
24. B
25. D
26. D

27. E
28. A
29. D
30. E
31. C
32. B
33. B
34. D
35. D
36. D
37. A
38. C
39. E
40. B
41. E
42. A
43. C
44. B
45. C
46. D
47. D
48. E
49. E
50. A
51. A
52. A
53. C
54. B
55. A
56. B
57. C
58. C
59. C
60. E

SSAT LL MATH 2

1. D
2. B
3. D
4. A
5. D
6. C
7. C
8. D
9. C
10. A

11. C
12. A
13. E
14. C
15. B
16. A
17. A
18. D
19. B
20. D
21. B
22. A
23. D
24. A
25. E

SSAT LL READING 3

1. C
2. C
3. B
4. B
5. D
6. A
7. C
8. B
9. E
10. D
11. B
12. D
13. A
14. B
15. B
16. C
17. A
18. C
19. E
20. B
21. B
22. A
23. B
24. E
25. B
26. D
27. E
28. D
29. A

30. C
31. E
32. C
33. D
34. B
35. C
36. E
37. C
38. B
39. D
40. A

SSAT LL MATH 4

1. A
2. A
3. C
4. E
5. A
6. A
7. C
8. C
9. B
10. C
11. A
12. C
13. A
14. E
15. C
16. E
17. B
18. A
19. D
20. B
21. B
22. E
23. A
24. C
25. B

10

Scoring Your Practice SSAT

Check Your Answers

Use the answer key to determine how many questions you answered correctly and how many you answered incorrectly. You may want to check yourself by adding together your number of correct answers, incorrect answers, and the number of questions you left blank. Make sure this total matches the total number of questions in the section.

Compute Your Raw Score

To compute your raw score, fill in the chart below. Your raw score equals the number of questions you answered correctly, minus one-fourth of the number of questions you answered incorrectly (the guessing penalty).

VERBAL: $\underset{\text{Right Answers}}{\underline{\hspace{2cm}}} - (\ \frac{1}{4}\ \times \underset{\text{Wrong Answers}}{\underline{\hspace{2cm}}}\ ) = \underset{\text{Raw Score}}{\underline{\hspace{2cm}}}$

MATH: $\underset{\text{Right Answers}}{\underline{\hspace{2cm}}} - (\ \frac{1}{4}\ \times \underset{\text{Wrong Answers}}{\underline{\hspace{2cm}}}\ ) = \underset{\text{Raw Score}}{\underline{\hspace{2cm}}}$

READING: $\underset{\text{Right Answers}}{\underline{\hspace{2cm}}} - (\ \frac{1}{4}\ \times \underset{\text{Wrong Answers}}{\underline{\hspace{2cm}}}\ ) = \underset{\text{Raw Score}}{\underline{\hspace{2cm}}}$

Find Your Raw Score on the Conversion Chart

On the following pages you will find a conversion chart for both the Upper Level and Lower Level test. Make sure you use the chart that corresponds to the test you took. Look in the appropriate column on the left to find your raw score and then read across to find your scaled score.

The best way to know what your scaled score means is to refer to the pacing section where you will find the percentile ranking for your scaled score. This will allow you to compare your performance with that of other students of your grade and gender.

SSAT UPPER LEVEL SCORE CONVERSION CHART

SSAT Raw Score

Verbal	Quan (over 2 sections)	Reading	Scaled Score
60	50	40	350
59	50	40	349
57	49	40	348
55	48	40	347
54	47	40	346
53	46	40	345
52	45	40	344
50	45	40	343
49	44	40	342
49	44	40	341
48	43	40	340
48	43	39	339
47	42	39	338
47	41	39	337
46	41	39	336
46	40	39	335
45	40	39	334
45	39	39	333
44	39	39	332
44	38	38	331
43	38	38	330
43	37	37	329
42	37	37	328
42	36	37	327
41	36	36	326
40	35	36	325
40	34	35	324
39	34	35	323
39	33	34	322
38	33	34	321
38	32	33	320
37	32	33	319
36	31	32	318
36	30	32	317
35	30	31	316
34	29	31	315
34	29	30	314
33	28	30	313
33	28	29	312
32	27	29	311
32	27	28	310

(continued on the next page)

SSAT UPPER LEVEL SCORE CONVERSION CHART

(CONTINUED)

SSAT Raw Score

Verbal	Quan (over 2 sections)	Reading	Scaled Score
31	26	28	309
31	26	27	308
30	25	27	307
29	25	26	306
29	24	26	305
28	24	25	304
28	23	25	303
27	23	24	302
27	22	24	301
26	22	23	300
26	21	23	299
25	21	22	298
25	20	22	297
24	19	21	296
24	19	21	295
23	18	20	294
23	18	19	293
22	17	19	292
21	17	18	291
21	16	18	290
20	16	17	289
20	15	17	288
19	15	16	287
18	14	16	286
18	14	15	285
17	13	15	284
17	13	14	283
16	12	14	282
16	12	13	281
15	11	13	280
15	11	12	279
14	10	12	278
14	9	12	277
13	9	11	276
12	8	11	275
12	8	10	274
11	7	10	273
11	7	9	272
10	6	9	271
10	6	8	270
9	5	8	269
9	5	7	268

(continued on the next page)

SSAT UPPER LEVEL SCORE CONVERSION CHART

(CONTINUED)

SSAT Raw Score

Verbal	Quan (over 2 sections)	Reading	Scaled Score
8	4	7	267
8	4	6	266
7	3	6	265
7	2	5	264
6	2	4	263
6	1	3	262
5	1	2	261
0	0	0	250-260

SSAT LOWER LEVEL SCORE CONVERSION CHART

SSAT Raw Score

Verbal	Quan (over 2 sections)	Reading	Scaled Score
50	50	40	320
49	50	39	319
48	50	39	318
47	49	38	317
45	49	38	316
44	48	37	315
44	48	36	314
43	47	36	313
43	46	35	312
42	46	35	311
41	45	34	310
41	44	34	309
40	43	33	308
39	43	33	307
39	42	32	306
38	41	32	305
37	41	31	304
37	40	31	303
36	39	30	302
36	39	29	301
35	38	29	300
34	37	28	299
33	37	28	298
33	36	27	297
32	36	27	296
32	35	27	295

(continued on next page)

SSAT LOWER LEVEL SCORE CONVERSION CHART

(CONTINUED)

SSAT Raw Score

Verbal	Quan (over 2 sections)	Reading	Scaled Score
31	34	26	294
31	33	26	293
30	33	25	292
29	32	24	291
29	32	24	290
28	31	23	289
27	30	23	288
27	29	23	287
26	28	22	286
26	27	22	285
25	27	21	284
25	26	21	283
24	26	20	282
23	25	20	281
23	24	19	280
22	24	19	279
21	23	18	278
21	23	18	277
20	22	17	276
19	21	17	275
19	21	16	274
18	20	16	273
18	19	15	272
17	18	14	271
17	18	14	270
16	17	14	269
15	16	13	268
14	16	13	267
14	15	12	266
13	14	12	265
12	13	11	264
12	13	11	263
11	12	10	262
11	12	9	261
10	11	9	260
9	10	8	259
8	9	8	258
8	9	8	257
7	8	7	256
7	8	7	255
6	7	6	254

(continued on next page)

SSAT LOWER LEVEL SCORE CONVERSION CHART

(CONTINUED)

SSAT Raw Score

Verbal	Quan (over 2 sections)	Reading	Scaled Score
6	6	6	253
5	6	5	252
5	5	4	251
4	4	4	250
4	4	4	249
3	3	3	248
2	2	3	247
2	2	2	246
1	1	2	245
0	0	1	244
0	0	1	243
0	0	0	242
0	0	0	241
0	0	0	230-240

WHAT ABOUT THE OVERALL SCORE?

In addition to scores in each of the three sections—verbal, quantitative (math), and reading—you will also receive an overall score, which is based on your verbal and quantitative performance. There is no conversion chart to allow you to determine your overall score, but to get a rough approximation, you can count on your overall score being roughly the average of your verbal and quantitative scaled score. Verbal counts slightly more than math, since there are more verbal questions than math questions, so your actual overall score will be slightly different from this average—usually a few points higher or lower in the direction of your verbal score.

PART III

The ISEE

11

Everything You Always Wanted to Know About the ISEE

THE FIRST STEP

Before you begin to think about preparing for the ISEE, you must complete one essential first step: *Sign up for the ISEE*. Your first step should be to get a copy of the most recent ISEE Student Guide, which comes from the Educational Records Bureau (ERB), the organization that writes and administers the ISEE. This publication is available directly from ERB or from the independent schools to which you are applying. The test is administered on a regular basis, but test dates differ from one city to the next. The Student Guide lists all available test dates and test centers. The regular registration deadline for the test (at United States testing centers) is usually three weeks before the test date, and the registration fee is $59.

In addition to these regularly scheduled test dates, it is possible to take the ISEE privately, by appointment, through a network of educational consultants. The fee for a private administration is $110, and a list of those consultants who administer the ISEE is available from ERB. Even if you choose to take the test privately, be sure you make your testing appointment as far in advance as possible.

Plan Ahead

Early registration will not only give you one fewer thing to worry about as the test approaches, but it will also get you your first-choice test center.

WHAT IS THE ISEE?

The Independent School Entrance Examination (ISEE) is a standardized test made up of a series of multiple-choice questions and a writing sample. The entire test lasts about 160 minutes, during which you will work on five different sections:

Verbal ability	40 questions	20 minutes
Quantitative ability	40 questions	35 minutes
Reading comprehension	40 questions	35 minutes
Mathematics achievement	50 questions	40 minutes
Writing sample (ungraded)	1 essay topic	30 minutes

Keep in mind that the sections will not necessarily appear in this order. The writing sample comes after the multiple-choice sections, but the sections within the multiple-choice portion of the test can appear in any order.

UPPER VS. MIDDLE LEVEL

There are, in effect, two different versions of the ISEE. The Middle Level test is taken by students who are, at the time of testing, in the fifth, sixth, and seventh grades. The Upper Level test is for students who take the test during the eighth, ninth, tenth, and eleventh grades.

There are few major differences between the Middle and Upper Level tests. There are some small differences in content; for instance, vocabulary on the Middle Level test is less challenging than it is on the Upper Level test. In math, you will see similar general concepts tested (arithmetic, algebra, geometry, charts and graphs) on both tests, but naturally the Middle Level test will ask slightly easier questions than the Upper Level test.

As you work through this book, you will notice that sets of practice problems do not distinguish between Upper and Middle questions. Instead, you will find practice sets that generally increase in difficulty as you move from earlier to later questions. Therefore, if you are taking the Middle Level test, don't worry if you have trouble with some of the later questions.

PACING

Most people believe that in order to do well on a test, it is important to try to answer every question. While this is true of most of the tests you take in school, it is not true of many standardized tests including the ISEE. On this test, it is very possible to score well without answering all of the questions. In fact, many students can improve their scores by spending their time working on fewer questions.

"Wait a second. I can get a better score by doing less work?" Yes. The reason for this is, in their effort to answer all the questions, many students spend very little time on easy questions and make careless errors. They then spend more of their time on harder questions that they are likely to answer incorrectly anyway. The ISEE does give you more points for answering a hard question correctly than for answering an easy one correctly. In spite of this, you should still spend most of your time making sure that you get as many points as possible from the easy and medium questions. Answer fewer questions, but get more of the questions that you do answer right. If you don't finish the test, that's fine, because by working slowly and carefully you got more points than you would have by rushing to answer more questions.

As we'll explain in a moment, you should pick an answer for every question on the test, taking random guesses on the questions you did not have time to solve. This last-minute guessing will earn you quick and easy points that you would surely miss if you left any questions blank.

Answer Every Question but Don't _Do_ Every Question

There is no penalty for wrong answers on the ISEE, so it is to your advantage to choose an answer for every question. This doesn't mean that you need to rush through the test to try to solve every question. Work at a pace that will maximize correct answers, and be ready to guess at the questions you didn't have time to answer.

PROCESS OF ELIMINATION

What is the capital of Malawi?

(A) New York   (B) Paris
(C) London   (D) Lilongwe

There are two ways to get this question right. First, you might know that the capital of Malawi is Lilongwe. If you do, good for you! The second is to know that the capital of Malawi is not New York, Paris, or London. You don't get more points for knowing the right answer from the start, so one way is just as good as the other. Try to get in the habit of looking at a question and asking, "What are the wrong answers?" instead of "What is the right answer?"

By using the Process of Elimination (or P.O.E.) this way, you will eliminate wrong answers and then have fewer answers from which to pick. The result is that you will pick right answers more often.

Should I Guess?

YES! But before you just make a random guess, always try to use POE to eliminate wrong answers.

Guessing

Some standardized tests, including the SSAT, include a component in their scoring that penalizes you for wrong answers. This is called a guessing penalty. *There is no guessing penalty on the ISEE.* Therefore, although you may not have time to look at or do every problem on the test, you should be certain to choose an answer for every question. For instance, if you only have time to attempt 30 out of 40 verbal questions, you should still guess an answer for each of the ten questions you did not have time to complete. We suggest that you simply choose your favorite letter, A through D, and make that your "letter of the day," which you will fill in on your answer sheet for every question you did not have time to answer.

In addition to this random guessing, you can also improve your score by taking educated guesses. If you encounter a verbal question, for instance, to which you do not know the right answer, don't just give up. Instead, look at the answer choices and try to identify wrong answers so you can eliminate them. Using P.O.E. this way turns guessing into a way to improve your score. Will you always guess correctly? No, but the odds of guessing correctly only get better with each answer choice you eliminate, so P.O.E. is a technique you should use often. Give it a try:

> Which of the following cities is the capital of
> Western Samoa?
>
> (A) Vila   (B) Boston
> (C) Apia   (D) Chicago

You may not know the right answer off the top of your head. But which cities are not the capital of Western Samoa? You probably know enough about the locations of (B) and (D) to know that neither Boston nor Chicago is the capital of Western Samoa.

So what's a good answer to this question? (A) or (C).

What's the right answer? It isn't important. You took a good guess and that's all that matters.

A Quick Summary

These points are important enough that we want to mention them again. Make sure you understand these points about the ISEE before you go any farther in this book.

- ◆ You do not have to solve every problem on the test. Slow down!

- ◆ You will not immediately know the correct answer to every question. Instead, use P.O.E. and look for wrong answers that you can eliminate.

- ◆ Set aside the last minute or two of each section to fill in a guess for each question you did not have time to answer. Don't leave anything blank!

12

ISEE Math

INTRODUCTION

This section will provide you with a review of all the math that you need to take the ISEE. When you get started, you may feel that the material is too easy. Don't worry. This test measures your basic math skills, so although you might feel a little frustrated reviewing things you have already learned, that is undoubtedly the best way to improve your score.

We recommend that you work straight through this math review chapter, first reviewing each concept and then doing each set of drills. If you have trouble with one section, mark the page so that you can come back later to go over it again. Keep in mind, though, that you shouldn't breeze over pages or sections just because they look familiar. Take the time to read over the entire chapter so you'll be sure to know all the math you'll need!

LOSE YOUR CALCULATOR

You will not be allowed to use a calculator on the ISEE. If you have developed a habit of reaching for your calculator whenever you need to add or multiply a couple of numbers, follow our advice: Put your calculator away now and don't take it out again until the test is behind you. Trust us, you'll be glad you did.

WRITE IT DOWN

Do not try to do math in your head. You are allowed to write in your test booklet. You should write in your test booklet. Even when you are just adding a few numbers together, write them down and do the work on paper. Not only will writing things down help eliminate careless errors; it will also give you something to refer to if you need to check over your work.

ONE PASS, TWO PASS

Within any math section, you will find three types of questions:

- those you can answer easily without too much time
- those which, if you had all the time in the world, you could do
- some questions which you have absolutely no idea how to tackle

When you work on a math section, start out with the first question. If it is one of the first types and you think you can do it without too much trouble, go ahead. If not, save it. Move on to the second question and decide whether to do that one or not.

Once you've made it all the way through the section, working slowly and carefully to do all the questions that come easily for you, then go back and try some of the ones that you think you can do, but know that it will take a little longer. Hopefully you will pace yourself so that time will run out while you're working on the second pass through the section. You won't be frustrated, though, because you'll know that you answered all the questions that were easy for you. Using a two-pass system and knowing that you can do the questions in whatever order you like is good, smart test taking.

GUESSTIMATING

Sometimes accuracy is important. Sometimes it isn't.

> Which of the following fractions is less than $\frac{1}{4}$?
>
> (A) $\frac{4}{18}$
>
> (B) $\frac{4}{12}$
>
> (C) $\frac{7}{7}$
>
> (D) $\frac{12}{5}$

Some Things are Easier than They Seem

Guesstimating, or finding approximate answers, can help you eliminate wrong answers and save lots of time.

Without doing a bit of calculation, think about this question. It asks you to find a fraction smaller than $\frac{1}{4}$. Even if you're not sure which one is actually smaller, you can certainly use P.O.E. to eliminate some wrong answers.

Start simple. $\frac{1}{4}$ is less than 1, right? Are there any fractions in the answer choices that are greater than 1? Get rid of (D).

Look at answer choice (C). $\frac{7}{7}$ equals 1. Can it be less than $\frac{1}{4}$? Eliminate (C). Already, without doing a bit of math, you have a 50-percent chance of guessing the right answer.

Here's another good example:

> A group of three men buys a one-dollar lottery ticket that wins $400. If the one dollar that they paid for the ticket is subtracted and the remainder of the prize money is divided equally among the men, how much will each man receive?
>
> (A) $62.50
> (B) $75.00
> (C) $100.00
> (D) $133.00

This isn't a terribly difficult question. To solve it mathematically, you would take $400, subtract $1, and then divide the remainder by three. But by using a little bit of logic, you don't have to do any of that.

The lottery ticket won $400. If there were four men, each one would have won about $100 (actually slightly less because the problem tells you to subtract the $1 price of the ticket, but you get the idea). So far so good? There weren't four men, though, there were only three. This means fewer men among whom to divide the winnings, so each one should get more than $100, right?

Look at the answer choices. Eliminate (A), (B), and (C). What's left? The right answer!

Guesstimating also works very well with some geometry questions, but just to give you something you can look forward to, we'll save that for the geometry chapter.

FUNDAMENTALS

MATH VOCABULARY

Many of the questions on the ISEE are word problems. If you're going to do well, you need to make sure you know what the words mean! This table lists some of the most popular math vocabulary words used on these tests. Make sure you know all of them!

TERM	DEFINITION	EXAMPLES
Integer	Any number that does not contain either a fraction or a decimal	14, 3, 0, -3
Positive number	Any number greater than zero	$\frac{1}{4}$, 1, 104
Negative number	Any number less than zero	$-\frac{1}{4}$, -1, -104
Even number	Any number which is evenly divisible by two	104, 16, 2, 0, -2, -104
Odd number	Any number which is not evenly divisible by two	115, 11, 1, -1, -11, -115
Prime number	Any number which is divisible only by 1 and itself. NOTE: One is not a prime number	2, 3, 5, 7, 13, 131
Digit	The numbers from 0 through 9	0, 2, 3, 7
Consecutive numbers	Any series of numbers listed in the order they appear on the number line	3, 4, 5 or -1, 0, 1, 2
Distinct numbers	Numbers that are different from one another	2, 7, and 19 are three distinct numbers. 4 and 4 are not distinct, because they are the same number.
Sum	The result of addition	The sum of 6 and 2 is 8 because 6 + 2 = 8.
Difference	The result of subtraction	The difference between 6 and 2 is 4 because 6 − 2 = 4.
Product	The result of multiplication	The product of 6 and 2 is 12 because 6 x 2 = 12.
Quotient	The result of division	The quotient when 6 is divided by 2 is 3 because 6 ÷ 2 = 3.

Practice—Math Vocabulary Test

1. How many integers are there between –1 and 6?_____

2. List three consecutive even integers:
   _____

3. How many odd integers are there between 1 and 9? _____

4. What is the tens digit in the number 182.09? _____

5. The product of any number and the smallest positive integer is: _____

6. What is the product of 5, 6, and 3?
   _____

7. What is the sum of 3, 11, and 16?
   _____

8. What is the difference between your answer to #6 and your answer to #7?
   _____

9. List three consecutive positive even numbers:_____

10. Is 11 a prime number? _____

11. What is the sum of the digits in the number 5,647? _____

12. The sum of five consecutive positive integers is 30. What is the square of the largest of the five positive integers?
    (A) 25
    (B) 36
    (C) 49
    (D) 64

ORDER OF OPERATIONS

How would you attack this problem?

$$16 - 45 \div (2 + 1)^2 \bullet 4 + 5 =$$

To solve a problem like this, use PEMDAS. The order of operations is:

Parentheses
Exponents
Done together { **Multiplication**
from left to right { **Division**
Addition } Done together
Subtraction } from left to right

First Things First

Make sure you remember PEMDAS whenever you see a question with more than one operation.

You can remember the order of operations using this phrase:
"Please Excuse My Dear Aunt Sally."

Now, let's give it a try:

$$16 - 45 \div \underline{(2+1)}^2 \cdot 4 + 5 =$$
$$16 - 45 \div (3)^2 \cdot 4 + 5 =$$

1. PARENTHESES:

$$16 - 45 \div \underline{(2+1)}^2 \cdot 4 + 5 =$$
$$16 - 45 \div (3)^2 \cdot 4 + 5 =$$

2. EXPONENTS:

$$16 - 45 \div \underline{(3)}^2 \cdot 4 + 5 =$$
$$16 - 45 \div 9 \cdot 4 + 5 =$$

3. MULTIPLICATION AND DIVISION (from left to right):

$$16 - \underline{45 \div 9} \cdot 4 + 5 =$$
$$16 - \underline{5 \cdot 4} + 5 =$$
$$16 - 20 + 5 =$$

4. ADDITION AND SUBTRACTION (from left to right):

$$\underline{16 - 20} + 5 =$$
$$-4 + 5 = \boxed{1}$$

Just take it one step at a time and the math is easy!

Practice — Order of Operations

1. $10 - 3 + 2 =$

2. $15 + (7 - 3) - 3 =$

3. $3 \times 2 + 3 \div 3 =$

4. $2 \times (4 + 6) \div 4 =$

5. $420 \div (5 \times 12 + 10) =$

6. $20 \times 5 \div 10 + 20 =$

7. $(3 + 5) \times 10 \times 7 \div 8 =$

8. $10 \times (8 + 1) \times (3 + 1) \div (8 - 2) =$

9. $12 \div 2 \div 2 \times 5 + 5 =$

10. $200 - 150 \div 3 \times 2 =$

FACTORS

Factors are all the numbers that divide evenly into your original number. For example, two is a factor of ten; it goes in five times. Three is not a factor of ten, because ten divided by three does not produce an integer quotient (and therefore does not "go in evenly"). When asked to find the factors of a number, just make a list.

The factors of 16 are:
    1 and 16
    2 and 8
    4 and 4
    Is 3 a factor of 16? _____

The factors of 18 are:
    1 and 18   (always start with 1 and the original number)
    2 and 9
    3 and 6
Knowing some rules of divisibility can save you some time.

A NUMBER IS DIVISIBLE BY	IF ...
2	If it ends in 0, 2, 4, 6, or 8.
3	If the sum of the digits is divisible by 3.
5	If it ends in 0 or 5.
9	If the sum of the digits is divisible by 9.
10	If it ends in 0.

Practice — Factors

1. How many factors does the number 24 have?

   (A) 8
   (B) 6
   (C) 4
   (D) 2

2. If 12 is a factor of a certain number, what must also be factors of that number?

   (A) 2 and 6 only
   (B) 3 and 4 only
   (D) 1, 2, 3, 4, and 6
   (E) 1, 2, 3, 4, 6, and 24

3. What is the smallest number that can be added to the number 1,024 to produce a result divisible by 9?

   (A) 1
   (B) 2
   (C) 3
   (E) 6

MULTIPLES

Factors are Small; Multiples are Big

The factors of a number are always equal to or less than that number. The multiples of a number are always equal to or greater than that number. Be sure not to confuse the two!

Multiples are the results when you multiply your number by any integer. Fifteen is a multiple of five, because five times three equals fifteen. Eighteen is a multiple of three, but not a multiple of five. Another way to think about multiples is to consider them "counting by a number."

The first seven positive multiples of 7 are:

7	(7×1)
14	(7×2)
21	(7×3)
28	(7×4)
35	(7×5)
42	(7×6)
49	(7×7)

Practice — Multiples

1. Which of the following is a multiple of 3?

   (A) 2
   (B) 6
   (C) 10
   (D) 14

2. Which of the following is not a multiple of 6?

   (A) 12
   (B) 18
   (C) 24
   (D) 23

3. Which of the following is a multiple of both 3 and 5?

   (A) 45
   (B) 25
   (C) 20
   (D) 10

4. A company's profit was $75,000 in 1972. In 1992, its profit was $450,000. The profit in 1992 was how many times as great as the profit in 1972?

   (A) 2
   (B) 4
   (C) 6
   (D) 60

FRACTIONS

A fraction really just tells you to divide. For instance, $\frac{5}{8}$ actually means five divided by eight (which equals 0.625 as a decimal).

Another way to think of this is to imagine a pie cut into eight pieces. $\frac{5}{8}$ tells you something about five of those eight pieces of pie.

The parts of a fraction are called the numerator and the denominator. The numerator is the number on top of the fraction, which refers to the part of the pie. The denominator is on the bottom of the fraction and tells you how many pieces there are in the entire pie.

$$\frac{\text{numerator}}{\text{denominator}}$$

Reducing Fractions

Imagine a pie cut into two big pieces. You eat one of the pieces. That means that you have eaten $\frac{1}{2}$ of the pie. Now imagine the same pie cut into four pieces; you eat two. That's $\frac{2}{4}$ this time. But look! The two fractions are equivalent!

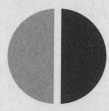 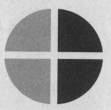

To reduce fractions, just divide the top number and the bottom number by the same amount. Start out with small numbers like 2, 3, 5, or 10, and reduce again if you need to.

$$\frac{12}{24} \begin{array}{c} \div 2 \\ \div 2 \end{array} = \frac{6}{12} \begin{array}{c} \div 2 \\ \div 2 \end{array} = \frac{3}{6} \begin{array}{c} \div 3 \\ \div 3 \end{array} = \frac{1}{2}$$

In this example, if you happened to see that both 12 and 24 were divisible by 12, then you could have saved two quick steps. Don't spend very much time, though, looking for the biggest number possible by which to reduce a fraction. Starting out with a small number and doing one extra set of reducing doesn't take very much time and will definitely help prevent careless errors.

Practice — Reducing fractions

1. $\frac{6}{8}$ =

2. $\frac{12}{60}$ =

3. $\frac{20}{30}$ =

4. $\frac{36}{96}$ =

5. $\frac{24}{32}$ =

6. $\frac{16}{56}$ =

7. $\frac{1056}{1056}$ =

8. $\dfrac{154}{126}$ =

9. What does it mean when the number on top is bigger than the one on the bottom?

Adding & subtracting fractions with a common denominator

To add or subtract fractions with a common denominator, just add or subtract the top numbers and leave the bottom number alone.

$$\frac{5}{7} + \frac{1}{7} = \frac{6}{7}$$

$$\frac{5}{7} - \frac{1}{7} = \frac{4}{7}$$

Adding & subtracting fractions when the denominators are different

In the past, you have probably tried to find common denominators so that you could just add or subtract straight across. There is an easier way; it is called the bowtie.

$$\frac{A}{B} \nearrow + \nwarrow \frac{C}{D} =$$

This diagram may make the bowtie look complicated, but it's not. There are three simple steps to adding and subtracting fractions.

Step 1: Multiply diagonally going up.
First find **B** x **C**. Write the product next to **C**.
Then find **D** x **A**. Write the product next to **A**.

Step 2: Multiply straight across the bottom. **B** x **D**.
Write the product as the denominator in your answer.

Step 3: To add, add the numbers written next to **A** and **C**.
Write the sum as the numerator in your answer.
To subtract, subtract the numbers written next to **A** and **C**.
Write the difference as the numerator in your answer.

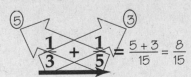

$$\frac{1}{3} + \frac{1}{5} = \frac{5+3}{15} = \frac{8}{15}$$

> ### No More "Smallest Common Denominators"
>
> Using the bowtie to add and subtract fractions eliminates the need for a smallest common denominator.

Practice—Adding & subtracting fractions

1. $\dfrac{3}{8} + \dfrac{2}{3} =$

2. $\dfrac{1}{3} + \dfrac{3}{8} =$

3. $\dfrac{4}{7} + \dfrac{2}{7} =$

4. $\dfrac{3}{4} - \dfrac{2}{3} =$

5. $\dfrac{7}{9} + \dfrac{5}{4} =$

6. $\dfrac{2}{5} - \dfrac{3}{4} =$

7. $\dfrac{10}{12} + \dfrac{7}{2} =$

8. $\dfrac{17}{27} - \dfrac{11}{27} =$

9. $\dfrac{3}{20} + \dfrac{2}{3} =$

10. $\dfrac{x}{3} + \dfrac{4x}{6} =$

Multiplying fractions

Multiplying is the easiest thing to do with fractions. All you need to do is multiply straight across the top and bottom.

$$\frac{3}{7} \times \frac{4}{5} = \frac{3 \times 4}{7 \times 5} = \frac{12}{35}$$

Dividing fractions

Dividing fractions is almost as simple as multiplying. You just have to flip the second fraction and then multiply.

$$\frac{3}{8} \div \frac{2}{5} = \frac{3}{8} \times \frac{5}{2} = \frac{15}{16}$$

When dividing, don't ask why; just flip the second fraction and multiply!

Practice — Multiplying & dividing fractions

1. $\dfrac{2}{3} \times \dfrac{1}{2} =$

2. $\dfrac{5}{8} \div \dfrac{1}{2} =$

3. $\dfrac{4}{5} \times \dfrac{3}{10} =$

4. $\dfrac{24}{15} \times \dfrac{10}{16} =$

5. $\dfrac{16}{25} \div \dfrac{4}{5} =$

Practice — Fraction problems

1. Joanna owns one-third of the pieces of furniture in the apartment she shares with her friends. If there is a total of twelve pieces of furniture in the apartment, how many pieces does Joanna own?
   (A) 4
   (B) 6
   (C) 8
   (D) 12

2. A tank of oil is one-third full. When full, the tank holds 90 gallons. How many gallons of oil are in the tank now?
   (A) 10
   (B) 20
   (C) 30
   (D) 40

3. Tigger the Cat sleeps three-fourths of every day. In a four-day period, he sleeps the equivalent of how many full days?
   (A) $\dfrac{1}{4}$
   (B) $\dfrac{3}{4}$
   (C) 1
   (D) 3

4. Which of the following is the greatest?
   (A) $\dfrac{1}{4} + \dfrac{2}{3}$
   (B) $\dfrac{3}{4} - \dfrac{1}{3}$
   (C) $\dfrac{1}{12} \div \dfrac{1}{3}$
   (D) $\dfrac{3}{4} \times \dfrac{1}{3}$

5. $\dfrac{1}{2} + \dfrac{2}{3} + \dfrac{3}{4} + \dfrac{1}{2} + \dfrac{1}{3} + \dfrac{1}{4} =$
   (A) $\dfrac{3}{4}$
   (B) 1
   (C) 6
   (D) 3

DECIMALS

Remember, decimals and fractions are just two different ways of writing the same thing. To change a fraction into a decimal, you just divide the bottom number into the top number.

Be sure you know the names of all the decimal places. Here's a quick reminder:

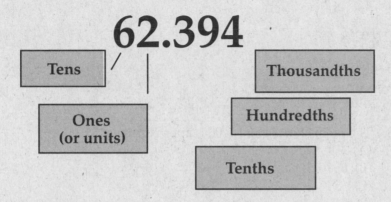

Adding decimals
To add decimals, just line up the decimal places and add.

$$48.02$$
$$+19.12$$
$$67.14$$

Subtracting decimals
To subtract, do the same thing. Line up the decimal places and subtract.

$$67.14$$
$$-48.02$$
$$19.12$$

Multiplying decimals
To multiply decimals, first count the number of digits to the right of the decimal point in the numbers you are multiplying. Then just multiply and move the decimal point in your answer from right to left by the same number of spaces.

$$0.5$$
$$\times 4.2 \text{ (two digits to the right of the decimal point)}$$
$$2.10$$

Dividing decimals
To divide, move the decimal points in both numbers the same number of spaces to the right, until you are working only with integers.

$$12.5 \div .25 = .25\overline{)12.5}$$

Now move both decimals over two places and solve the problem.

$$25\overline{)1250} \quad 50$$

Practice — Decimals

1. $1.43 + 17.27 =$

2. $2.49 + 1.7 =$

3. $7.08 - 2.3 =$

4. $4.25 \times 2.5 =$

5. $.02 \times .90 =$

6. $180 \div .03 =$

7. $.10 \div .02 =$

8. The product of .34 and 1000 is approximately
    (A) 350
    (B) 65
    (C) 35
    (D) 3.5

9. $2.398 =$

    (A) $2 \times \dfrac{9}{100} \times \dfrac{3}{10} \times \dfrac{8}{1000}$

    (B) $2 + \dfrac{3}{10} + \dfrac{9}{1000} + \dfrac{8}{100}$

    (C) $2 + \dfrac{9}{100} + \dfrac{8}{1000} + \dfrac{3}{10}$

    (D) None of the above

EXPONENTS

Exponents are just another way to indicate multiplication. For instance, 3^2 simply means to multiply 3 by itself 2 times, so $3^2 = 3 \times 3 = 9$. Even higher exponents aren't very complicated.

For example: $2^5 = 2 \times 2 \times 2 \times 2 \times 2 = 32$.

The questions on the SSAT and the ISEE don't generally use exponents higher than four or five, so this is likely to be as complicated as it gets.

The rule for exponents is simple: When in doubt, write it out! Don't try to figure out two times two times two times two times two in your head (just look at how silly it looks written down using words!); instead, write it as a math problem and just work through it one step at a time.

What would you do if you were asked to solve this problem?

$$Q^3 \times Q^2 =$$

When in Doubt, Write it Out!

Don't try to compute exponents in your head. Write them out and multiply!

Let's look at this one carefully. Q^3 means $Q \times Q \times Q$ and Q^2 means $Q \times Q$. Put them together and you've got:

$$(Q \times Q \times Q) \times (Q \times Q) =$$

How many Qs is that? Count them. Five! Be careful when multiplying exponents like this that you don't get confused and multiply the actual exponents, which would give you Q^6. If you are ever unsure, don't spend a second worrying; just write out the exponent and count the number of things you are multiplying.

PRACTICE — Exponents

1. $2^3 =$

2. $2^4 =$

3. $3^3 =$

4. $4^3 =$

5. $2^3 \times 2^3 \times 2^2 =$
    (A) 64
    (B) 2^8
    (C) 2^{10}
    (D) 2^{18}

6. For what integer value of m does
    $2m + 4 = m^3$?
    (A) 1
    (B) 2
    (C) 3
    (D) 4

ALGEBRA

MANIPULATING AN EQUATION

To solve an equation, your goal is to isolate the variable, meaning that you want to get the variable on one side of the equation and everything else on the other side.

$$3x + 5 = 17$$

To do this, follow these two steps:

Step 1: Move elements around using addition and subtraction. Get variables on one side and numbers on the other. Simplify.

Step 2: Divide both sides of the equation by the *coefficient*, the number in front of the variable. If that number is a fraction, multiply everything by the denominator.

Equal Rights for Equations!

You can do anything you want to one side of the equation, as long as you make sure to do exactly the same thing to the other side.

For example:

$3x + 5 = 17$
$-5 = -5$ Subtract 5 to get rid of the numbers on the left side
$3x = 12$
$\div 3 = \div 3$ Divide by 3 to get rid of the 3 on the left side
$x = 4$ Done!

Always remember:

Whatever you do to one side, you must also do to the other.

Practice — Manipulate!

1. If $6 + 2 = 11 - x$, then $x =$

2. If $4x = 20$, then $x =$

3. If $5x - 20 = 10$, then $x =$

4. If $4x + 3 = 31$, then $x =$

5. If $m + 5 = 3m - 3$, then $m =$

6. If $2.5x = 20$, then $x =$

7. If $0.2x + 2 = 3.6$, then $x =$

8. If $6 = 8x + 4$, then $x =$

9. If $3(x + y) = 21$, then $x + y =$

10. If $3x + 3y = 21$, then $x + y =$

11. If $2.5 \times 40 - 5y = 65$, then $y =$

12. One-fifth of the students in a class chose recycling as the topic for their science project. If four students chose recycling, how many students are in the class?
    (A) 4
    (B) 10
    (C) 16
    (D) 20

13. If $6x - 4 = 38$, then $x + 10 =$
    (A) 7
    (B) 10
    (C) 16
    (D) 17

14. If $3x - 6 = 21$, then what is $x \div 9$?
    (A) 0
    (B) 1
    (C) 3
    (D) 9

15. Only one-fifth of the chairs in a classroom are in working order. If three extra chairs are brought in, there are 19 working seats available. How many chairs were originally in the room?
    (A) 80
    (B) 22
    (C) 19
    (D) 16

FUNCTIONS

A function is just a set of instructions written in a strange way.

$\# x = 3x(x + 1)$

On the left:	there is usually a variable with a strange symbol next to or around it
In the middle:	an equal sign
On the right:	are the instructions. These tell you what to do with the variable.
$\# x = 3x(x + 1)$	*What does # 5 equal?*
$\# 5 = 3 \bullet 5(5 + 1)$	*Just replace each x with a 5!*

Here the function (which is indicated by the # sign) simply tells you to substitute a 5 wherever there is an x in the original set of instructions. Functions look confusing because of the strange symbols, but once you know what to do with them, they are just like manipulating an equation.

Sometimes more than one question will refer to the same function. The following drill, for example, contains two questions about one function. In cases such as this, the first question tends to be easier than the second.

Practice — Functions

Questions 1–2 refer to the following definition.
For all real numbers n, $\S n = 10n - 10$

1. $\S 7 =$
   (A) 7
   (B) 17
   (C) 60
   (D) 70

2. If $\S n = 120$, then $n =$
   (A) 12
   (B) 13
   (C) 120
   (D) 130

Questions 3–5 refer to the following definition.
For all real numbers d and y, $d \, \text{¿} \, y = (d \bullet y) - (d + y)$.
[Example: $3 \, \text{¿} \, 2 = (3 \bullet 2) - (3 + 2) = 6 - 5 = 1$]

3. $10 \, \text{¿} \, 2 =$
   (A) 20
   (B) 16
   (C) 12
   (D) 8

4. If $K \, (4 \, \text{¿} \, 3) = 30$, then $K =$
   (A) 3
   (B) 4
   (C) 5
   (D) 6

5. $(2 \, \text{¿} \, 4) \bullet (3 \, \text{¿} \, 6) =$
   (A) $(9 \, \text{¿} \, 3) + 3$
   (B) $(6 \, \text{¿} \, 4) + 1$
   (C) $(5 \, \text{¿} \, 3) + 4$
   (D) $(8 \, \text{¿} \, 4) + 2$

PERCENTAGES

Solving percent problems is easy when you know how to translate them from "percent language" into "math language." Once you've done the translation, you guessed it: You just manipulate the equation.

What is 40% of 72?

PERCENT LANGUAGE	MATH LANGUAGE
% or "percent"	Out of 100 ($\frac{}{100}$)
Of	Times (as in Multiplication) ($\times$)
What	Your favorite variable (p)
Is, are, were	Equals ($=$)

> **Learn a Foreign Language**
>
> "Percent language" is easy to learn because there are only four words you need to remember!

Whenever you see words from this table, just translate them into math language and go to work on the equation.

For example:

$$24 \text{ is } 60 \text{ percent of what?}$$

$$24 = \frac{60}{100} \times m$$

Practice — Translating & solving percent questions

1. 30 is what percent of 250?

2. What is 12% of 200?

3. What is 25% of 10% of 200?

4. 75% of 20% of what is 12?

Practice — Word problems involving percentages

1. If a harvest yielded 60 bushels of corn, 20 bushels of wheat, and 40 bushels of soybeans, what percent of the total harvest was corn?
   (A) 30%
   (B) 33%
   (C) 40%
   (D) 50%

2. At a local store, an item that usually sells for $45 is currently on sale for $30. What discount does that represent?
   (A) 66%
   (B) 33%
   (C) 25%
   (D) 10%

3. Which of the following is most nearly 35% of 19.95?
   (A) $13.50
   (B) $9.95
   (C) $7.00
   (D) $3.50

4. Of the fifty hotels in the Hilltop Hotels chain, five have indoor swimming pools and fifteen have outdoor swimming pools. What percent of all Hilltop Hotels have either an indoor or an outdoor swimming pool?
   (A) 5%
   (B) 15%
   (C) 20%
   (D) 40%

5. For what price item does 40% off equal a $20 discount?
   (A) $800.00
   (B) $100.00
   (C) $50.00
   (D) None of the above.

6. A pair of shoes is offered on a special blowout sale. The original price of the shoes is reduced from $50 to $20. What is the percent change in the price of the shoes?
   (A) 60%
   (B) 50%
   (C) 40%
   (D) 30%

7. Lisa buys a silk dress regularly priced at $60, a cotton sweater regularly priced at $40, and four pairs of socks regularly priced at $5 each. If the dress and the socks are on sale for 20% off the regular price and the sweater is on sale for 10% off the regular price, what is the total amount of her purchase?
   (A) $90.00
   (B) $96.00
   (C) $100.00
   (D) $102.00

8. Thirty percent of $17.95 is closest to
   (A) $2.00
   (B) $3.00
   (C) $6.00
   (D) $9.00

9. Fifty percent of the 20 students in Mrs. Weale's fifth grade class are boys. If ninety percent of these boys ride the bus to school, which of the following is the number of boys in Mrs. Weale's class who ride the bus to school?
   (A) 9
   (B) 10
   (C) 12
   (D) 18

10. On a test with 25 questions, Angela scored an 88%. How many questions did she answer correctly?
    (A) 3
    (B) 4
    (C) 16
    (D) 22

RATIOS

A ratio is like a recipe, because it tells you how much of different ingredients go into a mixture.

For example:

To make punch, mix two parts grape juice with three parts orange juice.

This ratio tells you that for every two units of grape juice, you will need to add three units of orange juice. It doesn't matter what the units are; if you were working with ounces, you would mix two ounces of grape juice with three ounces of orange juice to get five ounces of punch. If you were working with gallons, you would mix two gallons of grape juice with three gallons of orange juice. How much punch would you have? Five gallons!

To work through a ratio question, first you need to organize the information you are given. Do this using the ratio box.

In a club with 35 members, the ratio of boys to girls is 3 : 2.

BOYS	GIRLS	TOTAL
3	2	5
× 7	× 7	× 7
21	14	35

To complete your ratio box, fill in the ratio at the top and the "real world" at the bottom. Then look for a "magic number" that you can multiply by the ratio to get to the real world. That's all there is to it!

Practice — Ratios

1. In a jar of lollipops, the ratio of red lollipops to blue lollipops is 3:5. If only red lollipops and blue lollipops are in the jar and if the total number of lollipops in the jar is 56, how many blue lollipops are in the jar?
    (A) 35
    (B) 21
    (C) 8
    (D) 5

2. At Jed's Country Hotel, there are three types of rooms: singles, doubles, and triples. If the ratio of singles to doubles to triples is 3:4:5, and the total number of rooms is 36, how many doubles are there?
    (A) 4
    (B) 12
    (C) 24
    (D) 36

3. Matt's Oak Superstore has exactly three times as many large oak desks as small oak desks in its inventory. If the store only sells these two types of desks, which could be the total number of desks in stock?
    (A) 10
    (B) 13
    (C) 16
    (D) 25

4. In Janice's tennis club, 8 of the 12 players are right-handed. What is the ratio of right-handed to left-handed players in Janice's club?
    (A) 1 : 2
    (B) 2 : 1
    (C) 1 : 6
    (D) 3 : 4

5. One-half of the 400 students at Golder Junior High School are girls. Of the girls at the school, the ratio of those who ride a school bus to those who walk is 7 : 3. What is the total number of girls who walk to school?
    (A) 10
    (B) 30
    (C) 60
    (D) 140

6. A pet goat eats two pounds of goat food and one pound of
   grass each day. When the goat has eaten a total of fifteen
   pounds, how many pounds of grass will it have eaten?
   (A) 3
   (B) 5
   (C) 15
   (D) 30

AVERAGES

There are three parts of every average problem: total, number, and average.
Most ISEE problems will give you two of the three pieces and ask you to find the
third. To help organize the information you are given, use the average pie.

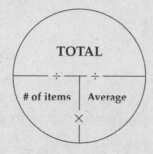

The average pie organizes all of your information visually. It is easy to see all
of the relationships between pieces of the pie:

- TOTAL = (# of items) × (Average)

- # of items = $\dfrac{\text{TOTAL}}{\text{Average}}$

- Average = $\dfrac{\text{TOTAL}}{\text{\# of items}}$

For example, if your friend went bowling and bowled three games, scoring
71, 90, and 100, here's how you would compute her average score using the
average pie:

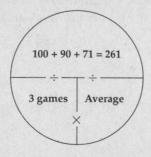

To find the average, you would simply write a fraction

that represents $\dfrac{\text{TOTAL}}{\text{\# of items}}$, in this case $\dfrac{261}{3}$.

The math becomes simple. 261 ÷ 3 = 87. Your friend bowled an average of 87.

Get used to working with the average pie by using it to solve these problems:

Practice — Average problems

1. The average of three numbers is eighteen. What is two times the sum of the three numbers?
   (A) 108
   (B) 54
   (C) 36
   (D) 18

2. If Set M contains four positive integers whose average is 7, what is the largest number that Set M could contain?
   (A) 6
   (B) 7
   (C) 25
   (D) 28

3. An art club of 4 boys and 5 girls makes craft projects. If the boys average 2 projects each and the girls average 3 projects each, what is the total number of projects produced by the club?
   (A) 14
   (B) 23
   (C) 26
   (D) 100

4. If a class of 6 students has an average grade of 72 before a seventh student joins the class, what must the seventh student's grade be in order to raise the class average to 76?
   (A) 100
   (B) 88
   (C) 80
   (D) 76

5. Catherine scores an 84, 85, and 88 on her first three exams. What must she score on her fourth exam to raise her average to an 89?
   (A) 89
   (B) 93
   (C) 97
   (D) 99

PLUGGING IN

The ISEE will often ask you questions about real-life situations where the numbers have been replaced with variables. One of the easiest ways to tackle these questions is with a powerful technique called *plugging in*.

> Mark is two inches taller than John, who is four inches shorter than Evan is. If *e* represents Evan's height in inches, then in terms of *j*, an expression for Mark's height is:
>
> (A) $e + 6$
> (B) $e + 4$
> (C) $e + 2$
> (D) $e - 2$

Take the Algebra Away and Arithmetic is all That's Left

When you plug in for variables, you won't need to write equations and won't have to solve algebra problems. Doing simple arithmetic is always easier than doing algebra.

The problem with this question is that we're not used to thinking of people's heights in terms of variables. Have you ever met someone who was *j* inches tall?

Whenever you see variables used in the question and in the answer choices, just plug in a number to replace the variable.

1. Choose a number for *e*.

2. Using that number, figure out Mark's and John's heights.

3. Put a box around Mark's height, since that's what the question asked you for.

4. Plug your number for *e* into the answer choices and choose the one that represents Mark's height.

Here's how it works:

> Mark is two inches taller than John, who is four inches shorter than Evan. If *e* represents Evan's height in inches, then <u>in terms of *j*</u>, an expression for Mark's height is:
>
> (A) $e + 6$
> (B) $e + 4$
> (C) $e + 2$
> (E) $e - 2$

Ignore this! Because you are plugging in, you don't need to pay any attention to "in terms of" any variable...

For Evan's height, let's pick 60 inches. This means that $e = 60$. Remember, there is no right or wrong number to pick. 50 would work just as well as 100.

But given that Evan is 60 inches tall, now we can figure out that since, John is four inches shorter than Evan, John's height must be $(60 - 4)$ or 56 inches.

The other piece of information we learn from the problem is that Mark is two inches taller than John. If John's height is 56 inches, that means Mark must be 58 inches tall.

So here's what we've got:

Evan 60 inches = e
John 56 inches
Mark 58 inches

Now, the question asks for Mark's height, which is 58 inches. The last step is to go through the answer choices substituting 60 for *e*, and choose the one that equals 58.

(A) $e + 6$ $60 + 6 = 66$ ELIMINATE
(B) $e + 4$ $60 + 4 = 64$ ELIMINATE
(C) $e + 2$ $60 + 2 = 62$ ELIMINATE
(D) $e - 2$ $60 - 2 = 58$ PICK THIS ONE!

This is a very long explanation of all the steps involved when you plug in. Don't be tempted to say, "Plugging in takes too long. I can do the problem just as fast if I write equations for each person's age." Writing equations is a fine way to do algebra in school, but on the ISEE it is a great way to make mistakes. Remember, the people who write these tests expect you to write equations; anytime you can do things differently than the way you are expected, you should.

Practice — Plugging in

1. At a charity fund-raiser, 200 people each donated *x* dollars. In terms of *x*, what was the total number of dollars that was donated?

    (A) $\dfrac{x}{200}$

    (B) $200x$

    (C) $\dfrac{200}{x}$

    (D) $200 + x$

2. If 10 magazines cost *d* dollars, how many magazines can be purchased for 3 dollars?

    (A) $\dfrac{3d}{10}$

    (B) $30d$

    (C) $\dfrac{d}{30}$

    (D) $\dfrac{30}{d}$

3. The zoo has four times as many monkeys as lions. There are four more lions than there are zebras at the zoo. If z represents the number of zebras in the zoo, then in terms of z, how many monkeys are there in the zoo?
(A) $4z$
(B) $z + 4$
(C) $4z + 16$
(D) $4z + 4$

Occasionally you may run into a plugging in question that doesn't contain variables. These questions usually ask about a percentage or a fraction of some unknown number or price. This is the one time that you should plug in, even when you don't see variables in the answer.

Also, be sure you plug in good numbers. Good doesn't mean right, because there's no such thing as a right or wrong number to plug in. A good number is one that makes the problem easier to work with. If a question asks about minutes and hours, try 30 or 60, not 128. Also, whenever you see the word percent, you guessed it: Plug in 100!

4. The price of a suit is reduced by half, and then the resulting price is reduced by 10%. The final price is what percent of the original price?
(A) 45%
(B) 40%
(C) 25%
(D) 10%

5. On Wednesday, Miguel ate one-fourth of a pumpkin pie. On Thursday, he ate one-half of what was left of the pie. What fraction of the entire pie did Miguel eat on Wednesday and Thursday?

(A) $\dfrac{3}{8}$

(B) $\dfrac{1}{2}$

(C) $\dfrac{5}{8}$

(D) $\dfrac{3}{4}$

6. If p pieces of candy costs c cents, 10 pieces of candy will cost

(A) $\dfrac{pc}{10}$ cents

(B) $\dfrac{10c}{p}$ cents

(C) $10pc$ cents

(D) $\dfrac{10p}{c}$ cents

7. If J is an odd integer, which of the following must be true?
   (A) $(J \div 3) > 1$
   (B) $(J - 2)$ is a positive integer.
   (C) $2 \cdot J$ is an even integer.
   (D) $J > 0$

8. If m is an even integer, n is an odd integer, and p is the product of m and n, which of the following is always true?
   (A) p is a fraction.
   (B) p is an odd integer.
   (C) p is divisible by 2.
   (D) p is greater than zero.

GEOMETRY

Guesstimating: A second look

Don't Forget to Guesstimate!

Guesstimating works best on geometry questions. Make sure you use your common sense, combined with P.O.E. to save time and energy.

Guesstimating worked well back in the introduction when we were just using it to estimate or "ballpark" the size of a number, but geometry problems are undoubtedly the best place to guesstimate whenever you can!

Unless a particular question tells you that a figure is not drawn to scale, you can safely assume that the figure *is* drawn to scale.

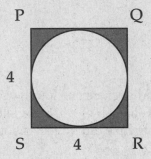

A circle in inscribed in square PQRS.
What is the area of the shaded region?

(A) $16 - 6\pi$
(B) $16 - 4\pi$
(C) $16 - 3\pi$
(D) 16π

Wow, a circle inscribed in a square—that sounds tough!

It isn't. Look at the picture. What fraction of the square looks like it is shaded? Half? Three-quarters? Less than half? In fact, about one-quarter of the area of the square is shaded. You've just done most of the work necessary to solve this problem.

Now, let's do a tiny bit of math. The length of one side of the square is 4, so the area of the square is 4 x 4 or 16. Don't worry if you feel a little lost; in the next few pages, we'll discuss area in much more detail.

So the area of the square is 16 and we said that the shaded region was about one-fourth of the square. One-fourth of 16 is 4, right? So we're looking for an answer choice which equals about (not necessarily exactly) 4. Let's look at the choices:

(A) $16 - 6\pi$
(B) $16 - 4\pi$
(C) $16 - 3\pi$
(D) 16π

This becomes a tiny bit complicated because the answers include π. For the purposes of guesstimating, and in fact for almost any purpose on either the SSAT or the ISEE, you should just remember that π is a little more than 3.

Let's look back at those answers:

(A) $16 - 6\pi$ is roughly equal to $16 - (6 \times 3) = -2$
(B) $16 - 4\pi$ is roughly equal to $16 - (4 \times 3) = 4$
(C) $16 - 3\pi$ is roughly equal to $16 - (3 \times 3) = 7$
(D) 16π is roughly equal to $(16 \times 3) = 48$

Now let's think about what these answers mean.

Answer choice (A) is geometrically impossible. A figure **cannot** have a negative area. Eliminate it.

Answer choice (B) means that the shaded region has an area of about 4. Sounds pretty good.

Answer choice (C) means that the shaded region has an area of about 7. The area of the entire square was 16, so that would mean that the shaded region was almost half the square. Possible, but doubtful.

Finally, answer choice (D) means that the shaded region has an area of about 48. What? The whole square had an area of 16. Is the shaded region three times as big as the square itself? No shot. Eliminate (E).

At this point you are left with only (B), which we feel pretty good about, and (C), which seems a little big. What should you do?

Pick (B) and pat yourself on the back, because you chose the right answer without doing a lot of unnecessary work. Also, remember how useful it was to guesstimate and make sure you do it whenever you see a geometry problem, unless the problem tells you that the figure is not drawn to scale!

PERIMETER

The perimeter is the distance around the outside of any figure. To find the perimeter of a figure, just add up the length of all the sides.

What are the perimeters of these figures?

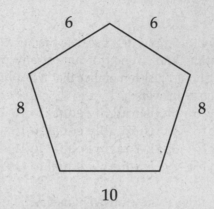

Perimeter = 6 + 6 + 8 + 8 + 10 = 38

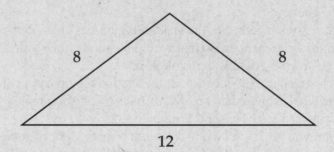

Perimeter = 8 + 8 + 12 = 28

Practice — Perimeter

1. A stop sign has 8 equal sides of length 4. What is its perimeter?
    (A) 4
    (B) 8
    (C) 32
    (D) It cannot be determined from the information given.

2. If the perimeter of a square is 56, what is the length of each side?
    (A) 4
    (B) 7
    (C) 14
    (D) 28

3. The perimeter of a square with a side of length 4 is how much less than the perimeter of a rectangle with sides of length 4 and width 6?
   (A) 2
   (B) 4
   (C) 6
   (D) 8

ANGLES

Straight lines

Angles that form a straight line always total 180°.

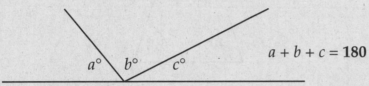

$$a + b + c = 180$$

The Rule of 180

There are 180 degrees in a straight line and in a triangle.

Triangles

All the angles in a triangle add up to 180°.

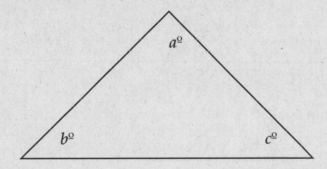

Four-sided figures

The angles in a square, rectangle, or any other four-sided figure always add up to 360°.

$$p + q + r + s = 360$$

The Rule of 360

There are 360 degrees in a four-sided figure and in a circle.

TRIANGLES

Isosceles triangles

Any triangle with two equal sides is an isosceles triangle.

If two sides of a triangle are equal, the angles opposite those sides are always equal.

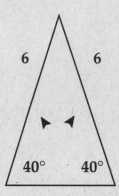

This particular isosceles triangle has two equal sides (of length 6) and therefore two equal angles (40° in this case).

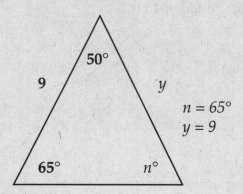

$n = 65°$
$y = 9$

Equilateral triangles

An equilateral triangle is a triangle with 3 equal sides. If all the sides are equal, then all the angles must be equal. Each angle in an equilateral triangle equals 60°.

Right triangles

A right triangle is a triangle with one 90° angle.

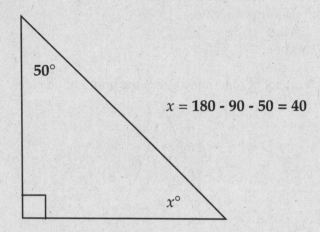

$$x = 180 - 90 - 50 = 40$$

This is a right triangle.

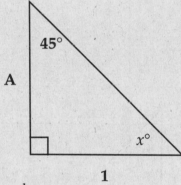

It is also an isosceles triangle.
What does that tell you?

The Pythagorean theorem

For all right triangles, $a^2 + b^2 = c^2$.

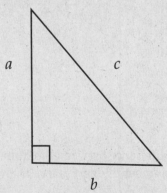

Always remember that c represents the *hypotenuse*, the longest side of the triangle, which is **always** opposite the right angle.

Test your knowledge of triangles with these problems. If the question describes a figure that isn't shown, make sure you draw the figure yourself!

Practice — Triangles

1. What is the perimeter of an equilateral triangle, one side of which measures 4 inches?
   (A) 4 inches
   (B) 8 inches
   (C) 12 inches
   (D) It cannot be determined from the information given.

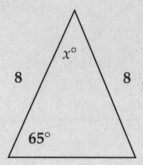

2. $x =$
   (A) 65
   (B) 50
   (C) 30
   (D) 8

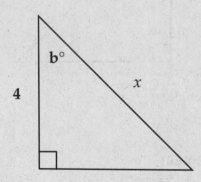

3. If $b = 45$, then $x^2 =$
   (A) 32
   (B) 25
   (C) 16
   (D) 5

4. One-half of the difference between the number of degrees in a square and the number of degrees in a triangle is
   (B) 45
   (C) 90
   (D) 180
   (E) 240

AREA

The area is the amount of space taken up by a two-dimensional figure. An easy way to think about area is as the amount of paper that a figure covers. The larger the area, the more paper the figure takes up.

In order to determine the area of a square or rectangle, multiply the length by the width. Remember the formula: **length x width**.

What is the area of a rectangle with length 9 and width 4?

In this case the length is 9 and the width is 4, so 9 x 4 = 36.

Area of rectangle ABCD = 6 x 8 = 48

To find the area of a triangle, you multiply $\frac{1}{2}$ times the length of the base times the length of the triangle's height, or $\frac{1}{2} b \cdot h$.

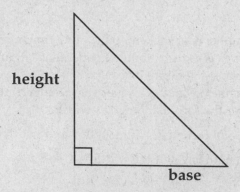

What is the area of a triangle with base 6 and height 3?

(A) 3
(B) 6
(C) 9
(D) 12
(E) 18

Just put the values you are given into the formula and do the math. That's all there is to it!

$$\frac{1}{2}b \bullet h = \text{area}$$

$$(\frac{1}{2})(6) \bullet 3 = \text{area}$$

$$3 \bullet 3 = 9$$

The only tricky point you may run into when finding the area of a triangle is when the triangle is not a right triangle. In this case, it becomes slightly more difficult to find the height, which is easiest to think of as the distance to the point of the triangle from the base. Here's an illustration to help:

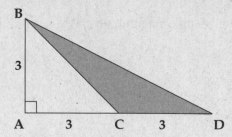

First look at triangle BAC, the unshaded right triangle on the left side. Finding its base and height is simple—they are both 3. So using our formula for

the area of a triangle, we can figure out that the area of triangle BAC is $4\frac{1}{2}$.

Now lets think about triangle BCD, the shaded triangle on the right. It isn't a right triangle, so finding the height will involve a little more thought. Remember the question, though: How far up from the base is the point of triangle BCD?

Think of the shaded triangle sitting on the floor of your room. How far up would its point stick from the ground? Yes, 3! The height of triangle BCD is exactly the same as the height of triangle BAC. Don't worry about drawing lines inside the shaded triangle or anything like that, just figure out how high its point is from the ground.

Okay, so just to finish up, to find the base of triangle BCD (the shaded one) you will use the same area formula, and just plug in 3 for the base and 3 for the height.

$$\frac{1}{2}b \bullet h = \text{area}$$

$$(\frac{1}{2})(3) \bullet 3 = \text{area}$$

And once you do the math, you'll see that the area of triangle BCD is $4\frac{1}{2}$.

Not quite convinced? Let's look at the question a little differently. The base of the entire figure (triangle DAB) is 6 and the height is 3. Using your trusty area formula, you can figure out that the area of triangle DAB is 9. You know the area of the unshaded triangle is $4\frac{1}{2}$, so what's left for the shaded part? You guessed it: $4\frac{1}{2}$.

VOLUME

Volume is very similar to area, except it takes into account a third dimension. To compute the volume of a figure, you simply find the area and multiply by a third dimension.

For instance, to find the volume of a rectangular object, you would multiply the length times the width (a.k.a. the area) by the height (the third dimension). So to find the volume of a quadrilateral, the only kind of figure you are likely to see in a volume question, you just use this formula: **length × width × height**

For example:

What is the volume of a rectangular fish tank with the following specifications:

length: 6 inches
height: 6 inches
width: 10 inches

There isn't much to it, just stick the numbers into the formula.
length x width x height = volume
$6 \times 10 \times 6 = 360$

Practice — Area & volume

1. If the area of a square is equal to its perimeter, what is the length of one side?
   (A) 8
   (B) 4
   (C) 2
   (D) 1

2. The area of a rectangle with width 4 and length 3 is equal to the area of a triangle with a base of 6 and a height of
   (A) 2
   (B) 3
   (C) 4
   (D) 12

3. Two cardboard boxes have equal volume. The dimensions of one box are 3 x 4 x 10. If the length of the other box is 6 and the width is 4, what is the height of the second box?
   (A) 2
   (B) 5
   (C) 10
   (D) 24

4. If the area of a square is $64p^2$, what is the length of one side of the square?
   (A) $64p^2$
   (B) $8p^2$
   (C) $64p$
   (D) $8p$

CHARTS & GRAPHS

Charts

Chart questions are simple, but you must be careful. Follow these three steps and you'll be well on the way to mastering any chart question.

Don't be in too Big a Hurry

When working with charts and graphs, make sure that you take a moment to look at the chart or graph, figure out what it tells you, and then go to the questions.

1. Read any text that accompanies the chart. It is important to know what the chart is showing and what scale the numbers are on.

2. Read the question.

3. Refer to the chart and find the specific information you need.

If there is more than one question about a single chart, the later questions will tend to be more difficult than the earlier ones. Be careful!

Here is a sample chart:

Club membership by state, 1995 and 1996

STATE	1995	1996
California	300	500
Florida	225	250
Illinois	200	180
Massachusetts	150	300
Michigan	150	200
New Jersey	200	250
New York	400	600
Texas	50	100

There are lots of different questions that you can answer based on the information in this chart. For instance:

> What is the difference between the number of members who came from New York in 1995 and the number of members who came from Illinois is 1996?

This question asks you to look up two simple pieces of information and then do a tiny bit of math.

First, the number of members who came from New York in 1995 was 400.

Second, the number of members who came from Illinois in 1996 was 180.

Finally, look back at the question. It asks you to find the difference between these numbers. 400 − 180 = 120. Done.

> What was the percent increase in members from New Jersey from 1995 to 1996?

You should definitely know how to do this one! Do you remember how to translate percentage questions? If not, go back to the algebra chapter!

In 1995 there were 200 club members from New Jersey. In 1996 there were 250 members from New Jersey. That represents an increase of 50 members. So to determine the percent increase, you will need to ask yourself "50 (the increase) is what percent of 200 (the original amount)?"

Translated, this becomes: $50 = \dfrac{g}{100} \times 200$

With a little bit of simple manipulation, this equation becomes: $50 = 2g$

. . . and . . .

$25 = g$

So from 1995 to 1996, there was a 25 percent increase in the number of members from New Jersey. Good work!

> Which state had as many club members in 1996 as a combination of Illinois, Massachusetts, and Michigan had in 1995?

First, take a second to look up the number of members who came from Illinois, Massachusetts, and Michigan in 1995 and add them together.

$$200 + 150 + 150 = 500$$

Which state had 500 members in 1996? California. That's all there is to it!

GRAPHS

Some questions will ask you to interpret a graph. You should be familiar with both pie and bar charts. These graphs are generally drawn to scale (meaning that the graphs give an accurate visual impression of the information), so you can always guess based on the figure if you need to.

The way to approach a graph question is exactly the same as the way to approach a chart question. Follow the same three steps:

1. Read any text that accompanies the graph. It is important to know what the graph is showing and what scale the numbers are on.

2. Read the question.

3. Refer to the graph and find the specific information you need.

This is how it works:

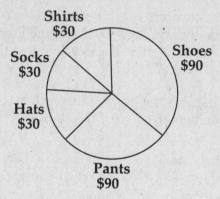

The graph in Figure 1 shows Emily's clothing expenditures for the month of October. On which type of clothing did she spend the most money?

(A) shoes
(B) shirts
(C) socks
(D) hats

This one is easy. You can look at the pieces of the pie and identify the largest, or you can look at the amounts shown in the graph and choose the largest one. Either way, the answer is (A), since Emily spent more money on shoes than on any other clothing items in October.

> Emily spent half of her clothing money on which two items?
>
> (A) shoes and pants
> (B) shoes and shirts
> (C) hats and socks
> (D) socks and shirts

Again, you can find the answer to this question two different ways. You can look for which two items together make up half the chart, or you can add up the total amount of money Emily spent, (which is $240,) and then figure out which two items made up half (or $120) of that amount. Either way is just fine, and either way the right answer is (B): shoes and shirts.

Practice — Chart and graph problems

Questions 1–2 refer to the following summary of energy costs by district.

DISTRICT	1990	1991
A	400	600
B	500	700
C	200	350
D	100	150
E	600	800

(ALL NUMBERS ARE IN THOUSANDS OF DOLLARS)

1. In 1991, which district spent twice as much on energy as district A spent in 1990?
   (A) B
   (B) C
   (C) D
   (D) E

2. Which district spent the most on electricity in 1990 and 1991 combined?
   (A) A
   (B) B
   (C) D
   (D) E

3. The total increase in energy expenditure in these districts, from 1990 to 1991, is how many dollars?

(A) $800,000
(B) $2,600
(C) $2,400
(D) $800

Questions 4–5 refer to Figure 2, which shows the number of compact discs owned by five students.

Figure 2

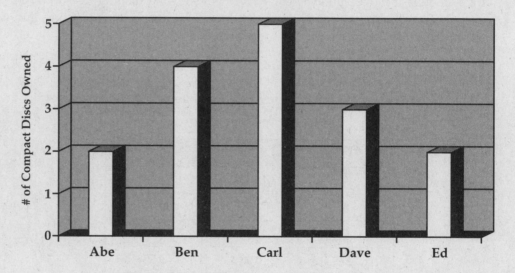

4. Carl owns as many CDs as which two other students combined?

(A) Abe and Dave
(B) Ben and Dave
(C) Abe and Ed
(D) Ben and Ed

5. Which one student owns one-fourth of the CDs accounted for in Figure 2?

(A) Abe
(B) Ben
(C) Dave
(D) Ed

Questions 6–8 refer to Matt's weekly time card, shown below.

DAY	IN	OUT	HOURS WORKED
Monday	2:00 pm	5:30 pm	3.5
Tuesday			
Wednesday	2:00 pm	6:00 pm	4
Thursday	2:00 pm	5:30 pm	3.5
Friday	2:00 pm	5:00 pm	3
Saturday			
Sunday			

6. If Matt's hourly salary is $6, what were his earnings for the week?
   (A) $84
   (B) $54
   (C) $14
   (D) $6

7. What is the average number of hours Matt worked on the days he worked during this particular week?
   (A) 3.5
   (B) 4
   (C) 7
   (D) 14

8. The hours that Matt worked on Monday accounted for what percent of the total number of hours he worked during this week?
   (A) 3.5
   (B) 20
   (C) 25
   (D) 35

QUANTITATIVE COMPARISON

QUANT COMP: SAME BOOK, DIFFERENT COVER

Quantitative comparison is a type of question—one slightly different from the traditional multiple-choice items you've seen so far—that tests exactly the same math concepts you have learned so far in this book. There is no new math for you to learn here, just a different mode of operation to answer this different type of question.

You will see a total of 20 quant comp questions in one of your ISEE math sections.

THE RULES OF THE GAME

To answer a quant comp question, your goal is very simple: Determine which column is larger and choose the appropriate answer choice. There are four possible answers:

(A) means that Column A is always greater.

(B) means that Column B is always greater.

(C) means that Column A is always equal to Column B.

(D) means that there is not enough information to determine a relationship between the columns that is always true.

So that you can use the Process of Elimination in quant comp, where there are no answer choices written out for you, we suggest that you write "A B C D" next to each question. Then when you eliminate an answer, you can cross it off.

DON'T DO TOO MUCH WORK

Quant comp is a strange, new question type for most students. Don't let it intimidate you, though. Always keep your goal in mind: to figure out which column is bigger. Do you care how much bigger one column is? We hope not.

Here's a good example:

Column A	Column B
2 x 4 x 6 x 8	3 x 5 x 7 x 9

Test-takers who don't appreciate the beauty of quant comp look at this one and immediately start multiplying. Look carefully, though, and compare the numbers in both columns.

Which is bigger–2 or 3?
Which is bigger–4 or 5?
Which is bigger–6 or 7?
Which is bigger–8 or 9?

They Look Different, but the Math is the Same

This final section will introduce you to quantitative comparison, a different type of question than the "regular" multiple-choice questions you've seen so far. Don't worry, though, these questions test your knowledge of exactly the same math skills you have already learned in this chapter.

In each case, column B contains bigger numbers. Now, when you multiply bigger numbers together, what happens? You guessed it—even bigger numbers!

Which column is bigger? Without doing a single bit of multiplication you know that (B) is the right answer. Good work!

(D) Means Different

Answer choice (D) is useful when the relationship between the columns can change. The most obvious time you will choose (D) is when you have variables in a quant comp problem. For example:

Column A	Column B
$g + 12$	$h - 7$

Which column is bigger here depends entirely on what g and h equal, and the problem doesn't give you that detail. This is a perfect time to choose (D).

Be careful, though, and don't be too quick to choose (D) whenever you see a variable.

Column A	Column B
$g + 12$	$g - 7$

With one small change, the answer is no longer (D). Since the variables are the same here, you can determine that no matter what number is represented by g, column A is bigger. So in this case the answer is (A).

One valuable thing to remember is that when a quant comp question contains no variables and no unknown quantities, the answer cannot be (D).

Column A	Column B
$6 \times 3 \times 4$	$4 \times 6 \times 3$

Even if you somehow forget how to multiply (don't worry, you won't forget), someone somewhere knows how to multiply, so you can get rid of (D).

By the way, look quickly at that last example. First you eliminate (D) because there are no variables. Do you need to multiply? Nope! The columns contain exactly the same numbers, just written in a different order. What's the answer? You got it: (C)!

Practice — Quant comp

	Column A	Column B
1.	17×3	$17 \times 2 + 17$

	Column A	Column B
2.	$\dfrac{1}{2}$	$\dfrac{3}{8}$

	Column A	Column B
3.	$b + 80$	$b + 82$

Rob is two inches shorter than Matt.
Joel is four inches taller than Matt.

	Column A	Column B
4.	Rob's height	Joel's height

	Column A	Column B
5.	16^3	4^6

Kimberly lives two miles from school.
Jennifer lives four miles from school.

	Column A	Column B
6.	The distance from Kimberly's house to school	The distance from Kimberly's house to Jennifer's house

Quant Comp Plugging In

Think back to the algebra section. Plugging in helped you deal with variables, right? The same technique works on quant comp questions. There are some special rules you'll need to follow, though, to make sure that you can reap all the benefits that plugging in has to offer you in the quant comp section.

<u>Column A</u>	<u>Column B</u>
x	x^2

Follow these three simple steps and you won't go wrong:

STEP 1: Write "A B C D" next to the problem.

STEP 2: Plug in an "easy" number for x. By easy number, we mean a nice simple integer, like 3. When you plug in 3 for x in the above example, column A is 3 and column B is 9, right? Think about the answer choices and what they mean. Column B is bigger, so can the correct answer be (A)? No, eliminate it. Can the correct answer be (C)? No, you can get rid of that one, too!

STEP 3: Plug in a "weird" number for x. A weird number is a little harder to define, but it is something that the most test-takers won't think of—for instance, zero, one, a fraction, or a negative number. In this case, try plugging in 1. Column A is 1 and column B is also 1. Now look at the answer choices you have left. Answer choice (B) means that column B is always greater. Is it? No. Cross off (B) and pick (D).

The thing to remember is that if you can come up with some cases where one answer seems correct and other cases where a different answer seems correct, you have to pick (D). Don't think too much about these questions, or you'll end up spending a lifetime looking for the perfect "weird" number. Just remember that you always have to plug in **twice** on Quant Comp questions.

Here's some practice to bring it all together for you:

Practice — Quant comp plugging in

	Column A	**Column B**

$$x < 1$$

1. x $\qquad\qquad\qquad$ x^2

Do you see the difference between this example and the one we did together? Since you know that x is less than 1, most of the "weird" numbers are eliminated.

---

b is an integer and $-1 < b < 1$

2. $\dfrac{b}{2}$ $\qquad\qquad\qquad$ $\dfrac{b}{8}$

---

3. p gallons $\qquad\qquad\qquad$ m quarts

---

x is a positive integer

4. $\dfrac{x}{4}$ $\qquad\qquad\qquad$ $\dfrac{x}{5}$

---

w is an integer less than 4.
p is an integer greater than 10.

5. $p \times w$ $\qquad\qquad\qquad$ w

---

6. $4c + 6$ $\qquad\qquad\qquad$ $3c + 12$

MATH REVIEW

Make sure you can confidently answer all of the following questions before you take the ISEE.

1. Is zero an integer? _____

2. Is zero positive or negative? _____

3. What operation do you perform to find a sum? _____

4. What operation do you perform to find a product? _____

5. What is the result called when you divide? _____

6. Is 312 divisible by 3? _____
   Is 312 divisible by 9? _____

   (Actually dividing isn't fair—use your divisibility rules!)

7. What does the "E" in PEMDAS stand for? _____

8. Is 3 a factor of 12? _____
   Is 12 a factor of 3? _____

9. Is 3 a multiple of 12? _____
   Is 12 a multiple of 3? _____

10. What is the tens digit in the number 304.275? _____

11. What is the tenths digit in the number 304.275? _____

12. $2^3 =$ _____

13. In "math language" the word "percent" means: _____

14. In "math language" the word "of" means: _____

15. In a ratio box, the last column on the right is always the _____.

16. Whenever you see a problem involving averages, draw the _____.

17. When a problem contains variables in the question and in the answers, I will _____.

18. To find the perimeter of a square, I _____ the length(s) of _____ side(s).

19. To find the area of a square, I _____ the length(s) of _____ sides.

20. There are _____ degrees in a straight line.

21. A triangle has _____ angles, which total _____ degrees.

22. A four-sided figure contains _____ degrees.

23. An isosceles triangle has _____ equal sides; a(n) _____ triangle has three equal sides.

24. The longest side of a right triangle is called the _____ and is located opposite the _____.

25. To find the area of a triangle, I use the formula: _____.

13

ISEE Verbal

THE VERBAL SECTION

Take a look at the verbal section of one of the practice ISEEs in this book. The verbal section on the ISEE consists of 40 questions, usually broken into:

- 20 synonym questions (questions 1–20)
- 20 sentence completion questions (questions 21–40)

That's 40 questions—but you only have 20 minutes! Should you try to spend 30 seconds on each question to get them all done? **No!**

You Mean I Don't Have To Do All The Questions?

Nope. You'll actually improve your score by answering fewer questions, as long as you're still using all of the allotted time.

Remember, this test is designed for students in three or four different grade levels. There will be vocabulary on some of these questions that is aimed at students older than you, and almost no one in your grade will get those questions right. The ISEE score you receive will compare you only to students in your own grade. The younger you are in your test level, the fewer questions you are expected to complete. Thus, fifth-graders and eighth-graders are expected to complete the fewest questions on the Middle Level and Upper Level Tests, respectively.

So why rush through the questions you can get right to get to the really tough ones that almost nobody gets? That approach only ensures that you will make hasty, careless errors. Work slowly on the questions that have vocabulary that you know, to make sure you get them right. Then try the ones that have some harder words in them.

If you pace yourself, you'll have much more time for each question than the student who thinks she has to get them all done.

Which Questions Should I Do?

Everybody's different. You know some words that your friends don't, and vice versa. What makes some verbal questions difficult is that you don't know the dictionary definitions of the words involved.

Do all the synonyms that are easy for you first. Then go back through and do the ones with words you "sorta" know. Then move on to sentence completions, leaving yourself more than half the time in the section.

Remember to skip a number on the answer sheet when you skip a question, and when there is just a minute or two remaining in the section, fill in an answer for any questions you didn't get to.

Knowing your own vocabulary is the key to deciding quickly if you can answer a question easily.

"Allotted time"?

If you can't define "allotted," make an index card for it! Look in the Vocabulary chapter for ideas on how to use index cards to learn new words.

Slow and Steady

Working slowly and getting questions right is how you score well. If you haven't already, look at chapter 3 to figure out how many questions you really need to complete.

Guess?

Yes. Fill in an answer even for the questions you don't read. Why? Because there is no penalty for a wrong answer, so you've got nothing to lose (and plenty to gain when you happen to be right!).

Know Yourself

Categorize the words you see in SSAT questions into:

- words you know
- words you "sorta" know
- words you really don't know

Be honest with yourself when it comes to deciding if you know a word or not, so you can tell which of the techniques you will learn is the best to use with the question in front of you. Keep your idea of the word's meaning flexible, because the test writers sometimes use the words in ways that you and I do not! (They claim to use dictionary definitions.)

Of course, the easiest way to get a verbal question right is by making sure all the words in it fall into the first category—words you know. The best way to do this is by learning new vocabulary **every day**. Check out the Vocabulary chapter (chapter 1) for the best ways to do this.

You can raise your verbal score moderately with the verbal techniques alone. If you want to see a substantial rise, you need to build up your vocabulary, too.

The Process of Elimination

P.O.E. is the key to getting verbal questions right. With math questions, there's always a "correct" answer. The other answers are simply wrong. In a Verbal question, however, things are not that simple. Words are a lot more slippery than numbers are. So verbal questions have "best" answers, not "correct" answers. The other answers aren't necessarily wrong, but the SSAT thinks they're not as good as the "best" one. This means that even more than on the quantitative sections, in the verbal and reading sections you're constantly trying to eliminate.

Get used to looking for "worse" answers. There are a lot more of them than there are "best" answers, so "worse" answers are easier to find!

When you find them, cross them out in the question booklet, to make sure you don't spend any more time looking at them. No matter which other techniques you use to answer a question, you're always eliminating wrong answers, instead of trying to magically pick out the best answer.

One thing to remember for the verbal section: You cannot eliminate answer choices that contain words you don't know. It doesn't matter that *you* don't know what a word means—it could still be the answer.

What If I Can't Narrow It Down To One Answer?

Should you guess? Yes. Even if you can't eliminate any choices, you should guess. We mentioned before that you should leave a minute or two at the end of the section to fill in an answer for any questions you did not get to. Why? **Because there's no guessing penalty on the ISEE**. Nothing is subtracted from your score for a wrong answer, and since there are four answer choices, you'll get approximately 25 percent correct of the questions on which you guess randomly.

P.O.E. and You

Process of Elimination is your best friend on this test. Even when none of the answers looks particularly right, you can usually eliminate at least one.

Shop Around

Try every answer choice in a verbal question to be sure you're picking the *best* answer there.

Don't Rule It Out

Don't eliminate answers with words you don't know.

That means that you should **never** leave a question blank. Pick a letter (A, B, C, or D) to fill in for your random guesses. It doesn't matter which letter you use, but stick with one "letter-of-the-day" so you don't have to think about it.

Of course, the number of questions you get right will increase if you can eliminate some answer choices before you guess, so we'll teach you techniques to do this.

WHERE DO I START?

Do synonyms first in the verbal section, right where you find them. Get them done in less than 10 minutes, so you have a little more than half the time in the section for sentence completions. Sentence completions take longer to read and work through, but they have more context to help you get the question right, even if you don't know all the words involved.

You'll be doing the questions in this order:

◆ Synonyms with words you know

◆ Synonyms with words you "sorta" know

◆ Sentence completions

◆ Fill in the letter-of-the-day for unanswered questions

Bubble Practice

Whenever you do a practice test, use the sample answer sheet so you get used to skipping around and making sure that you're always on the same number on the test booklet and answer sheet.

THE VERBAL PLAN

PACING AND VERBAL STRATEGY

What's the order in which I do questions in the verbal section?

1. _____

2. _____

3. _____

When I have 2 minutes left, what do I do? _____

How long should I spend on synonyms? _____

What's the technique I'll be using all the time, regardless of whatever else I'm using to answer a question?_____

How many answer choices must I have eliminated in order to guess productively? _____

Can I eliminate answer choices that contain words I don't know?
_____

If you had trouble with any of these questions, just review this short chapter before moving on.

KNOWING MY VOCABULARY

Look at each of the following words and decide if it's a word that you know, "sorta" know, or really don't know. If you know it, write down its definition.

insecticide (noun) _____

trifle (verb) _____

repugnant (adjective) _____

mollify (verb) _____

camouflage (verb) _____

historic (adjective) _____

Check the ones you thought you knew or "sorta" knew, and make index cards for the ones you didn't know.

SYNONYMS

WHAT IS A SYNONYM?

Be Honest

Do you really know the definition of the word? The SSAT uses dictionary definitions, and these may differ from your own sometimes. If you're not positive, you may want to use the techniques for when you 'sorta' know the word.

On the ISEE, a synonym question asks you to choose the answer choice that comes closest in meaning to the stem word (the word in capital letters). Often the best answer won't mean the exact same thing as the stem word, but it will be closer than any of the other choices.

You need to decide which vocabulary category the synonym stem word falls into for you, so you know which technique to use. Do all the synonyms for which you know the stem word first, and then go back and do the ones you "sorta" know.

WHEN YOU KNOW THE STEM WORD

Write down your own definition

Come up with a simple definition—a word or a phrase. Write it next to the stem word. Then look at the answers, eliminate the ones that are farthest from your definition, and choose the closest one.

It's very simple. Don't let the test writers put words in your mouth. Make sure you're armed with your own definition before you look at their answer choices. They often like to put in a word that is a close second to the "best" answer; if you've got your own synonym ready, you'll be able to make the distinction.

Don't Waste Time

Make sure you cross out answers you've eliminated, so you don't look at them again.

If you need to, cover the answers with your hand, so you can think of your definition before looking. Eventually you may not have to write down your definitions, but you should start out that way.

As you compare the choices to your definition, cross out the ones that are definitely not right with your pencil. Crossing out answer choices is something you should *always* do—it saves you time, because you don't go back to choices you've already decided were not the "best."

As always, don't eliminate words you don't know.

Try this one:

> WITHER: _____ (definition)
> (A) play
> (B) spoil
> (C) greatly improve
> (D) wilt

The stem word means "shrivel" or "dry up." Which answer is closest? (D). You may have been considering (B), but (D) is closer.

Practice — Write your own definition

Just write your definition—a word or two—for each of these stem words.

1. BIZARRE: _____

2. PREFACE: _____

3. GENEROUS: _____

4. MORAL: _____

5. ALTER: _____

6. REVOLVE: _____

7. HOPEFUL: _____

8. LINGER: _____

9. ASSIST: _____

10. CONSTRUCT: _____

11. STOOP: _____

12. CANDID: _____

13. TAUNT: _____

14. COARSE: _____

15. VAIN : _____

16. SERENE: _____

17. UTILIZE: _____

18. VIGOROUS: _____

19. PROLONG: _____

20. BENEFIT: _____

Write another definition

Why would you ever need to change your definition? Let's see:

MANEUVER:
(A) avoidance
(B) deviation
(C) find
(D) contrivance

Parts of Speech?

If you need to, go back and review parts of speech in the 'Word Parts' section of chapter 1.

Your definition might be something like "move" or "control," if you know the word from hearing it applied to cars. You're thinking about "maneuver" as a verb, and that definition isn't in the answer choices. "Maneuver" can also be a noun. It means "a plan, scheme, or trick." Now go back and eliminate. It's (D).

The ISEE sometimes uses secondary definitions, which can be the same part of speech or a different part of speech from the primary definition. Just stay flexible in your definitions, and you'll be fine.

Practice — Write another definition

Write down as many definitions as you can think of for the following words. Your definitions may be the same part of speech or different. If you have a hard time thinking of different meanings, look the word up.

1. POINT: _____   _____

2. INDUSTRY: _____   _____

3. FLAG: _____   _____

4. FLUID: _____   _____

5. CHAMPION: _____   _____

6. TABLE: _____   _____

7. SERVICE: _____   _____

Practice — Easy synonym techniques

Try these synonyms.

◆ Use the definition for the stem word that you wrote down before.

◆ Look at the answer choices and eliminate the ones that are farthest from your definition.

◆ If there are stem words you don't know well enough to define, just skip them and come back after you've learned techniques for stem words you "sorta" know.

1. BIZARRE:
(A) lonely
(B) unable
(C) odd
(D) found

2. PREFACE:
   (A introduce
   (B) state
   (C) propose
   (D) jumble

3. GENEROUS:
   (A) skimpy
   (B) faulty
   (C) ample
   (D) unusual

4. MORAL:
   (A) imitation
   (B) full
   (C) genuine
   (D) upright

5. ALTER:
   (A) sew
   (B) make up
   (C) react
   (D) change

6. REVOLVE:
   (A) push against
   (B) go forward
   (C) leave behind
   (D) turn around

7. HOPEFUL:
   (A) discouraging
   (B) promising
   (C) fulfilling
   (D) deceiving

8. LINGER:
   (A) hurry
   (B) abate
   (C) dawdle
   (D) attempt

9. ASSIST:
   (A) work
   (B) discourage
   (C) hinder
   (D) help

10. CONSTRUCT:
   (A) build
   (B) type
   (C) live in
   (D) engage

11. STOOP:
   (A) raise
   (B) elevate
   (C) condescend
   (D) realize

12. CANDID:
   (A) picture
   (B) honest
   (C) prepared
   (D) unfocused

13. TAUNT:
   (A) delay
   (B) stand
   (C) show
   (D) tease

14. COARSE:
   (A) smooth
   (B) crude
   (C) polite
   (D) furious

15. VAIN:
   (A) conceited
   (B) beautiful
   (C) talented
   (D) helpless

16. SERENE:
   (A) helpful
   (B) normal
   (C) calm
   (D) disastrous

17. UTILIZE:
   (A) pass on
   (B) resort to
   (C) rely on
   (D) make use of

18. VIGOROUS:
    (A) slothful
    (B) aimless
    (C) energetic
    (D) glorious

19. PROLONG:
    (A) delay
    (B) lengthen
    (C) exceed
    (D) assert

20. BENEFIT:
    (A) cooperate
    (B) struggle
    (C) assist
    (D) appeal

WHEN YOU "SORTA" KNOW THE STEM WORD

Why should you do synonyms quickly? Why are they harder than sentence completions, even though they're faster?

Synonyms are harder to beat than sentence completions because the ISEE gives you no context with which to figure out words that you "sorta" know. But that doesn't mean you're done after the easy synonyms. You can get the medium ones, too. You just need to create your own context to figure out words you don't know very well.

Also, keep in mind that your goal is to eliminate the worst answers, in order to make an educated guess. You'll be able to do this for every synonym that you "sorta" know, and even if you eliminate just one choice, you've increased your chances of guessing correctly. You'll gain points, overall.

Make your own context

You can create your own context for the word by figuring out how you've heard it used before. Think of the other words you've heard used with the stem word. Is there a certain phrase that comes to mind? What does that phrase mean?

If you still can't come up with a definition for the stem word, just use the context in which you've heard the word to eliminate answers that wouldn't fit at all in that same context.

How about this stem word:

    ABOMINABLE:

Where have you heard "abominable"? The Abominable Snowman, of course. Think about it—you know it's a monster-like creature. Which answer choices can you eliminate?

ABOMINABLE:
(A) terrifying   *the terrifying snowman? maybe*
(B) detestable   *the detestable snowman? sure*
(Ø) rude   *the rude snowman? probably not*
(Ø) talkative   *the talkative snowman? no way*

You can throw out everything but (A) and (B). You can guess, with a much better shot at getting the answer right than guessing from four choices. Or you can think about where else you've heard the stem word. Have you ever heard something called an "abomination"? Was it something that terrified people or was it something people hated? (B) is the answer.

Try this one. Where have you heard this stem word? Try the answers in that context.

SURROGATE:

(A) requested
(B) paranoid
(C) numerous
(D) substitute

Have you heard the stem word in "surrogate mother"? If you have, you can definitely eliminate (A), (B), and (C). A surrogate mother is a substitute mother.

Try one more:

ENDANGER:

(A) rescue
(B) frighten
(C) confuse
(D) threaten

Everyone's associations are different, but you've probably heard of "endangered species" or "endangered lives." Use either of those phrases to eliminate answer choices that can't fit into it. Rescued species? Frightened species? Confused species? Threatened species? (D) works best.

Practice—Making your own context

Write down the phrase in which you've heard each word.

1. COMMON   _____
2. COMPETENT   _____
3. ABRIDGE   _____
4. UNTIMELY   _____
5. HOMOGENIZE   _____
6. DELINQUENT   _____
7. INALIENABLE   _____
8. PALTRY   _____

9. AUSPICIOUS _____

10. PRODIGAL _____

Practice — Using your own context

1. COMMON:
   (A) beautiful
   (B) novel
   (C) typical
   (D) constant

2. COMPETENT:
   (A) angry
   (B) peaceful
   (C) well-written
   (D) capable

3. ABRIDGE:
   (A) complete
   (B) span
   (C) reach
   (D) shorten

4. UNTIMELY:
   (A) late
   (B) punctual
   (C) inappropriate
   (D) continuous

5. HOMOGENIZE:
   (A) group together
   (B) send
   (C) isolate
   (D) enfold

6. DELINQUENT:
   (A) underage
   (B) negligent
   (C) superior
   (D) advanced

7. INALIENABLE:
   (A) misplaced
   (B) universal
   (C) assured
   (D) democratic

8. PALTRY:
   (A) meager
   (B) colored
   (C) thick
   (D) abundant

9. AUSPICIOUS:
   (A) supple
   (B) minor
   (C) favorable
   (D) ominous

10. PRODIGAL:
    (A) wasteful
    (B) amusing
    (C) disadvantaged
    (D) lazy

Use word parts to piece together a definition

Prefixes, roots, and suffixes can help you figure out what a word means. You should use this technique in addition to word association, since not all word parts retain their original meanings.

You may have never seen this stem word before, but if you've been working on your Vocabulary chapter, you know that the root "pac" or "peac" means peace. You can see the same root in "Pacific," "pacifier," and the word "peace" itself. So what's the answer to this synonym?

PACIFIST:

(A) innocent person
(B) person opposed to war
(C) warmonger
(D) wanderer

It's (B). In the following stem word, we see "cred," a word part that means "belief" or "faith." You can see this word part in "incredible," "credit," and "credibility." The answer is now simple.

CREDIBLE:

(A) obsolete
(B) believable
(C) fabulous
(D) mundane

(B) again. What are the word parts in the following stem word?

MONOTONOUS:

(A) lively
(B) educational
(C) nutritious
(D) repetitious

"Mono" means "one." "Tone" has to do with sound. If something keeps striking one sound, how would you describe it? (D) is the answer.

The only way you'll be able to use word parts is if you know them. Get cracking on the Vocabulary chapter!

Use "positive/negative"

Another way to use what you "sorta" know about a stem word is to ask yourself whether it is positive or negative. Then decide if each of the answer choices is positive or negative. Eliminate any answers that do not match. If the stem word is positive, then the answer must be positive. If the stem word is negative, then so must be the answer. Write "+" or "−" or "neither" next to each word as you make your decisions.

If someone said you were belligerent, would you be complimented? No, because "belligerent" is a negative word. You might know that from hearing the word, but you might also know what the word part "bell" means. Now decide whether each answer choice is positive or negative:

BELLIGERENT: −

(A) frisky   +
(B) friendly   +
(C) antagonistic   −
(D) persuasive   +

You can eliminate (A), (B), and (D), because you're looking for a synonym, so if the stem is negative, then the answer must also be negative.

Try this one:

ZENITH:

(A) distance
(B) failure
(C) high point
(D) complaint

How do you know "zenith" is positive? Probably because it's the brand name of a television set, and brand names will generally be positive words. The only really positive answer choice here is (C), and that's the answer.

Practice — Decide positive/negative

1. LUGUBRIOUS   ___   6. HARMONIC: ___

2. DISDAIN: ___   7. INCORRIGIBLE: ___

3. CACOPHONOUS: ___   8. ELOQUENT: ___

4. COMPASSIONATE: ___   9. AGILE: ___

5. SLANDER: ___   10. TOIL: ___

Practice — Use positive/negative

In these synonyms, you know only that the stem word is positive or negative. Eliminate as many answers as you can, based on what you know.

1. GOOD WORD: (A) harmful (B) helpful (C) unusual (D) horrid

2. GOOD WORD: (A) useful (B) handy (C) difficult (D) regular

3. BAD WORD: (A) disgusting (B) reliable (C) furious (D) sturdy

4. BAD WORD: (A) beneficial (B) placid (C) coarse (D) noisy

5. BAD WORD: (A) faulty (B) vague (C) grateful (D) angry

6. GOOD WORD: (A) malignant (B) unhealthy (C) friendly (D) forward thinking

7. GOOD WORD: (A) incapable (B) useful (C) ferocious (D) flavorful

8. BAD WORD: (A) assistant (B) culprit (C) patron (D) rival

9. GOOD WORD: (A) diverse (B) winning (C) ruined (D) infrequent

10. GOOD WORD: (A) honorable (B) despicable (C) elite (D) unsurpassed

11. BAD WORD: (A) dangerous (B) illegal (C) sophisticated (D) delicious

12. BAD WORD: (A) rascal (B) vermin (C) benefactor (D) addict

13. GOOD WORD: (A) slovenly (B) gluttonous (C) envious (D) beatific

14. GOOD WORD: (A) visionary (B) despot (C) malefactor (D) ingrate

15. GOOD WORD: (A) significant (B) mediocre (C) provincial (D) opulent

16. BAD WORD: (A) apathetic (B) assertive (C) committed (D) insipid

17. BAD WORD: (A) banal (B) unrealistic (C) vague (D) decisive

18. BAD WORD: (A) tyrant (B) rebel (C) leader (D) participant

19. GOOD WORD: (A) quack (B) expert (C) narrator (D) reporter

20. GOOD WORD: (A) turmoil (B) amity (C) benign (D) virulent

WORDS YOU REALLY DON'T KNOW

Don't spend time on a synonym with a stem word you've never seen, if you don't know any of its word parts. Simply make sure that you fill your letter-of-the-day in for that question.

THE SYNONYMS PLAN

Words I know

When I know the stem word, I _____

If I don't see a definition close to mine, I _____

Words I "sorta" know

When I "sorta" know the stem word, I can use the following techniques:

_____

_____

_____

Words I really don't know

If I've never seen the stem word before, I _____

Can I eliminate answers that contain words I don't know? _____ _____

　　If you have trouble with any of these questions, review this chapter before you move on.

Practice — All synonyms techniques

1. PRINCIPLE:
   (A) leader
   (B) standard
   (C) theory
   (D) chief

2. CAPTURE:
   (A) secure
   (B) lose
   (C) steal
   (D) halt

3. BEFRIEND:
   (A) sever ties
   (B) close down
   (C) approach
   (D) enjoy

4. AUTOMATIC:
   (A) involuntary
   (B) enjoyable
   (C) forceful
   (D) hapless

5. APTITUDE:
   (A) difficulty
   (B) reason
   (C) mistake
   (D) ability

6. CAPITAL:
   (A) primary
   (B) regressive
   (C) capable
   (D) central

7. REPRESS:
   (A) defy
   (B) faithful
   (C) ruling
   (D) prevent

8. ENDURE:
   (A) take in
   (B) stick with
   (C) add to
   (D) run from

9. TRANSMIT:
   (A) eliminate
   (B) watch
   (C) send
   (D) annoy

10. DIALOGUE:
    (A) speech
    (B) conversation
    (C) monologue
    (D) sermon

11. EULOGY:
    (A) attack
    (B) tribute
    (C) complement
    (D) encouragement

12. BAN:
    (A) remove
    (B) impose
    (C) forbid
    (D) specify

13. APATHY:
    (A) involvement
    (B) compassion
    (C) contempt
    (D) indifference

14. OMNISCIENT:
    (A) agile
    (B) logical
    (C) knowledgeable
    (D) invulnerable

15. TRANSGRESS:
    (A) offend
    (B) eradicate
    (C) include
    (D) violate

16. VIVACIOUS:
    (A) nimble
    (B) lively
    (C) easily amused
    (D) direct

17. HYPERBOLE:
    (A) isolation
    (B) identification
    (C) exaggeration
    (D) sharp curve

18. CONGENITAL:
    (A) innocent
    (B) inborn
    (C) graceful
    (D) acquired

19. SUCCINCT:
    (A) subterranean
    (B) confusing
    (C) blatant
    (D) direct

20. CRAFTY:
    (A) apt
    (B) sly
    (C) agile
    (D) wicked

21. FLUENT:
    (A) spoken
    (B) quiet
    (C) flowing
    (D) fast

22. IDENTICAL:
    (A) broken
    (B) duplicate
    (C) foolish
    (D) related

23. POPULAR:
    (A) rude
    (B) accepted
    (C) understood
    (D) respected

24. WHARF:
    (A) beach
    (B) raft
    (C) flat ship
    (D) dock

25. FAITHFUL:
    (A) hopeful
    (B) unrealistic
    (C) truthful
    (D) devoted

26. OBSTACLE:
    (A) path
    (B) great distance
    (C) ditch
    (D) impediment

27. CONVOLUTED:
    (A) interesting
    (B) expensive
    (C) twisted
    (D) forged

28. ALIGN:
    (A) repair
    (B) command
    (C) straighten
    (D) replace

29. VETO:
    (A) reject
    (B) discuss
    (C) define
    (D) submit

30. MANGLE:
    (A) shine
    (B) wear
    (C) torture
    (D) mutilate

31. FEEBLE:
    (A) fair
    (B) ineffective
    (C) tough
    (D) hardened

32. SLUGGISH:
    (A) aggressive
    (B) slow
    (C) inconsiderate
    (D) wicked

33. REDUNDANT:
    (A) poor
    (B) superfluous
    (C) abundant
    (D) fancy

34. LAMPOON:
    (A) article
    (B) biography
    (C) journey
    (D) satire

35. TREPIDATION:
    (A) boldness
    (B) irony
    (C) rashness
    (D) fear

36. ASSESS:
    (A) deny
    (B) accept
    (C) size up
    (D) dismiss

37. GHASTLY:
    (A) responsible
    (B) erroneous
    (C) horrible
    (D) favorable

38. CENSURE:
    (A) editing
    (B) understanding
    (C) approval
    (D) disapproval

39. DISMANTLE:
    (A) discourse with
    (B) break down
    (C) yield to
    (D) drive away

40. CACOPHONY:
    (A) melody
    (B) harmony
    (C) music
    (D) dissonance

SENTENCE COMPLETIONS

WHAT IS A SENTENCE COMPLETION?

On an ISEE sentence completion, you need to pick the answer that best fills the blank (or blanks) in the sentence they've given you. Just like on the synonyms, you have to choose the best word (or words) from the answer choices, and sometimes it's not a perfect fit.

Often, though, you'll actually find more than one choice that could fit in the blank. How do you decide which is "best" to choose?

Just like on the synonyms, you need to make sure the ISEE test writers don't get to put words in your mouth. That's how they confuse you, especially on the medium and hard questions. You need to have your own answer ready, before you look at theirs.

Come up with your own word

The easiest way to make sure you don't get caught up in the ISEE's tricky answers is to cover them with your hand until you've thought of your own word for the blank. Why waste your time plugging all their answers into the sentence, anyway? Let's look at one.

> Quite _____ conditions continue to exist in many mountain towns in America where houses do not have running water or electricity.

What word would you put in the blank? Something like "basic" or "old-fashioned" or "harsh"? Write down any words that occur to you. Which part of the sentence let you know which words could fit? "Where houses do not have running water or electricity" gave you the clue.

When you've come up with one or two words you would put in the blank, write them down. (You may not always have to write them, but during practice you should, so you can compare your answers to the answers in this book.) Then uncover the answers.

> (A) common
> (B) primitive
> (C) orderly
> (D) lively

Which looks most like your words? (B). Any of the other words could appear in this sentence in real life, right? However, since the only context you have is the sentence itself, you have to use what the sentence gives you to get the "best" answer for the ISEE.

Use the clue

Try this one:

> Museums are good places for students of
>
> _____.

What word did you come up with? Art? History? Science? Those words are all different! Don't worry, you will not get a sentence completion like this, because there's not enough information to go on—any answer choice could be defended! There will always be a clue to tell you what can go in the blank.

> Museums that house paintings and sculptures are good places for students of
>
> _____.

What's your word? Something like "art." What told you it was art, and not history or science? Underline the part of the sentence that gave you the clue. The clue is the most important part of the sentence—the part that tells you what to put in the blank.

Try another one. Underline the clue and fill in the blank.

> The businessman was _____ because sales were down and costs were up, and his demeanor showed his unhappiness.

Just Use the Sentence

Don't try to use outside knowledge to fill in the blank. Use only what the sentence tells you.

Recycle

Often you can use the very same word(s) you see in the clue — or something close!

Don't be afraid to just reuse the clue in the blank—this guy is unhappy! When it fits, use the clue itself. Now eliminate answers.

(A) despondent

(B) persuasive

(C) indifferent

(D) unresponsive

Even if you're not sure what "despondent" means, do the other words mean "unhappy"? No. (A) is the answer.

Cover the answers, underline the clue, and fill in the blank before looking at the choices:

> In order to join the soccer team, a student absolutely had to be able to practice two hours a day; however, buying the uniform was_____.
>
> (A) obligatory
>
> (B) universal
>
> (C) natural
>
> (D) optional

Your word was probably something like "not required" or "unnecessary." (Don't worry if you're using a short phrase instead of a word—anything that expresses the meaning of what should go in the blank is fine.) But the clue was "absolutely had to," and your words are the opposite of that. What's going on?

Up until now, all the sentences we've seen have had a clue that was pretty much the same as the word in the blank. But sometimes the word in the blank is actually different from the clue—more like an opposite. How can you tell when this is true? Well, which word in the sentence just above told you? "However." "However" let you know that the word in the blank would be the opposite of the clue (the clue was "absolutely had to").

There are lots of little words that can tell you if the blank is the same as the clue, or different.

Use direction words

Direction words tell you if the blank continues in the same direction as the clue, or if it changes direction.

Which of these responses do you want to hear when you've just asked someone to the prom?

> I really like you, *but* _____.
>
> I really like you, *and* _____.

Why is the first one so awful to hear? "But" lets you know that the sentence is going to suddenly change direction, and not be about liking you anymore. Why is the second one so much better? "And" lets you know that the sentence is going to continue in the same direction, and continue to be all about liking you.

Some other direction words are below. Add any others you can think of.

Different Direction	Same Direction
but	and
however	thus
although	therefore
rather	so
instead	because
despite	in addition
yet	consequently

Cover the answers, underline the clue, circle the direction words, and fill in your own word.

When people first began investigating the human brain they were unscientific in their methods, but eventually they began to develop methods that were _____.

(A) objective
(B) inconclusive
(C) lucrative
(D) widespread

Which choice is closest to yours? If you underlined "unscientific" and circled "but," then you could have written "scientific" in the blank. (A) is closest.

Practice — Coming up with your own word
Underline the clues, circle the direction words, and come up with one or two words for each of these sentences.

1. The leading man's rehearsals were so _____ that the director and producer were already imagining what a hit the movie would be.

2. Once very _____ , computers are now found in almost every home.

3. After playing more than a dozen different concert halls, the orchestra was praised by critics for its _____ rendition of Beethoven's famous Fifth Symphony.

4. Although Miles had been unable to sleep the night before, he seemed remarkably _____ when he gave his presentation.

5. Julie was _____ to have been in the right place at the right time; the drama coach gave her the lead in our class play.

6. Mr. Jones is an intelligent and _____ teacher; his knowledge is matched only by his concern for his students.

7. To the casual observer, all fingerprints may appear to be _____ ; but in fact each individual's prints are unique.

8. Hardly one to _____ , Josh tackled every project as soon as he got it.

9. In Charles Dickens's *Christmas Carol*, Scrooge is a particularly _____ character, refusing to give his assistant Bob Cratchit a raise despite his enormous wealth.

10. Alfred Wegener's theory that the continents are slowly drifting apart has recently been confirmed by instruments that measure very small _____ in land masses.

11. Despite their seemingly _____ architecture, the pyramids of Giza are actually intricate marvels of ancient engineering.

12. Unlike animals, which must seek sustenance in their surrounding environment, plants are able to _____ their own food.

13. Great variations in successive layers of polar ice make it possible for scientists to determine how the climate has _____ over the past millennia.

14. Because of the rigors of mountain climbing, the team needs equipment that is both _____ and reliable when setting out for the peak.

15. To qualify for the foreign study program, good language skills are absolutely necessary; however, prior travel to the host country is _____ .

16. The task was very _____ because certain parts needed to be carried out over and over again.

17. Because the ground there was steep and dangerous, the mountain guide told us that it was _____ to approach the edge.

18. Most members of the drama club, though reserved in real life, are quite _____ once they get on stage.

19. Physicians offer recommendations about food groups and eating habits in order to help their patients follow a more _____ diet.

20. Fundraising is only effective when _____ individuals are available, showing their concern by their readiness to give.

21. Not one to be easily intimidated, the corporal remained _____ while the opposing army pressed toward his troops' position.

22. Unlike her confident companion, she tended to be _____ when she found herself among strangers.

23. Although the rest of the class laughed at her antics, the teacher was _____ by Shelly's constant interruptions.

24. In order to avoid being penalized for tardiness, it is a good idea to be _____ with your assignments.

25. Carpentry and cabinetmaking are such difficult trades that they require great _____ with woodworking tools.

26. One of the most ecologically diverse places on earth, the tropical rain forests of Brazil are home to an incredible _____ of insect species.

27. Higher math is a very _____ discipline; it requires just as much imagination and insight as do any of the arts.

28. Many tribes in New Guinea are known for their _____ societies; all property belongs to all members of the tribe.

29. Because their roots are external and their leaf bases clasp, palm trees are rigid and upright, yet _____ enough to bend in strong winds.

30. Though some assert that all behavior is learned, there are others who hold that some behaviors are _____ , existing before any learning occurs.

31. A very outgoing and _____ individual, the mayor loved to talk to her fellow citizens.

32. Staring wide-eyed, the crowd was _____ by the magician's amazing feats of illusion.

Practice — Eliminating answers based on your word

Using what you wrote in the sentences above, eliminate answers that cannot fit.

1. The leading man's rehearsals were so _____ that the director and producer were already imagining what a hit the movie would be.
   (A) indignant
   (B) overacted
   (C) trite
   (D) imaginative

2. Once very _____ , computers are now found in almost every home.
   (A) common
   (B) unusual
   (C) obtainable
   (D) simple

3. After playing more than a dozen different concert halls, the orchestra was praised by critics for its _____ rendition of Beethoven's famous Fifth Symphony.
   (A) unimaginative
   (B) typical
   (C) moving
   (D) loud

4. Although Miles had been unable to sleep the night before, he seemed remarkably _____ when he gave his presentation.
   (A) worn
   (B) tired
   (C) presentable
   (D) alert

5. Julie was _____ to have been in the right place at the right time; the drama coach gave her the lead in our class play.
   (A) fortunate
   (B) inspired
   (C) creative
   (D) impressive

6. Mr. Jones is an intelligent and _____ teacher; his knowledge is matched only by his concern for his students.
   (A) caring
   (B) experienced
   (C) unusual
   (D) original

7. To the casual observer, all fingerprints may appear to be
   _____; but in fact each individual's prints are unique.
   (A) different
   (B) complicated
   (C) personal
   (D) similar

8. Hardly one to _____ , Josh tackled every project as
   soon as he got it.
   (A) strive
   (B) volunteer
   (C) procrastinate
   (D) disagree

9. In Charles Dickens's *Christmas Carol*, Scrooge is a particularly
   _____ character, refusing to give his assistant Bob
   Cratchit a raise despite his enormous wealth.
   (A) circumspect
   (B) miserly
   (C) generous
   (D) demure

10. Alfred Wegener's theory that the continents are slowly drifting
    apart has recently been confirmed by instruments that measure
    very small _____ in land masses.
    (A) locomotion
    (B) adhesion
    (C) punishment
    (D) erosion

11. Despite their seemingly _____ architecture, the
    pyramids of Giza are actually intricate marvels of ancient
    engineering.
    (A) revolutionary
    (B) complex
    (C) archaic
    (D) simplistic

12. Unlike animals, which must seek sustenance in their surround-
    ing environment, plants are able to _____ their own
    food.
    (A) find
    (B) digest
    (C) gather
    (D) manufacture

13. Great variations in successive layers of polar ice make it possible for scientists to determine how the climate has _____ over the past millennia.
    (A) migrated
    (B) altered
    (C) tended
    (D) petrified

14. Because of the rigors of mountain climbing, the team needs equipment that is both _____ and reliable when setting out for the peak.
    (A) weighty
    (B) consistent
    (C) sturdy
    (D) innovative

15. To qualify for the foreign study program, good language skills are absolutely necessary; however, prior travel to the host country is _____.
    (A) inevitable
    (B) mandatory
    (C) plausible
    (D) optional

16. The task was very _____ , because certain parts needed to be carried out over and over again.
    (A) standard
    (B) enjoyable
    (C) tiresome
    (D) common

17. Because the ground there was steep and dangerous, the mountain guide told us that it was _____ to approach the edge.
    (A) encouraged
    (B) forbidden
    (C) important
    (D) possible

18. Most members of the drama club, though reserved in real life, are quite _____ once they get on stage.
    (A) dynamic
    (B) quarrelsome
    (C) threatening
    (D) behaved

19. Physicians offer recommendations about food groups and eating habits in order to help their patients follow a more _____ diet.
    (A) total
    (B) hearty
    (C) balanced
    (D) fulfilling

20. Fundraising is only effective when _____ individuals are available, showing their concern by their readiness to give.
    (A) popular
    (B) famous
    (C) selfless
    (D) meaningful

21. Not one to be easily intimidated, the corporal remained _____ while the opposing army pressed toward his troops' position.
    (A) commanding
    (B) composed
    (C) aggressive
    (D) communicative

22. Unlike her confident companion, she tended to be _____ when she found herself among strangers.
    (A) lively
    (B) friendly
    (C) crowded
    (D) bashful

23. Although the rest of the class laughed at her antics, the teacher was _____ by Shelly's constant interruptions.
    (A) irked
    (B) amused
    (C) consoled
    (D) confused

24. In order to avoid being penalized for tardiness, it is a good idea to be _____ with your assignments.
    (A) original
    (B) punctual
    (C) precise
    (D) thorough

25. Carpentry and cabinetmaking are such difficult trades that they require great _____ with woodworking tools.
(A) adeptness
(B) alertness
(C) awareness
(D) assertiveness

26. One of the most ecologically diverse places on earth, the tropical rain forests of Brazil are home to an incredible _____ of insect species.
(A) size
(B) collection
(C) range
(D) group

27. Higher math is a very _____ discipline; it requires just as much imagination and insight as do any of the arts.
(A) logical
(B) creative
(C) new
(D) surprising

28. Many tribes in New Guinea are known for their _____ societies; all property belongs to all members of the tribe.
(A) primitive
(B) communal
(C) ancient
(D) savage

29. Because their roots are external and their leaf bases clasp, palm trees are rigid and upright, yet _____ enough to bend in strong winds.
(A) tropical
(B) vibrant
(C) elastic
(D) flamboyant

30. Though some assert that all behavior is learned, there are others who hold that some behaviors are _____ , existing before any learning occurs.
(A) ostentatious
(B) innate
(C) durable
(D) cultural

31. A very outgoing and _____ individual, the mayor loved to talk to her fellow citizens.
    (A) garrulous
    (B) majestic
    (C) classy
    (D) rambunctious

32. Staring wide-eyed, the crowd was _____ by the magician's amazing feats of illusion.
    (A) rewarded
    (B) conjoined
    (C) stupefied
    (D) pleased

Use positive/negative

Sometimes you'll have trouble coming up with a word of your own. Don't sweat it; you can still eliminate answers.

> Gregor was a gifted violinist who was_____ about practicing, showing a dedication to his art that even surpassed his talent.

If you can't come up with an exact word, decide if it's good or bad. In the sentence above, is Gregor good about practicing, or is he bad about practicing? Underline the clue that tells you, and put a little "+" sign if the word is good, and a "—" sign if the word is bad. (You can put an "N" if it's neither.) Gregor is good about practicing, so which of the following answer choices can you eliminate? We've marked whether they're positive or negative, so cross out the ones you know are wrong.

(A)	diligent	+
(B)	ornery	−
(C)	practical	+
(D)	ambivalent	neither

(B) and (D) cannot fit, because they don't match what we know about the word in the blank (it's positive). Between (A) and (C), which best expresses the same thing as the clue? (A). If you're not sure what "diligent" means, make an index card for it. (And if you're not sure what to do with the index card, get cracking on the Vocabulary chapter!)

Practice — Using positive/negative

Decide if the blank is positive, negative, or neutral. Try to come up with a word of your own, if you can.

1. Our manager was normally so _____ that it surprised everyone when he failed so badly on the test.

2. Frozen vegetables, though perhaps not as nutritious as fresh, can be a _____ way to get vitamins into a dietary plan.

3. The five-person team of adventurers almost _____ after ten grueling days in stormy weather.

4. David enjoyed the Matisse exhibit at the museum; Matisse was one of his _____ artists.

5. Petra was so _____ while giving her speech in front of the class that her stomach began to ache.

6. The Neanderthals of Krapina were _____ hunters, possessing great strength and prowess.

7. Mr. Lambert _____ the class for not studying enough for the science exam.

8. The two knights engaged in a _____ fight; it would not end until one of them lay dead on the ground.

9. If Wanda had a better sense of her accomplishments, she would stop making such _____ remarks about herself.

10. As their diet became enriched by energy-laden fat, the populations of early hunters _____ and spread throughout the plains.

Practice — Eliminating based on positive/negative

Use your judgments on the sentences above to eliminate answers that cannot fit.

1. Our manager was normally so _____ that it surprised everyone when he failed so badly on the test.
   (A) successful
   (B) conceited
   (C) hateful
   (D) spiteful

2. Frozen vegetables, though perhaps not as nutritious as fresh, can be a _____ way to get vitamins into a dietary plan.
   (A) poor
   (B) inadequate
   (C) convenient
   (D) lenient

3. The five-person team of adventurers almost _____ after ten grueling days in stormy weather.
   (A) struggled
   (B) perished
   (C) paused
   (D) lapsed

4. David enjoyed the Matisse exhibit at the museum; Matisse was one of his _____ artists.
   (A) unusual
   (B) respected
   (C) unknown
   (D) cherished

5. Petra was so _____ while giving her speech in front of the class that her stomach began to ache.
   (A) loud
   (B) calm
   (C) anxious
   (D) relaxed

6. The Neanderthals of Krapina were _____ hunters, possessing great strength and prowess.
   (A) formidable
   (B) unsuitable
   (C) unstable
   (D) researched

7. Mr. Lambert _____ the class for not studying enough for the science exam.
   (A) congratulated
   (B) warned
   (C) chastised
   (D) corrected

8. The two knights engaged in a _____ fight; it would not end until one of them lay dead on the ground.
   (A) divided
   (B) humiliating
   (C) tenuous
   (D) perilous

9. If Wanda had a better sense of her accomplishments, she would stop making such _____ remarks about herself.
    (A) deprecating
    (B) indelicate
    (C) rebellious
    (D) fertile

10. As their diet became enriched by energy-laden fat, the populations of early hunters _____ and spread throughout the plains.
    (A) divided
    (B) congregated
    (C) thrived
    (D) restored

Tackle two-blank sentences one blank at a time

Two-blank sentences are usually longer than one-blanks. Does that mean they're harder? Nope. Actually, if you take two-blank sentences slowly, one blank at a time, they can be easier to get right! Check it out:

> Since Europe has been polluting its rivers, the _____ of many species of fish has been severely _____.

Cover your answers, and look for the clues and direction words. Which blank do you do first? Whichever is easier for you; whichever you have more information for, in the form of clues and direction words. For this example, let's go with the second blank, since we know something bad has been happening to the fish. How do we know? The clues are "polluting its rivers" and "severely," and the direction word is "since," which keeps everything moving in the same direction. We can at least put a "—" sign next to the second blank. Now, when you uncover the answers to check them, only uncover the words for the blank you're working on. Don't even look at the words for the first blank here! You're only going to eliminate answers based on what cannot fit in the second blank.

> (A) XXXX . . . augmented
> (B) XXXX . . . observed
> (C) XXXX . . . approached
> (D) XXXX . . . threatened

You can eliminate (B) and (C), because they're not negative enough. Cross them out so you don't look at them again. Do you know what (A) means? If not, you can't eliminate it. Never eliminate words you don't know.

Now look back at the sentence and fill in a word or two for the first blank. What is it that can be negatively affected by pollution? Once you've got a word or two, look at the choices that are left for the first blank.

(A) acceptance...augmented
~~(B) audacity...observed~~
~~(C) equanimity...approached~~
(D) habitat...threatened

Which sounds better? You may have had a word like "environment" or "survival" filled in. (D) definitely fits better than (A). Notice that if you didn't know what "augmented," "audacity," or "equanimity" meant, you could still get this question right. That's because on two-blank sentence completions, as soon as you eliminate an answer choice based on one of its words, the whole thing is gone—you never have to look at it again, and it doesn't matter what the other word in it is. (However, if "augmented," "audacity," or "equanimity" comes up in a one-blank sentence, you do need to know it in order to eliminate it—so make some index cards for those words.)

Think of all the time you'd waste if you tried plugging the words for each answer choice into the sentence. You'd be reading the sentence four or five times! Plus, you'd find more than one answer choice that sounded okay, and you'd have nothing to compare them to.

Two-blank sentence completions are your friends on the ISEE. Treat your friends right—do them one blank at a time, coming up with your own words.

Take It Easy

As long as you do two-blank sentence completions the way we've shown you, they'll be easier, because you won't need to know all the vocab.

Practice — Two-blank sentence completions

Cover the answers, underline the clues, circle the direction words, and come up with a word for one of the blanks. Eliminate answers based on that blank alone, and then go back up to the sentence to work on the other blank. Then eliminate again.

1. Psychologists have long _____ the connection between violence on television and actual crime; the wealth of different _____ makes it very hard to reach a consensus.
   (A) found . . . facts
   (B) debated . . . opinions
   (C) agreed . . . articles
   (D) argued . . . criminals

2. Jason felt quite _____ about his ability to score well; he had studied _____ the night before.
   (A) frightened . . . thoroughly
   (B) happy . . . poorly
   (C) confident . . . diligently
   (D) resistant . . . lately

3. Although the pilot checked all his instruments before takeoff, the _____ of one of them almost caused the plane to _____ .
   (A) malfunction . . . crash
   (B) misuse . . . land
   (C) safety . . . abort
   (D) refusal . . . fly

4. Her treatment of the subject was so _____ that the class was convinced she had only _____ the material the night before.
   (A) spotty . . . skimmed
   (B) thorough . . . .misunderstood
   (C) partial . . . .memorized
   (D) confused . . . learned

5. Communities need to work not _____ , but _____ ; as a group they can solve problems more easily.
   (A) in groups . . . communally
   (B) at home . . . detached
   (C) always . . . constantly
   (D) in isolation . . . together

6. Despite the best efforts of his coach, Josh remained _____ in his _____ streak.
   (A) mired . . . losing
   (B) upbeat . . . winning
   (C) free . . . consistent
   (D) taken . . . sportsman

7. Due to the author's _____ handwriting, the typist had a difficult time _____ the manuscript.
   (A) perfect . . . transcribing
   (B) careful . . . reading
   (C) illegible . . . deciphering
   (D) readable . . . translating

8. The maid, while _____ to the guests of the hotel, was rather _____ with her employers.
   (A) indifferent . . . curt
   (B) submissive . . . pleasant
   (C) obsequious . . . obstinate
   (D) reliable . . . obedient

9. The owner is difficult to work for, less for her critical and _____ nature than for her _____.
   (A) exacting . . . procrastination
   (B) perfect . . . assistance
   (C) meticulous . . . effort
   (D) carefree . . . complaints

10. Smithers hoped that the committee would not _____ a course of action that would _____ an already bad situation in the workplace.
    (A) relate . . . assist
    (B) formulate . . . amend
    (C) recommend . . . exacerbate
    (D) present . . . mediate

Guess aggressively when you've worked on a sentence

When you've narrowed a sentence completion down to two or three answers, it's probably because you don't know the vocabulary in some of those answers. Just take a guess and move on—you're not going to be able to divine the meanings of the words (and trust us, the proctor will not let you pull out a dictionary). You've increased your chances of getting the question right by eliminating one or two choices, and there's no guessing penalty, so fill in a bubble and move on.

When to skip a question

What if you come across a sentence that is so confusing, you can't even decide if the blank(s) should be positive or negative, much less come up with a word of your own? Skip it—but make sure you fill in your letter-of-the-day.

Be sure to leave a minute at the end of the verbal section to fill in your letter-of-the-day on any questions you have not gotten to.

THE SENTENCE COMPLETIONS PLAN

One-blank sentence completions

For each and every sentence completion, the first thing I do is _____ the answers.

I look for the _____ , and I mark it by _____ it.

I look for any _____ words, and I _____ them.

Then I _____.

If I have trouble coming up with a word for the blank, I decide if the blank is _____ or _____ (or neither).

Then I _____ the answer choices, and _____ .

Two-blank sentence completions

For each and every sentence completion, the first thing I do is _____ the answers.

I look for the _____ and I mark it by _____ it.

I look for any _____ words, and I _____ them.

If the sentence completion has two blanks, I do them _____ .

Which blank do I do first? _____

I come up with a word for one of the blanks, and when I uncover the answer choices, I only uncover _____ and I eliminate based on those.

Then I go back to the sentence and _____ for the other blank, uncover the answer choices that are left, and eliminate.

Which letter should I use?

No matter what you may have heard, it doesn't matter which letter you use to fill in answers for questions you don't work on.

P.O.E. and guessing

Can I eliminate answer choices just because they contain words I do not know?

_____

What do I do if I can only eliminate one or two answer choices? _____

_____

What do I do if the sentence or the vocabulary looks so difficult that I can't come up with a word or decide if the blank is positive or negative? _____

_____

What do I spend my last minute on? _____

_____

Why should I never leave a question unanswered, even if I did not work on that question at all? _____

If you have trouble answering any of these questions, go back and review this chapter before going on.

Practice — All sentence completion techniques

1. One of the simple guidelines of public speaking is that good presentations require _____ preparation.
   (A) thorough
   (B) fretful
   (C) partial
   (D) solitary

2. Franklin D. Roosevelt was an effective _____ , taking time out each week to speak to the people of the United States by radio in casual "fireside chats."
   (A) writer
   (B) warrior
   (C) communicator
   (D) legislator

3. Compared to Asia, the huge continent to its east, Europe is actually quite _____ in size, though not in its impressive and numerous cultural contributions.
   (A) mammoth
   (B) modest
   (C) irregular
   (D) predictable

4. Known for their _____ skills at goldsmithing, the
    Incas produced some of the most beautiful and _____
    gold figurines of all time.
    (A) primitive ... expensive
    (B) early ... religious
    (C) expert ... intricate
    (D) novice ... strong

5. It is hard to imagine that so much modern machinery, from
    huge oil tankers, cars, and jet engines all the way down to
    _____ nuts, bolts, and screws, is made from
    _____ material: steel.
    (A) minuscule ... the same
    (B) tremendous ... .the common
    (C) countless ... the perfect
    (D) flimsy ... the unique

6. Even though she was known to be quite outgoing, Janet could
    be _____ if she didn't know everyone in the room.
    (A) timid
    (B) extroverted
    (C) diverse
    (D) separate

7. Unlike the convex lens, which brings light rays together, the
    concave lens actually _____ light rays.
    (A) merges
    (B) dissolves
    (C) assists
    (D) spreads out

8. Once a common and important means of _____ ,
    sailing has become more of a sport and a _____ than a
    primary way of getting around.
    (A) conveyance ... profession
    (B) transportation ... hobby
    (C) relaxation ... business
    (D) socialization ... vocation

9. Usually cool and collected, the coach grew _____
    when he saw his best player needlessly injured in the illegal
    play.
    (A) indifferent
    (B) furious
    (C) realistic
    (D) impatient

10. Because he was the best at spelling, Michael was
_____ to be our _____ at the county spelling
bee.
(A) assigned . . . delegate
(B) picked . . . manager
(C) chosen . . . representative
(D) elected . . . washout

11. The ruler of the kingdom was known to be quite a
_____ ; he was domineering and cruel to all his
subjects.
(A) leader
(B) tyrant
(C) democrat
(D) highbrow

12. Martha could no longer keep _____ ; with unusual
_____ , she spoke out passionately against the injus-
tices at her school.
(A) pace . . . speed
(B) quiet . . . timidity
(C) up . . . facility
(D) silent . . vigor

13. Most house fires can be avoided through such simple
_____ as proper education and a well-placed fire
extinguisher.
(A) previews
(B) presentations
(C) precautions
(D) preventions

14. The dishonest employee _____ his company, abscond-
ing with more than two thousand dollars' worth of supplies.
(A) relieved
(B) reported
(C) swindled
(D) demoted

15. With a multitude of nationalities present, this campus is one of
the most _____ and _____ in the whole
country.
(A) diverse . . . fascinating
(B) uniform . . . tremendous
(C) multifaceted . . . bland
(D) homogeneous . . . ethnic

16. Almost worse than the cast that covered it, the scar on
    Jennifer's leg was quite _____.
    (A) pleasant
    (B) ghastly
    (C) beneficial
    (D) ingenious

17. Theories of the origin of the universe are far from
    _____ ; after all, no one was around to witness the
    event.
    (A) hypothetical
    (B) plausible
    (C) credible
    (D) definitive

18. Standing on their feet and applauding, the audience was
    _____ the actor's _____ performance of Abe
    Lincoln in Illinois.
    (A) rebellious at . . . fanatic
    (B) thrilled by . . . weak
    (C) impressed with . . . uninspired
    (D) electrified by . . . marvelous

19. The situation called for _____ measures; the solution
    would not be simple and straightforward.
    (A) complex
    (B) unique
    (C) elementary
    (D) firsthand

20. The day was hardly a _____ one; everything that
    could possibly go wrong did.
    (A) reluctant
    (B) blithe
    (C) resistant
    (D) frenetic

READING

WHAT'S READING ALL ABOUT ON THE ISEE?

You have to read the ISEE reading passages differently from the way you read
anything else. The passages the test writers use are dense with information.

Generally, when you read a textbook or any other book, you notice one or
two phrases you want to remember in each paragraph. You can underline those
phrases to show that they seem important, so you can easily find them later.

On the ISEE, however, the passages are chosen precisely because there is a lot of information in only a few paragraphs. It's all packed in together. So if you read your normal way, then you read the first sentence and you try to remember it. You read the second sentence and try to remember it. You read the third sentence and, as you try to remember it, you forget the first two.

You have to read with a different goal in mind for the ISEE. This may sound crazy, but don't try to learn or remember anything. You don't get any points for reading the passage well!

What do you get points for? Answering questions correctly. On the questions and answers, you need to slow down and make sure you're checking each answer carefully before eliminating it. Don't worry about finishing the section, especially if you're in one of the lower grades taking that test. Working slowly and carefully will gain you points here.

Read Quickly, Answer Slowly

Your goal is to spend more time answering questions (and less time reading the passage).

THE PASSAGES

What are the passages like?

There are around 9 passages in a reading section, and there are 40 questions. Of these, 20 questions are based on science passages, and 20 questions are based on social studies passages.

You can choose which passages to do. The reading section purposely has more passages and questions than many students can complete in 35 minutes. Don't let the test writers choose which ones you'll get to. Choose for yourself by flipping through them and doing the ones that look easiest first. You'll also do better on topics that interest you.

Also, do you tend to do better on science passages, or do you do better on social studies passages? Investigate this as you do practice questions and the practice ISEE.

Social studies passages can be about the history of a person, a group, or an event. Science passages explain some phenomenon or theory. Both types of passages are much like your school textbooks—unemotional and striving to be objective.

HOW DO I READ THE PASSAGES?

Quickly! Don't try to remember the details in the passage. Your goal is to read the passage quickly to get the main idea.

The ISEE reading section is an open-book test—you can look back at the passage to answer questions about the details.

Label the paragraphs

As you read ISEE passages, you will find that although many of them look like one big paragraph, they can be broken up into smaller pieces. After you read a few sentences, ask yourself what you just read. Put it in your own words—just a couple of words—and label the side of the paragraph with your summary. This way you'll have something to guide you back to the relevant part of the passage when you answer a question.

Imagine your grandparents are coming to visit, and they're staying in your room. Your parents tell you to clean up your room, and get all that junk off the floor. Now, that junk is important to you. Okay, so maybe you don't need your rollerblades every day, or all those old notes from your best friend, but you do need to be able to get to them. So you get a bunch of boxes, and you throw your rollerblades, ballet slippers, dress shoes, and ice skates in one box. In another, you throw all your old notes, letters, cards, and schoolwork. In another, you throw all your hand-held videogames, CDs, computer software, and floppy disks. Before you put the boxes in the closet, what must you do to be sure you don't have to go through every one of them the next time you want to play Tetris? You need to label them. "Shoes," "papers," and "computer/CDs" should do it.

The same thing is true of the paragraphs you read on the ISEE. You need to be able to go back to the passage and find the answer to a question quickly—you don't want to have to look through the entire passage to find it! The key to labeling the paragraphs is practice—you need to do it quickly, coming up with one or two words that accurately remind you of what's in each part of the passage. You'll find that some passages really should be broken up into more paragraphs, and your labels can show you where the breaks occur.

For very short passages, you can skip right to the next step.

State the main idea

After you have read the entire passage, ask yourself two questions:

- **What?** What is the passage about?

- **So what?** What's the author's point about this topic?

The answers to these questions will show you the main idea of the passage. Scribble down this main idea in just a few words. The answer to **What?** is the thing that was being talked about—"bees" or "weather forecasting." The answer to **So what?** gives you the rest of the sentence; "Bees do little dances that tell other bees where to go for pollen," or "Weather forecasting is complicated by many problems."

Don't assume you will find the main idea in the first sentence. While often the main idea is in the beginning of the passage, it is not always in the first sentence. The beginning may just be a lead-in to the main point.

Practice — Getting through the passage

As you quickly read the passage, label the sections that should be separate paragraphs. When you finish the passage, answer **What?** and **So what?** to get the main idea.

> Contrary to popular belief, the first European known to lay eyes on America was not Christopher Columbus or Amerigo Vespucci but a little-known Viking by the name of Bjarni Herjolfsson. In the summer of 986, Bjarni sailed from Norway to Iceland, heading for the Viking settlement where his father Heriulf resided. When he arrived in Iceland, Bjarni discovered that his father had already sold his land and estates and set out for the latest Viking settlement on the subarctic island called Greenland. Discovered by a notorious murderer and criminal named Eric the Red, Greenland lay at the limit of the known world. Dismayed, Bjarni set out for this new colony. Since the Vikings traveled without chart or compass, it was not uncommon for them to lose their way in the unpredictable northern seas. Beset by fog, the crew lost their bearings. When the fog finally cleared, they found themselves before a land that was level and covered with woods. They traveled farther up the coast, finding more flat, wooded country. Farther north, the landscape revealed glaciers and rocky mountains. Though Bjarni realized this was an unknown land, he was no intrepid explorer. Rather, he was a practical man who had simply set out to find his father. Refusing his crew's request to go ashore, he promptly turned his bow back out to sea. After four days' sailing, Bjarni landed at Herjolfsnes on the southwestern tip of Greenland, the exact place he had been seeking all along.

What is this passage about? _____

So what? What's the author's point? _____

What type of passage is this? _____

Check your answers to be sure you're on the right track.

THE QUESTIONS

Now we're getting to the important part of the reading section. This is where you need to spend time, in order to avoid careless errors. After reading a passage, you'll have a group of questions that is in no particular order. The first thing you need to decide is whether the question you're answering is general or specific.

GENERAL QUESTIONS

General questions are about the passage as a whole. There are five types:

Main idea

- ◆ Which of the following best expresses the main point?
- ◆ The passage is primarily about
- ◆ The main idea of the passage is
- ◆ The best title for this passage would be

Tone/attitude

- The author's tone is
- The attitude of the author is one of

General interpretation

- The author's tone/attitude indicates
- The author would most likely agree with
- This passage deals with X by
- The passage implies that
- Which of the following words best describes the passage?
- It can be inferred from the passage that
- The style of the passage is most like
- Where would you be likely to find this passage?
- What is the author's opinion of X?
- The passage is best described as a

Purpose

- The purpose of the passage is
- The author wrote this passage in order to

Prediction

- Which is likely to happen next?
- The author will most likely discuss next

Notice that these questions all require you to know the main idea, but the ones at the beginning of the list don't require anything else, and the ones toward the end require you to interpret a little more.

Answering a general question

Keep your answers to "**What? So What?**" in mind. The answer to a general question will concern the main idea. If you need more, go back to your paragraph labels. The labels will allow you to look at the passage again without getting bogged down in the details.

- For a straight **main idea** question, just ask yourself, "What was the "What? So what?" for this passage?"
- For a **tone/attitude question**, ask yourself, "How did the author feel about the subject?"
- For a **general interpretation** question, ask yourself, "Which answer stays closest to what the author said and how he said it?"
- For a **general purpose** question, ask yourself, "Why did the author write this?"

- For a **prediction** question, ask yourself, "How was the passage arranged?" Take a look at your paragraph labels, and reread the last sentence.

Answer the question in your own words before looking at the answer choices. As always, you want to arm yourself with your own answer before looking at the ISEE's tricky answers.

Practice — Answering a general question

Use the passage about Vikings that you just read and labeled. Reread your main idea and answer the following questions. Use the questions above to help you paraphrase your own answer before looking at the choices.

What was the answer to "What? So what?" for this passage?

1. This passage is primarily about
    (A) the Vikings and their civilization
    (B) the waves of Viking immigration
    (C) sailing techniques of Bjarni Herjolfsson
    (D) one Viking's glimpse of the new world

Which answer is closest to what the author said, overall?

2. With which of the following statements about Viking explorers would the author most probably agree?
    (A) Greenland and Iceland were the Vikings' final discoveries.
    (B) Viking explorers were cruel and savage.
    (C) The Vikings' most startling discovery was an accidental one.
    (D) Bjarni Herjolfsson was the first settler of America.

Why did the author write this passage? Think about the main idea.

3. What was the author's purpose in writing this passage?
    (A) To turn the reader against Italian adventurers
    (B) To show his disdain for Eric the Red
    (C) To demonstrate the Vikings' nautical skills
    (D) To correct a common misconception about the European discovery of America

SPECIFIC QUESTIONS

Specific questions are about a detail or a section of the passage. There are four main types:

Fact

- According to the passage/author
- The author states that
- Which of these questions is answered by the passage?
- All of the following are mentioned EXCEPT

Definition in context

- What does the passage mean by X?
- X probably represents/means
- Which word best replaces the word X without changing the meaning?

Specific interpretation

- ◆ The author implies in line X

- ◆ It can be inferred from paragraph X

- ◆ The most likely interpretation of X is

Purpose

- ◆ The author uses X in order to

- ◆ Why does the author say X?

Again, the questions above range from flat-out requests for information found in the passage (just like the straight "main idea" general questions) to questions that require some interpretation of what you find in the passage (like the general questions that ask what the author is "likely to agree with").

Answering a specific question

For specific questions, always reread the part of the passage concerned. Remember, this is an open-book test!

Of course, you don't want to have to reread the entire passage. What part are they focusing on? To find the relevant part:

- ◆ Use your **paragraph labels** to go straight to the information you need.

- ◆ Use the line or paragraph reference, if there is one, but be careful. With a **line reference** ("In line 10 . . . "), be sure to read the whole surrounding paragraph, not just the line. If the question says "In line 10 . . . " then you need to read lines 5 through 15 to actually find the answer.

- ◆ Use words that stand out in the question and passage. Names, places, and long words will be easy to find back in the passage. We call these **lead words** because they lead you back to the right place in the passage.

Once you're in the right area, answer the question in your own words. Then look at the answer choices and eliminate any that aren't like yours.

Answering special specific questions

Definition-in-context questions

Creating your own answer before looking at the choices makes definition-in-context questions especially easy. Remember, they want to know how the word or phrase is being used in context, so come up with your own word that fits in the sentence before looking at the answer choices. Try one:

> In line 15, the word "spot" most closely means

Cross out the word they're asking about, and replace it with your own.

A raptor must also have a sharp, often hooked beak so that it may tear the flesh of its prey. Because they hunt from the sky, these birds must have extremely sharp eyesight, which allows them to *spot* potential prey from a great distance.

Now look at the answer choices and eliminate the ones that are not at all like yours.

(A) taint
(B) mark
(C) hunt
(D) detect

You probably came up with something like "see." The closest answer to "see" is (D). Notice that "taint" and "mark" are possible meanings of "spot," but they don't work in this context. Those answer choices are there to catch students who do not go back to the passage to see how the word is used and to replace it with their own.

Definition-in-context questions are so quick that if you only have a few minutes left, you should definitely do them first.

I, II, III Questions

The questions that have three roman numerals are confusing and time-consuming. They look like this:

According to the passage, which of the following is true?

I.   The sky is blue.
II. Nothing rhymes with "orange."
III. Smoking cigarettes increases lung capacity.

(A) I only
(B) II only
(C) I and II only
(D) I, II and III

On the ISEE, you will need to look up each of the three statements in the passage. This will always be time-consuming, but you can make them less confusing by making sure that you look up just one statement at a time.

For instance, in the question above, say you look back at the passage and see that the passage says "I" is true. Write a big "T" next to it. What can you eliminate? (B). Now you check out "II," and you find that sure enough, they've said that, too. "II" gets a big "T" and you cross off (A). Next, looking in the paragraph that you labeled "smoking is bad," you find that the passage actually says that smoking decreases lung capacity. What can you eliminate? (D).

You may want to skip a I, II, III question because it will be time-consuming, especially if you're on your last passage and there are other questions you can do instead.

EXCEPT/LEAST/NOT QUESTIONS

This is another confusing type of question. The test writers are reversing what you need to look for, asking you which answer is **false**.

> All of the following can be inferred from the
> passage EXCEPT:

Before you go any further, cross out the "EXCEPT." Now you have a much more positive question to answer. Of course, as always, you will go through all the answer choices, but for this type of question you will put a little "T" or "F" next to the answers as you check them out. Let's say we've checked out these answers:

> (A) Americans are patriotic.   T
> (B) Americans have great ingenuity.   T
> (C) Americans love war.   F
> (D) Americans do what they can to help one another.   T

Which one stands out? The one with the "F." That's your answer. You made a confusing question much simpler than the test writers wanted it to be. If you don't go through all the choices and mark them, you run the risk of accidentally picking one of the choices that you know is true, because that's what you usually look for on reading questions.

You should skip an EXCEPT/LEAST/NOT question if you're on your last passage and there are other questions you can do instead.

Practice — Answering a specific question

Use the passage about Vikings that you just read and labeled. Use your paragraph labels and the lead words in each question to get to the part of the passage you need, and then put the answer in your own words before going back to the answer choices.

1. According to the passage, Bjarni Herjolfsson left Norway to
    (A) found a new colony
    (B) open trading lanes
    (C) visit his relations
    (D) map the North Sea

What's the lead word here? Norway. 'Norway' should also be in one of your labels.

2. Bjarni's reaction upon landing in Iceland can best be described as
    (A) disappointed
    (B) satisfied
    (C) amused
    (D) indifferent

What's the lead word here?_____ Again, this should be in one of your labels.

3. "The crew lost their bearings," probably means that
    (A) the ship was damaged beyond repair
    (B) the crew became disoriented
    (C) the crew decided to mutiny
    (D) the crew went insane

Go back and read this part. Replace the words they've quoted with your own.

What's the lead word here?_____ Is it in one of your labels? What does that part of the passage say about Greenland? Paraphrase before looking at the answers!

4. It can be inferred from the passage that prior to Bjarni Herjolfsson's voyage, Greenland
    (A) was covered in grass and shrubs
    (B) was overrun with Vikings
    (C) was rich in fish and game
    (D) was as far west as the Vikings had traveled

THE ANSWERS

Before you ever look at an answer choice, you've come up with your own answer, in your own words. What do you do next?

Well, you're looking for the closest answer to yours, but it's a lot easier to eliminate answers than to try to magically zoom in on the "best" one. Work through the answers using process of elimination. As soon as you eliminate an answer, cross off the letter in your test booklet so that you no longer think of that choice as a possibility.

How do I eliminate answer choices?

On a general question:
Eliminate an answer that is:

- too small. The passage may mention it, but it's only a detail—not a main idea.

- not mentioned in the passage.

- in contradiction to the passage— it says the opposite of what you read.

- too big. The answer tries to say that more was discussed than really was.

- too extreme. An extreme answer is too negative or too positive, or it uses absolute words like "all," "every," "never," or "always." Eliminating extreme answers makes tone/attitude questions especially easy and quick.

- going against common sense. The passage is not likely to back up answers that just don't make sense at all.

On a specific question:
Eliminate an answer that is:

- too extreme

- contradicting passage details

- not mentioned in the passage

- against common sense

If you look back at the questions you did for the Viking passage, you'll see that many of the wrong answer choices fit into the categories above.

What kinds of answers do I keep?
"Best" answers are likely to be:

- paraphrases of the words in the passage.
- traditional and conservative in their outlook.
- moderate, using words like "may," "can," and "often"

Practice — Eliminating answers

The following phrases are answer choices. You haven't read the passage, or even the question, which goes with each of them. However, you can decide if each one is a possible correct answer, or if you can eliminate it, based on the above criteria. Cross out any that you can eliminate.

Index Card Alert
What's the definition of 'criteria'?

For a general question:

(A) The author refutes each argument exhaustively.

(B) The author admires the courage of most Americans.

(C) Creativity finds full expression in a state of anarchy.

(D) The passage criticizes Western society for not allowing freedom of expression to artists.

(E) The ancient Egyptians were barbaric.

(F) The author proves that Native American writing does not have a multicultural perspective.

(G) The author emphasizes the significance of diversity in the United States.

(H) The passage reports the record cold temperatures in Boston in 1816.

For a general tone/attitude question:

(I) respectful

(J) confused

(K) angry condemnation

(L) admiring

(M) mournful

(N) objective

(O) thrilled optimism

(P) exaggeration

(Q) disgusted

(R) neutral

(S) condescending

(T) indifferent

For a specific question:

(U) They were always in danger of being deprived of their power.

(V) Voters were easily misled by mudslinging campaigns.

(W) One-celled organisms could be expected to act in fairly predictable ways.

(X) Only a show of athletic ability can excite an audience.

(Y) Economic events can have political repercussions.

When you've got it down to two:

If you've eliminated all but two answers, don't get stuck and waste time. Keep the main idea in the back of your mind and step back.

- Reread the question.
- Look at what makes the two answers different.
- Go back to the passage.
- Which answer is worse? Eliminate it.

THE READING PLAN

The passages

As I read the passage, I _____ where the paragraphs should be.

After I read an entire passage, I ask myself _____ ? and _____ ?

The questions

The five main types of general questions, and the questions I can ask myself in order to answer them, are:

_____   _____

_____   _____

_____   _____

_____   _____

_____   _____

To find the answer to a specific question, I can use three clues:

_____

_____

_____

If the question says "in line 22," where do I begin reading for the answer? _____

The answers

On a general question, I eliminate answers that are:

_____

_____

_____

_____

_____

_____

On a specific question, I eliminate answers that are:

_____

_____

_____

When I've got it down to two possible answers, I:

_____

_____

_____

_____

If you had any trouble with these questions, reread this chapter before going further.

Practice — All reading techniques

The term "tides" has come to represent the cyclical rising and falling of ocean waters, most notably evident along the shoreline as the border between land and sea moves in and out with the passing of the day. The primary reason for this constant redefinition of the boundaries of the sea is the gravitational force of the moon. This force of lunar gravity is not as strong as earth's own gravitational pull, which keeps our bodies and our homes from being pulled off the ground, through the sky, and into space toward the moon. It is a strong enough force, however, to exert a certain gravitational pull as the moon passes over the earth's surface. This pull causes the water level to rise (as the water is literally pulled ever-so-slightly toward the moon) in those parts of the ocean that are exposed to the moon and its gravitational forces. When the water level in one part of the ocean rises, it must naturally fall in another, and this is what causes water level to change, dramatically at times, along any given piece of coastline.

1. Which one of the following is the most obvious effect of the tides?
   (A) A part of the beach that was once dry is now underwater.
   (B) Floods cause great damage during heavy rainstorms.
   (C) The moon is not visible.
   (D) Water falls.

2. The word "lunar" most nearly means
   (A) weak
   (B) strong
   (C) destructive
   (D) related to the moon

3. It can be inferred from the passage that if one were to travel to the moon
   (A) that water would be found on its surface
   (B) that an object, if dropped, would float away from the surface of the moon
   (C) that tides are more dramatic during the day than during the night
   (D) that an object, if dropped, would fall to the moon's surface

4. The author's primary purpose in writing this passage is to
   (A) prove the existence of water on the moon
   (B) refute claims that tides are caused by the moon
   (C) explain the main cause of the ocean's tides
   (D) argue that humans should not interfere with the processes of nature

Additional practice

Read the opinion and editorial pages and the Science section of a major newspaper to get practice reading short passages with lots of information in them. Also complete all reading practice exercises you can get from the Educational Records Bureau. For even more reading passages and questions, check out a book with practice SAT questions from the College Board. (They will be slightly longer than the passages on the ISEE, but still good practice.)

ESSAY

What Is the ISEE Essay?

The ISEE's final section is the essay. How important is it to your ISEE scores? It doesn't affect them one bit. The ISEE people do not score the writing sample. They do, however, copy it and send it to schools along with each of your score reports. Keep in mind that although it does not matter what the ISEE people think of the essay that you write, you are writing it for the admissions officers at the schools to which you are applying.

The ISEE gives you 30 minutes to write an essay on an assigned topic.

The Topic

The topic can be a proverb or saying with which you need to either agree or disagree. It may also be a more open ended question. Here are some examples of ISEE topics:

> No pain, no gain. Do you agree or disagree with this saying?
>
> Actions speak louder than words. Do you agree or disagree?
>
> The greatest sorrows are those we cause ourselves. Is this true?
>
> How can we help the elderly in our community?
>
> What I value most in life is

As you can see, sometimes the topic can be interpreted in many ways—it's very vague. The test writers leave the topic open to interpretation on purpose. Don't worry about interpreting it the "correct" way. Go with whatever you think it means. Often there will be a "prompt," a small paragraph that will explain the topic a little further.

Index Card Alert
What exactly is a 'proverb'?

You cannot write an essay on a different topic. If you have trouble understanding the topic, try putting it in your own words. With the first example above, "No pain, no gain," how would you explain what it means to someone else?

You might explain "No pain, no gain" by saying, "In order to accomplish something worthwhile, you often have to make sacrifices." This will be an excellent phrase to use in your introduction!

THE PROMPT

The prompt that you'd see along with the first three essay topics above would look something like this:

> Do you agree or disagree with the topic statement? Support your
> position with specific examples from personal experience, the
> experience of others, current events, history, or literature.

You **must** decide if you agree or disagree. No straddling the fence here, even if you could really care less about the topic. You have to muster an opinion.

Index Card Alert

What does 'muster' mean?

The prompt for a topic of "How can we help the elderly in our community?" or "What I value most in life is . . . " would look more like this:

> Write an essay discussing (topic). Support your position
> with specific examples from personal experience, the
> experience of others, current events, or history.

In the prompt, besides specifying that you need to agree or disagree, the ISEE has also told you that you need to support your opinion with examples. They've listed different types that you can use. However, all examples are not equal. You want to form the strongest possible argument, and for that you need the strongest examples you can think of. How can you be sure you'll have some at hand? Prepare them in advance!

Any of the types of examples mentioned in the assignment—history, current events, literature, or personal experience—can be strong support for your opinion or position. You may think that personal experience is the way to go, since it's what you know best, so you'll always be able to think of something, right? Well, you may have had many meaningful things happen to you, or you may even think you'll be able to pretend you have. However, sometimes an essay can be made much stronger with the addition of a more scholarly example from history, current events, or literature.

If creativity strikes on the day of the test, and you come up with the perfect story to support your opinion, then go for it. But what if nothing comes to you? If you're prepared with some examples you can use, you'll be less anxious on the day of the test, because you'll have something to write, no matter what the topic is.

PREPARE YOUR EXAMPLES

Brainstorm some examples that you can use on any essay topic the ISEE throws at you. The essay topics are always vague, and if you have a bunch of solid examples you've reviewed in advance, you'll save a lot of time at the test. Your potential examples will be in the forefront of your mind, and you can choose one or two that are supportive of your opinion on whatever your topic may be.

Prepare history and current event examples

For history and current event examples, stay away from potentially controversial issues and events. Also avoid those that have recently been turned into movies or TV shows.

- What have you studied in school?

- What have you heard people talking about in the news?

- Get specific. Come up with as many details as you can—names, dates, general order of events, issues involved. Go back to your school notes, if you need to, for details you've forgotten. Details will make your example stronger and help you to explain exactly how it supports your opinion.

CURRENT EVENTS	HISTORY
_____	_____
_____	_____
_____	_____
_____	_____
_____	_____
_____	_____
_____	_____

If you're having trouble thinking of events and issues, see if any of these are something you know about:

homelessness	the Salem Witch Trials
censorship	the Civil War
smoking in public	the American Revolution
environmental issues	the breakup of the USSR
drunk driving	slavery
gun control	World War I or World War II
underage drinking	any historical event or war

If you want to start from our list above, you must remember that you need to flesh out the details on these issues and events. For example, you don't want to say "Environmental issues are a good example of . . . " because "environmental issues" can cover a whole host of concerns and viewpoints. Break it down. What do you know about the issues? There's the greenhouse effect (what does that mean?), endangered species (why do they matter?), air pollution (what is being done about it?), water pollution (how does it happen?), nuclear power (what are the pros and cons?), and so forth. In the same way, you need to think about "slavery." What were the conditions under slavery? Who rebelled or helped runaway slaves? When was slavery in practice in the United States? Who and what led to its demise?

Index Card Alert

What is a 'demise'?

For any big issue or event, break down what is involved. Get specific! It may help to talk it out with your parents while jotting down notes on what you're saying. If you just studied the Salem Witch Trials, for instance, try explaining to your parents what happened (even if they already know), and the significance of the events. You'll get deeper into the example so you can be sure to have a paragraph or two to write about it. Doing all the practice writing samples we've included will help, also.

Prepare literature examples

Books, short stories, poems, and plays you've read for school (and perhaps some you've read on your own) provide you with events and characters that can support your opinion. The key is, the work must be "literature," a work that most educators would consider a classic. Movies and television shows do not count. It's very difficult to use a work that isn't well known, because the reader will probably be unfamiliar with it, and you'll need to spend precious minutes explaining plot.

Think back now (instead of during the test!) to recall those works of literature you have read and can use in your ISEE writing sample. Write down the author of each, and the characters and main events in the work. Again, refer to your old school notes or the book itself to refresh your memory.

LITERATURE

_____

_____

_____

_____

_____

_____

_____

If you've read anything by Homer, Shakespeare, Dickens, Steinbeck, Hemingway, Conrad—those are classics you can use. There are many, many more; ask your English teacher if you're in doubt about a particular work you've read.

In your essay:

◆ Stick to the classics.

◆ Name the author.

- Underline the titles of books, plays, and epic poems.
- Put quotation marks around short stories, essays, articles, and poems.
- You probably know these words from school: *plot, protagonist, antagonist, climax,* and *theme.* Use them!

Prepare personal experience examples

Use personal experiences that are "deep." Academic and athletic achievements, family history, and personal aspirations work well. Avoid boyfriend/girlfriend stories. Use experiences that have taught you something.

PERSONAL EXPERIENCE

_____

_____

_____

_____

_____

These are sometimes the hardest examples to make strong, because what is meaningful to you may not be to someone else. Ask your parents or a teacher what they think of the ones you've written down.

PLAN YOUR ESSAY

When the essay section begins, in order to form an opinion and organize your essay, take three minutes to note some examples you could use on the topic. Do this on the test booklet or on scratch paper—not on the lined essay answer sheet. Don't take too long, and don't worry about being original—just come up with examples that really support an opinion.

Try this with our topics from before:

No pain, no gain.

Agree   Disagree

_____   _____

_____   _____

_____   _____

Actions speak louder than words.

Agree   Disagree

_____   _____

_____   _____

_____   _____

The greatest sorrows are those we cause ourselves.

Agree   Disagree

_____   _____

_____   _____

_____   _____

For which side do you have stronger examples? Remember, you need just **two or three** good ones that you can write a few paragraphs about. Cross out the other side. You now have your outline!

For the more open ended essay topics, brainstorm. Come up with anything you can for the topic, and then go back and cross out the weaker examples, or the ones you don't know as much about, and go with what you have left.

How can we help the elderly in our community?

_____   _____

_____   _____

_____   _____

_____   _____

What I most value in life is . . .

_____   _____

_____   _____

_____   _____

_____   _____

For these last two topics, once you've decided on two or three solid examples, number them so you know the order in which you will use them. Again, there's your outline!

How do you flesh out your outline and make it into an essay in the next 22 minutes? Stick to basic essay structure.

ORGANIZE YOUR ESSAY

Opening Paragraph: Introduction

- ◆ Put the topic in your own words. Show them you understand it.

- ◆ State your opinion.

- ◆ Introduce your examples.

Body Paragraph: First Example

- ◆ State your first example and explain how it supports your opinion.

Body Paragraph: Second Example

- ◆ State your second example and explain how it supports your opinion, *or* state another way in which your first example supports your opinion.

Final Paragraph: Conclusion

- ◆ Paraphrase your opinion.

- ◆ End with "The Kicker," a final sentence that shows the wider significance of your opinion.

This looks very familiar, right? You've probably been writing the five-paragraph essay or some variant thereof for many years. You may be way beyond it now, but for this timed essay, it's the best way to be sure you've got a structure to rely on. If you practice getting all of the above elements into your essay, and you also have examples planned, then you've left very little to chance. You know everything you're going to write, except the topic.

You can, of course, have more body paragraphs than are laid out above, and you definitely should if you're using three examples. However, no matter how much more you want to write, be sure to leave yourself at least three minutes to write a conclusion. It's better to have just one example with a conclusion than two examples without a conclusion!

The "Kicker" in your conclusion is something that relates the topic of the essay to more than just the examples you've used. It shows how the topic applies to life, society, the world—the bigger picture. Look at sample essay #2 to see a typical "Kicker." Even if you don't have a way to show how the position you took relates to the grand scheme of things, you must wrap up with some sort of conclusion, even if it only restates your opinion.

Let's practice writing some of these paragraphs.

Introductions

Write a quick opening paragraph for each of the essays you just outlined. Show that you understand the topic, state your opinion, and introduce your examples. Spend five minutes on each. Remember, the introduction is where the reader gets his first impression of you, so be extra careful here in spelling, punctuation, and grammar.

Some words you can use if you're agreeing with the topic: *sustain, support, advocate, uphold, endorse, espouse, maintain, bolster, strengthen, fortify,* and *align with.*

Some words you can use if you're disagreeing with the topic: *refute, counter, oppose, controvert, contest, dispute,* and *differ.*

If you want to use one of these words but it is unfamiliar to you, look it up, try using it, and then ask a parent or teacher to read your sentence or paragraph and tell you if you've used it correctly.

No pain, no gain.

_____

_____

_____

_____

_____

Actions speak louder than words.

_____

_____

_____

_____

The greatest sorrows are those we cause ourselves.

_____

_____

_____

_____

How can we help the elderly in our community?

_____

_____

_____

_____

What I most value in life is . . .

_____

_____

_____

_____

_____

Body

The body of your essay will consist of paragraphs that explain how your examples support your opinion. As we've said, details help you make a strong case. They allow you to give the reader concrete information and description, and that helps the reader understand what it is in your example that bolsters your case.

For example, the issue of air pollution supports my agreement with "The greatest sorrows are those we cause ourselves." When you read that sentence, you probably made some connection in your mind between "air pollution" and "humans causing their own problems." But you've made a very vague connection. You only sort of know what I mean. My job, as the writer, is to convince you that the two are intimately connected. Thus, I tell you about the hundreds of millions of tons of particles that are pumped into the air every day from factories—the very factories from which we demand products that we think will make our lives easier. And I also have to tell you how those particles are causing us pain by describing the prevalence of asthma and allergies in children and adults, and the rising incidence of cancers in metropolitan areas.

There are lots of other details I could have used instead of the ones I did, but I needed to use some sort of description and explanation to make it perfectly clear that air pollution is something that humans do to themselves, and how great a danger it is.

Explaining your examples is the most important thing you must do while writing the body paragraphs. Assume the burden of responsibility for making your points clear to the reader.

Something else to think about while writing these paragraphs is how you and your reader get from one paragraph to another. You want the reader to see a smooth transition from one paragraph to the next, so she knows she's still reading the same essay. Thus, if your first example for "The greatest sorrows are those we cause ourselves" is historical, and your second example is the air pollution one, you'll want to smoothly switch from one to the other. The beginning of the air pollution paragraph could be something like, "Humans continue to harm themselves, into the present day. One of the ways they do this is by poisoning their own air . . . "

In order to make the transition from one paragraph to another, you can point out similarities or differences that the two examples have, or in some way show that they are related. You don't want to spend time thinking about this at the test, though. If nothing comes to mind, you can fall back on "Another example of . . . is . . . " You can also take a peek at most basic writing, grammar, and style handbooks, if you want to see some more transition words and phrases in action.

Get a Second Opinion

Get as many people as possible to read your practice essays and tell you if there are parts that are not clear, or points that could be developed better. Make sure they know you only have 30 minutes to write.

For now, reread your introductions and choose one to continue. Spend 15 minutes developing your examples in body paragraphs.

_____

_____

_____

_____

_____

_____

_____

_____

_____

_____

_____

_____

_____

_____

_____

_____

_____

_____

_____

_____

_____

_____

_____

_____

_____

_____

Conclusions

Write a quick closing paragraph for each of the five topics we've been using. Remember to paraphrase (don't use the same words you used in your introduction) and try writing a "Kicker" that broadens the essay outward, and makes it more meaningful. If you can't come up with a "Kicker," don't worry—just write something that wraps up. Try to spend just three to five minutes on each conclusion.

Some words you can use to show you're concluding your essay: *therefore, in sum, clearly, consequently, thus,* or *in conclusion.*

_____

_____

_____

_____

_____

_____

_____

_____

_____

_____

_____

_____

_____

_____

_____

_____

_____

_____

_____

_____

_____

_____

_____

THE BASICS

Basic things to keep in mind:

- Write legibly. Practice handwriting essays in pen. Nothing turns a reader off more quickly than an essay that's messy or difficult to decipher. Think about how many essays a school admissions officer has to read!

- If you need to delete words, draw one neat line through them.

- Indent your paragraphs substantially, so the reader can see at a glance that you've organized your essay.

- Stay within the lines and margins.

- Stick to the assigned topic.

- Keep your sentences easy to understand. If you see you've written a long, complicated sentence, think about breaking it up. You want the reader to be able to understand your points.

- Use some big vocabulary words, if you're sure you really know them.

- Watch for the punctuation and grammar mistakes that you've made in the past, and still tend to make. (If you're not sure which mistakes you make, ask your English teacher!)

- If you're not sure how to spell a word, think of another one you can use.

- Write as much as you can. If an admissions officer sees a half-page essay instead of two pages, he'll think you don't have much to say. Even though you'll be writing this essay after two hours of multiple-choice questions, try to gear up to be prolific.

- Try to leave a minute or two to read over your essay when you're done. Catch any careless errors, and neatly correct them.

Index Card Alert

What does 'prolific' mean?

Now let's look at some sample essays. As you read them, decide which one follows the assignment and our guidelines better.

SAMPLE ESSAY 1

Topic: No pain, no gain.

Prompt: Do you agree or disagree with the topic statement? Support your position with specific examples from personal experience, the experience of others, current events, history, or literature.

I agree with the statement "No pain, no gain." In this competitive society, an individual cannot expect to accomplish all of his goals without suffering first. This suffering provides a person with the incentive to learn from his or her mistakes and try harder to obtain what he or she desires. The following examples will help to make this idea clearer.

An athlete must always keep his body in ~~shape~~ top form. If the person doesn't, then his competitors will knock him out of the sport with ease. The athlete just practice many hours per day by pushing himself beyond his limits. For example, the weightlifter must lift weights that start out light and get heavier as he progresses. When the weightlifter can lift a certain amount with ease, he is forced to try a heavier amount, which may hurt at first. However, in the long run the weightlifter will be stronger than before.

In American Colonial days, colonists were in some ways tortured by the mother country, England. The Stamp Acts, tea taxes, Quartering Acts, etc., imposed by England angered the ~~people~~ colonists because they hurt their trade, causing the colonists to become more dependent on England. In the long run, however, these actions by England helped the colonists to win their independence. Each time England imposed another law, the colonists grew more angry. Finally, the people got up the courage to rebel. Thus, they gained their independence.

WHAT DO YOU THINK OF SAMPLE ESSAY 1?

Use these questions to evaluate sample essay 1:

- ◆ Is the essay legible?
- ◆ Does the essay have an introduction that is a separate paragraph?
- ◆ Does the author understand the topic?
- ◆ Is the author's opinion stated clearly?
- ◆ Does the author use examples to support his opinion?
- ◆ How many examples? What kind? How convincing are they?
- ◆ *Does the author explain* how *the examples support his opinion?*
- ◆ Has the author moved smoothly from one paragraph to the next?
- ◆ Is the essay organized? Does each example have a paragraph?
- ◆ Are the paragraphs well-indented?
- ◆ Has the author stayed neatly within the lines?
- ◆ Has the author used impressive vocabulary correctly?
- ◆ Does the essay have a conclusion that is a separate paragraph?
- ◆ Does the conclusion summarize the points in the essay without being just a word-for-word repeat of the intro?

For Those Who Can Help You

You can show these questions to people who read your practice essays, and ask them to answer the questions as they apply to your essays, too.

SAMPLE ESSAY 2

It is absolutely true that one cannot accomplish anything without bearing some sort of pain, whether it is physical or emotional. This has been true throughout history, and remains true in our world today. One example of this is drug testing, during which animals must be hurt or killed so that new, lifesaving drugs may be developed. Another example is the Civil Rights movement, during which many people had to sacrifice a great deal for the greater good.

Before a new medicine or drug can be used on human beings, it must undergo a tremendous amount of testing on animals, to ensure that it is safe and effective. During this process, most of the animals die or are hurt so badly that they must be killed. Many people protest that it is not fair to harm all these animals, but I think this is a very good example of "no pain, no gain." Animals' pain is an unfortunate but necessary step in our making medical gains.

During the American Civil Rights movement, such people as Rosa Parks and Martin Luther King, Jr. had to undergo tremendous physical and emotional pain in order to move the country toward racial equality. Rosa Parks knew that she would be arrested for sitting in the "whites only" part of the bus, but she did it anyway, knowing that it was necessary to pay the price for advancing civil rights. She was not only arrested, but she and her whole family were harassed, receiving death threats for a long time. She did not let these dangers stop her from continuing to protest, boycott, and speak for the movement. Martin Luther King, Jr. also made many sacrifices to work for racial equality, and he died striving to further the cause, but his life and death resulted in great gains.

In summary, nothing positive can happen without some pain. We must learn to take the good with the bad, and realize that we can not gain the former without accepting the latter. It is only through this realization that we can continue to advance as individuals, citizens, and human beings.

WHAT DO YOU THINK OF SAMPLE ESSAY 2?

Use these questions to evaluate sample essay 2:

- ◆ Is the essay legible?
- ◆ Does the essay have an introduction that is a separate paragraph?
- ◆ Does the author understand the topic?
- ◆ Is the author's opinion stated clearly?
- ◆ Does the author use examples to support her opinion?
- ◆ How many examples? What kind? How convincing are they?
- ◆ Does the author explain *how* the examples support her opinion?
- ◆ Has the author moved smoothly from one paragraph to the next?
- ◆ Is the essay organized? Does each example have a paragraph?
- ◆ Are the paragraphs well indented?

- Has the author stayed neatly within the lines?

- Has the author used impressive vocabulary correctly?

- Does the essay have a conclusion that is a separate paragraph?

- Does the conclusion summarize the points in the essay without being just a word-for-word repeat of the intro?

Which writing sample was better? _____

Take a look at the answer key for our evaluations of these essays.

THE ESSAY PLAN

The first three minutes

How do I spend the first three minutes?

_____

_____

Writing the essay

Opening Paragraph: _____

What do I include here? _____

_____

_____

Body Paragraphs: _____

What do I include here? _____

_____

Final Paragraph: _____

What do I include here? _____

_____

When I've only got three minutes left, what must I be sure to do?

_____

If you have any trouble answering these questions, reread this chapter before going further.

Practice — Prepare examples

Create index cards for the examples you've already written down, and any other examples you think of. Index cards will allow you to flip through your examples the morning of the test so they're really fresh in your mind.

- On each card, write down details that you can use in your essay. Go through your old school notes to jog your memory. You'll be glad you did.

- For a current event or historical example, write down names, dates, chronology, and the issues involved.

- For a literature example, write down titles, authors, character names and a summary of the plot.

Practice — Coming up with examples

It's not what you do, but how well you do it.

Agree   Disagree

_____   _____

_____   _____

_____   _____

Neither a borrower nor a lender be.

Agree   Disagree

_____   _____

_____   _____

_____   _____

Winning isn't everything.

Agree   Disagree

_____   _____

_____   _____

_____   _____

It is better to give than to receive.

Agree   Disagree

_____   _____

_____   _____

_____   _____

Look before you leap.

Agree   Disagree

_____   _____

_____   _____

_____   _____

American students still lag substantially behind students in other countries on tests of mathematics and science. How can we change this?

_____   _____

_____   _____

_____   _____

_____   _____

_____   _____

_____   _____

Practice — Writing essays

Time yourself for each of the following essays. When you're done with each, ask yourself the same questions you used to evaluate the sample "No pain, no gain" essay.

Ask a parent or teacher to read it, also, but be sure to let them know that what they're reading is a timed 25-minute essay, so they should read primarily for content and organization. Ask them not to grade it, but to tell you what you did well and what you could do better.

If your grammar, spelling, or punctuation is such that your reader has a hard time understanding the essay, you should to pick up a basic handbook so you can identify your weak points and work on them. However, don't be concerned about a few minor errors. If you have solid examples that support your main idea, and you've organized them well and written clearly and legibly, then you've covered the most important areas. Developing your writing style by learning to vary the length of your sentences, or reviewing the basics of grammar, usage, spelling, and punctuation can be useful, also, and will add to the polish of your essay. However, only if you have plenty of preparation time should you check out handbooks of style and usage.

If you'd like to do more essays than those that follow, then use the topics that you developed examples for above.

Topic: Haste makes waste.

Prompt: Do you agree or disagree with the topic statement? Support your position with specific examples from personal experience, the experience of others, current events, history, or literature.

_____

_____

_____

_____

_____

_____

_____

_____

_____

_____

_____

_____

_____

_____

_____

_____

_____

_____

_____

_____

_____

_____

_____

_____

_____

Topic: Be careful what you ask for, because you may get it.

Prompt: Do you agree or disagree with the topic statement? Support your position with specific examples from personal experience, the experience of others, current events, history, or literature.

Topic: People rarely stand up for what they believe.

Prompt: Do you agree or disagree with the topic statement? Support your position with specific examples from personal experience, the experience of others, current events, history, or literature.

Topic: Be careful what you ask for, because you may get it.

Prompt: Do you agree or disagree with the topic statement? Support your position with specific examples from personal experience, the experience of others, current events, history, or literature.

Topic: The opinions of one's peers can be influential on one's behavior. Is this good or bad?

Assignment: Support your position with specific examples from personal experience, the experience of others, current events, history, or literature.

14

Key to ISEE Drills

FUNDAMENTALS

Math vocabulary test

1.	6	0, 1, 2, 3, 4, and 5
2.	2, 4, 6	Many sets of integers would answer this question correctly.
3.	3	3, 5, and 7
4.	8	
5.	That number	The smallest positive integer is 1, and any number times 1 is itself.
6.	90	$5 + 6 + 3 = 90$
7.	30	$3 + 11 + 16 = 30$
8.	60	$90 - 30 = 60$
9.	2, 4, 6	Your answer to #2, as long as your integers are positive, answers this one too!
10.	Yes	
11.	22	$5 + 6 + 4 + 7 = 22$
12.	D	

Order of operations

1. 9
2. 16
3. 7
4. 5
5. 6
6. 30
7. 70
8. 60
9. 20
10. 100

Factors

1. A
2. D
3. B

Multiples

1. B
2. D
3. A
4. C

Reducing fractions

1. $\dfrac{3}{4}$

2. $\dfrac{1}{5}$

3. $\dfrac{2}{3}$

4. $\dfrac{3}{8}$

5. $\dfrac{3}{4}$

6. $\dfrac{2}{7}$

7. 1

8. $\dfrac{11}{9}$

9. If the number on top is bigger than the number on the bottom, the fraction is greater than 1.

Adding & subtracting fractions

1. $\dfrac{25}{24}$

2. $\dfrac{17}{24}$

3. $\dfrac{6}{7}$ Did you use the bowtie here? There was a common denominator already!

4. $\dfrac{1}{12}$

5. $\dfrac{73}{36}$ or $2\dfrac{1}{36}$

6. $-\dfrac{7}{20}$

7. $\dfrac{13}{3}$

8. $\dfrac{2}{9}$

9. $\dfrac{49}{60}$

10. $\dfrac{18x}{18} = x$

Multiplying & dividing fractions

1. $\dfrac{1}{3}$

2. $\dfrac{5}{4}$ or $1\dfrac{1}{4}$

3. $\dfrac{6}{25}$

4.   1

5. $\dfrac{4}{5}$

Fraction problems

1.   A
2.   C
3.   D
4.   A
5.   D

Did you use the bowtie to add all those fractions?
If so, look for an easier way to combine things: $\dfrac{1}{2} + \dfrac{1}{2} = 1$ and $\dfrac{2}{3} + \dfrac{1}{3} = 1$, etc.

Decimals

1.   18.7
2.   4.19
3.   4.78
4.   10.625
5.   .018
6.   6000
7.   5
8.   A
9.   C

Exponents

1.   8
2.   16
3.   27
4.   64
5.   B
6.   B

ALGEBRA

Manipulate!

1. 3
2. 5
3. 6
4. 7
5. 4
6. 8
7. 8
8. $\dfrac{1}{4}$
9. 7
10. 7   Problems 9 and 10 are really the same question. Did you see it?
11. 7
12. D
13. D   Be careful! If you chose (A), you did all the work, but didn't answer the right question!
14. B   Be careful of answer choice (D)!
15. A

Functions

1. C
2. B
3. D
4. D
5. A

Translating & solving percent questions

1. 12
2. 24
3. 5
4. 80

Word problems involving percentages

1. D
2. B
3. C
4. D
5. C
6. A
7. C
8. C
9. A
10. D

Ratios

1.   A
2.   B
3.   C
4.   B
5.   C
6.   B

Average problems

1.   A   Be careful of (B)—what does the question ask for?
2.   C
3.   B
4.   A
5.   D

Plugging In

1.   B
2.   D
3.   C
4.   A
5.   C   If you had trouble, try plugging in 8 for the number of pieces in the pie, drawing a pie with eight pieces, and crossing pieces off as Miguel eats them.
6.   B
7.   C
8.   C

GEOMETRY

Perimeter

1.   C
2.   C
3.   B

Triangles

1.   C
2.   B
3.   A
4.   C

Area & volume

1.   B
2.   C
3.   B
4.   D

Charts & Graphs

Chart and graph problems
1. D
2. D
3. A   Be careful of (D)—look at the little note underneath the chart!
4. A
5. B
6. A
7. A
8. C

Quantitative Comparison

Quant comp
1. C
2. A
3. B
4. B
5. C
6. D

Quant comp plugging in
1. B
2. C
3. D
4. A
5. D
6. D

Math Review
1. Yes.
2. It is neither positive nor negative.
3. Addition
4. Multiplication
5. The quotient
6. Yes; no
7. Exponents
8. Yes; no
9. No; Yes
10. Zero
11. Two
12. $2 + 2 + 2 = 8$
13. over 100 $(\dfrac{\quad}{100})$
14. Multiplication – +
15. Total
16. Average pie

17.   Plug in a number
18.   Add; all four
19.   Multiply; two (or one, since all the sides of a square
              are the same)
20.   180
21.   3; 180
22.   360
23.   2; equilateral
24.   Hypotenuse; right angle

25.   Area (of a triangle) $= \frac{1}{2} +$ base + height

Synonyms

Write your own definition

Possible definitions:
1.   Weird
2.   Introduction
3.   Giving
4.   Doing the right thing
5.   Change
6.   Spin
7.   Optimistic
8.   Stick around
9.   Help
10.   Build
11.   Bend
12.   Honest
13.   Tease
14.   Rough
15.   Self-centered
16.   Quiet
17.   Use
18.   Full of life
19.   Stretch out
20.   Positive result

Easy synonym techniques
1.   C
2.   A
3.   C
4.   D
5.   D
6.   D
7.   B
8.   C
9.   D
10.   A
11.   C
12.   B

13.	D
14.	B
15.	A
16.	C
17.	D
18.	C
19.	B
20.	C

Making your own context

Possible contexts:

1.	Common cold; common man
2.	Competent to stand trial
3.	Abridged dictionary
4.	Untimely demise; untimely remark
5.	Homogenized milk
6.	Juvenile delinquent; delinquent payments
7.	Inalienable rights
8.	Paltry sum
9.	Auspicious beginning; auspicious occasion
10.	Prodigal son

Using your own context

1.	C
2.	D
3.	D
4.	C
5.	A
6.	B
7.	C
8.	A
9.	C
10.	A

Decide positive/negative

1.	–
2.	–
3.	–
4.	+
5.	–
6.	+
7.	–
8.	+
9.	+
10.	–

Use positive/negative

Answers remaining should be:

1. B C
2. A B D
3. A C
4. C D
5. A B D
6. C D
7. B D
8. B D
9. A B
10. A C D
11. A B
12. A B D
13. C D
14. A
15. A D
16. A D
17. A B C
18. A B
19. B C D
20. B C

All synonyms techniques

1. B
2. A
3. C
4. A
5. D
6. A
7. D
8. B
9. C
10. B
11. B
12. C
13. D
14. C
15. D
16. B
17. C
18. B
19. D
20. B
21. C
22. B
23. B
24. D
25. D
26. D
27. C

28.	C
29.	A
30.	D
31.	B
32.	B
33.	B
34.	D
35.	D
36.	C
37.	C
38.	D
39.	B
40.	D

SENTENCE COMPLETIONS

Coming up with your word

These words are just to give you an idea of what you could have. Any words that accurately fill the blank based on the clue and the direction will do.

1.	Good
2.	Rare
3.	Remarkable
4.	Awake
5.	Lucky
6.	Caring
7.	Alike
8.	Procrastinate
9.	Frugal
10.	Movement
11.	Simple
12.	Produce
13.	Changed
14.	Lightweight; solid
15.	Optional
16.	Repetitive
17.	Dangerous
18.	Outgoing
19.	Healthy
20.	Generous
21.	Steadfast
22.	Intimidated; shy
23.	Annoyed
24.	On time
25.	Skill
26.	Variety
27.	Creative
28.	Sharing
29.	Flexible
30.	Innate
31.	Affable
32.	Awestruck

Eliminating answers based on your word

1. D
2. B
3. C
4. D
5. A
6. A
7. D
8. C
9. B
10. A
11. D
12. D
13. B
14. C
15. D
16. C
17. B
18. A
19. C
20. C
21. B
22. D
23. A
24. B
25. A
26. C
27. B
28. B
29. C
30. B
31. A
32. C

Using positive/negative

1. +
2. +
3. −
4. +
5. −
6. +
7. −
8. −
9. −
10. +

Eliminating based on positive/negative
1. A
2. C
3. B
4. D
5. C
6. A
7. C
8. D
9. A
10. C

Two blank sentence completions
1. B
2. C
3. A
4. A
5. D
6. A
7. C
8. C
9. A
10. C

All sentence completion techniques
1. A
2. C
3. B
4. C
5. A
6. A
7. D
8. B
9. B
10. C
11. B
12. D
13. C
14. C
15. A
16. B
17. D
18. D
19. A
20. B

READING

Getting through the passage

You should have brief labels like the following:

1st Label: Norway—>Iceland
2nd Label: Iceland—>Greenland
3rd Label: Lost
4th Label: Saw America; landed Greenland
What? A Viking
So What? Found America early
Passage type? History of an event—special studies

Answering a general question

1. D
2. C
3. D

Answering a specific question

1. C
2. A   Lead word: Iceland
3. B
4. D   Lead word: Greenland

Eliminating answers

Eliminate on a general question:

A   Too big—You can't do that in a few paragraphs.
C   Extreme
D   Extreme
E   Extreme
F   Extreme
H   Too small—This is only a detail.

Eliminate on a tone/attitude question:

J
K
M
O   Still too extreme, even though it's positive!
P
Q
S
T   Why would anyone write about something she doesn't care about?

Eliminate on a specific question:

U   Extreme
V   Extreme
X   Extreme and against common sense

All reading techniques

What? Tides
So what? Are caused by the moon.
1.   A
2.   D
3.   D
4.   C

Essay

Essay sample #1 evaluation

Sample 1 has several good points: It is legible, has a separate introduction that clearly states the author's opinion and shows that he understands the topic, and has two examples to support his opinion. However, the examples are weak and not fully developed. The first example is a generalized statement of which the author does not even claim to have personal experience, and the second example needs to be explained a bit further. There are separate paragraphs, showing that the author has organized his ideas, but there are no transitions from paragraph to paragraph. There are a few spelling errors and strikeouts, but this essay's biggest problem is its lack of any conclusion for the essay as a whole. Sample 1 is an essay that is a little below average.

Essay sample #2 evaluation

Sample 2 is a slightly longer essay that is also legible, with only a few spelling errors. It has a separate introduction that states the author's opinion, shows that she understands the topic, and introduces the examples that will support her opinion. In this essay, the author used two strong examples. One is a current event, and the other is historical. They are both explained so that the reader knows some details about each, and gains some understanding of the 'pains' and 'gains' involved in each. Transitions between sections could be smoother, but the essay is organized and the reader can quickly see that by looking at the indentations. Finally, the reader is left with a conclusion that both summarizes the author's opinion, and also broadens the essay outward, showing the importance of the topic. Sample 2 is a slightly above average essay, and could be made even better with additional details and a smoother style.

PART IV

ISEE Practice Tests

15

Upper Level ISEE
Practice Test

Upper Level Practice Test

Upper Level ISEE
Section 1
Time-20 minutes
40 Questions

This section consists of 40 questions for which you are allowed 20 minutes. There are two types of questions included, and directions for each type.

DIRECTIONS: Each question is made up of a word in capital letters followed by four choices. You should circle the one word that is most nearly the same in meaning as the word in capital letters.

1. GRAVE
   (A) deadly
   (B) open
   (C) solemn
   (D) final

2. FOMENT
   (A) instigate
   (B) dissemble
   (C) articulate
   (D) praise

3. INARTICULATE
   (A) tongue-tied
   (B) creative
   (C) overly sensitive
   (D) friendly

4. JARGON
   (A) fast speaking
   (B) odor
   (C) definition
   (D) terminology

5. THESIS
   (A) paper
   (B) report
   (C) belief
   (D) study

6. DEBUNK
   (A) build
   (B) justify
   (C) discredit
   (D) impress

7. DISDAIN
   (A) hope
   (B) contempt
   (C) find
   (D) annoy

8. RETICENT
   (A) anxious
   (B) aware
   (C) informed
   (D) reserved

9. PREVALENT
   (A) old-fashioned
   (B) minority
   (C) predominant
   (D) fascinating

10. SATIATE
   (A) fill
   (B) starve
   (C) serve
   (D) deny

GO ON TO THE NEXT PAGE.

11. CANDID
    (A) defiant
    (B) stingy
    (C) frank
    (D) dejected

12. EMULATE
    (A) brush off
    (B) imitate
    (C) perplex
    (D) permit

13. TAINT
    (A) master
    (B) infect
    (C) annoy
    (D) handle

14. CONFORM
    (A) perpetuate
    (B) jar
    (C) harmonize
    (D) contract

15. DETRIMENTAL
    (A) desolate
    (B) injurious
    (C) emphatic
    (D) considerate

16. METICULOUS
    (A) finicky
    (B) maddening
    (C) favorable
    (D) gigantic

17. JUXTAPOSE
    (A) place side by side
    (B) put behind
    (C) keep away
    (D) question

18. HETEROGENEOUS
    (A) similar
    (B) generous
    (C) unusual
    (D) mixed

19. MITIGATE
    (A) harden
    (B) bend
    (C) untangle
    (D) ease

20. ELUSIVE
    (A) unhappy
    (B) real
    (C) treacherous
    (D) slippery

GO ON TO THE NEXT PAGE.

DIRECTIONS: Each question below is made up of a sentence with one or two blanks. The sentences with one blank indicate that one word is missing. The sentences with two blanks indicate that two words are missing. Each sentence is followed by four choices. You should circle the one word or pair of words that will best complete the meaning of the sentence as whole.

21. Jane felt _____ about whether to go the party or not; on one hand it seemed like fun, but on the other, she was very tired.
    (A) happy
    (B) ambivalent
    (C) apathetic
    (D) irritated

22. Even though the critics praised the author's _____ use of words, they found the text _____ at a mere 100 pages.
    (A) improper...laconic
    (B) precise...short
    (C) hackneyed...threadbare
    (D) sure...banal

23. Like the more famous Susan B. Anthony, M. Carey Thomas _____ feminism and women's right to be treated equally.
    (A) degraded
    (B) gained
    (C) found
    (D) championed

24. It is unfortunate but true that some of the most _____ nations in the world are capable of some of the most brutal and barbaric acts.
    (A) advanced
    (B) ill-mannered
    (C) large
    (D) primitive

25. Although Marie was a talented and _____ performer, her gifts were often _____ because she didn't know how to promote herself.
    (A) promising...satisfied
    (B) faithful...supported
    (C) insulting...overlooked
    (D) versatile...ignored

26. The _____ given on the Fourth of July was a tradition for years after the American Revolution; the _____ men in town would stand up in front of their communities and speak about what made America great.
    (A) invitation...ordinary
    (B) concert...musical
    (C) oration... important
    (D) experiment...famous

27. Thomas Jefferson was a man of _____ talents: He was known for his skills as a writer, a musician, architect, and inventor as well as politician.
    (A) overblown
    (B) diverse
    (C) mundane
    (D) professed

28. Monica could remain _____ no longer; the injustices she witnessed moved her to speak up.
    (A) diplomatic
    (B) active
    (C) furious
    (D) helpful

29. Louisa May Alcott's *Little Women* is really quite _____; much of the story is based on her experiences as a young woman growing up in Concord, Massachusetts.
    (A) moving
    (B) visual
    (C) autobiographical
    (D) fictional

GO ON TO THE NEXT PAGE.

30. Although she was the daughter of a wealthy slaveholder, Angelina Grimke _____ slavery and _____ her whole life for the cause of abolition.
    (A) represented...fought
    (B) detested...worked
    (C) hated...wasted
    (D) desired...picketed

31. Though his lectures could be monotonous, Mr. Carey was actually quite _____ when he spoke to students in small, informal groups.
    (A) prosaic
    (B) vapid
    (C) fascinating
    (D) pious

32. Craig had _____ that the day would not go well, and just as he'd thought, he had two pop quizzes.
    (A) an interest
    (B) a premonition
    (C) an antidote
    (D) a report

33. Morality is not _____; cultures around the world have different ideas about how people should be treated.
    (A) debatable
    (B) universal
    (C) helpful
    (D) realistic

34. Marshall's worst habit was that he _____; putting off all his work until it was overwhelming.
    (A) obfuscated
    (B) procrastinated
    (C) celebrated
    (D) proliferated

35. Many of today's consumers are _____ expensive computer equipment, purchasing complicated machinery that they may not even need.
    (A) captivated by
    (B) jealous of
    (C) sullen about
    (D) misled by

36. Because Martha was naturally _____, she would see the bright side of any situation, but Jack had a _____ personality and always waited for something bad to happen.
    (A) cheerful... upbeat
    (B) frightened ... mawkish
    (C) optimistic. . . dismal
    (D) realistic. . . . unreasonable

37. Rhubarb is actually quite_____ requiring a large amount of sugar to make it _____.
    (A) nutritious... sickening
    (B) bitter... palatable
    (C) flavorful... fattening
    (D) unpopular... sticky

38. The panelist was extremely _____ to the other members of the discussion, referring to them as "ignorant demagogues."
    (A) deferential
    (B) contentious
    (C) respectful
    (D) garrulous

39. Coach Jones believed his feelings about the team were _____; he didn't need to explicitly state them.
    (A) overt
    (B) reasonable
    (C) fractious
    (D) tacit

40. Unwilling to commit to any field of study or type of work, Margie was labeled a _____ by her advisors at school.
    (A) dilettante
    (B) firebrand
    (C) logician
    (D) opportunist

STOP

IF YOU FINISH BEFORE TIME IS CALLED,
YOU MAY CHECK YOUR WORK ON THIS SECTION ONLY.
DO NOT TURN TO ANY OTHER SECTION IN THE TEST.

Upper Level ISEE
Section 2
Time-35 Minutes
25 Questions

Following each problem in this section, there are four suggested answers. Work each problem in your head or in the blank space provided at the right of the page. Then look at the four suggested answers and decide which one is best.

<u>Note:</u> Figures that accompany problems in this section are drawn as accurately as possible EXCEPT when it is stated in a specific problem that its figure is not drawn to scale.

Sample Problem:

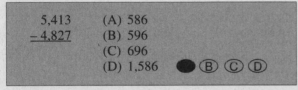

1. Which of the following is greatest?

    (A) .0100
    (B) .0099
    (C) .1900
    (D) .0199

2. Which of the following is NOT the product of two prime numbers?

    (A) 33
    (B) 35
    (C) 45
    (D) 91

3. If x, y, and z are consecutive even integers, then what is the difference between x and z?

    (A) 0
    (B) 1
    (C) 2
    (D) 4

GO ON TO THE NEXT PAGE.

2

Questions 4-5 refer to the following chart.

CLOTHING CLOSE OUT

Dresses	Originally $120	Now $90
Coats	Originally $250	Now $180
Shoes	Originally $60	Now $40
Hats	Originally $40	Now $20

4. Which of the items for sale has the greatest percent discount?

   (A) Dresses
   (B) Coats
   (C) Shoes
   (D) Hats

5. Purchasing which item will save the buyer the most dollars?

   (A) Dresses
   (B) Coats
   (C) Shoes
   (D) Hats

6. Amy is three years older than Beth and five years younger than Jo. If Beth is *b* years old, how old is Jo, in terms of *b?*

   (A) $2b + 3$
   (B) $2b - 3$
   (C) $b + 4$
   (D) $b + 8$

GO ON TO THE NEXT PAGE.

7. If x is divided by 5, the remainder is 4. If y is divided by 5, the remainder is 1. What is the remainder when $(x + y)$ is divided by 5?

   (A) 0
   (B) 1
   (C) 2
   (D) 3

USE THIS SPACE FOR FIGURING.

2

8. What is the perimeter of the square ABCD?

   (A) 5
   (B) 15
   (C) 20
   (D) 25

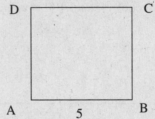

9. At a party, 4 pizzas with 8 slices each were served. If each of the 9 guests had 3 pieces of pizza each, how many slices remained?

   (A) 4
   (B) 5
   (C) 6
   (D) 7

10. Jamie had x dollars in the bank. He withdrew $\frac{1}{2}$ to buy a car. He withdrew $\frac{1}{3}$ of what was left to buy a couch. What fraction of the original amount remained in his account?

    (A) $\frac{1}{6}$

    (B) $\frac{1}{5}$

    (C) $\frac{1}{4}$

    (D) $\frac{1}{3}$

GO ON TO THE NEXT PAGE.

11. J is a whole number divisible by 4. J is also divisible by 3. Which of the following is NOT a possible value for J?

    (A) 12
    (B) 24
    (C) 30
    (D) 36

USE THIS SPACE FOR FIGURING.

2

12. The product of .48 and 100 is approximately

    (A) 0.5
    (B) 4.8
    (C) 5
    (D) 50

13. Which of the following is less than $\frac{6}{7}$?

    (A) $\frac{2}{3}$

    (B) $\frac{8}{9}$

    (C) $\frac{7}{6}$

    (D) $\frac{17}{19}$

14. Square ACEG is composed of 4 squares with sides of 1 meter each. Traveling only on the lines of the squares, how many different routes from A to D that are exactly 3 meters long are possible?

    (A) 2
    (B) 3
    (C) 4
    (D) 5

GO ON TO THE NEXT PAGE.

15. If, in triangle ABC, the measure of angle *B* is greater than 90°, and *AB* = *BC,* what is a possible measure for angle *C* in degrees?

    (A) 35
    (B) 45
    (C) 60
    (D) It cannot be determined from the information given.

USE THIS SPACE FOR FIGURING.

2

16. Chumway Motors discounts the cost of a car by 10% and then runs another special one-day deal offering an additional 20% off the discounted price. What discount does this represent from the original price of the car?

    (A) 28%
    (B) 30%
    (C) 40%
    (D) 72%

17. David scored 82, 84, and 95 on his three first math tests. What score does he need on his fourth test to bring his average up to a 90?

    (A) 90
    (B) 92
    (C) 96
    (D) 99

18. $\frac{1}{3}$ is most nearly equivalent to

    (A) 0.13
    (B) 0.3
    (C) 0.4
    (D) 0.5

GO ON TO THE NEXT PAGE.

19. 25% of 10% of 200 is

USE THIS SPACE FOR FIGURING.

2

(A) 250
(B) 100
(C) 50
(D) 5

20. The ratio of yellow paint to red paint to white paint needed to make a perfect mixture of orange paint is 3 to 2 to 1. If 36 gallons of orange paint are needed to paint a cottage, how many gallons of red paint will be needed?

(A) 2
(B) 6
(C) 12
(D) 15

Directions for Quantitative Comparison Questions

<u>Questions 21–40</u> each consist of two quantities in boxes, one in Column A and one in Column B. You are to compare the two quantities and on the answer sheet fill in oval

  A if the quantity in Column A is greater;
  B if the quantity in Column B is greater;
  C if the two quantities are equal;
  D if the relationship cannot be determined from
     the information given.

<u>Notes:</u>

1. In some questions, information is given about one or both of the quantities to be compared. In such cases, the given information is centered above the two columns and is not boxed.
2. In a given question, a symbol that appears in both columns represents the same thing in Column A as it does in Column B.
3. Letters such as *x*, *n*, and *k* stand for real numbers.

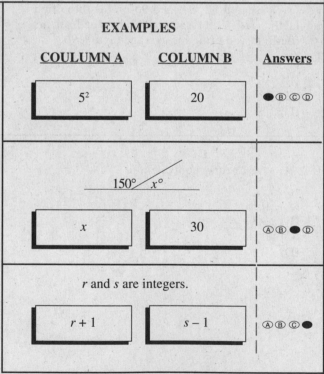

GO ON TO THE NEXT PAGE.

	COLUMN A	**COLUMN B**

USE THIS SPACE FOR FIGURING.

2

21. 25% of 50   50% of 25

In a group of 150
fiction books, 60
percent are fiction.

22. Half the number of fiction books   The difference between the number of fiction books and the number of non-fiction books

---

Dawn has a drawer filled
with socks. The ratio of brown
socks to blue socks is 2:3

23. $\dfrac{2}{3}$ The fractional part of the socks in Dawn's drawer which are brown

---

24. x^2 x^3

---

25. The average of the three smallest positive even integers   The average of the three smallest positive integers

---

26. $2x$ 120

GO ON TO THE NEXT PAGE.

	__COLUMN A__	__COLUMN B__

$$(x + 2)(x - 2) = 0$$

27.	x	2

28.	$\sqrt{36} + \sqrt{16}$	$\sqrt{52}$

29.	3^{12}	9^6

The volume of
a solid cube is 27.

30.	The height of the cube.	3

$$abc > 0$$
$$a < 0$$

31.	bc	0

$$\frac{x + 2}{y + 2} = \frac{x}{y}$$

32.	x	$y + 2$

Triangle LMN is
isosceles and the
sum of angle L
and angle M is 160.

33.	The measure of the largest angle of triangle LMN	90°

	COLUMN A	**COLUMN B**

USE THIS SPACE FOR FIGURING.

2

8 thingees = 64 gizmos

34.	$\frac{1}{2}$ thingee	4 gizmos

35.	The sum of the integers from 1 to 100, inclusive	The sum of the even integers from 1 to 200, inclusive

NO = OP = 2

36.	NP	2

$$\frac{x}{4} = 1.5$$

37.	x	5

$x > 0$

38.	x	x^2

A hiker completed a hike walking at an average rate of 4 miles per hour. Had she averaged 5 miles per hour, the trip would have been completed two hours earlier than it was.

39.	The number of hours in which the hike was completed	10

GO ON TO THE NEXT PAGE.

COLUMN A	COLUMN B	USE THIS SPACE FOR FIGURING.

x is a positive integer
y is the result of $100x$

40. The sum of the   The sum of the
     digits in x digits in y

2

STOP
**IF YOU FINISH BEFORE TIME IS CALLED,
YOU MAY CHECK YOUR WORK ON THIS SECTION ONLY.
DO NOT TURN TO ANY OTHER SECTION IN THE TEST.**

Upper Level ISEE
Section 3
Time-35 minutes
40 Questions

DIRECTIONS: Each passage below is followed by questions based on its content. Answer the questions following a passage on the basis of what is *stated* or *implied* in that passage.

The Aztecs were the last Native Americans to rule Mexico. Their great civilization, founded more than seven hundred years ago, was a barbarous and ambitious one. When the Aztecs invaded Central Mexico in the 13th century, it was not to gain territory, but to gather the thousands of people they would need to sacrifice to their gods. The priests used stone knives to kill almost a thousand people a week to offer up their hearts to their sun god, Huitzilopochtli.

It seems hard to reconcile that sort of violence with the great advances the Aztecs made in civilization. They instituted a system of government of tribunals, through which they ruled various provinces. Their artists and craftsman produced a great variety of cultural objects. Their architecture is still admired. Their culture thrived until its defeat by the Spanish conquistadors, led by Cortez in 1519.

---

1. The passage suggests that the Aztecs made important contributions in all the following fields EXCEPT
   (A) architecture
   (B) art
   (C) religion
   (D) government

2. The primary purpose of the passage is to
   (A) debunk the religious theories put forth by the Aztecs
   (B) argue that the Aztecs were more important than most people think
   (C) discuss religious rituals of Native American cultures
   (D) provide a summary of the rise and fall of the Aztecs

3. The passage implies that Cortez
   (A) greatly admired the Aztec civilization
   (B) was a Spanish conquistador
   (C) fell victim to the human sacrifices made by Aztec priests
   (D) destroyed many Aztec artifacts

4. According to the passage, the reason the Aztecs invaded Central Mexico was to
   (A) gather more land for their empire
   (B) build new temples to their gods
   (C) institute a new governmental system
   (D) assemble people to be used as human sacrifice

5. Which of the following best describes the author's attitude toward the Aztecs?
   (A) indifference
   (B) admiration
   (C) objectivity
   (D) revulsion

GO ON TO THE NEXT PAGE.

> A simple microscope is able to magnify an object more than a magnifying glass by its use of two lenses. There are many types of microscopes, from the simple optical microscope to the electron microscope. While a simple, inexpensive optical microscope may magnify an object from about fifty times its size to about one to two thousand times its size, the expensive electron microscope can magnify an object by up to about 250,000 times.
>
> The electron microscope works not with glass lenses, but with magnetic lenses. It uses electrons instead of light to produce an image. Just as a ray of light bends as it passes through a curved lens, streams of electrons bend as they pass by a magnetic lens. Very small objects do not affect light at all, but they do affect electrons. Because of that, an electron microscope can distinguish objects which are very small and very close together.

3

6. The primary purpose of the passage is to
   - (A) explain the difference between the electron and optical microscope
   - (B) give the reasons that an electron microscope is so expensive
   - (C) show the difference between a glass and a magnetic lens
   - (D) report on the history of microscopes

7. The passage implies that the greatest advantage of the electron microscope is
   - (A) its expense
   - (B) its versatility
   - (C) its use of magnets
   - (D) its greater ability to magnify

8. According to the passage, the primary reason that a regular optical microscope cannot be used to magnify very small objects is because
   - (A) it uses light instead of electrons to project an image
   - (B) it can only magnify up to 250,000 times original size
   - (C) it does not use magnetic fields
   - (D) the light rays it uses bend

9. As used in line 8, the word "pass" most closely means
   - (A) forgo
   - (B) proceed
   - (C) permit
   - (D) open

10. According to the passage, for which of the following would an electron microscope be more useful than an optical microscope?
    - (A) Examining fingerprints
    - (B) Measuring the width of a strand of hair
    - (C) Enlarging the image of a skin pore by 50,000 times
    - (D) Examining the seed of a tomato

GO ON TO THE NEXT PAGE.

The world changed on the morning of December 17th in 1903. At Kitty Hawk, North Carolina, Orville and Wilbur Wright made the world's first controlled, powered flight. Although the actual flight lasted a very short time—only twelve seconds—it represented the beginning of man's ascent into the sky.

The science of aviation did not take long to progress. By 1909, Louis Bleriot flew 26 miles over the English Channel from France to England. Charles Lindbergh made the first solo flight across the Atlantic Ocean in his Spirit of St. Louis, in 1927. In 1947, just twenty years after that, pilot Chuck Yeager flew the rocket powered Bell X-1 faster than the speed of sound. Today, the supersonic Concorde transports passengers over the ocean at the speed of sound on a daily basis. It makes the trip in fewer than four hours. Today, many people take airplanes every day to reach all the corners of the earth.

11. The best title for the passage is
    (A) A Short History of Aviation
    (B) Man's Future in the Skies
    (C) The Life of Orville and Wilbur Wright
    (D) Chuck Yeager—Man of Speed

12. According to the passage, the reason the flight taken by the Wright Brothers was so important was that
    (A) it took place in North Carolina
    (B) it lasted only a short time
    (C) it was very powerful
    (D) it was the first time such a flight had taken place

13. The word "supersonic" in line 7 most probably means
    (A) expensive
    (B) faster than the speed of sound
    (C) daily
    (D) luxurious

14. According to the author, one of the most impressive things about the science of aviation is that
    (A) it progressed very quickly
    (B) it costs so much money
    (C) it took place primarily in America
    (D) planes now travel on a daily basis

GO ON TO THE NEXT PAGE.

3

Not all bees live in colonies. Some bees live all alone in a nest built for one. Most of us, however, when we think of bees and wasps, think of huge groups of insects, working together in a cohesive social unit. The hive is, in many ways, a perfect example of a social system. Inside the hive, bees raise their young and store honey. The queen honeybee, for example, may lay up to 1,500 eggs a day in the summer. The drone bee mates with the queen and dies. The worker bees gather food, care for the hive and the young and protect the hive. The stored pollen and honey will feed the colony throughout the cold winter months. Inside a hive there is one queen, a few hundred drones and as many as 40,000 workers. The expression "busy as a bee" is certainly true when you consider the work that bees perform.

15. According to the passage, the purpose of the drones is to
    (A) gather food
    (B) care for the hive
    (C) mate with the queen
    (D) supervise the workers

16. According to the passage, the purpose of the honey and pollen is to
    (A) fertilize flowers
    (B) attract a queen to the hive
    (C) provide a place for the queen to lay her eggs
    (D) provide nourishment for the hive

17. The passage implies that the hive is an example of a social system because
    (A) the queen rules over all the bees
    (B) each member of the hive performs a different job, yet they work together
    (C) there is no strife in the hive
    (D) there are workers to do all the work

18. The word "cohesive" in line 2 most closely means
    (A) sticky
    (B) connected
    (C) hard working
    (D) ritualistic

19. The tone of the passage is most like that found in a
    (A) diary entry of a modern naturalist
    (B) laboratory report
    (C) general science textbook
    (D) letter to a friend

GO ON TO THE NEXT PAGE.

1

3

A wealthy patron of the arts, Isabella Stewart Gardner, was born in New York in 1840. She married John Lowell Gardner, a wealthy heir, and settled in Boston, Massachusetts. When her only son died as a young child, she devoted her life to the arts. Assisted by Bernard Berenson, a young art critic, she began collecting important works of art. After her husband died in 1898, she purchased land for the construction of a museum and worked for years supervising its creation. She actually lived in the museum until her death in 1924. Her museum became a gathering place for artists, writers, and celebrities. She was considered quite eccentric, often shunning Boston "society" in favor of more colorful characters. She willed her wonderful museum to the city of Boston, to be preserved as a public museum. Today, if you visit the city of Boston, you can admire the work of Isabella Gardner.

20. As used in line 7, the word "colorful" means
    (A) vivid
    (B) beautiful
    (C) offbeat
    (D) brilliant

21. The passage suggests that Isabella Gardner began collecting art
    (A) to spend her husband's money
    (B) after the death of her husband
    (C) after the death of her son
    (D) to impress art critics

22. According to the passage, the museum built by Isabella Gardner was used for all of the following EXCEPT
    (A) her home
    (B) a place for artists to congregate
    (C) a place for art to be viewed
    (D) a school for aspiring artists

23. Which of the following best describes the author's attitude toward Isabella Stewart Gardner?
    (A) Jealous
    (B) Critical
    (C) Admiring
    (D) Fanatic

GO ON TO THE NEXT PAGE.

3

Carrie Nation gained notoriety as a hatchet-wielding woman during the early part of the twentieth century. She was married to an alcoholic and spent many years trying to reform him. When that seemed impossible, she left him and married David Nation. Some time after their marriage, Carrie and David Nation moved to Kansas. The sale of alcohol was illegal in Kansas, yet there were many establishments that sold alcoholic drinks. Carrie organized the Women's Christian Temperance Union, which vehemently, and sometimes violently, fought the saloons. She believed that since saloons were illegal, she was within her rights to destroy them, so she wrecked saloons with her hatchet. Carrie was arrested thirty times, in many cities around the country. Some say her eccentric behavior was inherited from her mentally ill mother. Whatever the cause, Carrie Nation was a well-known personality in the early 1900s and her efforts most probably helped the cause of temperance, which led to the national prohibition of alcohol in 1920.

24. The word "cause" as used in line 9 most closely means
    (A) goal
    (B) reason
    (C) excuse
    (D) rebellion

25. The main purpose of the passage is to
    (A) explain the causes that led to the national prohibition of alcohol in 1920
    (B) examine the reasons that Carrie Nation was so eccentric
    (C) present an overview of the life and actions of a famous woman
    (D) report on the Women's Christian Temperance Union

26. The passage implies that which of the following was a reason for Carrie Nation's attitude toward temperance?
    (A) Her mother's mental illness
    (B) Her inability to have children
    (C) Her first husband's alcoholism
    (D) Her move to Kansas

27. Which of the following best expresses the author's attitude toward Carrie Nation?
    (A) Admiration
    (B) Disgust
    (C) Neutrality
    (D) Indifference

28. According to the author, what was the most probable legacy of Carrie Nation's actions?
    (A) The national prohibition of alcohol
    (B) The destruction of saloons by women around the country
    (C) The legislation prohibiting the destruction of saloons
    (D) The inquiry into the genetic link to mental illness

GO ON TO THE NEXT PAGE.

3

When you hear a weather report, watch television, or make a phone call, you are frequently doing so because of a satellite. The word *satellite* refers to anything that orbits around a planet in space. The moon is one of our satellites. However, in addition to the moon, there are many objects floating around the earth that we have put there for our uses. Some satellites take pictures of the Earth from high up in space, giving us useful pictures of our planet. They may be used to spot weather patterns that could not have been seen from a lower vantage point. Television reporters may use an uplink to send their images to a satellite that circles high above the earth, which will send the images back down to a television station halfway around the world. Spy satellites may observe military installations around the world and report back with detailed pictures. Circling hundreds of miles above the Earth are many of these satellites, performing all sorts of jobs.

29. According to the passage, all of the following are uses of satellites EXCEPT
    (A) taking pictures
    (B) sending television images
    (C) spying
    (D) protecting the atmosphere

30. The passage suggests that which of the following would be classified as a satellite?
    (A) A meteor shower
    (B) The sun
    (C) The planet Neptune
    (D) One of the moons of Jupiter

31. The author implies that spy satellites are useful because
    (A) they send radio transmissions
    (B) they take pictures and send them back quickly
    (C) they detect potential weather problems
    (D) they decide the proper course of action

32. The main purpose of the passage is to
    (A) discuss reasons that satellites are superior to other forms of communication
    (B) define the term "satellite" and describe some of their uses
    (C) explain the reasons that satellites work so well
    (D) give an example of the only real beneficial use of satellites

33. Which of the following can be inferred is the reason that weather satellites are preferable to weather balloons?
    (A) They can take a larger picture from higher up.
    (B) They are faster.
    (C) They are less expensive in the long run.
    (D) They don't need people to run them.

GO ON TO THE NEXT PAGE.

3

It seems hard to imagine a world without plastics. So many of the items we use every day are made of plastic. The first plastic was synthesized in 1909. A synthetic material is any that is manufactured from chemicals in factories, as opposed to those which are naturally occurring materials, like cotton or wood. Plastics are made primarily from petroleum products and have many advantages over natural products. For one thing, they may be less expensive to produce. More important, however, is that they are light and malleable. Parts for automobiles, aircraft, and many appliances can be easily crafted by plastics. Special kinds of plastics are used for different jobs. Nylon, an elastic synthetic resin, is a type of plastic that can be used to make clothing.

34. As used in line 6, the word "crafted" most closely means
    (A) swapped
    (B) made
    (C) sculpted
    (D) tricked

35. According to the author, one of the primary advantages of plastic is its
    (A) cost
    (B) color
    (C) flexibility
    (D) ability to make cloth

36. The primary purpose of the passage is to
    (A) discuss the advantages of plastic
    (B) warn about the ecological dangers associated with plastic
    (C) make a plea for the use of petroleum products
    (D) tout the usefulness of nylon

GO ON TO THE NEXT PAGE.

3

The digestive system of the cow is complex indeed. Unlike humans, who have a simple stomach, the cow has a large, four-chambered stomach. Cows eat plants (primarily grass), which are swallowed and partly digested in one of the four chambers, called the rumen. The cow will then regurgitate, or bring back up, the partially digested plant fibers in a small mass called "cud." The cud is chewed further and swallowed again, this time into the second chamber, or reticulum. It passes then to the third and fourth chambers, until it is completely digested. It may sound unpleasant, but the cow is able to extract a maximum of nutrients from its food by digesting in this manner. The whole process may take more than three days.

37. The best title for the passage might be
    (A) The Cow's Great Gift to Man: Milk
    (B) Digestive Systems and their Purposes
    (C) The Diet of the Cow
    (D) The Digestive System of the Cow

38. According to the passage, the primary benefit of the cow's digestive system is that
    (A) it allows the cow to eat more slowly
    (B) it doesn't require as much food as other systems
    (C) it allows the cow to absorb more nutrients
    (D) it is complex and original

39. The passage suggests which of the following about humans?
    (A) They depend on cows.
    (B) They do not have four-chambered stomachs.
    (C) They do not eat grass.
    (D) They require the same nutrients as cows do.

40. Which of the following best describes the author's attitude toward the cow's digestive system?
    (A) She believes it is needlessly complicated.
    (B) She is disgusted by the process of digestion.
    (C) She is worried that the cow will be slaughtered.
    (D) She admires the efficiency of the system.

STOP

IF YOU FINISH BEFORE TIME IS CALLED,
YOU MAY CHECK YOUR WORK ON THIS SECTION ONLY.
DO NOT TURN TO ANY OTHER SECTION IN THE TEST.

Upper Level ISEE
Section 4
Time-40 Minutes
50 Questions

Following each problem in this section, there are five suggested answers. Work each problem in your head or in the blank space provided at the right of the page. Then look at the five suggested answers and decide which one is best.

<u>Note:</u> Figures that accompany problems in this section are drawn as accurately as possible EXCEPT when it is stated in a specific problem that its figure is not drawn to scale.

Sample Problem:

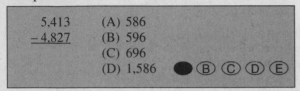

1. Which of the following pairs of numbers are the two different prime factors of 36?

   (A) 2 and 3
   (B) 3 and 4
   (C) 3 and 12
   (D) 4 and 9

USE THIS SPACE FOR FIGURING.

2. For what non-zero value of x will the expression

   $\dfrac{x - 3}{4x}$ be equal to 0?

   (A) -3
   (B) -2
   (C) 0
   (D) 3

3. Two positive whole numbers are in a ratio of 3 to 4. If the smaller of the two numbers is 9, what is the average of the two numbers?

    (A) 4
    (B) 10
    (C) 10.5
    (D) 12

4. The four angles in Figure 1 share a common vertex on a straight line. What is the value of *b* when *a* equals 42?

    (A)   38 degrees
    (B)   40 degrees
    (C)   42 degrees
    (D)   46 degrees

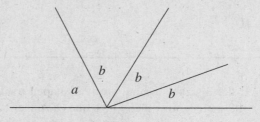

FIGURE 1

5. What is 85% of 50?

    (A) 135
    (B) 150.75
    (C) 42.5
    (D) 39

6. A set of three positive integers has a sum of 11 and a product of 36. If the smallest of the three numbers is 2, what is the largest?

    (A) 2
    (B) 4
    (C) 6
    (D) 9

GO ON TO THE NEXT PAGE.

7. What is two-thirds of one-half?

(A) $\dfrac{1}{3}$

(B) $\dfrac{7}{6}$

(C) $\dfrac{1}{2}$

(D) $\dfrac{2}{3}$

USE THIS SPACE FOR FIGURING.

8. If the distance around an oval-shaped track is 400 meters, how many laps does a runner have to run to cover a distance of 4 kilometers? 1 kilometer = 1,000 meters)

(A) 4
(B) 10
(C) 15
(D) 1,000

9. In triangle ABC, the length of side AB is

(A) 5
(B) 7
(C) 11
(D) 14

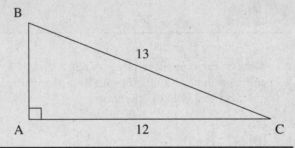

10. If $f = 2$, and $f^{\,j} = 2f$, what is the value of j?

(A) 0
(B) 1
(C) 2
(D) 3

11. Frank earns $300 a week every week that he works for the first 4 weeks of the summer. He earns $500 a week every week for the last 6 weeks of the summer. What was Frank's average weekly salary for the full ten weeks of summer?

    (A) $400
    (B) $420
    (C) $450
    (D) $500

USE THIS SPACE FOR FIGURING.

4

12. If $\sqrt{a} + \sqrt{b} + \sqrt{c} = 15$, and $a = 36$ and $b = 25$, what is the value of c?

    (A) 4
    (B) 16
    (C) 49
    (D) 81

13. There are x students is Mrs. Sproul's class, 4 fewer than twice as many as are in Mrs. Puccio's class. If there are y students in Mrs. Puccio's class then what is the value of y in terms of x?

    (A) $\dfrac{x}{2} + 2$
    (B) $2x + 4$
    (C) $2x - 4$
    (D) $\dfrac{x}{2} - 4$

14. An automobile traveling 50 miles per hour will take how many hours to travel 1,000 miles?

    (A) 2
    (B) 5
    (C) 10
    (D) 20

GO ON TO THE NEXT PAGE.

15. What is the average of Alex's bowling scores if she bowls a 110, 170, and 200 for her three games?

(A) 120
(B) 160
(C) 190
(D) 210

USE THIS SPACE FOR FIGURING.

Questions 16–17 refer to the following definition.

$\#x = x^2$ if x is negative
$\#x = 2x$ is x is positive

16. # (–6) – # (6) =

(A) –24
(B) 16
(C) 24
(D) 30

17. What is the value of #[#x – #y] when $x = 3$ and $y = -4$?

(A) –10
(B) 12
(C) 32
(D) 100

18. In Figure 2, what is the value of x in terms of y?

(A) y
(B) $90 - y$
(C) $90 + y$
(D) $180 - y$

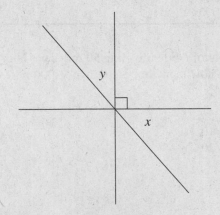

FIGURE 2

19. $\dfrac{4a^4b^6c^3}{2a^3b^5c^2} =$

USE THIS SPACE FOR FIGURING.

$\boxed{4}$

(A) $\dfrac{2ac}{b}$

(B) $\dfrac{ac}{b}$

(C) $\dfrac{2b}{c}$

(D) $2abc$

20. In Mr. Johanessen's class, $\dfrac{1}{4}$ of the students failed the final exam. Of the remaining class, $\dfrac{1}{3}$ scored an A. What fraction of the whole class passed the test, but scored below an A?

(A) $\dfrac{5}{12}$

(B) $\dfrac{1}{4}$

(C) $\dfrac{7}{12}$

(D) $\dfrac{1}{2}$

21. A room in a house had a width that is $\dfrac{1}{2}$ of its length. If the perimeter of the room is 180 feet, what is the length of the room in feet?

(A) 60
(B) 50
(C) 40
(D) 30

GO ON TO THE NEXT PAGE.

22. When buying new clothes for school, Rena spends $20 more than Karen and $50 more than Lynn does. If Rena spends r dollars, then what is the cost of all three of their purchases, in terms of r?

    (A) $r + 70$

    (B) $\dfrac{r + 70}{3}$

    (C) $3r - 70$

    (D) $r + 210$

23. In a group of 100 children, there are 34 more girls than there are boys. How many boys are in the group?

    (A) 33
    (B) 37
    (C) 67
    (D) 68

24. If $6x - 7 = 17$, then $x + 6 =$

    (A) 6
    (B) 10
    (C) 14
    (D) 24

25. At Nicholas's Computer World, computers usually sold for $1,500 are now being sold for $1,200. What fraction of the original price is the new price?

    (A) $\dfrac{1}{10}$

    (B) $\dfrac{1}{5}$

    (C) $\dfrac{3}{4}$

    (D) $\dfrac{4}{5}$

26. A dressing of oil and vinegar is 20% vinegar and 80% oil. A chef adds x cups of vinegar and $4x$ cups of oil. The new mixture will have what percent vinegar?

   (A) 10%
   (B) 20%
   (C) 50%
   (D) It cannot be determined from the information given.

USE THIS SPACE FOR FIGURING.

4

27. If $\dfrac{3}{x} = \dfrac{y}{4}$ x, then

   (A) $xy = 12$
   (B) $3y = 4x$
   (C) $\dfrac{x}{y} = \dfrac{4}{3}$
   (D) $3x = 4y$

28. The ratio of boys to girls at Delaware Township School is 3 to 2. If there is a total of 600 students at the school, how many are girls?

   (A) 120
   (B) 240
   (C) 360
   (D) 400

29. 150% of 40 is

   (A) 30
   (B) 40
   (C) 50
   (D) 60

GO ON TO THE NEXT PAGE.

30. Jane studied for her math exam for 4 hours last night. If she studied $\frac{3}{4}$ as long for her English exam, how many hours did she study all together?

    (A) 3
    (B) $4\frac{3}{4}$
    (C) 6
    (D) 7

31. $\dfrac{.966}{.42} =$

    (A) 0.23
    (B) 2.3
    (C) 23
    (D) 230

32. Nicole was able to type 35 words per minute. If she increased her speed by 20%, her new typing speed would be

    (A) 38 words per minute
    (B) 42 words per minute
    (C) 55 words per minute
    (D) 70 words per minute

33. The first term in a series of numbers is 50. Each subsequent term is one-half the term before it if the term is even, or one-half rounded up to the next whole number if the term is odd. What is the third term in this sequence?

    (A) 13
    (B) 24
    (C) 30
    (D) 40

34. If the average of 7 and x is equal to the average of 5, 9, and x, what is the value of x?

    (A) 2
    (B) 5
    (C) 7
    (D) 9

USE THIS SPACE FOR FIGURING.

4

35. On the number line, if segment BD has a length of 18, segment AB has a length of 5, and segment CD has a length of 12, then segment AC has a length of

    (A) 6
    (B) 11
    (C) 17
    (D) 23

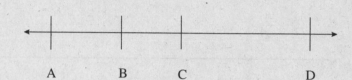

36. The decimal representation of $2 + 40 + \dfrac{1}{100}$ is

    (A) 24.1
    (B) 24.01
    (C) 42.1
    (D) 42.01

37. What is the least possible integer divisible by 2, 3, 4, and 5?

    (A) 30
    (B) 40
    (C) 60
    (D) 90

38. If a car travels at x miles per hour, in terms of x and y, how long does it take it to travel y miles?

    (A) 2x,y
    (B) xy
    (C) y,x
    (D) x,y

GO ON TO THE NEXT PAGE.

USE THIS SPACE FOR FIGURING.

39. $\dfrac{4}{15} + \dfrac{3}{11} =$

(A) $\dfrac{12}{17}$

(B) $\dfrac{89}{165}$

(C) $\dfrac{44}{45}$

(D) $\dfrac{4}{55}$

40. James buys one halibut steak and two salmon steaks for $30.00. Dave buys two halibut steaks and four salmon steaks for $60.00. If halibut steaks cost x dollars each, and salmon steaks cost y dollars each, what is the value of x?

(A) $5.00
(B) $8.00
(C) $10.00
(D) It cannot be determined from the information given.

Questions 41-42 refer to the following definition.

USE THIS SPACE FOR FIGURING.

4

For all positive integer values of x,

$(x) = \dfrac{1}{2}x$ if x is even;

$(x) = 2x$ if x is odd.

41. $(1 + 5) =$

   (A) 2
   (B) 3
   (C) 4
   (D) 6

42. Which of the following equals $(4z + 1)$?

   (A) $2z + \dfrac{1}{2}$
   (B) $2z + 1$
   (C) $4z + 2$
   (D) $8z + 2$

43. There are eight buildings in Celeste's apartment complex. Each building is directly connected to each of the others with a tunnel. How many tunnels are there?

   (A) 8
   (B) 28
   (C) 36
   (D) 56

44. Zoo A has 3 monkeys. Zoo B has 8 monkeys. Zoo C has 16 monkeys. What is the average number of monkeys at the three zoos?

   (A) 3
   (B) 7
   (C) 9
   (D) 27

GO ON TO THE NEXT PAGE.

45. A steak costs \$4 more than a hamburger, and a hamburger costs \$4 more than a grilled cheese sandwich. If six grilled cheese sandwiches cost $2x$ dollars, how much will 4 steaks and 2 hamburgers cost?

(A) $2x + 40$
(B) $2x + 48$
(C) $6x + 34$
(D) $12x + 40$

46. If the base of an isosceles triangle is decreased by 40% and its height is increased by 10%, then what is the percent change in the area of the triangle?

(A) 17
(B) 30
(C) 34
(D) 40

47. $100xy$ is what percent of xy?

(A) 10
(B) 100
(C) 1,000
(D) 10,000

48. If Matt's home is four miles from school and Laura's home is eight miles from school, then the distance from Matt's home to Laura's home is

(A) 4 miles
(B) 8 miles
(C) 12 miles
(D) It cannot be determined from the information given.

49. Two partners divide a profit of $2,000, so that the difference between the two amounts is half of their average. What is the ratio of the larger to the smaller amount?

    (A) 5:3
    (B) 6:1
    (C) 4:1
    (D) 2:1

USE THIS SPACE FOR FIGURING.

4

50. What is the total value, in cents, of j coins worth 10 cents each and $j + 5$ coins, worth 25 cents each?

    (A) $35j + 125$
    (B) $35j + 5$
    (C) $10j + 130$
    (D) $2j + 5$

STOP

IF YOU FINISH BEFORE TIME IS CALLED,
YOU MAY CHECK YOUR WORK ON THIS SECTION ONLY.
DO NOT TURN TO ANY OTHER SECTION IN THE TEST.

USE THIS SPACE FOR FIGURING.

4

NO TEST MATERIAL ON THIS PAGE.

Upper Level ISEE
Section 5
Time—30 minutes
1 Topic

You have 30 minutes to complete a brief writing sample. This writing exercise will not be scored but is used by admission officers to assess your writing skills.

Directions: Read the following topic carefully. Take a few minutes to think about the topic and organize your thoughts before you begin writing. Be sure that your handwriting is legible and that you stay within the lines and margins.

Topic:	Each state in America has raised the drinking age to 21, and this action has decreased the number of alcohol-related car accidents. Some evidence suggests that the number of accidents would further decrease if the driving age were raised also, requiring drivers to be 18 years old.	Prompt:	Should the driving age be raised to 18? Support your position with specific examples from personal experience, the experience of others, current events, history or literature.

16

Middle Level
ISEE Practice Test

Middle Level Practice Test

Middle Level ISEE
Section 1
Time—20 minutes
40 Questions

This section consists of 40 questions for which you are allowed 20 minutes. There are two types of questions included, and directions for each type.

DIRECTIONS: Each question is made up of a word in capital letters followed by four choices. You should circle the one word that is most nearly the same in meaning as the word in capital letters.

1. UNUSUAL
   (A) friendly
   (B) peculiar
   (C) happy
   (D) new

2. ASSISTANCE
   (A) call
   (B) service
   (C) teaching
   (D) disability

3. REALITY
   (A) dream
   (B) rarity
   (C) fact
   (D) security

4. DIMINUTION
   (A) assessment
   (B) leniency
   (C) restitution
   (D) reduction

5. CONTENTED
   (A) mammoth
   (B) diplomatic
   (C) disgusted
   (D) satisfied

6. BOUND
   (A) relieved
   (B) confused
   (C) badgered
   (D) obliged

7. ADVANCED
   (A) remedied
   (B) juxtaposed
   (C) fearsome
   (D) highly evolved

8. CONTAINED
   (A) wooden
   (B) raging
   (C) held
   (D) burned out

9. RESPECT
   (A) esteem
   (B) disdain
   (C) reliance
   (D) faith

10. DILIGENT
    (A) lazy
    (B) hardworking
    (C) obsessive
    (D) defensive

11. EASE
    (A) harm
    (B) hamper
    (C) relieve
    (D) fulfill

GO ON TO THE NEXT PAGE.

12. VOW
    (A) claim
    (B) please
    (C) pledge
    (D) argue

13. IMPACT
    (A) bruise
    (B) argument
    (C) impression
    (D) consideration

14. MATERIALIZE
    (A) dash
    (B) take form
    (C) forget
    (D) plunder

15. REUNITED
    (A) torn
    (B) merged
    (C) fallen again
    (D) combined again

16. DISCLOSE
    (A) reveal
    (B) keep secret
    (C) threaten
    (D) take away

17. CONGEAL
    (A) weaken
    (B) coagulate
    (C) help
    (D) recede

18. REDUCTION
    (A) enlargement
    (B) framework
    (C) arrangement
    (D) cutback

19. HOSTILE
    (A) apathetic
    (B) fertile
    (C) malicious
    (D) taciturn

20. RUTHLESS
    (A) unsparing
    (B) counterfeit
    (C) unofficial
    (D) victorious

GO ON TO THE NEXT PAGE.

DIRECTIONS: Each question below is made up of a sentence with one or two blanks. The sentences with one blank indicate that one word is missing. The sentences with two blanks indicate that two words are missing. Each sentence is followed by four choices. You should circle the one word or pair of words that will best complete the meaning of the sentence as whole.

1

21. Myron was able to remain completely _____ ; he never took sides in any of the disagreements around the house.
    (A) neutral
    (B) bias
    (C) one-sided
    (D) thoughtful

22. Since the great drought left the soil completely useless, the people of that country were forced to _____ food from other countries.
    (A) export
    (B) import
    (C) sell
    (D) report on

23. Because he was annoyed by even the smallest grammatical error, Mr. Jones reviewed all the students' papers _____ before grading them.
    (A) inefficiently
    (B) meticulously
    (C) crudely
    (D) helplessly

24. Some researchers claim to have taught apes basic sign language, but skeptics are concerned that the apes are only _____, not truly understanding the signs they use.
    (A) revealing
    (B) communicating
    (C) copying
    (D) instructing

25. The teacher's authority was not _____; students frequently _____ and had to be sent to the principal for discipline.
    (A) helpful...reviewed
    (B) didactic...answered
    (C) realistic...supported
    (D) complete...misbehaved

26. Even though the accident led to serious damage to our property, our _____ lawyer didn't present a convincing argument and we received no compensation.
    (A) incompetent
    (B) fatalistic
    (C) discerning
    (D) professional

27. After months of _____ disputes, the warring countries decided to sit down at a table and have a _____ discussion.
    (A) irate...angry
    (B) mild...friendly
    (C) petty...hostile
    (D) bitter...civilized

28. While working on the assignment, Miriam _____, to her great delight, _____ that not even her own family would have suspected.
    (A) hid...a feeling
    (B) thought...an inkling
    (C) discovered...a talent
    (D) considered...an instinct

29. In order to be a good doctor, you don't need to be _____ yourself, just as a good architect does not have to live in a fancy house.
    (A) educated
    (B) thoughtful
    (C) healthy
    (D) handsome

30. Pete _____ his coach when he followed up his winning season with a _____ performance this year.
    (A) thrilled...poor
    (B) upset...charming
    (C) disappointed...lackluster
    (D) relieved...pale

GO ON TO THE NEXT PAGE.

31. Ms. Santos is both _____ and fair; she demands perfection from her students but is even-handed in her criticism.
    (A) sloppy
    (B) unhappy
    (C) overbearing
    (D) precise

32. During his years in the Senate, Jones felt _____ about speaking up at all, while most of the other Senators were aggressive and argumentative.
    (A) timid
    (B) blithe
    (C) contented
    (D) favorable

33. The salesman's speech was so _____ that nearly everyone in the room purchased something.
    (A) monotonous
    (B) persuasive
    (C) unique
    (D) damaging

34. The corporation did not have a _____ system for promotions; each department was free to use its own discretion in advancing employees.
    (A) forgiving
    (B) uniform
    (C) dignified
    (D) favorable

35. Paul believed that life should be _____; every day should be filled with exciting, unpredictable, and completely_____ activities.
    (A) a model...pragmatic
    (B) an adventure...spontaneous
    (C) unique...anticipated
    (D) manipulated...forced

36. Though Mr. Fenster was known to be _____ toward his neighbors, he always welcomed their children as trick-or-treaters at Halloween.
    (A) belligerent
    (B) courteous
    (C) cheerful
    (D) direct

37. Although the supervisor was a tough _____ during the work day, if you saw her on the weekends, she was quite _____.
    (A) taskmaster...friendly
    (B) thinker...strict
    (C) tyrant...angry
    (D) teacher...thoughtless

38. In her new novel, the author managed to go beyond stereotypes to draw characters that are as _____ as they are _____.
    (A) stale...rethought
    (B) fresh...distinct
    (C) rumored...fearful
    (D) interesting...biased

39. The school used a policy of nepotism, admitting _____ of alumni over other applicants.
    (A) friends
    (B) neighbors
    (C) relatives
    (D) students

40. Our teacher advised us not to get too caught up in the _____ of the information in the textbook, or we could lose the important "big picture" of its theory by getting bogged down in the details.
    (A) scope
    (B) thought
    (C) principles
    (D) minutiae

STOP

IF YOU FINISH BEFORE TIME IS CALLED,
YOU MAY CHECK YOUR WORK ON THIS SECTION ONLY.
DO NOT TURN TO ANY OTHER SECTION IN THE TEST.

Middle Level ISEE
Section 2
Time-35 Minutes
25 Questions

Following each problem in this section, there are five suggested answers. Work each problem in your head or in the blank space provided at the right of the page. Then look at the four suggested answers and decide which one is best

Note: Figures that accompany problems in this section are drawn as accurately as possible EXCEPT when it is stated in a specific problem that its figure is not drawn to scale.

Sample Problem:

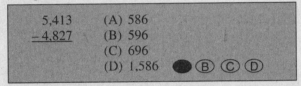

5,413	(A) 586
−4,827	(B) 596
	(C) 696
	(D) 1,586 ● Ⓑ Ⓒ Ⓓ

USE THIS SPACE FOR FIGURING.

1. $54 \times 3 =$

    (A) 123
    (B) 150
    (C) 162
    (D) 172

---

2. What is the area of a square with a side of length 2?

    (A) 2
    (B) 4
    (C) 6
    (D) 8

---

3. $3 \times 2 \times 1 - (4 \times 3 \times 2) =$

    (A) 18
    (B) 6
    (C) −6
    (D) −18

GO ON TO THE NEXT PAGE.

4. Vicky scored 80, 90, and 94 on her three tests.
    What was her average score?

    (A) 81
    (B) 88
    (C) 90
    (D) 93

USE THIS SPACE FOR FIGURING.

2

Questions 5-6 refer to the following graph.

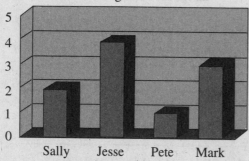

Books Bought at School Fair

5. Who bought the most books at the school fair?

    (A) Sally
    (B) Jesse
    (C) Pete
    (D) Mark

6. Sally and Mark together bought how many
    more books than Jesse?

    (A) 1
    (B) 2
    (C) 3
    (D) 5

7. Marc raked leaves for three hours on Saturday.
    If he charged $5.00 per hour, how much did he
    earn on Saturday?

    (A) $5.00
    (B) $10.00
    (C) $15.00
    (D) $20.00

GO ON TO THE NEXT PAGE.

8. $\frac{1}{2} + \frac{3}{4} =$

(A) $\frac{3}{8}$

(B) $\frac{5}{4}$

(C) $\frac{3}{2}$

(D) $\frac{5}{2}$

9. What is the value of the digit 7 in the number 4,678.02?

(A) 7
(B) 70
(C) 700
(D) 7000

10. $\frac{.5 + .5 + .5}{3} =$

(A) .5
(B) .10
(C) 1
(D) 1.5

11. $\frac{7}{.35} =$

(A) .2
(B) 2
(C) 20
(D) 200

12. Which of the following is closest in value to 5?

(A) 4.5
(B) 5.01
(C) 5.009
(D) 5.101

GO ON TO THE NEXT PAGE.

13. Janice went to the butcher and bought six pounds of hamburger. If the bill was $18.50, which of the following is closest to the cost per pound of the hamburger?

    (A) $2.00
    (B) $3.00
    (C) $5.00
    (D) $6.00

USE THIS SPACE FOR FIGURING.

2

14. Which is the greatest prime factor of 18?

    (A) 1
    (B) 2
    (C) 3
    (D) 9

15. Laurie was reading a book that had an illustration on every odd-numbered page. If there are 32 numbered pages in the book, how many illustrations are there?

    (A) 15
    (B) 16
    (C) 17
    (D) 31

16. When a number is divided by 8, the quotient is 11 and the remainder is 2. What is the number?

    (A) 11
    (B) 22
    (C) 72
    (D) 90

17. Kelly went into a store and purchased three candy bars for fifty cents each. If she gave the clerk a $5.00 bill, how much was her change?

    (A) $1.50
    (B) $2.00
    (C) $3.00
    (D) $3.50

GO ON TO THE NEXT PAGE.

The following graph shows the amount of rainfall in Miller County for the years 1942-1946.

Average Inches of Rainfall in Miller County, 1942-1946

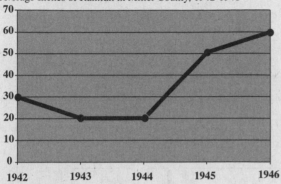

USE THIS SPACE FOR FIGURING.

2

18. When did the greatest increase in rainfall occur in Miller County?

    (A) Between 1942 and 1943
    (B) Between 1943 and 1944
    (C) Between 1944 and 1945
    (D) Between 1945 and 1946

19. The temperature at 6 a.m. was 32 degrees. If the temperature increased at a constant rate of 3 degrees per hour all day, what was the temperature at 1 p.m.?

    (A) 35 degrees
    (B) 43 degrees
    (C) 47 degrees
    (D) 53 degrees

20. What is the volume of a box with length 4 cm, width 3 cm, and height 2 cm?

    (A) 6 cubic centimeters
    (B) 9 cubic centimeters
    (C) 12 cubic centimeters
    (D) 24 cubic centimeters

GO ON TO THE NEXT PAGE.

Directions for Quantitative Comparison Questions

Questions 21–40 each consist of two quantities in boxes, one in Column A and one in Column B. You are to compare the two quantities and on the answer sheet fill in oval

    A if the quantity in Column A is greater;
    B if the quantity in Column B is greater;
    C if the two quantities are equal;
    D if the relationship cannot be determined from the information given.

Notes:

1. In some questions, information is given about one or both of the quantities to be compared. In such cases, the given information is centered above the two columns and is not boxed.
2. In a given question, a symbol that appears in both columns represents the same thing in Column A as it does in Column B.
3. Letters such as x, n, and k stand for real numbers.

EXAMPLES

COULUMN A	COLUMN B	Answers
5^2	20	●ⒷⒸⒹ

150° $x°$

| x | 30 | ⒶⒷ●Ⓓ |

r and s are integers.

| $r + 1$ | $s - 1$ | ⒶⒷⒸ● |

COLUMN A	COLUMN B

21. $\dfrac{3}{7}$ $\dfrac{1}{3}$

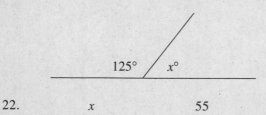

125° $x°$

22. x 55

GO ON TO THE NEXT PAGE.

	COLUMN A	**COLUMN B**

USE THIS SPACE FOR FIGURING.

2

23. $23 + 23 + 23 + 23$ 23×4

24.   The average of 2,   The average of 1,
      8, 12, and k 4, 9, and k

A rectangle with
sides x and y has
an area of 12.

25.   The length of x The length of y

26.   The least integer   The greatest integer
      greater than 4   less than 6

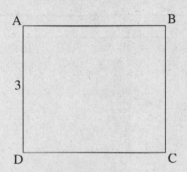

The quadrilateral ABCD
has an area of 12

27.   The perimeter of   15
      ABCD

Plants cost $5.50 each.

28.   The cost of three $16.50
      plants

GO ON TO THE NEXT PAGE.

COLUMN A   **COLUMN B**

USE THIS SPACE FOR FIGURING.

2

Martha had $20. She
gave half of her money
to her sister, Linda.
Linda now has $30.

29. The amount of   The amount of
money Martha   money Linda had
now has   originally

$$6 \times 12 = 55 + x$$

30. x 7

31. The area of a   The area of a square
rectangle with   with a side of 3
length 3 and
width 4

Number of cookies
eaten each day

Wednesday	3
Thursday	2
Friday	1
Saturday	3

32. The average number The number of
of cookies eaten for cookies eaten
the week   on Tuesday

33. $5 + (6 \times 2)$ $(5 + 6) \times 2$

GO ON TO THE NEXT PAGE.

COLUMN A   **COLUMN B**

USE THIS SPACE FOR FIGURING.

2

Amy bought 5 oranges and 6 peaches. The total price of the fruit was $1.10.

34. The cost of one orange | The cost of one peach

---

x represents an integer whose value is greater than 0.

35. $x + 15$ $x + 12$

Annette painted 21 pictures to sell at the school fair. She sold $\frac{1}{3}$ to Joe and 4 more to Ben.

36. The total number pictures sold | The number of pictures left

---

a represents an odd integer greater than 9 and less than 15

b represents an even integer greater than 9 and less than 15

37. $a \times 3$ $b \times 4$

---

38. The remainder when 30 is divided by 12 | The remainder when 30 is divided by 9

GO ON TO THE NEXT PAGE.

__COLUMN A__	__COLUMN B__

USE THIS SPACE FOR FIGURING.

2

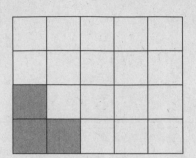

39. | The fractional part of the figure that is shaded | $\dfrac{3}{20}$ |

Melvin brought home a large pizza.

40. | The number of slices left if Melvin eats 50% of the pizza | The number of slices left if Melvin eats one-third of the pizza |

STOP

IF YOU FINISH BEFORE TIME IS CALLED,
YOU MAY CHECK YOUR WORK ON THIS SECTION ONLY.
DO NOT TURN TO ANY OTHER SECTION IN THE TEST.

Middle Level ISEE
Section 3
Time-35 minutes
40 Questions

DIRECTIONS: Each passage below is followed by questions based on its content. Answer the questions following a passage on the basis of what is *stated* or *implied* in that passage.

When most people think of the history of transportation, they think of the invention of the wheel as the starting point. The wheel was invented around 3,500 BC, more than 5,000 years ago. Before then, transportation was a difficult process, especially if you had anything to carry. During prehistoric times, the only way to get around was to walk. Children and possessions were strapped to the back if they needed to be carried. If the load was too heavy for one person, it could be strapped to a pole and carried by two. The sledge was developed as a way to drag a heavy load. These were originally just logs or pieces of animal skin upon which a load was strapped and dragged. In time, runners were put on the sledge, and it evolved to what is now called a sled. Around 5,000 BC, the first animals were domesticated, or tamed. Then, donkeys and oxen were used to carry heavy loads and pull sledges. It wasn't until almost 1,500 years later that wheeled vehicles appeared. It is believed that the wheel was invented in Mesopotamia, in the Middle East. About 300 years later, the Egyptians invented the sailboat. These two inventions changed transportation forever.

1. The passage suggests that prehistoric man used all of the following for carrying things EXCEPT

   (A) poles
   (B) animals
   (C) primitive sleds
   (D) children

2. The primary purpose of the passage is to

   (A) give a detailed history of transportation
   (B) describe some of the things early man used for transportation
   (C) explain the evolution of the sled
   (D) describe the reasons that led to transportation discoveries

3. The passage implies that early man

   (A) was incapable of inventing the wheel any earlier than 3500 BC
   (B) was interested in farming
   (C) was outgoing and friendly
   (D) was interested in finding ways to help carry things

4. According to the passage, the reason animals were domesticated was

   (A) to provide family pets
   (B) to help carry large loads
   (C) to ward off danger
   (D) to move people and possessions around quickly

5. Which of the following described the author's attitude toward the invention of the wheel?

   (A) admiration
   (B) indifference
   (C) disdain
   (D) regret

GO ON TO THE NEXT PAGE.

Bison and buffalo are not the same animal. For years, the American bison were mistakenly referred to as buffalo. Buffalo are actually found in Asia, Africa, and South America. Bison roamed the Northern American western plains by the millions just a couple of centuries ago. Because they were so widely hunted, however, their numbers fell greatly. In fact, as of a century ago, there were only about 500 left. They were deemed near extinction, and due to conservation efforts, their numbers have increased. There are approximately 50,000 bison living today in protected parks. Though they may never be as abundant as they once were, they are not in danger of extinction as long as they remain protected.

3

6. The passage implies that the primary difference between the buffalo and the bison is

   (A) their geographic location
   (B) their size
   (C) their number
   (D) when they existed

7. The primary purpose of the passage is to

   (A) explain the difference between the bison and the buffalo
   (B) applaud conservation efforts
   (C) give some background on the American bison
   (D) explain why people confuse the buffalo and the bison

8. According to the passage, the primary reason that the American bison is no longer near extinction is

   (A) lack of interest in hunting them
   (B) conservation efforts
   (C) loss of value of their fur
   (D) the migration of the animals

9. As used in line 6, the word "deemed" most closely means

   (A) found
   (B) hunted
   (C) ruled
   (D) eaten

10. According to the passage, what can be hoped for as long as the American bison is protected?

   (A) They will be as plentiful as they once were.
   (B) They will disturb the delicate ecological balance in the plains.
   (C) They will probably not die out.
   (D) They will face even greater dangers.

GO ON TO THE NEXT PAGE.

Diamonds, emeralds, rubies, and other stones are called gemstones because they are used to make jewelry. They are valued for many reasons: their beauty, rarity, and strength. Gemstones are minerals that occur naturally. The value of a gemstone is measured in various ways. It is measured by the stone's color, clearness, size, and how well the stone has been cut. A jeweler cuts a stone to bring out its beauty. A gemstone sparkles because it is cut to have angled sides, or facets. The facets reflect the light that enters into the stone, causing it to sparkle. The gem cutter's job is a difficult one; to split the stone, cut facets into the stone, and polish it. You may not recognize a diamond before a jeweler has worked on it. A diamond in nature may resemble a colorless piece of rock. After it has been cut and polished, it may be a valuable addition to a jeweler's collection.

3

11. According to the information in the passage, the purpose of facets is to

(A) reflect light
(B) cut down the size of the stone
(C) realize the stone's intended shape
(D) help the stone to set securely in a piece of jewelry

12. The best title for the passage would be

(A) The Lonely Life of a Jeweler
(B) Gemstones: From Rocks to Jewelry
(C) Diamonds: Once a Piece of Rock
(D) The Value of Diamonds

13. According to the passage, all of the following are important to the value of a gemstone EXCEPT

(A) its color
(B) its size
(C) its clarity
(D) its country of origin

14. According to the passage, certain stones are called gemstones because

(A) they are rare
(B) they are large
(C) they are used for jewelry
(D) they are beautiful

GO ON TO THE NEXT PAGE.

When most people think of the Tasmanian Devil, they imagine a cartoon animal, spinning about furiously and acting crazy. There is a real animal called the Tasmanian Devil, and it does not resemble its cartoon counterpart very much at all. Tasmania is a small island off the coast of Australia. It has a population of about half a million people. Tasmania is famous for its fruit, livestock, and vegetables. It is also well known for its dense forest, in which many species, including the Tasmanian Devil, dwell. The Tasmanian Devil is a marsupial—it carries its young in a pouch on its body. It looks somewhat like a mouse and is in fact related to the mouse. The Tasmanian Devil is known to be quite vicious if it is cornered or attacked. There were Tasmanian Devils on mainland Australia at one point, but the Dingoes, or wild dogs of Australia, hunted the Tasmanian Devil and the Tasmanian Wolf out of existence in Australia.

15. According to the passage, Tasmania is

   (A) the part of Australia where the Tasmanian Devil lives
   (B) a large forest in Australia
   (C) an island near Australia
   (D) a famous wildlife refuge

16. The passage implies that the Tasmanian Devil is vicious

   (A) if it is threatened
   (B) in the presence of the Dingo
   (C) in its natural habitat
   (D) when hunting for food

17. According to the passage, the Tasmanian Devil no longer lives on mainland Australia due to

   (A) the food shortage
   (B) a natural predator
   (C) a disaster
   (D) its migration to the island of Tasmania

18. The primary purpose of the passage is to

   (A) give a brief history of the Tasmanian Devil
   (B) explain the reasons that the Tasmanian Devil was hunted out of mainland Australia
   (C) talk about the varied wildlife on Tasmania
   (D) discuss the marsupials of Australia

GO ON TO THE NEXT PAGE.

3

The Greek philosopher Aristotle had many students, but perhaps none so famous as Alexander the Great. As a child, Alexander was known for his intelligence and bravery. The lessons he learned from Aristotle left him with a lifelong love of books and learning. But it was not his love of books that made him famous. Alexander, in 336 BC, became the king of a small Greek kingdom called Macedonia. He was only twenty at the time. He went on to invade country after country: Persia (now known as Iran), Egypt, and all the way to parts of India and Pakistan. Alexander conquered most of what was then the civilized world. He brought with him the Greek way of thinking and doing things. He is considered one of the great generals and kings of history and is responsible for the spread of Greek culture throughout much of the world.

19. As used in line 6, the word "civilized" most closely means

   (A) well-mannered
   (B) educated
   (C) barbaric
   (D) friendly

20. The tone of the passage is most like that found in

   (A) a diary entry from an historian
   (B) a philosophy journal
   (C) a reference book
   (D) a letter from an archeologist

21. Which of the following would be the best title for the passage?

   (A) Aristotle: Teacher of the Kings
   (B) Alexander the Great: King and Conqueror
   (C) Greek Culture
   (D) The History of Macedonia

22. According to the passage, one of the things that was so impressive about Alexander was

   (A) his intelligence and culture
   (B) his handsome features
   (C) his great integrity
   (D) his ability to teach

GO ON TO THE NEXT PAGE.

3

It may seem to you as you gaze up into the night sky that the stars move from one night to the next. While the position of a star may vary a bit over the years, in general the movement of the stars is due to the rotation of the earth, not the movement of the stars. The earth rotates on its axis from west to east every day. Because you are not aware of the movement of the earth, it looks to you as though the stars are moving from east to west in the sky. The only star that does not appear to have any motion is Polaris, or what is commonly called the North Star. The reason it does not appear to move is that it lies almost directly above the North Pole. Because it is fixed in position, the North Star has long been used as a tool for navigation. No matter where you are, no matter what night, if you can locate the North Star, you can figure out which direction is North. Sailors out on the sea used it to direct them. Polaris is a very bright star, so it can be located easily.

23. As used in line 5, the word "appear" most closely means

    (A) seem
    (B) show up
    (C) reveal
    (D) occur

24. According to the passage, the reason the stars appear to move is due to

    (A) the distance between the earth and the stars
    (B) the effect of the sun
    (C) gravity
    (D) the rotation of the earth

25. The reason the North Star is used for navigation is

    (A) its brightness
    (B) it is easy to locate
    (C) its fixed position
    (D) it is low to the horizon

26. According to the passage, the reason Polaris does not appear to move is that

    (A) it moves more slowly than the other stars
    (B) it is brighter than the other stars
    (C) it lies above the North Pole
    (D) it is not near the earth's axis of rotation

27. According to the passage, most stars appear to move

    (A) from east to west
    (B) from west to east
    (C) toward the north
    (D) around the North Star

GO ON TO THE NEXT PAGE.

3

Everyone has had attacks of the hiccups, or hiccoughs, at one point in his or her life. Few people, however, think about what is happening to them and how hiccups begin and end.

The diaphragm is a large muscle, shaped like a dome, that sits at the base of the chest cavity. As one breathes, the diaphragm gently contracts and relaxes to help the process. Occasionally, an irritation near the diaphragm or a disease may cause the muscle to spasm, or contract suddenly. The spasm will suck air into the lungs with a quick force past the vocal cords. A small flap called the epiglottis tops the vocal cords so that food will not accidentally enter into the wind pipe. The sudden spasm of the diaphragm causes the epiglottis to close quickly. Imagine the pull of air into the vocal cords from the spastic diaphragm hitting the closed epiglottis. This moves the vocal cords, causing the "hic" sound of the hiccup. Although most people don't really worry about the hiccups, attacks may last for days. The exhaustion of hiccuping for days on end has been fatal in certain rare cases. Home remedies abound—from breathing into paper bags to squeezing on pressure points that supposedly relax the diaphragm.

28. According to the passage, one possible cause of hiccups is

    (A) a sudden rush of air
    (B) the closing of the epiglottis
    (C) an irritant near the diaphragm
    (D) breathing in and out of a paper bag

29. As used in line 11 "attacks" most closely means

    (A) threats
    (B) bouts
    (C) assaults
    (D) advances

30. The passage suggests that which of the following make the "hic" sound of the hiccup?

    (A) The diaphragm
    (B) The stomach
    (C) The lungs
    (D) The vocal cords

31. According to the passage, the hiccups can be fatal due to

    (A) the irritant to the diaphragm
    (B) fatigue from days of hiccuping
    (C) home remedies that are toxic
    (D) the humiliation of hiccuping for days on end

GO ON TO THE NEXT PAGE.

3

During the winter months in many regions, food can be extremely scarce. For the wildlife of these areas, this can be a great problem unless they have some mechanism that allows them to adapt. Some animals migrate to warmer climates. Others hibernate to conserve energy and decrease the need for food. Prior to hibernation, an animal will generally feed to build up a store of fat. The animal's system will "feed" off the fat stores throughout the long cold winter months. When the animal hibernates, its body temperature decreases and its body functions slow down considerably. The dormouse's heartbeat, for example, slows down to just a beat every few minutes. Its breathing becomes slow and its body temperature drops to just a few degrees above the temperature of ground around it. All these changes decrease the need for fuel and allow the animal to survive long periods without any food. It is a mistake to think that all hibernating animals sleep for the whole winter. In fact, many animals hibernate for short spurts during the winter. They may wake for an interval of mild weather. Scientists have now discovered the chemical that triggers hibernation. If this chemical is injected in an animal in the summer months, it can cause them to go into summer hibernation.

32. As used in line 3, the word "conserve" most closely means

    (A) expend
    (B) help
    (C) reserve
    (D) waste

33. According to the author, each of the following happens to a hibernating animal EXCEPT

    (A) its heartbeat slows
    (B) its body temperature drops
    (C) it goes into a dream state
    (D) its breathing becomes slow

34. The primary purpose of the passage is to

    (A) discuss the discovery of the chemical that causes hibernation
    (B) debunk some common myths about hibernation
    (C) compare the hibernating dormouse to other hibernating animals
    (D) explore some basic information about hibernation

35. Which of the following can be inferred as a reason a hibernating animal may interrupt its hibernation?

    (A) A week in which the temperature was well above freezing
    (B) A week in which there was no snow
    (C) An overabundance of food
    (D) A day or two of stormy weather

36. According to the author, if the chemical that triggers hibernation is injected into an animal when it would not normally hibernate, it may

    (A) cause body functions to slow to a halt
    (B) cause an out-of-season hibernation
    (C) allow the animal to shed extra fat stores
    (D) decrease an animal's need for food

GO ON TO THE NEXT PAGE.

3

The theater is one of the richest art forms around. The excitement of opening night can be felt by the people waiting to watch a performance and by the performers and workers backstage waiting for the curtain to go up. Live theater is thrilling for that reason—no one really knows how well it will go until the play is performed live. Many people collaborate to bring a play to life. There are playwrights, directors, set designers, costumers, lighting technicians, and, of course, the actors. If the play is a musical, the skills of a songwriter, a choreographer (the person who composes the dances), and musicians are also required. The word theater comes from the Greek "theatron," which means "a place for seeing." Although most people think of the theater in terms of a play performed on the stage, theater has taken on a much broader meaning in the modern world. Theater may come to life on a street corner, or in a classroom. The excitement of theater is in its very nature—an art form that changes as it is interpreted in different ways by different people. That is probably why the works of the greatest playwright of all time, William Shakespeare, are still performed and enjoyed today, both in classic and new interpretations.

37. The best title for the passage might be

(A) A Brief History of Theatrical Productions
(B) Shakespeare: Our Greatest Playwright
(C) Modern Theater: Adventures in Acting
(D) The Excitement of the Theater

38. According to the passage, the primary reason that theater is so exciting is that

(A) plays are often well written
(B) it is performed live
(C) there are so many people working on it
(D) it derives from Greek

39. The passage suggests which of the following about modern theater?

(A) It has been interpreted in a more varied fashion.
(B) It is less exciting than classic theater.
(C) There are mostly Shakespearean plays performed.
(D) It always draws great attention from the audience.

40. The author's attitude toward theater can best be described as

(A) admiring
(B) ambivalent
(C) apathetic
(D) neutral

STOP

IF YOU FINISH BEFORE TIME IS CALLED,
YOU MAY CHECK YOUR WORK ON THIS SECTION ONLY.
DO NOT TURN TO ANY OTHER SECTION IN THE TEST.

3

NO TEST MATERIAL ON THIS PAGE.

Middle Level ISEE
Section 4
Time-40 Minutes
50 Questions

Following each problem in this section, there are four suggested answers. Work each problem in your head or in the blank space provided at the right of the page. Then look at the four suggested answers and decide which one is best.

Note: Figures that accompany problems in this section are drawn as accurately as possible EXCEPT when it is stated in a specific problem that its figure is not drawn to scale.

Sample Problem:

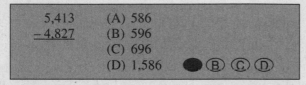

1. In the decimal 0.0987, the digit 9 is equivalent to which of the following?

   (A) $\dfrac{9}{10}$

   (B) $\dfrac{9}{100}$

   (C) $\dfrac{9}{1000}$

   (D) $\dfrac{9}{10000}$

USE THIS SPACE FOR FIGURING.

2. $4 \times 128 =$

   (A) 52
   (B) 320
   (C) 482
   (D) 512

GO ON TO THE NEXT PAGE.

3. Which numeral represents thirty thousand, four hundred and twenty three?

    (A) 30,423
    (B) 34.023
    (C) 3,423
    (D) 34.230

USE THIS SPACE FOR FIGURING.

4. $\dfrac{5}{7} + \dfrac{2}{11} =$

    (A) $\dfrac{10}{17}$

    (B) $\dfrac{10}{77}$

    (C) $\dfrac{7}{18}$

    (D) $\dfrac{69}{77}$

5. $7\dfrac{1}{2}$ hours is how many minutes more than $6\dfrac{1}{4}$ hours?

    (A) 45
    (B) 60
    (C) 75
    (D) 90

6. What is the perimeter of equilateral triangle
    ABC?

    (A) 12
    (B) 15
    (C) 18
    (D) It cannot be determined from the
         information given.

USE THIS SPACE FOR FIGURING.

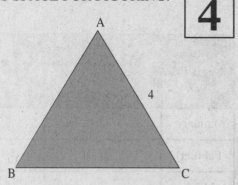

7. Matthew's brother has 26 comic books. Matthew
    has twice as many comic books as his brother
    has. How many comic books does Matthew
    have?

    (A) 13
    (B) 26
    (C) 42
    (D) 52

8. Which of the following is 20% of 200?

    (A) 20
    (B) 30
    (C) 40
    (D) 100

GO ON TO THE NEXT PAGE.

Questions 9–11 refer to the following chart.

4

MONTH	Average Temperature (in degrees Celsius)	Average Snowfall (in centimeters)
January	2	3
February	6	3
March	3	4
April	13	1

9. What was the total amount of snowfall for the four-month period shown?

   (A) 44 cm
   (B) 40 cm
   (C) 11 cm
   (D) 10 cm

10. In which month was the average snowfall the greatest?

   (A) April
   (B) March
   (C) February
   (D) January

11. What was the average temperature for each month in the four-month period?

   (A) 24 degrees
   (B) 20 degrees
   (C) 11 degrees
   (D) 6 degrees

12. $\dfrac{100}{0.25} =$

   (A) 4
   (B) 40
   (C) 400
   (D) 4000

13. $5 \times 31 = 100 +$

 (A) 55
 (B) 51
 (C) 50
 (D) 36

USE THIS SPACE FOR FIGURING.

4

14. Over the course of five games, Henrietta has scored 19 points. Which of the following is the best approximation of her average point score per game?

 (A) 5
 (B) 4
 (C) 3
 (D) 2

15. Gwen planted six tomato plants. Half of them died. She then planted one more. How many tomato plants does Gwen have now?

 (A) 3
 (B) 4
 (C) 5
 (D) 6

16. The Public Library charges one dollar to rent a video overnight, with a fifty-cent charge for each day the video is late. If Treacy returns a video three days late, how much does she owe all together?

 (A) $1.50
 (B) $2.00
 (C) $2.50
 (D) $3.50

17. $0.45 \times 100 =$

 (A) 4500
 (B) 450
 (C) 45
 (D) 4.5

GO ON TO THE NEXT PAGE.

18. In triangle FGH, the value of angle x, in degrees, is

    (A) 30
    (B) 45
    (C) 50
    (D) 90

USE THIS SPACE FOR FIGURING.

19. If a dozen eggs cost $1.20, then 3 eggs cost

    (A) 30¢
    (B) 36¢
    (C) 48¢
    (D) $3.60

20. Boris and his friend Bruce collect baseball cards. If Bruce has 12 baseball cards and Boris has three times as many baseball cards as Bruce, what is the average number of cards in the boys' collections?

    (A) 7.5
    (B) 18
    (C) 24
    (D) 48

21. What is the perimeter of a rectangle with length 3 and width 2?

    (A) 6
    (B) 8
    (C) 10
    (D) 12

USE THIS SPACE FOR FIGURING. 4

22. $\frac{3}{5} \times \frac{2}{7} =$

  (A) $\frac{3}{8}$

  (B) $\frac{6}{35}$

  (C) $\frac{31}{35}$

  (D) $\frac{21}{35}$

23. If Kenny can run three miles in 45 minutes, how long will it take him to run five miles?

  (A) 1 hour
  (B) 1 hour and 15 minutes
  (C) 1 hour and 30 minutes
  (D) 2 hours

24. Which fraction is greater than $\frac{5}{11}$?

  (A) $\frac{3}{8}$

  (B) $\frac{2}{7}$

  (C) $\frac{4}{9}$

  (D) $\frac{4}{7}$

25. Which is the least prime factor of 35?

  (A) 2
  (B) 3
  (C) 5
  (D) 7

GO ON TO THE NEXT PAGE.

26. If the perimeter of a square is 36, what is its area?

    (A) 16
    (B) 36
    (C) 64
    (D) 81

USE THIS SPACE FOR FIGURING.

4

27. Maureen studied for two hours before school. After school she studied for twice as long as she had before school. What was the total number of hours she studied in the day?

    (A) 4
    (B) 6
    (C) 8
    (D) 12

28. $711 \times 15 =$

    (A) 10, 665
    (B) 1.665
    (C) 726
    (D) 356

29. $0.347 =$

    (A) $\dfrac{7}{10} + \dfrac{4}{100} + \dfrac{3}{1000}$

    (B) $\dfrac{3}{100} + \dfrac{4}{10} + \dfrac{7}{100}$

    (C) $\dfrac{4}{100} + \dfrac{3}{10} + \dfrac{7}{1000}$

    (D) $\dfrac{3}{10} + \dfrac{4}{1000} + \dfrac{7}{100}$

30. Which is the prime factorization of 36?

    (A) $3 \times 3 \times 3 \times 2$
    (B) $3 \times 3 \times 2 \times 2$
    (C) $3 \times 2 \times 2 \times 2$
    (D) $6 \times 3 \times 2$

Questions 31–34 refer to the following chart.

USE THIS SPACE FOR FIGURING.

4

Train fares from Monroeville to Perkins' Corner

Fares	Weekday Peak	Weekday Off-Peak	Weekend & Holiday
One Way	$6.00	$5.00	$4.50
Round Trip	$12.00	$10.00	$9.00
10-Trip Ticket	$54.00	$45.00	$40.00
Children Under 11	$1.00	$0.50	Free with Paying Adult

31. How much would it cost two adults and one child under the age of 11 to travel one way from Monroeville to Perkins' Corner on a weekend?

    (A) $25.00
    (B) $20.50
    (C) $18.00
    (D) $9.00

32. Which one-way fare would be most expensive?

    (A) One adult travelling during the weekday peak fare period
    (B) Two adults travelling on the weekend
    (C) One adult and two children travelling during the weekday off-peak fare period
    (D) One adult and three children under the age of 11 travelling on the weekend

33. The price of a weekday peak fare ten-trip ticket is what percent less than the cost of purchasing ten one-way weekday peak fare tickets?

    (A) 10%
    (B) 20%
    (C) 50%
    (D) 100%

GO ON TO THE NEXT PAGE.

34. How much more does it cost for one adult to travel one way during the weekday peak fare period than for one adult to make the trip on the weekend?

    (A) $0.50
    (B) $0.75
    (C) $1.00
    (D) $1.50

4

35. Mr. Schroder swims laps at the Community Pool. It takes him 5 minutes to swim one lap. If he swims for 60 minutes without stopping, how many laps will he swim?

    (A) 8
    (B) 10
    (C) 12
    (D) 14

36. $10^3 =$

    (A) 10 x 3
    (B) 10 + 10 + 10
    (C) 10 x 10 x 10
    (D) $\dfrac{10}{3}$

37. If one pound equals 16 ounces, which of the following is equivalent to 2.5 pounds?

    (A) 18 ounces
    (B) 24 ounces
    (C) 32 ounces
    (D) 40 ounces

38. Mr. Hoffman has a rectangular box which is 10 centimeters wide, 30 centimeters long, and 4 centimeters high. What is the volume of the box?

    (A) 44 cm³
    (B) 120 cm³
    (C) 300 cm³
    (D) 1200 cm³

39. Dr. Heldman sees an average of nine patients an hour for eight hours on Monday and for six hours on Tuesday. What is the average number of patients she sees on each day?

    (A) 54
    (B) 63
    (C) 72
    (D) 126

40. What is the length in millimeters of a piece of rope that is 358 centimeters long?
    (1 centimeter = 10 millimeters)

    (A) 3.58
    (B) 35.8
    (C) 3,580
    (D) 35,800

41. Which of the following is the product of two consecutive even integers?

    (A) 0
    (B) 15
    (C) 22
    (D) 30

42. All of the following are multiples of 6 EXCEPT

    (A) 46
    (B) 90
    (C) 738
    (D) 1206

43. Jed wants to build a shelf to store his rare book collection. If he has 6 books, each of which is 2 inches thick, and 16 books, each of which is $1\frac{1}{2}$ inches thick, how many inches long must the shelf be?

    (A) 12
    (B) 18
    (C) 24
    (D) 36

USE THIS SPACE FOR FIGURING.

4

GO ON TO THE NEXT PAGE.

44. The perimeter of a square whose area is 169 centimeters is

    (A) 52
    (B) 48
    (C) 44
    (D) 42

USE THIS SPACE FOR FIGURING.

45. If three-fourths of the 240 employees at Tigger's Toys are at a party, how many of the employees are NOT at the party?

    (A) 60
    (B) 80
    (C) 120
    (D) 180

46. Jose and Greg are going on a 20-mile walk for charity. If they walk $\frac{1}{4}$ of the distance in the first two hours, and $\frac{1}{5}$ of the entire distance in the next hour and a half, how many miles do they have left to walk?

    (A) 9
    (B) 10
    (C) 11
    (D) 12

47. What is the perimeter of the shaded area in Figure 1?

    (A) 15
    (B) 16
    (C) 24
    (D) It cannot be determined from the information given

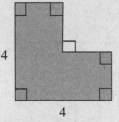

4

4

FIGURE 1

48. A field hockey player scored an average of 3 goals per game for 12 games. How many points did she score in all twelve games?

    (A) 4
    (B) 20
    (C) 24
    (D) 36

USE THIS SPACE FOR FIGURING.

49. What is the volume of a box with length 8, width 4, and height $\frac{1}{4}$?

    (A) 8
    (B) $12\frac{1}{4}$
    (C) 32
    (D) 128

50. The price of a $30 hat is decreased by 20%. What is the new price of the hat?

    (A) $10.00
    (B) $12.00
    (C) $20.00
    (D) $24.00

STOP

IF YOU FINISH BEFORE TIME IS CALLED, YOU MAY CHECK YOUR WORK ON THIS SECTION ONLY. DO NOT TURN TO ANY OTHER SECTION IN THE TEST.

USE THIS SPACE FOR FIGURING.

$$\boxed{4}$$

NO TEST MATERIAL ON THIS PAGE.

Middle Level ISEE
Section 5
Time-30 minutes
1 Topic

You have 25 minutes to complete a brief writing sample. This writing exercise will not be scored but is used by admission officers to assess your writing skills.

Directions: Read the following topic carefully. Take a few minutes to think about the topic and organize your thoughts before you begin writing. Be sure that your handwriting is legible and that you stay within the lines and margins.

Topic: Television has been blamed for an increase in violence, the decline of the educational system, and the dulling of the American mind. On the other hand, it does provide educational programs and fast access to news and world events.	**Prompt:** Do the positive effects of television outweigh its negative influence on people? Support your position with specific examples from personal experience, the experience of others, current events, history, or literature.

Upper Level Practice Test

Be sure each mark *completely* fills the answer space.
Start with number 1 for each new section of the test. You may find more answer spaces than you need.
If so, please leave them blank.

SECTION 1

1 Ⓐ Ⓑ Ⓒ Ⓓ Ⓔ	13 Ⓐ Ⓑ Ⓒ Ⓓ Ⓔ	25 Ⓐ Ⓑ Ⓒ Ⓓ Ⓔ	37 Ⓐ Ⓑ Ⓒ Ⓓ Ⓔ	49 Ⓐ Ⓑ Ⓒ Ⓓ Ⓔ
2 Ⓐ Ⓑ Ⓒ Ⓓ Ⓔ	14 Ⓐ Ⓑ Ⓒ Ⓓ Ⓔ	26 Ⓐ Ⓑ Ⓒ Ⓓ Ⓔ	38 Ⓐ Ⓑ Ⓒ Ⓓ Ⓔ	50 Ⓐ Ⓑ Ⓒ Ⓓ Ⓔ
3 Ⓐ Ⓑ Ⓒ Ⓓ Ⓔ	15 Ⓐ Ⓑ Ⓒ Ⓓ Ⓔ	27 Ⓐ Ⓑ Ⓒ Ⓓ Ⓔ	39 Ⓐ Ⓑ Ⓒ Ⓓ Ⓔ	51 Ⓐ Ⓑ Ⓒ Ⓓ Ⓔ
4 Ⓐ Ⓑ Ⓒ Ⓓ Ⓔ	16 Ⓐ Ⓑ Ⓒ Ⓓ Ⓔ	28 Ⓐ Ⓑ Ⓒ Ⓓ Ⓔ	40 Ⓐ Ⓑ Ⓒ Ⓓ Ⓔ	52 Ⓐ Ⓑ Ⓒ Ⓓ Ⓔ
5 Ⓐ Ⓑ Ⓒ Ⓓ Ⓔ	17 Ⓐ Ⓑ Ⓒ Ⓓ Ⓔ	29 Ⓐ Ⓑ Ⓒ Ⓓ Ⓔ	41 Ⓐ Ⓑ Ⓒ Ⓓ Ⓔ	53 Ⓐ Ⓑ Ⓒ Ⓓ Ⓔ
6 Ⓐ Ⓑ Ⓒ Ⓓ Ⓔ	18 Ⓐ Ⓑ Ⓒ Ⓓ Ⓔ	30 Ⓐ Ⓑ Ⓒ Ⓓ Ⓔ	42 Ⓐ Ⓑ Ⓒ Ⓓ Ⓔ	54 Ⓐ Ⓑ Ⓒ Ⓓ Ⓔ
7 Ⓐ Ⓑ Ⓒ Ⓓ Ⓔ	19 Ⓐ Ⓑ Ⓒ Ⓓ Ⓔ	31 Ⓐ Ⓑ Ⓒ Ⓓ Ⓔ	43 Ⓐ Ⓑ Ⓒ Ⓓ Ⓔ	55 Ⓐ Ⓑ Ⓒ Ⓓ Ⓔ
8 Ⓐ Ⓑ Ⓒ Ⓓ Ⓔ	20 Ⓐ Ⓑ Ⓒ Ⓓ Ⓔ	32 Ⓐ Ⓑ Ⓒ Ⓓ Ⓔ	44 Ⓐ Ⓑ Ⓒ Ⓓ Ⓔ	56 Ⓐ Ⓑ Ⓒ Ⓓ Ⓔ
9 Ⓐ Ⓑ Ⓒ Ⓓ Ⓔ	21 Ⓐ Ⓑ Ⓒ Ⓓ Ⓔ	33 Ⓐ Ⓑ Ⓒ Ⓓ Ⓔ	45 Ⓐ Ⓑ Ⓒ Ⓓ Ⓔ	57 Ⓐ Ⓑ Ⓒ Ⓓ Ⓔ
10 Ⓐ Ⓑ Ⓒ Ⓓ Ⓔ	22 Ⓐ Ⓑ Ⓒ Ⓓ Ⓔ	34 Ⓐ Ⓑ Ⓒ Ⓓ Ⓔ	46 Ⓐ Ⓑ Ⓒ Ⓓ Ⓔ	58 Ⓐ Ⓑ Ⓒ Ⓓ Ⓔ
11 Ⓐ Ⓑ Ⓒ Ⓓ Ⓔ	23 Ⓐ Ⓑ Ⓒ Ⓓ Ⓔ	35 Ⓐ Ⓑ Ⓒ Ⓓ Ⓔ	47 Ⓐ Ⓑ Ⓒ Ⓓ Ⓔ	59 Ⓐ Ⓑ Ⓒ Ⓓ Ⓔ
12 Ⓐ Ⓑ Ⓒ Ⓓ Ⓔ	24 Ⓐ Ⓑ Ⓒ Ⓓ Ⓔ	36 Ⓐ Ⓑ Ⓒ Ⓓ Ⓔ	48 Ⓐ Ⓑ Ⓒ Ⓓ Ⓔ	60 Ⓐ Ⓑ Ⓒ Ⓓ Ⓔ

SECTION 2

1 Ⓐ Ⓑ Ⓒ Ⓓ Ⓔ	6 Ⓐ Ⓑ Ⓒ Ⓓ Ⓔ	11 Ⓐ Ⓑ Ⓒ Ⓓ Ⓔ	16 Ⓐ Ⓑ Ⓒ Ⓓ Ⓔ	21 Ⓐ Ⓑ Ⓒ Ⓓ Ⓔ
2 Ⓐ Ⓑ Ⓒ Ⓓ Ⓔ	7 Ⓐ Ⓑ Ⓒ Ⓓ Ⓔ	12 Ⓐ Ⓑ Ⓒ Ⓓ Ⓔ	17 Ⓐ Ⓑ Ⓒ Ⓓ Ⓔ	22 Ⓐ Ⓑ Ⓒ Ⓓ Ⓔ
3 Ⓐ Ⓑ Ⓒ Ⓓ Ⓔ	8 Ⓐ Ⓑ Ⓒ Ⓓ Ⓔ	13 Ⓐ Ⓑ Ⓒ Ⓓ Ⓔ	18 Ⓐ Ⓑ Ⓒ Ⓓ Ⓔ	23 Ⓐ Ⓑ Ⓒ Ⓓ Ⓔ
4 Ⓐ Ⓑ Ⓒ Ⓓ Ⓔ	9 Ⓐ Ⓑ Ⓒ Ⓓ Ⓔ	14 Ⓐ Ⓑ Ⓒ Ⓓ Ⓔ	19 Ⓐ Ⓑ Ⓒ Ⓓ Ⓔ	24 Ⓐ Ⓑ Ⓒ Ⓓ Ⓔ
5 Ⓐ Ⓑ Ⓒ Ⓓ Ⓔ	10 Ⓐ Ⓑ Ⓒ Ⓓ Ⓔ	15 Ⓐ Ⓑ Ⓒ Ⓓ Ⓔ	20 Ⓐ Ⓑ Ⓒ Ⓓ Ⓔ	25 Ⓐ Ⓑ Ⓒ Ⓓ Ⓔ

SECTION 3

1 Ⓐ Ⓑ Ⓒ Ⓓ Ⓔ	9 Ⓐ Ⓑ Ⓒ Ⓓ Ⓔ	17 Ⓐ Ⓑ Ⓒ Ⓓ Ⓔ	25 Ⓐ Ⓑ Ⓒ Ⓓ Ⓔ	33 Ⓐ Ⓑ Ⓒ Ⓓ Ⓔ
2 Ⓐ Ⓑ Ⓒ Ⓓ Ⓔ	10 Ⓐ Ⓑ Ⓒ Ⓓ Ⓔ	18 Ⓐ Ⓑ Ⓒ Ⓓ Ⓔ	26 Ⓐ Ⓑ Ⓒ Ⓓ Ⓔ	34 Ⓐ Ⓑ Ⓒ Ⓓ Ⓔ
3 Ⓐ Ⓑ Ⓒ Ⓓ Ⓔ	11 Ⓐ Ⓑ Ⓒ Ⓓ Ⓔ	19 Ⓐ Ⓑ Ⓒ Ⓓ Ⓔ	27 Ⓐ Ⓑ Ⓒ Ⓓ Ⓔ	35 Ⓐ Ⓑ Ⓒ Ⓓ Ⓔ
4 Ⓐ Ⓑ Ⓒ Ⓓ Ⓔ	12 Ⓐ Ⓑ Ⓒ Ⓓ Ⓔ	20 Ⓐ Ⓑ Ⓒ Ⓓ Ⓔ	28 Ⓐ Ⓑ Ⓒ Ⓓ Ⓔ	36 Ⓐ Ⓑ Ⓒ Ⓓ Ⓔ
5 Ⓐ Ⓑ Ⓒ Ⓓ Ⓔ	13 Ⓐ Ⓑ Ⓒ Ⓓ Ⓔ	21 Ⓐ Ⓑ Ⓒ Ⓓ Ⓔ	29 Ⓐ Ⓑ Ⓒ Ⓓ Ⓔ	37 Ⓐ Ⓑ Ⓒ Ⓓ Ⓔ
6 Ⓐ Ⓑ Ⓒ Ⓓ Ⓔ	14 Ⓐ Ⓑ Ⓒ Ⓓ Ⓔ	22 Ⓐ Ⓑ Ⓒ Ⓓ Ⓔ	30 Ⓐ Ⓑ Ⓒ Ⓓ Ⓔ	38 Ⓐ Ⓑ Ⓒ Ⓓ Ⓔ
7 Ⓐ Ⓑ Ⓒ Ⓓ Ⓔ	15 Ⓐ Ⓑ Ⓒ Ⓓ Ⓔ	23 Ⓐ Ⓑ Ⓒ Ⓓ Ⓔ	31 Ⓐ Ⓑ Ⓒ Ⓓ Ⓔ	39 Ⓐ Ⓑ Ⓒ Ⓓ Ⓔ
8 Ⓐ Ⓑ Ⓒ Ⓓ Ⓔ	16 Ⓐ Ⓑ Ⓒ Ⓓ Ⓔ	24 Ⓐ Ⓑ Ⓒ Ⓓ Ⓔ	32 Ⓐ Ⓑ Ⓒ Ⓓ Ⓔ	40 Ⓐ Ⓑ Ⓒ Ⓓ Ⓔ

SECTION 4

1 Ⓐ Ⓑ Ⓒ Ⓓ Ⓔ	6 Ⓐ Ⓑ Ⓒ Ⓓ Ⓔ	11 Ⓐ Ⓑ Ⓒ Ⓓ Ⓔ	16 Ⓐ Ⓑ Ⓒ Ⓓ Ⓔ	21 Ⓐ Ⓑ Ⓒ Ⓓ Ⓔ
2 Ⓐ Ⓑ Ⓒ Ⓓ Ⓔ	7 Ⓐ Ⓑ Ⓒ Ⓓ Ⓔ	12 Ⓐ Ⓑ Ⓒ Ⓓ Ⓔ	17 Ⓐ Ⓑ Ⓒ Ⓓ Ⓔ	22 Ⓐ Ⓑ Ⓒ Ⓓ Ⓔ
3 Ⓐ Ⓑ Ⓒ Ⓓ Ⓔ	8 Ⓐ Ⓑ Ⓒ Ⓓ Ⓔ	13 Ⓐ Ⓑ Ⓒ Ⓓ Ⓔ	18 Ⓐ Ⓑ Ⓒ Ⓓ Ⓔ	23 Ⓐ Ⓑ Ⓒ Ⓓ Ⓔ
4 Ⓐ Ⓑ Ⓒ Ⓓ Ⓔ	9 Ⓐ Ⓑ Ⓒ Ⓓ Ⓔ	14 Ⓐ Ⓑ Ⓒ Ⓓ Ⓔ	19 Ⓐ Ⓑ Ⓒ Ⓓ Ⓔ	24 Ⓐ Ⓑ Ⓒ Ⓓ Ⓔ
5 Ⓐ Ⓑ Ⓒ Ⓓ Ⓔ	10 Ⓐ Ⓑ Ⓒ Ⓓ Ⓔ	15 Ⓐ Ⓑ Ⓒ Ⓓ Ⓔ	20 Ⓐ Ⓑ Ⓒ Ⓓ Ⓔ	25 Ⓐ Ⓑ Ⓒ Ⓓ Ⓔ

Upper Level Practice Test

Be sure each mark *completely* fills the answer space.
Start with number 1 for each new section of the test. You may find more answer spaces than you need.
If so, please leave them blank.

SECTION 1

1 Ⓐ Ⓑ Ⓒ Ⓓ Ⓔ	13 Ⓐ Ⓑ Ⓒ Ⓓ Ⓔ	25 Ⓐ Ⓑ Ⓒ Ⓓ Ⓔ	37 Ⓐ Ⓑ Ⓒ Ⓓ Ⓔ	49 Ⓐ Ⓑ Ⓒ Ⓓ Ⓔ
2 Ⓐ Ⓑ Ⓒ Ⓓ Ⓔ	14 Ⓐ Ⓑ Ⓒ Ⓓ Ⓔ	26 Ⓐ Ⓑ Ⓒ Ⓓ Ⓔ	38 Ⓐ Ⓑ Ⓒ Ⓓ Ⓔ	50 Ⓐ Ⓑ Ⓒ Ⓓ Ⓔ
3 Ⓐ Ⓑ Ⓒ Ⓓ Ⓔ	15 Ⓐ Ⓑ Ⓒ Ⓓ Ⓔ	27 Ⓐ Ⓑ Ⓒ Ⓓ Ⓔ	39 Ⓐ Ⓑ Ⓒ Ⓓ Ⓔ	51 Ⓐ Ⓑ Ⓒ Ⓓ Ⓔ
4 Ⓐ Ⓑ Ⓒ Ⓓ Ⓔ	16 Ⓐ Ⓑ Ⓒ Ⓓ Ⓔ	28 Ⓐ Ⓑ Ⓒ Ⓓ Ⓔ	40 Ⓐ Ⓑ Ⓒ Ⓓ Ⓔ	52 Ⓐ Ⓑ Ⓒ Ⓓ Ⓔ
5 Ⓐ Ⓑ Ⓒ Ⓓ Ⓔ	17 Ⓐ Ⓑ Ⓒ Ⓓ Ⓔ	29 Ⓐ Ⓑ Ⓒ Ⓓ Ⓔ	41 Ⓐ Ⓑ Ⓒ Ⓓ Ⓔ	53 Ⓐ Ⓑ Ⓒ Ⓓ Ⓔ
6 Ⓐ Ⓑ Ⓒ Ⓓ Ⓔ	18 Ⓐ Ⓑ Ⓒ Ⓓ Ⓔ	30 Ⓐ Ⓑ Ⓒ Ⓓ Ⓔ	42 Ⓐ Ⓑ Ⓒ Ⓓ Ⓔ	54 Ⓐ Ⓑ Ⓒ Ⓓ Ⓔ
7 Ⓐ Ⓑ Ⓒ Ⓓ Ⓔ	19 Ⓐ Ⓑ Ⓒ Ⓓ Ⓔ	31 Ⓐ Ⓑ Ⓒ Ⓓ Ⓔ	43 Ⓐ Ⓑ Ⓒ Ⓓ Ⓔ	55 Ⓐ Ⓑ Ⓒ Ⓓ Ⓔ
8 Ⓐ Ⓑ Ⓒ Ⓓ Ⓔ	20 Ⓐ Ⓑ Ⓒ Ⓓ Ⓔ	32 Ⓐ Ⓑ Ⓒ Ⓓ Ⓔ	44 Ⓐ Ⓑ Ⓒ Ⓓ Ⓔ	56 Ⓐ Ⓑ Ⓒ Ⓓ Ⓔ
9 Ⓐ Ⓑ Ⓒ Ⓓ Ⓔ	21 Ⓐ Ⓑ Ⓒ Ⓓ Ⓔ	33 Ⓐ Ⓑ Ⓒ Ⓓ Ⓔ	45 Ⓐ Ⓑ Ⓒ Ⓓ Ⓔ	57 Ⓐ Ⓑ Ⓒ Ⓓ Ⓔ
10 Ⓐ Ⓑ Ⓒ Ⓓ Ⓔ	22 Ⓐ Ⓑ Ⓒ Ⓓ Ⓔ	34 Ⓐ Ⓑ Ⓒ Ⓓ Ⓔ	46 Ⓐ Ⓑ Ⓒ Ⓓ Ⓔ	58 Ⓐ Ⓑ Ⓒ Ⓓ Ⓔ
11 Ⓐ Ⓑ Ⓒ Ⓓ Ⓔ	23 Ⓐ Ⓑ Ⓒ Ⓓ Ⓔ	35 Ⓐ Ⓑ Ⓒ Ⓓ Ⓔ	47 Ⓐ Ⓑ Ⓒ Ⓓ Ⓔ	59 Ⓐ Ⓑ Ⓒ Ⓓ Ⓔ
12 Ⓐ Ⓑ Ⓒ Ⓓ Ⓔ	24 Ⓐ Ⓑ Ⓒ Ⓓ Ⓔ	36 Ⓐ Ⓑ Ⓒ Ⓓ Ⓔ	48 Ⓐ Ⓑ Ⓒ Ⓓ Ⓔ	60 Ⓐ Ⓑ Ⓒ Ⓓ Ⓔ

SECTION 2

1 Ⓐ Ⓑ Ⓒ Ⓓ Ⓔ	6 Ⓐ Ⓑ Ⓒ Ⓓ Ⓔ	11 Ⓐ Ⓑ Ⓒ Ⓓ Ⓔ	16 Ⓐ Ⓑ Ⓒ Ⓓ Ⓔ	21 Ⓐ Ⓑ Ⓒ Ⓓ Ⓔ
2 Ⓐ Ⓑ Ⓒ Ⓓ Ⓔ	7 Ⓐ Ⓑ Ⓒ Ⓓ Ⓔ	12 Ⓐ Ⓑ Ⓒ Ⓓ Ⓔ	17 Ⓐ Ⓑ Ⓒ Ⓓ Ⓔ	22 Ⓐ Ⓑ Ⓒ Ⓓ Ⓔ
3 Ⓐ Ⓑ Ⓒ Ⓓ Ⓔ	8 Ⓐ Ⓑ Ⓒ Ⓓ Ⓔ	13 Ⓐ Ⓑ Ⓒ Ⓓ Ⓔ	18 Ⓐ Ⓑ Ⓒ Ⓓ Ⓔ	23 Ⓐ Ⓑ Ⓒ Ⓓ Ⓔ
4 Ⓐ Ⓑ Ⓒ Ⓓ Ⓔ	9 Ⓐ Ⓑ Ⓒ Ⓓ Ⓔ	14 Ⓐ Ⓑ Ⓒ Ⓓ Ⓔ	19 Ⓐ Ⓑ Ⓒ Ⓓ Ⓔ	24 Ⓐ Ⓑ Ⓒ Ⓓ Ⓔ
5 Ⓐ Ⓑ Ⓒ Ⓓ Ⓔ	10 Ⓐ Ⓑ Ⓒ Ⓓ Ⓔ	15 Ⓐ Ⓑ Ⓒ Ⓓ Ⓔ	20 Ⓐ Ⓑ Ⓒ Ⓓ Ⓔ	25 Ⓐ Ⓑ Ⓒ Ⓓ Ⓔ

SECTION 3

1 Ⓐ Ⓑ Ⓒ Ⓓ Ⓔ	9 Ⓐ Ⓑ Ⓒ Ⓓ Ⓔ	17 Ⓐ Ⓑ Ⓒ Ⓓ Ⓔ	25 Ⓐ Ⓑ Ⓒ Ⓓ Ⓔ	33 Ⓐ Ⓑ Ⓒ Ⓓ Ⓔ
2 Ⓐ Ⓑ Ⓒ Ⓓ Ⓔ	10 Ⓐ Ⓑ Ⓒ Ⓓ Ⓔ	18 Ⓐ Ⓑ Ⓒ Ⓓ Ⓔ	26 Ⓐ Ⓑ Ⓒ Ⓓ Ⓔ	34 Ⓐ Ⓑ Ⓒ Ⓓ Ⓔ
3 Ⓐ Ⓑ Ⓒ Ⓓ Ⓔ	11 Ⓐ Ⓑ Ⓒ Ⓓ Ⓔ	19 Ⓐ Ⓑ Ⓒ Ⓓ Ⓔ	27 Ⓐ Ⓑ Ⓒ Ⓓ Ⓔ	35 Ⓐ Ⓑ Ⓒ Ⓓ Ⓔ
4 Ⓐ Ⓑ Ⓒ Ⓓ Ⓔ	12 Ⓐ Ⓑ Ⓒ Ⓓ Ⓔ	20 Ⓐ Ⓑ Ⓒ Ⓓ Ⓔ	28 Ⓐ Ⓑ Ⓒ Ⓓ Ⓔ	36 Ⓐ Ⓑ Ⓒ Ⓓ Ⓔ
5 Ⓐ Ⓑ Ⓒ Ⓓ Ⓔ	13 Ⓐ Ⓑ Ⓒ Ⓓ Ⓔ	21 Ⓐ Ⓑ Ⓒ Ⓓ Ⓔ	29 Ⓐ Ⓑ Ⓒ Ⓓ Ⓔ	37 Ⓐ Ⓑ Ⓒ Ⓓ Ⓔ
6 Ⓐ Ⓑ Ⓒ Ⓓ Ⓔ	14 Ⓐ Ⓑ Ⓒ Ⓓ Ⓔ	22 Ⓐ Ⓑ Ⓒ Ⓓ Ⓔ	30 Ⓐ Ⓑ Ⓒ Ⓓ Ⓔ	38 Ⓐ Ⓑ Ⓒ Ⓓ Ⓔ
7 Ⓐ Ⓑ Ⓒ Ⓓ Ⓔ	15 Ⓐ Ⓑ Ⓒ Ⓓ Ⓔ	23 Ⓐ Ⓑ Ⓒ Ⓓ Ⓔ	31 Ⓐ Ⓑ Ⓒ Ⓓ Ⓔ	39 Ⓐ Ⓑ Ⓒ Ⓓ Ⓔ
8 Ⓐ Ⓑ Ⓒ Ⓓ Ⓔ	16 Ⓐ Ⓑ Ⓒ Ⓓ Ⓔ	24 Ⓐ Ⓑ Ⓒ Ⓓ Ⓔ	32 Ⓐ Ⓑ Ⓒ Ⓓ Ⓔ	40 Ⓐ Ⓑ Ⓒ Ⓓ Ⓔ

SECTION 4

1 Ⓐ Ⓑ Ⓒ Ⓓ Ⓔ	6 Ⓐ Ⓑ Ⓒ Ⓓ Ⓔ	11 Ⓐ Ⓑ Ⓒ Ⓓ Ⓔ	16 Ⓐ Ⓑ Ⓒ Ⓓ Ⓔ	21 Ⓐ Ⓑ Ⓒ Ⓓ Ⓔ
2 Ⓐ Ⓑ Ⓒ Ⓓ Ⓔ	7 Ⓐ Ⓑ Ⓒ Ⓓ Ⓔ	12 Ⓐ Ⓑ Ⓒ Ⓓ Ⓔ	17 Ⓐ Ⓑ Ⓒ Ⓓ Ⓔ	22 Ⓐ Ⓑ Ⓒ Ⓓ Ⓔ
3 Ⓐ Ⓑ Ⓒ Ⓓ Ⓔ	8 Ⓐ Ⓑ Ⓒ Ⓓ Ⓔ	13 Ⓐ Ⓑ Ⓒ Ⓓ Ⓔ	18 Ⓐ Ⓑ Ⓒ Ⓓ Ⓔ	23 Ⓐ Ⓑ Ⓒ Ⓓ Ⓔ
4 Ⓐ Ⓑ Ⓒ Ⓓ Ⓔ	9 Ⓐ Ⓑ Ⓒ Ⓓ Ⓔ	14 Ⓐ Ⓑ Ⓒ Ⓓ Ⓔ	19 Ⓐ Ⓑ Ⓒ Ⓓ Ⓔ	24 Ⓐ Ⓑ Ⓒ Ⓓ Ⓔ
5 Ⓐ Ⓑ Ⓒ Ⓓ Ⓔ	10 Ⓐ Ⓑ Ⓒ Ⓓ Ⓔ	15 Ⓐ Ⓑ Ⓒ Ⓓ Ⓔ	20 Ⓐ Ⓑ Ⓒ Ⓓ Ⓔ	25 Ⓐ Ⓑ Ⓒ Ⓓ Ⓔ

Upper Level Practice Test

Be sure each mark *completely* fills the answer space.
Start with number 1 for each new section of the test. You may find more answer spaces than you need.
If so, please leave them blank.

SECTION 1

1 Ⓐ Ⓑ Ⓒ Ⓓ Ⓔ   13 Ⓐ Ⓑ Ⓒ Ⓓ Ⓔ   25 Ⓐ Ⓑ Ⓒ Ⓓ Ⓔ   37 Ⓐ Ⓑ Ⓒ Ⓓ Ⓔ   49 Ⓐ Ⓑ Ⓒ Ⓓ Ⓔ
2 Ⓐ Ⓑ Ⓒ Ⓓ Ⓔ   14 Ⓐ Ⓑ Ⓒ Ⓓ Ⓔ   26 Ⓐ Ⓑ Ⓒ Ⓓ Ⓔ   38 Ⓐ Ⓑ Ⓒ Ⓓ Ⓔ   50 Ⓐ Ⓑ Ⓒ Ⓓ Ⓔ
3 Ⓐ Ⓑ Ⓒ Ⓓ Ⓔ   15 Ⓐ Ⓑ Ⓒ Ⓓ Ⓔ   27 Ⓐ Ⓑ Ⓒ Ⓓ Ⓔ   39 Ⓐ Ⓑ Ⓒ Ⓓ Ⓔ   51 Ⓐ Ⓑ Ⓒ Ⓓ Ⓔ
4 Ⓐ Ⓑ Ⓒ Ⓓ Ⓔ   16 Ⓐ Ⓑ Ⓒ Ⓓ Ⓔ   28 Ⓐ Ⓑ Ⓒ Ⓓ Ⓔ   40 Ⓐ Ⓑ Ⓒ Ⓓ Ⓔ   52 Ⓐ Ⓑ Ⓒ Ⓓ Ⓔ
5 Ⓐ Ⓑ Ⓒ Ⓓ Ⓔ   17 Ⓐ Ⓑ Ⓒ Ⓓ Ⓔ   29 Ⓐ Ⓑ Ⓒ Ⓓ Ⓔ   41 Ⓐ Ⓑ Ⓒ Ⓓ Ⓔ   53 Ⓐ Ⓑ Ⓒ Ⓓ Ⓔ
6 Ⓐ Ⓑ Ⓒ Ⓓ Ⓔ   18 Ⓐ Ⓑ Ⓒ Ⓓ Ⓔ   30 Ⓐ Ⓑ Ⓒ Ⓓ Ⓔ   42 Ⓐ Ⓑ Ⓒ Ⓓ Ⓔ   54 Ⓐ Ⓑ Ⓒ Ⓓ Ⓔ
7 Ⓐ Ⓑ Ⓒ Ⓓ Ⓔ   19 Ⓐ Ⓑ Ⓒ Ⓓ Ⓔ   31 Ⓐ Ⓑ Ⓒ Ⓓ Ⓔ   43 Ⓐ Ⓑ Ⓒ Ⓓ Ⓔ   55 Ⓐ Ⓑ Ⓒ Ⓓ Ⓔ
8 Ⓐ Ⓑ Ⓒ Ⓓ Ⓔ   20 Ⓐ Ⓑ Ⓒ Ⓓ Ⓔ   32 Ⓐ Ⓑ Ⓒ Ⓓ Ⓔ   44 Ⓐ Ⓑ Ⓒ Ⓓ Ⓔ   56 Ⓐ Ⓑ Ⓒ Ⓓ Ⓔ
9 Ⓐ Ⓑ Ⓒ Ⓓ Ⓔ   21 Ⓐ Ⓑ Ⓒ Ⓓ Ⓔ   33 Ⓐ Ⓑ Ⓒ Ⓓ Ⓔ   45 Ⓐ Ⓑ Ⓒ Ⓓ Ⓔ   57 Ⓐ Ⓑ Ⓒ Ⓓ Ⓔ
10 Ⓐ Ⓑ Ⓒ Ⓓ Ⓔ   22 Ⓐ Ⓑ Ⓒ Ⓓ Ⓔ   34 Ⓐ Ⓑ Ⓒ Ⓓ Ⓔ   46 Ⓐ Ⓑ Ⓒ Ⓓ Ⓔ   58 Ⓐ Ⓑ Ⓒ Ⓓ Ⓔ
11 Ⓐ Ⓑ Ⓒ Ⓓ Ⓔ   23 Ⓐ Ⓑ Ⓒ Ⓓ Ⓔ   35 Ⓐ Ⓑ Ⓒ Ⓓ Ⓔ   47 Ⓐ Ⓑ Ⓒ Ⓓ Ⓔ   59 Ⓐ Ⓑ Ⓒ Ⓓ Ⓔ
12 Ⓐ Ⓑ Ⓒ Ⓓ Ⓔ   24 Ⓐ Ⓑ Ⓒ Ⓓ Ⓔ   36 Ⓐ Ⓑ Ⓒ Ⓓ Ⓔ   48 Ⓐ Ⓑ Ⓒ Ⓓ Ⓔ   60 Ⓐ Ⓑ Ⓒ Ⓓ Ⓔ

SECTION 2

1 Ⓐ Ⓑ Ⓒ Ⓓ Ⓔ   6 Ⓐ Ⓑ Ⓒ Ⓓ Ⓔ   11 Ⓐ Ⓑ Ⓒ Ⓓ Ⓔ   16 Ⓐ Ⓑ Ⓒ Ⓓ Ⓔ   21 Ⓐ Ⓑ Ⓒ Ⓓ Ⓔ
2 Ⓐ Ⓑ Ⓒ Ⓓ Ⓔ   7 Ⓐ Ⓑ Ⓒ Ⓓ Ⓔ   12 Ⓐ Ⓑ Ⓒ Ⓓ Ⓔ   17 Ⓐ Ⓑ Ⓒ Ⓓ Ⓔ   22 Ⓐ Ⓑ Ⓒ Ⓓ Ⓔ
3 Ⓐ Ⓑ Ⓒ Ⓓ Ⓔ   8 Ⓐ Ⓑ Ⓒ Ⓓ Ⓔ   13 Ⓐ Ⓑ Ⓒ Ⓓ Ⓔ   18 Ⓐ Ⓑ Ⓒ Ⓓ Ⓔ   23 Ⓐ Ⓑ Ⓒ Ⓓ Ⓔ
4 Ⓐ Ⓑ Ⓒ Ⓓ Ⓔ   9 Ⓐ Ⓑ Ⓒ Ⓓ Ⓔ   14 Ⓐ Ⓑ Ⓒ Ⓓ Ⓔ   19 Ⓐ Ⓑ Ⓒ Ⓓ Ⓔ   24 Ⓐ Ⓑ Ⓒ Ⓓ Ⓔ
5 Ⓐ Ⓑ Ⓒ Ⓓ Ⓔ   10 Ⓐ Ⓑ Ⓒ Ⓓ Ⓔ   15 Ⓐ Ⓑ Ⓒ Ⓓ Ⓔ   20 Ⓐ Ⓑ Ⓒ Ⓓ Ⓔ   25 Ⓐ Ⓑ Ⓒ Ⓓ Ⓔ

SECTION 3

1 Ⓐ Ⓑ Ⓒ Ⓓ Ⓔ   9 Ⓐ Ⓑ Ⓒ Ⓓ Ⓔ   17 Ⓐ Ⓑ Ⓒ Ⓓ Ⓔ   25 Ⓐ Ⓑ Ⓒ Ⓓ Ⓔ   33 Ⓐ Ⓑ Ⓒ Ⓓ Ⓔ
2 Ⓐ Ⓑ Ⓒ Ⓓ Ⓔ   10 Ⓐ Ⓑ Ⓒ Ⓓ Ⓔ   18 Ⓐ Ⓑ Ⓒ Ⓓ Ⓔ   26 Ⓐ Ⓑ Ⓒ Ⓓ Ⓔ   34 Ⓐ Ⓑ Ⓒ Ⓓ Ⓔ
3 Ⓐ Ⓑ Ⓒ Ⓓ Ⓔ   11 Ⓐ Ⓑ Ⓒ Ⓓ Ⓔ   19 Ⓐ Ⓑ Ⓒ Ⓓ Ⓔ   27 Ⓐ Ⓑ Ⓒ Ⓓ Ⓔ   35 Ⓐ Ⓑ Ⓒ Ⓓ Ⓔ
4 Ⓐ Ⓑ Ⓒ Ⓓ Ⓔ   12 Ⓐ Ⓑ Ⓒ Ⓓ Ⓔ   20 Ⓐ Ⓑ Ⓒ Ⓓ Ⓔ   28 Ⓐ Ⓑ Ⓒ Ⓓ Ⓔ   36 Ⓐ Ⓑ Ⓒ Ⓓ Ⓔ
5 Ⓐ Ⓑ Ⓒ Ⓓ Ⓔ   13 Ⓐ Ⓑ Ⓒ Ⓓ Ⓔ   21 Ⓐ Ⓑ Ⓒ Ⓓ Ⓔ   29 Ⓐ Ⓑ Ⓒ Ⓓ Ⓔ   37 Ⓐ Ⓑ Ⓒ Ⓓ Ⓔ
6 Ⓐ Ⓑ Ⓒ Ⓓ Ⓔ   14 Ⓐ Ⓑ Ⓒ Ⓓ Ⓔ   22 Ⓐ Ⓑ Ⓒ Ⓓ Ⓔ   30 Ⓐ Ⓑ Ⓒ Ⓓ Ⓔ   38 Ⓐ Ⓑ Ⓒ Ⓓ Ⓔ
7 Ⓐ Ⓑ Ⓒ Ⓓ Ⓔ   15 Ⓐ Ⓑ Ⓒ Ⓓ Ⓔ   23 Ⓐ Ⓑ Ⓒ Ⓓ Ⓔ   31 Ⓐ Ⓑ Ⓒ Ⓓ Ⓔ   39 Ⓐ Ⓑ Ⓒ Ⓓ Ⓔ
8 Ⓐ Ⓑ Ⓒ Ⓓ Ⓔ   16 Ⓐ Ⓑ Ⓒ Ⓓ Ⓔ   24 Ⓐ Ⓑ Ⓒ Ⓓ Ⓔ   32 Ⓐ Ⓑ Ⓒ Ⓓ Ⓔ   40 Ⓐ Ⓑ Ⓒ Ⓓ Ⓔ

SECTION 4

1 Ⓐ Ⓑ Ⓒ Ⓓ Ⓔ   6 Ⓐ Ⓑ Ⓒ Ⓓ Ⓔ   11 Ⓐ Ⓑ Ⓒ Ⓓ Ⓔ   16 Ⓐ Ⓑ Ⓒ Ⓓ Ⓔ   21 Ⓐ Ⓑ Ⓒ Ⓓ Ⓔ
2 Ⓐ Ⓑ Ⓒ Ⓓ Ⓔ   7 Ⓐ Ⓑ Ⓒ Ⓓ Ⓔ   12 Ⓐ Ⓑ Ⓒ Ⓓ Ⓔ   17 Ⓐ Ⓑ Ⓒ Ⓓ Ⓔ   22 Ⓐ Ⓑ Ⓒ Ⓓ Ⓔ
3 Ⓐ Ⓑ Ⓒ Ⓓ Ⓔ   8 Ⓐ Ⓑ Ⓒ Ⓓ Ⓔ   13 Ⓐ Ⓑ Ⓒ Ⓓ Ⓔ   18 Ⓐ Ⓑ Ⓒ Ⓓ Ⓔ   23 Ⓐ Ⓑ Ⓒ Ⓓ Ⓔ
4 Ⓐ Ⓑ Ⓒ Ⓓ Ⓔ   9 Ⓐ Ⓑ Ⓒ Ⓓ Ⓔ   14 Ⓐ Ⓑ Ⓒ Ⓓ Ⓔ   19 Ⓐ Ⓑ Ⓒ Ⓓ Ⓔ   24 Ⓐ Ⓑ Ⓒ Ⓓ Ⓔ
5 Ⓐ Ⓑ Ⓒ Ⓓ Ⓔ   10 Ⓐ Ⓑ Ⓒ Ⓓ Ⓔ   15 Ⓐ Ⓑ Ⓒ Ⓓ Ⓔ   20 Ⓐ Ⓑ Ⓒ Ⓓ Ⓔ   25 Ⓐ Ⓑ Ⓒ Ⓓ Ⓔ

Upper Level Practice Test

Be sure each mark *completely* fills the answer space.
Start with number 1 for each new section of the test. You may find more answer spaces than you need.
If so, please leave them blank.

SECTION 1

1 Ⓐ Ⓑ Ⓒ Ⓓ Ⓔ	13 Ⓐ Ⓑ Ⓒ Ⓓ Ⓔ	25 Ⓐ Ⓑ Ⓒ Ⓓ Ⓔ	37 Ⓐ Ⓑ Ⓒ Ⓓ Ⓔ	49 Ⓐ Ⓑ Ⓒ Ⓓ Ⓔ
2 Ⓐ Ⓑ Ⓒ Ⓓ Ⓔ	14 Ⓐ Ⓑ Ⓒ Ⓓ Ⓔ	26 Ⓐ Ⓑ Ⓒ Ⓓ Ⓔ	38 Ⓐ Ⓑ Ⓒ Ⓓ Ⓔ	50 Ⓐ Ⓑ Ⓒ Ⓓ Ⓔ
3 Ⓐ Ⓑ Ⓒ Ⓓ Ⓔ	15 Ⓐ Ⓑ Ⓒ Ⓓ Ⓔ	27 Ⓐ Ⓑ Ⓒ Ⓓ Ⓔ	39 Ⓐ Ⓑ Ⓒ Ⓓ Ⓔ	51 Ⓐ Ⓑ Ⓒ Ⓓ Ⓔ
4 Ⓐ Ⓑ Ⓒ Ⓓ Ⓔ	16 Ⓐ Ⓑ Ⓒ Ⓓ Ⓔ	28 Ⓐ Ⓑ Ⓒ Ⓓ Ⓔ	40 Ⓐ Ⓑ Ⓒ Ⓓ Ⓔ	52 Ⓐ Ⓑ Ⓒ Ⓓ Ⓔ
5 Ⓐ Ⓑ Ⓒ Ⓓ Ⓔ	17 Ⓐ Ⓑ Ⓒ Ⓓ Ⓔ	29 Ⓐ Ⓑ Ⓒ Ⓓ Ⓔ	41 Ⓐ Ⓑ Ⓒ Ⓓ Ⓔ	53 Ⓐ Ⓑ Ⓒ Ⓓ Ⓔ
6 Ⓐ Ⓑ Ⓒ Ⓓ Ⓔ	18 Ⓐ Ⓑ Ⓒ Ⓓ Ⓔ	30 Ⓐ Ⓑ Ⓒ Ⓓ Ⓔ	42 Ⓐ Ⓑ Ⓒ Ⓓ Ⓔ	54 Ⓐ Ⓑ Ⓒ Ⓓ Ⓔ
7 Ⓐ Ⓑ Ⓒ Ⓓ Ⓔ	19 Ⓐ Ⓑ Ⓒ Ⓓ Ⓔ	31 Ⓐ Ⓑ Ⓒ Ⓓ Ⓔ	43 Ⓐ Ⓑ Ⓒ Ⓓ Ⓔ	55 Ⓐ Ⓑ Ⓒ Ⓓ Ⓔ
8 Ⓐ Ⓑ Ⓒ Ⓓ Ⓔ	20 Ⓐ Ⓑ Ⓒ Ⓓ Ⓔ	32 Ⓐ Ⓑ Ⓒ Ⓓ Ⓔ	44 Ⓐ Ⓑ Ⓒ Ⓓ Ⓔ	56 Ⓐ Ⓑ Ⓒ Ⓓ Ⓔ
9 Ⓐ Ⓑ Ⓒ Ⓓ Ⓔ	21 Ⓐ Ⓑ Ⓒ Ⓓ Ⓔ	33 Ⓐ Ⓑ Ⓒ Ⓓ Ⓔ	45 Ⓐ Ⓑ Ⓒ Ⓓ Ⓔ	57 Ⓐ Ⓑ Ⓒ Ⓓ Ⓔ
10 Ⓐ Ⓑ Ⓒ Ⓓ Ⓔ	22 Ⓐ Ⓑ Ⓒ Ⓓ Ⓔ	34 Ⓐ Ⓑ Ⓒ Ⓓ Ⓔ	46 Ⓐ Ⓑ Ⓒ Ⓓ Ⓔ	58 Ⓐ Ⓑ Ⓒ Ⓓ Ⓔ
11 Ⓐ Ⓑ Ⓒ Ⓓ Ⓔ	23 Ⓐ Ⓑ Ⓒ Ⓓ Ⓔ	35 Ⓐ Ⓑ Ⓒ Ⓓ Ⓔ	47 Ⓐ Ⓑ Ⓒ Ⓓ Ⓔ	59 Ⓐ Ⓑ Ⓒ Ⓓ Ⓔ
12 Ⓐ Ⓑ Ⓒ Ⓓ Ⓔ	24 Ⓐ Ⓑ Ⓒ Ⓓ Ⓔ	36 Ⓐ Ⓑ Ⓒ Ⓓ Ⓔ	48 Ⓐ Ⓑ Ⓒ Ⓓ Ⓔ	60 Ⓐ Ⓑ Ⓒ Ⓓ Ⓔ

SECTION 2

1 Ⓐ Ⓑ Ⓒ Ⓓ Ⓔ	6 Ⓐ Ⓑ Ⓒ Ⓓ Ⓔ	11 Ⓐ Ⓑ Ⓒ Ⓓ Ⓔ	16 Ⓐ Ⓑ Ⓒ Ⓓ Ⓔ	21 Ⓐ Ⓑ Ⓒ Ⓓ Ⓔ
2 Ⓐ Ⓑ Ⓒ Ⓓ Ⓕ	7 Ⓐ Ⓑ Ⓒ Ⓓ Ⓔ	12 Ⓐ Ⓑ Ⓒ Ⓓ Ⓔ	17 Ⓐ Ⓑ Ⓒ Ⓓ Ⓔ	22 Ⓐ Ⓑ Ⓒ Ⓓ Ⓔ
3 Ⓐ Ⓑ Ⓒ Ⓓ Ⓔ	8 Ⓐ Ⓑ Ⓒ Ⓓ Ⓔ	13 Ⓐ Ⓑ Ⓒ Ⓓ Ⓔ	18 Ⓐ Ⓑ Ⓒ Ⓓ Ⓔ	23 Ⓐ Ⓑ Ⓒ Ⓓ Ⓔ
4 Ⓐ Ⓑ Ⓒ Ⓓ Ⓔ	9 Ⓐ Ⓑ Ⓒ Ⓓ Ⓔ	14 Ⓐ Ⓑ Ⓒ Ⓓ Ⓔ	19 Ⓐ Ⓑ Ⓒ Ⓓ Ⓔ	24 Ⓐ Ⓑ Ⓒ Ⓓ Ⓔ
5 Ⓐ Ⓑ Ⓒ Ⓓ Ⓔ	10 Ⓐ Ⓑ Ⓒ Ⓓ Ⓔ	15 Ⓐ Ⓑ Ⓒ Ⓓ Ⓔ	20 Ⓐ Ⓑ Ⓒ Ⓓ Ⓔ	25 Ⓐ Ⓑ Ⓒ Ⓓ Ⓔ

SECTION 3

1 Ⓐ Ⓑ Ⓒ Ⓓ Ⓔ	9 Ⓐ Ⓑ Ⓒ Ⓓ Ⓔ	17 Ⓐ Ⓑ Ⓒ Ⓓ Ⓔ	25 Ⓐ Ⓑ Ⓒ Ⓓ Ⓔ	33 Ⓐ Ⓑ Ⓒ Ⓓ Ⓔ
2 Ⓐ Ⓑ Ⓒ Ⓓ Ⓔ	10 Ⓐ Ⓑ Ⓒ Ⓓ Ⓔ	18 Ⓐ Ⓑ Ⓒ Ⓓ Ⓔ	26 Ⓐ Ⓑ Ⓒ Ⓓ Ⓔ	34 Ⓐ Ⓑ Ⓒ Ⓓ Ⓔ
3 Ⓐ Ⓑ Ⓒ Ⓓ Ⓔ	11 Ⓐ Ⓑ Ⓒ Ⓓ Ⓔ	19 Ⓐ Ⓑ Ⓒ Ⓓ Ⓔ	27 Ⓐ Ⓑ Ⓒ Ⓓ Ⓔ	35 Ⓐ Ⓑ Ⓒ Ⓓ Ⓔ
4 Ⓐ Ⓑ Ⓒ Ⓓ Ⓔ	12 Ⓐ Ⓑ Ⓒ Ⓓ Ⓔ	20 Ⓐ Ⓑ Ⓒ Ⓓ Ⓔ	28 Ⓐ Ⓑ Ⓒ Ⓓ Ⓔ	36 Ⓐ Ⓑ Ⓒ Ⓓ Ⓔ
5 Ⓐ Ⓑ Ⓒ Ⓓ Ⓕ	13 Ⓐ Ⓑ Ⓒ Ⓓ Ⓔ	21 Ⓐ Ⓑ Ⓒ Ⓓ Ⓔ	29 Ⓐ Ⓑ Ⓒ Ⓓ Ⓔ	37 Ⓐ Ⓑ Ⓒ Ⓓ Ⓔ
6 Ⓐ Ⓑ Ⓒ Ⓓ Ⓔ	14 Ⓐ Ⓑ Ⓒ Ⓓ Ⓔ	22 Ⓐ Ⓑ Ⓒ Ⓓ Ⓔ	30 Ⓐ Ⓑ Ⓒ Ⓓ Ⓔ	38 Ⓐ Ⓑ Ⓒ Ⓓ Ⓔ
7 Ⓐ Ⓑ Ⓒ Ⓓ Ⓔ	15 Ⓐ Ⓑ Ⓒ Ⓓ Ⓔ	23 Ⓐ Ⓑ Ⓒ Ⓓ Ⓔ	31 Ⓐ Ⓑ Ⓒ Ⓓ Ⓔ	39 Ⓐ Ⓑ Ⓒ Ⓓ Ⓔ
8 Ⓐ Ⓑ Ⓒ Ⓓ Ⓔ	16 Ⓐ Ⓑ Ⓒ Ⓓ Ⓔ	24 Ⓐ Ⓑ Ⓒ Ⓓ Ⓔ	32 Ⓐ Ⓑ Ⓒ Ⓓ Ⓔ	40 Ⓐ Ⓑ Ⓒ Ⓓ Ⓔ

SECTION 4

1 Ⓐ Ⓑ Ⓒ Ⓓ Ⓔ	6 Ⓐ Ⓑ Ⓒ Ⓓ Ⓔ	11 Ⓐ Ⓑ Ⓒ Ⓓ Ⓔ	16 Ⓐ Ⓑ Ⓒ Ⓓ Ⓔ	21 Ⓐ Ⓑ Ⓒ Ⓓ Ⓔ
2 Ⓐ Ⓑ Ⓒ Ⓓ Ⓔ	7 Ⓐ Ⓑ Ⓒ Ⓓ Ⓔ	12 Ⓐ Ⓑ Ⓒ Ⓓ Ⓔ	17 Ⓐ Ⓑ Ⓒ Ⓓ Ⓔ	22 Ⓐ Ⓑ Ⓒ Ⓓ Ⓔ
3 Ⓐ Ⓑ Ⓒ Ⓓ Ⓔ	8 Ⓐ Ⓑ Ⓒ Ⓓ Ⓔ	13 Ⓐ Ⓑ Ⓒ Ⓓ Ⓔ	18 Ⓐ Ⓑ Ⓒ Ⓓ Ⓔ	23 Ⓐ Ⓑ Ⓒ Ⓓ Ⓔ
4 Ⓐ Ⓑ Ⓒ Ⓓ Ⓔ	9 Ⓐ Ⓑ Ⓒ Ⓓ Ⓔ	14 Ⓐ Ⓑ Ⓒ Ⓓ Ⓔ	19 Ⓐ Ⓑ Ⓒ Ⓓ Ⓔ	24 Ⓐ Ⓑ Ⓒ Ⓓ Ⓔ
5 Ⓐ Ⓑ Ⓒ Ⓓ Ⓔ	10 Ⓐ Ⓑ Ⓒ Ⓓ Ⓔ	15 Ⓐ Ⓑ Ⓒ Ⓓ Ⓔ	20 Ⓐ Ⓑ Ⓒ Ⓓ Ⓔ	25 Ⓐ Ⓑ Ⓒ Ⓓ Ⓔ

Upper Level Practice Test

Be sure each mark *completely* fills the answer space.
Start with number 1 for each new section of the test. You may find more answer spaces than you need.
If so, please leave them blank.

SECTION 1

1 Ⓐ Ⓑ Ⓒ Ⓓ Ⓔ	13 Ⓐ Ⓑ Ⓒ Ⓓ Ⓔ	25 Ⓐ Ⓑ Ⓒ Ⓓ Ⓔ	37 Ⓐ Ⓑ Ⓒ Ⓓ Ⓔ	49 Ⓐ Ⓑ Ⓒ Ⓓ Ⓔ
2 Ⓐ Ⓑ Ⓒ Ⓓ Ⓔ	14 Ⓐ Ⓑ Ⓒ Ⓓ Ⓔ	26 Ⓐ Ⓑ Ⓒ Ⓓ Ⓔ	38 Ⓐ Ⓑ Ⓒ Ⓓ Ⓔ	50 Ⓐ Ⓑ Ⓒ Ⓓ Ⓔ
3 Ⓐ Ⓑ Ⓒ Ⓓ Ⓔ	15 Ⓐ Ⓑ Ⓒ Ⓓ Ⓔ	27 Ⓐ Ⓑ Ⓒ Ⓓ Ⓔ	39 Ⓐ Ⓑ Ⓒ Ⓓ Ⓔ	51 Ⓐ Ⓑ Ⓒ Ⓓ Ⓔ
4 Ⓐ Ⓑ Ⓒ Ⓓ Ⓔ	16 Ⓐ Ⓑ Ⓒ Ⓓ Ⓔ	28 Ⓐ Ⓑ Ⓒ Ⓓ Ⓔ	40 Ⓐ Ⓑ Ⓒ Ⓓ Ⓔ	52 Ⓐ Ⓑ Ⓒ Ⓓ Ⓔ
5 Ⓐ Ⓑ Ⓒ Ⓓ Ⓔ	17 Ⓐ Ⓑ Ⓒ Ⓓ Ⓔ	29 Ⓐ Ⓑ Ⓒ Ⓓ Ⓔ	41 Ⓐ Ⓑ Ⓒ Ⓓ Ⓔ	53 Ⓐ Ⓑ Ⓒ Ⓓ Ⓔ
6 Ⓐ Ⓑ Ⓒ Ⓓ Ⓔ	18 Ⓐ Ⓑ Ⓒ Ⓓ Ⓔ	30 Ⓐ Ⓑ Ⓒ Ⓓ Ⓔ	42 Ⓐ Ⓑ Ⓒ Ⓓ Ⓔ	54 Ⓐ Ⓑ Ⓒ Ⓓ Ⓔ
7 Ⓐ Ⓑ Ⓒ Ⓓ Ⓔ	19 Ⓐ Ⓑ Ⓒ Ⓓ Ⓔ	31 Ⓐ Ⓑ Ⓒ Ⓓ Ⓔ	43 Ⓐ Ⓑ Ⓒ Ⓓ Ⓔ	55 Ⓐ Ⓑ Ⓒ Ⓓ Ⓔ
8 Ⓐ Ⓑ Ⓒ Ⓓ Ⓔ	20 Ⓐ Ⓑ Ⓒ Ⓓ Ⓔ	32 Ⓐ Ⓑ Ⓒ Ⓓ Ⓔ	44 Ⓐ Ⓑ Ⓒ Ⓓ Ⓔ	56 Ⓐ Ⓑ Ⓒ Ⓓ Ⓔ
9 Ⓐ Ⓑ Ⓒ Ⓓ Ⓔ	21 Ⓐ Ⓑ Ⓒ Ⓓ Ⓔ	33 Ⓐ Ⓑ Ⓒ Ⓓ Ⓔ	45 Ⓐ Ⓑ Ⓒ Ⓓ Ⓔ	57 Ⓐ Ⓑ Ⓒ Ⓓ Ⓔ
10 Ⓐ Ⓑ Ⓒ Ⓓ Ⓔ	22 Ⓐ Ⓑ Ⓒ Ⓓ Ⓔ	34 Ⓐ Ⓑ Ⓒ Ⓓ Ⓔ	46 Ⓐ Ⓑ Ⓒ Ⓓ Ⓔ	58 Ⓐ Ⓑ Ⓒ Ⓓ Ⓔ
11 Ⓐ Ⓑ Ⓒ Ⓓ Ⓔ	23 Ⓐ Ⓑ Ⓒ Ⓓ Ⓔ	35 Ⓐ Ⓑ Ⓒ Ⓓ Ⓔ	47 Ⓐ Ⓑ Ⓒ Ⓓ Ⓔ	59 Ⓐ Ⓑ Ⓒ Ⓓ Ⓔ
12 Ⓐ Ⓑ Ⓒ Ⓓ Ⓔ	24 Ⓐ Ⓑ Ⓒ Ⓓ Ⓔ	36 Ⓐ Ⓑ Ⓒ Ⓓ Ⓔ	48 Ⓐ Ⓑ Ⓒ Ⓓ Ⓔ	60 Ⓐ Ⓑ Ⓒ Ⓓ Ⓔ

SECTION 2

1 Ⓐ Ⓑ Ⓒ Ⓓ Ⓔ	6 Ⓐ Ⓑ Ⓒ Ⓓ Ⓔ	11 Ⓐ Ⓑ Ⓒ Ⓓ Ⓔ	16 Ⓐ Ⓑ Ⓒ Ⓓ Ⓔ	21 Ⓐ Ⓑ Ⓒ Ⓓ Ⓔ
2 Ⓐ Ⓑ Ⓒ Ⓓ Ⓔ	7 Ⓐ Ⓑ Ⓒ Ⓓ Ⓔ	12 Ⓐ Ⓑ Ⓒ Ⓓ Ⓔ	17 Ⓐ Ⓑ Ⓒ Ⓓ Ⓔ	22 Ⓐ Ⓑ Ⓒ Ⓓ Ⓔ
3 Ⓐ Ⓑ Ⓒ Ⓓ Ⓔ	8 Ⓐ Ⓑ Ⓒ Ⓓ Ⓔ	13 Ⓐ Ⓑ Ⓒ Ⓓ Ⓔ	18 Ⓐ Ⓑ Ⓒ Ⓓ Ⓔ	23 Ⓐ Ⓑ Ⓒ Ⓓ Ⓔ
4 Ⓐ Ⓑ Ⓒ Ⓓ Ⓔ	9 Ⓐ Ⓑ Ⓒ Ⓓ Ⓔ	14 Ⓐ Ⓑ Ⓒ Ⓓ Ⓔ	19 Ⓐ Ⓑ Ⓒ Ⓓ Ⓔ	24 Ⓐ Ⓑ Ⓒ Ⓓ Ⓔ
5 Ⓐ Ⓑ Ⓒ Ⓓ Ⓔ	10 Ⓐ Ⓑ Ⓒ Ⓓ Ⓔ	15 Ⓐ Ⓑ Ⓒ Ⓓ Ⓔ	20 Ⓐ Ⓑ Ⓒ Ⓓ Ⓔ	25 Ⓐ Ⓑ Ⓒ Ⓓ Ⓔ

SECTION 3

1 Ⓐ Ⓑ Ⓒ Ⓓ Ⓔ	9 Ⓐ Ⓑ Ⓒ Ⓓ Ⓔ	17 Ⓐ Ⓑ Ⓒ Ⓓ Ⓔ	25 Ⓐ Ⓑ Ⓒ Ⓓ Ⓔ	33 Ⓐ Ⓑ Ⓒ Ⓓ Ⓔ
2 Ⓐ Ⓑ Ⓒ Ⓓ Ⓔ	10 Ⓐ Ⓑ Ⓒ Ⓓ Ⓔ	18 Ⓐ Ⓑ Ⓒ Ⓓ Ⓔ	26 Ⓐ Ⓑ Ⓒ Ⓓ Ⓔ	34 Ⓐ Ⓑ Ⓒ Ⓓ Ⓔ
3 Ⓐ Ⓑ Ⓒ Ⓓ Ⓔ	11 Ⓐ Ⓑ Ⓒ Ⓓ Ⓔ	19 Ⓐ Ⓑ Ⓒ Ⓓ Ⓔ	27 Ⓐ Ⓑ Ⓒ Ⓓ Ⓔ	35 Ⓐ Ⓑ Ⓒ Ⓓ Ⓔ
4 Ⓐ Ⓑ Ⓒ Ⓓ Ⓔ	12 Ⓐ Ⓑ Ⓒ Ⓓ Ⓔ	20 Ⓐ Ⓑ Ⓒ Ⓓ Ⓔ	28 Ⓐ Ⓑ Ⓒ Ⓓ Ⓔ	36 Ⓐ Ⓑ Ⓒ Ⓓ Ⓔ
5 Ⓐ Ⓑ Ⓒ Ⓓ Ⓔ	13 Ⓐ Ⓑ Ⓒ Ⓓ Ⓔ	21 Ⓐ Ⓑ Ⓒ Ⓓ Ⓔ	29 Ⓐ Ⓑ Ⓒ Ⓓ Ⓔ	37 Ⓐ Ⓑ Ⓒ Ⓓ Ⓔ
6 Ⓐ Ⓑ Ⓒ Ⓓ Ⓔ	14 Ⓐ Ⓑ Ⓒ Ⓓ Ⓔ	22 Ⓐ Ⓑ Ⓒ Ⓓ Ⓔ	30 Ⓐ Ⓑ Ⓒ Ⓓ Ⓔ	38 Ⓐ Ⓑ Ⓒ Ⓓ Ⓔ
7 Ⓐ Ⓑ Ⓒ Ⓓ Ⓔ	15 Ⓐ Ⓑ Ⓒ Ⓓ Ⓔ	23 Ⓐ Ⓑ Ⓒ Ⓓ Ⓔ	31 Ⓐ Ⓑ Ⓒ Ⓓ Ⓔ	39 Ⓐ Ⓑ Ⓒ Ⓓ Ⓔ
8 Ⓐ Ⓑ Ⓒ Ⓓ Ⓔ	16 Ⓐ Ⓑ Ⓒ Ⓓ Ⓔ	24 Ⓐ Ⓑ Ⓒ Ⓓ Ⓔ	32 Ⓐ Ⓑ Ⓒ Ⓓ Ⓔ	40 Ⓐ Ⓑ Ⓒ Ⓓ Ⓔ

SECTION 4

1 Ⓐ Ⓑ Ⓒ Ⓓ Ⓔ	6 Ⓐ Ⓑ Ⓒ Ⓓ Ⓔ	11 Ⓐ Ⓑ Ⓒ Ⓓ Ⓔ	16 Ⓐ Ⓑ Ⓒ Ⓓ Ⓔ	21 Ⓐ Ⓑ Ⓒ Ⓓ Ⓔ
2 Ⓐ Ⓑ Ⓒ Ⓓ Ⓔ	7 Ⓐ Ⓑ Ⓒ Ⓓ Ⓔ	12 Ⓐ Ⓑ Ⓒ Ⓓ Ⓔ	17 Ⓐ Ⓑ Ⓒ Ⓓ Ⓔ	22 Ⓐ Ⓑ Ⓒ Ⓓ Ⓔ
3 Ⓐ Ⓑ Ⓒ Ⓓ Ⓔ	8 Ⓐ Ⓑ Ⓒ Ⓓ Ⓔ	13 Ⓐ Ⓑ Ⓒ Ⓓ Ⓔ	18 Ⓐ Ⓑ Ⓒ Ⓓ Ⓔ	23 Ⓐ Ⓑ Ⓒ Ⓓ Ⓔ
4 Ⓐ Ⓑ Ⓒ Ⓓ Ⓔ	9 Ⓐ Ⓑ Ⓒ Ⓓ Ⓔ	14 Ⓐ Ⓑ Ⓒ Ⓓ Ⓔ	19 Ⓐ Ⓑ Ⓒ Ⓓ Ⓔ	24 Ⓐ Ⓑ Ⓒ Ⓓ Ⓔ
5 Ⓐ Ⓑ Ⓒ Ⓓ Ⓔ	10 Ⓐ Ⓑ Ⓒ Ⓓ Ⓔ	15 Ⓐ Ⓑ Ⓒ Ⓓ Ⓔ	20 Ⓐ Ⓑ Ⓒ Ⓓ Ⓔ	25 Ⓐ Ⓑ Ⓒ Ⓓ Ⓔ

Middle Level Practice Test

Be sure each mark *completely* fills the answer space.
Start with number 1 for each new section of the test. You may find more answer spaces than you need.
If so, please leave them blank.

SECTION 1

1 Ⓐ Ⓑ Ⓒ Ⓓ Ⓔ	13 Ⓐ Ⓑ Ⓒ Ⓓ Ⓔ	25 Ⓐ Ⓑ Ⓒ Ⓓ Ⓔ	37 Ⓐ Ⓑ Ⓒ Ⓓ Ⓔ	49 Ⓐ Ⓑ Ⓒ Ⓓ Ⓔ
2 Ⓐ Ⓑ Ⓒ Ⓓ Ⓔ	14 Ⓐ Ⓑ Ⓒ Ⓓ Ⓔ	26 Ⓐ Ⓑ Ⓒ Ⓓ Ⓔ	38 Ⓐ Ⓑ Ⓒ Ⓓ Ⓔ	50 Ⓐ Ⓑ Ⓒ Ⓓ Ⓔ
3 Ⓐ Ⓑ Ⓒ Ⓓ Ⓔ	15 Ⓐ Ⓑ Ⓒ Ⓓ Ⓔ	27 Ⓐ Ⓑ Ⓒ Ⓓ Ⓔ	39 Ⓐ Ⓑ Ⓒ Ⓓ Ⓔ	51 Ⓐ Ⓑ Ⓒ Ⓓ Ⓔ
4 Ⓐ Ⓑ Ⓒ Ⓓ Ⓔ	16 Ⓐ Ⓑ Ⓒ Ⓓ Ⓔ	28 Ⓐ Ⓑ Ⓒ Ⓓ Ⓔ	40 Ⓐ Ⓑ Ⓒ Ⓓ Ⓔ	52 Ⓐ Ⓑ Ⓒ Ⓓ Ⓔ
5 Ⓐ Ⓑ Ⓒ Ⓓ Ⓔ	17 Ⓐ Ⓑ Ⓒ Ⓓ Ⓔ	29 Ⓐ Ⓑ Ⓒ Ⓓ Ⓔ	41 Ⓐ Ⓑ Ⓒ Ⓓ Ⓔ	53 Ⓐ Ⓑ Ⓒ Ⓓ Ⓔ
6 Ⓐ Ⓑ Ⓒ Ⓓ Ⓔ	18 Ⓐ Ⓑ Ⓒ Ⓓ Ⓔ	30 Ⓐ Ⓑ Ⓒ Ⓓ Ⓔ	42 Ⓐ Ⓑ Ⓒ Ⓓ Ⓔ	54 Ⓐ Ⓑ Ⓒ Ⓓ Ⓔ
7 Ⓐ Ⓑ Ⓒ Ⓓ Ⓔ	19 Ⓐ Ⓑ Ⓒ Ⓓ Ⓕ	31 Ⓐ Ⓑ Ⓒ Ⓓ Ⓔ	43 Ⓐ Ⓑ Ⓒ Ⓓ Ⓔ	55 Ⓐ Ⓑ Ⓒ Ⓓ Ⓔ
8 Ⓐ Ⓑ Ⓒ Ⓓ Ⓔ	20 Ⓐ Ⓑ Ⓒ Ⓓ Ⓔ	32 Ⓐ Ⓑ Ⓒ Ⓓ Ⓔ	44 Ⓐ Ⓑ Ⓒ Ⓓ Ⓔ	56 Ⓐ Ⓑ Ⓒ Ⓓ Ⓔ
9 Ⓐ Ⓑ Ⓒ Ⓓ Ⓔ	21 Ⓐ Ⓑ Ⓒ Ⓓ Ⓔ	33 Ⓐ Ⓑ Ⓒ Ⓓ Ⓔ	45 Ⓐ Ⓑ Ⓒ Ⓓ Ⓔ	57 Ⓐ Ⓑ Ⓒ Ⓓ Ⓔ
10 Ⓐ Ⓑ Ⓒ Ⓓ Ⓔ	22 Ⓐ Ⓑ Ⓒ Ⓓ Ⓔ	34 Ⓐ Ⓑ Ⓒ Ⓓ Ⓔ	46 Ⓐ Ⓑ Ⓒ Ⓓ Ⓔ	58 Ⓐ Ⓑ Ⓒ Ⓓ Ⓔ
11 Ⓐ Ⓑ Ⓒ Ⓓ Ⓔ	23 Ⓐ Ⓑ Ⓒ Ⓓ Ⓔ	35 Ⓐ Ⓑ Ⓒ Ⓓ Ⓔ	47 Ⓐ Ⓑ Ⓒ Ⓓ Ⓔ	59 Ⓐ Ⓑ Ⓒ Ⓓ Ⓔ
12 Ⓐ Ⓑ Ⓒ Ⓓ Ⓔ	24 Ⓐ Ⓑ Ⓒ Ⓓ Ⓔ	36 Ⓐ Ⓑ Ⓒ Ⓓ Ⓔ	48 Ⓐ Ⓑ Ⓒ Ⓓ Ⓔ	60 Ⓐ Ⓑ Ⓒ Ⓓ Ⓔ

SECTION 2

1 Ⓐ Ⓑ Ⓒ Ⓓ Ⓔ	6 Ⓐ Ⓑ Ⓒ Ⓓ Ⓔ	11 Ⓐ Ⓑ Ⓒ Ⓓ Ⓔ	16 Ⓐ Ⓑ Ⓒ Ⓓ Ⓔ	21 Ⓐ Ⓑ Ⓒ Ⓓ Ⓔ
2 Ⓐ Ⓑ Ⓒ Ⓓ Ⓔ	7 Ⓐ Ⓑ Ⓒ Ⓓ Ⓔ	12 Ⓐ Ⓑ Ⓒ Ⓓ Ⓔ	17 Ⓐ Ⓑ Ⓒ Ⓓ Ⓔ	22 Ⓐ Ⓑ Ⓒ Ⓓ Ⓔ
3 Ⓐ Ⓑ Ⓒ Ⓓ Ⓔ	8 Ⓐ Ⓑ Ⓒ Ⓓ Ⓔ	13 Ⓐ Ⓑ Ⓒ Ⓓ Ⓔ	18 Ⓐ Ⓑ Ⓒ Ⓓ Ⓔ	23 Ⓐ Ⓑ Ⓒ Ⓓ Ⓕ
4 Ⓐ Ⓑ Ⓒ Ⓓ Ⓔ	9 Ⓐ Ⓑ Ⓒ Ⓓ Ⓔ	14 Ⓐ Ⓑ Ⓒ Ⓓ Ⓔ	19 Ⓐ Ⓑ Ⓒ Ⓓ Ⓔ	24 Ⓐ Ⓑ Ⓒ Ⓓ Ⓔ
5 Ⓐ Ⓑ Ⓒ Ⓓ Ⓔ	10 Ⓐ Ⓑ Ⓒ Ⓓ Ⓔ	15 Ⓐ Ⓑ Ⓒ Ⓓ Ⓔ	20 Ⓐ Ⓑ Ⓒ Ⓓ Ⓔ	25 Ⓐ Ⓑ Ⓒ Ⓓ Ⓔ

SECTION 3

1 Ⓐ Ⓑ Ⓒ Ⓓ Ⓔ	9 Ⓐ Ⓑ Ⓒ Ⓓ Ⓔ	17 Ⓐ Ⓑ Ⓒ Ⓓ Ⓔ	25 Ⓐ Ⓑ Ⓒ Ⓓ Ⓔ	33 Ⓐ Ⓑ Ⓒ Ⓓ Ⓔ
2 Ⓐ Ⓑ Ⓒ Ⓓ Ⓕ	10 Ⓐ Ⓑ Ⓒ Ⓓ Ⓔ	18 Ⓐ Ⓑ Ⓒ Ⓓ Ⓔ	26 Ⓐ Ⓑ Ⓒ Ⓓ Ⓔ	34 Ⓐ Ⓑ Ⓒ Ⓓ Ⓔ
3 Ⓐ Ⓑ Ⓒ Ⓓ Ⓔ	11 Ⓐ Ⓑ Ⓒ Ⓓ Ⓔ	19 Ⓐ Ⓑ Ⓒ Ⓓ Ⓔ	27 Ⓐ Ⓑ Ⓒ Ⓓ Ⓔ	35 Ⓐ Ⓑ Ⓒ Ⓓ Ⓔ
4 Ⓐ Ⓑ Ⓒ Ⓓ Ⓔ	12 Ⓐ Ⓑ Ⓒ Ⓓ Ⓔ	20 Ⓐ Ⓑ Ⓒ Ⓓ Ⓔ	28 Ⓐ Ⓑ Ⓒ Ⓓ Ⓔ	36 Ⓐ Ⓑ Ⓒ Ⓓ Ⓔ
5 Ⓐ Ⓑ Ⓒ Ⓓ Ⓔ	13 Ⓐ Ⓑ Ⓒ Ⓓ Ⓔ	21 Ⓐ Ⓑ Ⓒ Ⓓ Ⓔ	29 Ⓐ Ⓑ Ⓒ Ⓓ Ⓔ	37 Ⓐ Ⓑ Ⓒ Ⓓ Ⓕ
6 Ⓐ Ⓑ Ⓒ Ⓓ Ⓔ	14 Ⓐ Ⓑ Ⓒ Ⓓ Ⓔ	22 Ⓐ Ⓑ Ⓒ Ⓓ Ⓔ	30 Ⓐ Ⓑ Ⓒ Ⓓ Ⓔ	38 Ⓐ Ⓑ Ⓒ Ⓓ Ⓔ
7 Ⓐ Ⓑ Ⓒ Ⓓ Ⓔ	15 Ⓐ Ⓑ Ⓒ Ⓓ Ⓔ	23 Ⓐ Ⓑ Ⓒ Ⓓ Ⓔ	31 Ⓐ Ⓑ Ⓒ Ⓓ Ⓔ	39 Ⓐ Ⓑ Ⓒ Ⓓ Ⓔ
8 Ⓐ Ⓑ Ⓒ Ⓓ Ⓔ	16 Ⓐ Ⓑ Ⓒ Ⓓ Ⓔ	24 Ⓐ Ⓑ Ⓒ Ⓓ Ⓔ	32 Ⓐ Ⓑ Ⓒ Ⓓ Ⓔ	40 Ⓐ Ⓑ Ⓒ Ⓓ Ⓔ

SECTION 4

1 Ⓐ Ⓑ Ⓒ Ⓓ Ⓔ	6 Ⓐ Ⓑ Ⓒ Ⓓ Ⓔ	11 Ⓐ Ⓑ Ⓒ Ⓓ Ⓔ	16 Ⓐ Ⓑ Ⓒ Ⓓ Ⓔ	21 Ⓐ Ⓑ Ⓒ Ⓓ Ⓔ
2 Ⓐ Ⓑ Ⓒ Ⓓ Ⓔ	7 Ⓐ Ⓑ Ⓒ Ⓓ Ⓔ	12 Ⓐ Ⓑ Ⓒ Ⓓ Ⓔ	17 Ⓐ Ⓑ Ⓒ Ⓓ Ⓔ	22 Ⓐ Ⓑ Ⓒ Ⓓ Ⓔ
3 Ⓐ Ⓑ Ⓒ Ⓓ Ⓔ	8 Ⓐ Ⓑ Ⓒ Ⓓ Ⓔ	13 Ⓐ Ⓑ Ⓒ Ⓓ Ⓔ	18 Ⓐ Ⓑ Ⓒ Ⓓ Ⓔ	23 Ⓐ Ⓑ Ⓒ Ⓓ Ⓔ
4 Ⓐ Ⓑ Ⓒ Ⓓ Ⓔ	9 Ⓐ Ⓑ Ⓒ Ⓓ Ⓔ	14 Ⓐ Ⓑ Ⓒ Ⓓ Ⓔ	19 Ⓐ Ⓑ Ⓒ Ⓓ Ⓔ	24 Ⓐ Ⓑ Ⓒ Ⓓ Ⓔ
5 Ⓐ Ⓑ Ⓒ Ⓓ Ⓔ	10 Ⓐ Ⓑ Ⓒ Ⓓ Ⓔ	15 Ⓐ Ⓑ Ⓒ Ⓓ Ⓔ	20 Ⓐ Ⓑ Ⓒ Ⓓ Ⓔ	25 Ⓐ Ⓑ Ⓒ Ⓓ Ⓔ

Middle Level Practice Test

Be sure each mark *completely* fills the answer space.
Start with number 1 for each new section of the test. You may find more answer spaces than you need.
If so, please leave them blank.

SECTION 1

1 Ⓐ Ⓑ Ⓒ Ⓓ Ⓔ	13 Ⓐ Ⓑ Ⓒ Ⓓ Ⓔ	25 Ⓐ Ⓑ Ⓒ Ⓓ Ⓔ	37 Ⓐ Ⓑ Ⓒ Ⓓ Ⓔ	49 Ⓐ Ⓑ Ⓒ Ⓓ Ⓔ
2 Ⓐ Ⓑ Ⓒ Ⓓ Ⓔ	14 Ⓐ Ⓑ Ⓒ Ⓓ Ⓔ	26 Ⓐ Ⓑ Ⓒ Ⓓ Ⓔ	38 Ⓐ Ⓑ Ⓒ Ⓓ Ⓔ	50 Ⓐ Ⓑ Ⓒ Ⓓ Ⓔ
3 Ⓐ Ⓑ Ⓒ Ⓓ Ⓔ	15 Ⓐ Ⓑ Ⓒ Ⓓ Ⓔ	27 Ⓐ Ⓑ Ⓒ Ⓓ Ⓔ	39 Ⓐ Ⓑ Ⓒ Ⓓ Ⓔ	51 Ⓐ Ⓑ Ⓒ Ⓓ Ⓔ
4 Ⓐ Ⓑ Ⓒ Ⓓ Ⓔ	16 Ⓐ Ⓑ Ⓒ Ⓓ Ⓔ	28 Ⓐ Ⓑ Ⓒ Ⓓ Ⓔ	40 Ⓐ Ⓑ Ⓒ Ⓓ Ⓔ	52 Ⓐ Ⓑ Ⓒ Ⓓ Ⓔ
5 Ⓐ Ⓑ Ⓒ Ⓓ Ⓔ	17 Ⓐ Ⓑ Ⓒ Ⓓ Ⓔ	29 Ⓐ Ⓑ Ⓒ Ⓓ Ⓔ	41 Ⓐ Ⓑ Ⓒ Ⓓ Ⓔ	53 Ⓐ Ⓑ Ⓒ Ⓓ Ⓔ
6 Ⓐ Ⓑ Ⓒ Ⓓ Ⓔ	18 Ⓐ Ⓑ Ⓒ Ⓓ Ⓔ	30 Ⓐ Ⓑ Ⓒ Ⓓ Ⓔ	42 Ⓐ Ⓑ Ⓒ Ⓓ Ⓔ	54 Ⓐ Ⓑ Ⓒ Ⓓ Ⓔ
7 Ⓐ Ⓑ Ⓒ Ⓓ Ⓔ	19 Ⓐ Ⓑ Ⓒ Ⓓ Ⓔ	31 Ⓐ Ⓑ Ⓒ Ⓓ Ⓔ	43 Ⓐ Ⓑ Ⓒ Ⓓ Ⓔ	55 Ⓐ Ⓑ Ⓒ Ⓓ Ⓔ
8 Ⓐ Ⓑ Ⓒ Ⓓ Ⓔ	20 Ⓐ Ⓑ Ⓒ Ⓓ Ⓔ	32 Ⓐ Ⓑ Ⓒ Ⓓ Ⓔ	44 Ⓐ Ⓑ Ⓒ Ⓓ Ⓔ	56 Ⓐ Ⓑ Ⓒ Ⓓ Ⓔ
9 Ⓐ Ⓑ Ⓒ Ⓓ Ⓔ	21 Ⓐ Ⓑ Ⓒ Ⓓ Ⓔ	33 Ⓐ Ⓑ Ⓒ Ⓓ Ⓔ	45 Ⓐ Ⓑ Ⓒ Ⓓ Ⓔ	57 Ⓐ Ⓑ Ⓒ Ⓓ Ⓔ
10 Ⓐ Ⓑ Ⓒ Ⓓ Ⓔ	22 Ⓐ Ⓑ Ⓒ Ⓓ Ⓔ	34 Ⓐ Ⓑ Ⓒ Ⓓ Ⓔ	46 Ⓐ Ⓑ Ⓒ Ⓓ Ⓔ	58 Ⓐ Ⓑ Ⓒ Ⓓ Ⓔ
11 Ⓐ Ⓑ Ⓒ Ⓓ Ⓔ	23 Ⓐ Ⓑ Ⓒ Ⓓ Ⓔ	35 Ⓐ Ⓑ Ⓒ Ⓓ Ⓔ	47 Ⓐ Ⓑ Ⓒ Ⓓ Ⓔ	59 Ⓐ Ⓑ Ⓒ Ⓓ Ⓔ
12 Ⓐ Ⓑ Ⓒ Ⓓ Ⓔ	24 Ⓐ Ⓑ Ⓒ Ⓓ Ⓔ	36 Ⓐ Ⓑ Ⓒ Ⓓ Ⓔ	48 Ⓐ Ⓑ Ⓒ Ⓓ Ⓔ	60 Ⓐ Ⓑ Ⓒ Ⓓ Ⓔ

SECTION 2

1 Ⓐ Ⓑ Ⓒ Ⓓ Ⓔ	6 Ⓐ Ⓑ Ⓒ Ⓓ Ⓔ	11 Ⓐ Ⓑ Ⓒ Ⓓ Ⓔ	16 Ⓐ Ⓑ Ⓒ Ⓓ Ⓔ	21 Ⓐ Ⓑ Ⓒ Ⓓ Ⓔ
2 Ⓐ Ⓑ Ⓒ Ⓓ Ⓔ	7 Ⓐ Ⓑ Ⓒ Ⓓ Ⓔ	12 Ⓐ Ⓑ Ⓒ Ⓓ Ⓔ	17 Ⓐ Ⓑ Ⓒ Ⓓ Ⓔ	22 Ⓐ Ⓑ Ⓒ Ⓓ Ⓔ
3 Ⓐ Ⓑ Ⓒ Ⓓ Ⓔ	8 Ⓐ Ⓑ Ⓒ Ⓓ Ⓔ	13 Ⓐ Ⓑ Ⓒ Ⓓ Ⓔ	18 Ⓐ Ⓑ Ⓒ Ⓓ Ⓔ	23 Ⓐ Ⓑ Ⓒ Ⓓ Ⓔ
4 Ⓐ Ⓑ Ⓒ Ⓓ Ⓔ	9 Ⓐ Ⓑ Ⓒ Ⓓ Ⓔ	14 Ⓐ Ⓑ Ⓒ Ⓓ Ⓔ	19 Ⓐ Ⓑ Ⓒ Ⓓ Ⓔ	24 Ⓐ Ⓑ Ⓒ Ⓓ Ⓔ
5 Ⓐ Ⓑ Ⓒ Ⓓ Ⓔ	10 Ⓐ Ⓑ Ⓒ Ⓓ Ⓔ	15 Ⓐ Ⓑ Ⓒ Ⓓ Ⓔ	20 Ⓐ Ⓑ Ⓒ Ⓓ Ⓔ	25 Ⓐ Ⓑ Ⓒ Ⓓ Ⓔ

SECTION 3

1 Ⓐ Ⓑ Ⓒ Ⓓ Ⓔ	9 Ⓐ Ⓑ Ⓒ Ⓓ Ⓔ	17 Ⓐ Ⓑ Ⓒ Ⓓ Ⓔ	25 Ⓐ Ⓑ Ⓒ Ⓓ Ⓔ	33 Ⓐ Ⓑ Ⓒ Ⓓ Ⓔ
2 Ⓐ Ⓑ Ⓒ Ⓓ Ⓔ	10 Ⓐ Ⓑ Ⓒ Ⓓ Ⓔ	18 Ⓐ Ⓑ Ⓒ Ⓓ Ⓔ	26 Ⓐ Ⓑ Ⓒ Ⓓ Ⓔ	34 Ⓐ Ⓑ Ⓒ Ⓓ Ⓔ
3 Ⓐ Ⓑ Ⓒ Ⓓ Ⓔ	11 Ⓐ Ⓑ Ⓒ Ⓓ Ⓔ	19 Ⓐ Ⓑ Ⓒ Ⓓ Ⓔ	27 Ⓐ Ⓑ Ⓒ Ⓓ Ⓔ	35 Ⓐ Ⓑ Ⓒ Ⓓ Ⓔ
4 Ⓐ Ⓑ Ⓒ Ⓓ Ⓔ	12 Ⓐ Ⓑ Ⓒ Ⓓ Ⓔ	20 Ⓐ Ⓑ Ⓒ Ⓓ Ⓔ	28 Ⓐ Ⓑ Ⓒ Ⓓ Ⓔ	36 Ⓐ Ⓑ Ⓒ Ⓓ Ⓔ
5 Ⓐ Ⓑ Ⓒ Ⓓ Ⓔ	13 Ⓐ Ⓑ Ⓒ Ⓓ Ⓔ	21 Ⓐ Ⓑ Ⓒ Ⓓ Ⓔ	29 Ⓐ Ⓑ Ⓒ Ⓓ Ⓔ	37 Ⓐ Ⓑ Ⓒ Ⓓ Ⓔ
6 Ⓐ Ⓑ Ⓒ Ⓓ Ⓔ	14 Ⓐ Ⓑ Ⓒ Ⓓ Ⓔ	22 Ⓐ Ⓑ Ⓒ Ⓓ Ⓔ	30 Ⓐ Ⓑ Ⓒ Ⓓ Ⓔ	38 Ⓐ Ⓑ Ⓒ Ⓓ Ⓔ
7 Ⓐ Ⓑ Ⓒ Ⓓ Ⓔ	15 Ⓐ Ⓑ Ⓒ Ⓓ Ⓔ	23 Ⓐ Ⓑ Ⓒ Ⓓ Ⓔ	31 Ⓐ Ⓑ Ⓒ Ⓓ Ⓔ	39 Ⓐ Ⓑ Ⓒ Ⓓ Ⓔ
8 Ⓐ Ⓑ Ⓒ Ⓓ Ⓔ	16 Ⓐ Ⓑ Ⓒ Ⓓ Ⓔ	24 Ⓐ Ⓑ Ⓒ Ⓓ Ⓔ	32 Ⓐ Ⓑ Ⓒ Ⓓ Ⓔ	40 Ⓐ Ⓑ Ⓒ Ⓓ Ⓔ

SECTION 4

1 Ⓐ Ⓑ Ⓒ Ⓓ Ⓔ	6 Ⓐ Ⓑ Ⓒ Ⓓ Ⓔ	11 Ⓐ Ⓑ Ⓒ Ⓓ Ⓔ	16 Ⓐ Ⓑ Ⓒ Ⓓ Ⓔ	21 Ⓐ Ⓑ Ⓒ Ⓓ Ⓔ
2 Ⓐ Ⓑ Ⓒ Ⓓ Ⓔ	7 Ⓐ Ⓑ Ⓒ Ⓓ Ⓔ	12 Ⓐ Ⓑ Ⓒ Ⓓ Ⓔ	17 Ⓐ Ⓑ Ⓒ Ⓓ Ⓔ	22 Ⓐ Ⓑ Ⓒ Ⓓ Ⓔ
3 Ⓐ Ⓑ Ⓒ Ⓓ Ⓔ	8 Ⓐ Ⓑ Ⓒ Ⓓ Ⓔ	13 Ⓐ Ⓑ Ⓒ Ⓓ Ⓔ	18 Ⓐ Ⓑ Ⓒ Ⓓ Ⓔ	23 Ⓐ Ⓑ Ⓒ Ⓓ Ⓔ
4 Ⓐ Ⓑ Ⓒ Ⓓ Ⓔ	9 Ⓐ Ⓑ Ⓒ Ⓓ Ⓔ	14 Ⓐ Ⓑ Ⓒ Ⓓ Ⓔ	19 Ⓐ Ⓑ Ⓒ Ⓓ Ⓔ	24 Ⓐ Ⓑ Ⓒ Ⓓ Ⓔ
5 Ⓐ Ⓑ Ⓒ Ⓓ Ⓔ	10 Ⓐ Ⓑ Ⓒ Ⓓ Ⓔ	15 Ⓐ Ⓑ Ⓒ Ⓓ Ⓔ	20 Ⓐ Ⓑ Ⓒ Ⓓ Ⓔ	25 Ⓐ Ⓑ Ⓒ Ⓓ Ⓔ

Middle Level Practice Test

Be sure each mark *completely* fills the answer space.
Start with number 1 for each new section of the test. You may find more answer spaces than you need.
If so, please leave them blank.

SECTION 1

1 Ⓐ Ⓑ Ⓒ Ⓓ Ⓔ	13 Ⓐ Ⓑ Ⓒ Ⓓ Ⓔ	25 Ⓐ Ⓑ Ⓒ Ⓓ Ⓔ	37 Ⓐ Ⓑ Ⓒ Ⓓ Ⓔ	49 Ⓐ Ⓑ Ⓒ Ⓓ Ⓔ
2 Ⓐ Ⓑ Ⓒ Ⓓ Ⓔ	14 Ⓐ Ⓑ Ⓒ Ⓓ Ⓔ	26 Ⓐ Ⓑ Ⓒ Ⓓ Ⓔ	38 Ⓐ Ⓑ Ⓒ Ⓓ Ⓔ	50 Ⓐ Ⓑ Ⓒ Ⓓ Ⓔ
3 Ⓐ Ⓑ Ⓒ Ⓓ Ⓔ	15 Ⓐ Ⓑ Ⓒ Ⓓ Ⓔ	27 Ⓐ Ⓑ Ⓒ Ⓓ Ⓔ	39 Ⓐ Ⓑ Ⓒ Ⓓ Ⓔ	51 Ⓐ Ⓑ Ⓒ Ⓓ Ⓔ
4 Ⓐ Ⓑ Ⓒ Ⓓ Ⓔ	16 Ⓐ Ⓑ Ⓒ Ⓓ Ⓔ	28 Ⓐ Ⓑ Ⓒ Ⓓ Ⓔ	40 Ⓐ Ⓑ Ⓒ Ⓓ Ⓔ	52 Ⓐ Ⓑ Ⓒ Ⓓ Ⓔ
5 Ⓐ Ⓑ Ⓒ Ⓓ Ⓔ	17 Ⓐ Ⓑ Ⓒ Ⓓ Ⓔ	29 Ⓐ Ⓑ Ⓒ Ⓓ Ⓔ	41 Ⓐ Ⓑ Ⓒ Ⓓ Ⓔ	53 Ⓐ Ⓑ Ⓒ Ⓓ Ⓔ
6 Ⓐ Ⓑ Ⓒ Ⓓ Ⓔ	18 Ⓐ Ⓑ Ⓒ Ⓓ Ⓔ	30 Ⓐ Ⓑ Ⓒ Ⓓ Ⓔ	42 Ⓐ Ⓑ Ⓒ Ⓓ Ⓔ	54 Ⓐ Ⓑ Ⓒ Ⓓ Ⓔ
7 Ⓐ Ⓑ Ⓒ Ⓓ Ⓔ	19 Ⓐ Ⓑ Ⓒ Ⓓ Ⓔ	31 Ⓐ Ⓑ Ⓒ Ⓓ Ⓔ	43 Ⓐ Ⓑ Ⓒ Ⓓ Ⓔ	55 Ⓐ Ⓑ Ⓒ Ⓓ Ⓔ
8 Ⓐ Ⓑ Ⓒ Ⓓ Ⓔ	20 Ⓐ Ⓑ Ⓒ Ⓓ Ⓔ	32 Ⓐ Ⓑ Ⓒ Ⓓ Ⓔ	44 Ⓐ Ⓑ Ⓒ Ⓓ Ⓔ	56 Ⓐ Ⓑ Ⓒ Ⓓ Ⓔ
9 Ⓐ Ⓑ Ⓒ Ⓓ Ⓔ	21 Ⓐ Ⓑ Ⓒ Ⓓ Ⓔ	33 Ⓐ Ⓑ Ⓒ Ⓓ Ⓔ	45 Ⓐ Ⓑ Ⓒ Ⓓ Ⓔ	57 Ⓐ Ⓑ Ⓒ Ⓓ Ⓔ
10 Ⓐ Ⓑ Ⓒ Ⓓ Ⓔ	22 Ⓐ Ⓑ Ⓒ Ⓓ Ⓔ	34 Ⓐ Ⓑ Ⓒ Ⓓ Ⓔ	46 Ⓐ Ⓑ Ⓒ Ⓓ Ⓔ	58 Ⓐ Ⓑ Ⓒ Ⓓ Ⓔ
11 Ⓐ Ⓑ Ⓒ Ⓓ Ⓔ	23 Ⓐ Ⓑ Ⓒ Ⓓ Ⓔ	35 Ⓐ Ⓑ Ⓒ Ⓓ Ⓔ	47 Ⓐ Ⓑ Ⓒ Ⓓ Ⓔ	59 Ⓐ Ⓑ Ⓒ Ⓓ Ⓔ
12 Ⓐ Ⓑ Ⓒ Ⓓ Ⓔ	24 Ⓐ Ⓑ Ⓒ Ⓓ Ⓔ	36 Ⓐ Ⓑ Ⓒ Ⓓ Ⓔ	48 Ⓐ Ⓑ Ⓒ Ⓓ Ⓕ	60 Ⓐ Ⓑ Ⓒ Ⓓ Ⓔ

SECTION 2

1 Ⓐ Ⓑ Ⓒ Ⓓ Ⓔ	6 Ⓐ Ⓑ Ⓒ Ⓓ Ⓔ	11 Ⓐ Ⓑ Ⓒ Ⓓ Ⓔ	16 Ⓐ Ⓑ Ⓒ Ⓓ Ⓔ	21 Ⓐ Ⓑ Ⓒ Ⓓ Ⓔ
2 Ⓐ Ⓑ Ⓒ Ⓓ Ⓔ	7 Ⓐ Ⓑ Ⓒ Ⓓ Ⓔ	12 Ⓐ Ⓑ Ⓒ Ⓓ Ⓔ	17 Ⓐ Ⓑ Ⓒ Ⓓ Ⓔ	22 Ⓐ Ⓑ Ⓒ Ⓓ Ⓔ
3 Ⓐ Ⓑ Ⓒ Ⓓ Ⓔ	8 Ⓐ Ⓑ Ⓒ Ⓓ Ⓔ	13 Ⓐ Ⓑ Ⓒ Ⓓ Ⓔ	18 Ⓐ Ⓑ Ⓒ Ⓓ Ⓔ	23 Ⓐ Ⓑ Ⓒ Ⓓ Ⓔ
4 Ⓐ Ⓑ Ⓒ Ⓓ Ⓔ	9 Ⓐ Ⓑ Ⓒ Ⓓ Ⓔ	14 Ⓐ Ⓑ Ⓒ Ⓓ Ⓔ	19 Ⓐ Ⓑ Ⓒ Ⓓ Ⓔ	24 Ⓐ Ⓑ Ⓒ Ⓓ Ⓔ
5 Ⓐ Ⓑ Ⓒ Ⓓ Ⓔ	10 Ⓐ Ⓑ Ⓒ Ⓓ Ⓔ	15 Ⓐ Ⓑ Ⓒ Ⓓ Ⓔ	20 Ⓐ Ⓑ Ⓒ Ⓓ Ⓔ	25 Ⓐ Ⓑ Ⓒ Ⓓ Ⓔ

SECTION 3

1 Ⓐ Ⓑ Ⓒ Ⓓ Ⓔ	9 Ⓐ Ⓑ Ⓒ Ⓓ Ⓔ	17 Ⓐ Ⓑ Ⓒ Ⓓ Ⓔ	25 Ⓐ Ⓑ Ⓒ Ⓓ Ⓔ	33 Ⓐ Ⓑ Ⓒ Ⓓ Ⓕ
2 Ⓐ Ⓑ Ⓒ Ⓓ Ⓔ	10 Ⓐ Ⓑ Ⓒ Ⓓ Ⓔ	18 Ⓐ Ⓑ Ⓒ Ⓓ Ⓔ	26 Ⓐ Ⓑ Ⓒ Ⓓ Ⓔ	34 Ⓐ Ⓑ Ⓒ Ⓓ Ⓔ
3 Ⓐ Ⓑ Ⓒ Ⓓ Ⓔ	11 Ⓐ Ⓑ Ⓒ Ⓓ Ⓔ	19 Ⓐ Ⓑ Ⓒ Ⓓ Ⓔ	27 Ⓐ Ⓑ Ⓒ Ⓓ Ⓔ	35 Ⓐ Ⓑ Ⓒ Ⓓ Ⓔ
4 Ⓐ Ⓑ Ⓒ Ⓓ Ⓔ	12 Ⓐ Ⓑ Ⓒ Ⓓ Ⓔ	20 Ⓐ Ⓑ Ⓒ Ⓓ Ⓔ	28 Ⓐ Ⓑ Ⓒ Ⓓ Ⓔ	36 Ⓐ Ⓑ Ⓒ Ⓓ Ⓔ
5 Ⓐ Ⓑ Ⓒ Ⓓ Ⓔ	13 Ⓐ Ⓑ Ⓒ Ⓓ Ⓔ	21 Ⓐ Ⓑ Ⓒ Ⓓ Ⓔ	29 Ⓐ Ⓑ Ⓒ Ⓓ Ⓔ	37 Ⓐ Ⓑ Ⓒ Ⓓ Ⓔ
6 Ⓐ Ⓑ Ⓒ Ⓓ Ⓔ	14 Ⓐ Ⓑ Ⓒ Ⓓ Ⓔ	22 Ⓐ Ⓑ Ⓒ Ⓓ Ⓔ	30 Ⓐ Ⓑ Ⓒ Ⓓ Ⓔ	38 Ⓐ Ⓑ Ⓒ Ⓓ Ⓔ
7 Ⓐ Ⓑ Ⓒ Ⓓ Ⓔ	15 Ⓐ Ⓑ Ⓒ Ⓓ Ⓔ	23 Ⓐ Ⓑ Ⓒ Ⓓ Ⓔ	31 Ⓐ Ⓑ Ⓒ Ⓓ Ⓔ	39 Ⓐ Ⓑ Ⓒ Ⓓ Ⓔ
8 Ⓐ Ⓑ Ⓒ Ⓓ Ⓔ	16 Ⓐ Ⓑ Ⓒ Ⓓ Ⓔ	24 Ⓐ Ⓑ Ⓒ Ⓓ Ⓔ	32 Ⓐ Ⓑ Ⓒ Ⓓ Ⓔ	40 Ⓐ Ⓑ Ⓒ Ⓓ Ⓔ

SECTION 4

1 Ⓐ Ⓑ Ⓒ Ⓓ Ⓔ	6 Ⓐ Ⓑ Ⓒ Ⓓ Ⓔ	11 Ⓐ Ⓑ Ⓒ Ⓓ Ⓔ	16 Ⓐ Ⓑ Ⓒ Ⓓ Ⓔ	21 Ⓐ Ⓑ Ⓒ Ⓓ Ⓔ
2 Ⓐ Ⓑ Ⓒ Ⓓ Ⓔ	7 Ⓐ Ⓑ Ⓒ Ⓓ Ⓔ	12 Ⓐ Ⓑ Ⓒ Ⓓ Ⓔ	17 Ⓐ Ⓑ Ⓒ Ⓓ Ⓔ	22 Ⓐ Ⓑ Ⓒ Ⓓ Ⓔ
3 Ⓐ Ⓑ Ⓒ Ⓓ Ⓔ	8 Ⓐ Ⓑ Ⓒ Ⓓ Ⓔ	13 Ⓐ Ⓑ Ⓒ Ⓓ Ⓔ	18 Ⓐ Ⓑ Ⓒ Ⓓ Ⓔ	23 Ⓐ Ⓑ Ⓒ Ⓓ Ⓔ
4 Ⓐ Ⓑ Ⓒ Ⓓ Ⓔ	9 Ⓐ Ⓑ Ⓒ Ⓓ Ⓔ	14 Ⓐ Ⓑ Ⓒ Ⓓ Ⓔ	19 Ⓐ Ⓑ Ⓒ Ⓓ Ⓔ	24 Ⓐ Ⓑ Ⓒ Ⓓ Ⓔ
5 Ⓐ Ⓑ Ⓒ Ⓓ Ⓔ	10 Ⓐ Ⓑ Ⓒ Ⓓ Ⓔ	15 Ⓐ Ⓑ Ⓒ Ⓓ Ⓔ	20 Ⓐ Ⓑ Ⓒ Ⓓ Ⓔ	25 Ⓐ Ⓑ Ⓒ Ⓓ Ⓔ

Middle Level Practice Test

Be sure each mark *completely* fills the answer space.
Start with number 1 for each new section of the test. You may find more answer spaces than you need.
If so, please leave them blank.

SECTION 1

1 Ⓐ Ⓑ Ⓒ Ⓓ Ⓔ	13 Ⓐ Ⓑ Ⓒ Ⓓ Ⓔ	25 Ⓐ Ⓑ Ⓒ Ⓓ Ⓔ	37 Ⓐ Ⓑ Ⓒ Ⓓ Ⓔ	49 Ⓐ Ⓑ Ⓒ Ⓓ Ⓔ
2 Ⓐ Ⓑ Ⓒ Ⓓ Ⓔ	14 Ⓐ Ⓑ Ⓒ Ⓓ Ⓔ	26 Ⓐ Ⓑ Ⓒ Ⓓ Ⓔ	38 Ⓐ Ⓑ Ⓒ Ⓓ Ⓔ	50 Ⓐ Ⓑ Ⓒ Ⓓ Ⓔ
3 Ⓐ Ⓑ Ⓒ Ⓓ Ⓔ	15 Ⓐ Ⓑ Ⓒ Ⓓ Ⓔ	27 Ⓐ Ⓑ Ⓒ Ⓓ Ⓔ	39 Ⓐ Ⓑ Ⓒ Ⓓ Ⓔ	51 Ⓐ Ⓑ Ⓒ Ⓓ Ⓔ
4 Ⓐ Ⓑ Ⓒ Ⓓ Ⓔ	16 Ⓐ Ⓑ Ⓒ Ⓓ Ⓔ	28 Ⓐ Ⓑ Ⓒ Ⓓ Ⓔ	40 Ⓐ Ⓑ Ⓒ Ⓓ Ⓔ	52 Ⓐ Ⓑ Ⓒ Ⓓ Ⓔ
5 Ⓐ Ⓑ Ⓒ Ⓓ Ⓔ	17 Ⓐ Ⓑ Ⓒ Ⓓ Ⓔ	29 Ⓐ Ⓑ Ⓒ Ⓓ Ⓔ	41 Ⓐ Ⓑ Ⓒ Ⓓ Ⓔ	53 Ⓐ Ⓑ Ⓒ Ⓓ Ⓔ
6 Ⓐ Ⓑ Ⓒ Ⓓ Ⓔ	18 Ⓐ Ⓑ Ⓒ Ⓓ Ⓔ	30 Ⓐ Ⓑ Ⓒ Ⓓ Ⓔ	42 Ⓐ Ⓑ Ⓒ Ⓓ Ⓔ	54 Ⓐ Ⓑ Ⓒ Ⓓ Ⓔ
7 Ⓐ Ⓑ Ⓒ Ⓓ Ⓔ	19 Ⓐ Ⓑ Ⓒ Ⓓ Ⓔ	31 Ⓐ Ⓑ Ⓒ Ⓓ Ⓔ	43 Ⓐ Ⓑ Ⓒ Ⓓ Ⓔ	55 Ⓐ Ⓑ Ⓒ Ⓓ Ⓔ
8 Ⓐ Ⓑ Ⓒ Ⓓ Ⓔ	20 Ⓐ Ⓑ Ⓒ Ⓓ Ⓔ	32 Ⓐ Ⓑ Ⓒ Ⓓ Ⓔ	44 Ⓐ Ⓑ Ⓒ Ⓓ Ⓔ	56 Ⓐ Ⓑ Ⓒ Ⓓ Ⓔ
9 Ⓐ Ⓑ Ⓒ Ⓓ Ⓔ	21 Ⓐ Ⓑ Ⓒ Ⓓ Ⓔ	33 Ⓐ Ⓑ Ⓒ Ⓓ Ⓔ	45 Ⓐ Ⓑ Ⓒ Ⓓ Ⓔ	57 Ⓐ Ⓑ Ⓒ Ⓓ Ⓔ
10 Ⓐ Ⓑ Ⓒ Ⓓ Ⓔ	22 Ⓐ Ⓑ Ⓒ Ⓓ Ⓔ	34 Ⓐ Ⓑ Ⓒ Ⓓ Ⓔ	46 Ⓐ Ⓑ Ⓒ Ⓓ Ⓔ	58 Ⓐ Ⓑ Ⓒ Ⓓ Ⓔ
11 Ⓐ Ⓑ Ⓒ Ⓓ Ⓔ	23 Ⓐ Ⓑ Ⓒ Ⓓ Ⓔ	35 Ⓐ Ⓑ Ⓒ Ⓓ Ⓔ	47 Ⓐ Ⓑ Ⓒ Ⓓ Ⓔ	59 Ⓐ Ⓑ Ⓒ Ⓓ Ⓔ
12 Ⓐ Ⓑ Ⓒ Ⓓ Ⓔ	24 Ⓐ Ⓑ Ⓒ Ⓓ Ⓔ	36 Ⓐ Ⓑ Ⓒ Ⓓ Ⓔ	48 Ⓐ Ⓑ Ⓒ Ⓓ Ⓔ	60 Ⓐ Ⓑ Ⓒ Ⓓ Ⓔ

SECTION 2

1 Ⓐ Ⓑ Ⓒ Ⓓ Ⓔ	6 Ⓐ Ⓑ Ⓒ Ⓓ Ⓔ	11 Ⓐ Ⓑ Ⓒ Ⓓ Ⓔ	16 Ⓐ Ⓑ Ⓒ Ⓓ Ⓔ	21 Ⓐ Ⓑ Ⓒ Ⓓ Ⓔ
2 Ⓐ Ⓑ Ⓒ Ⓓ Ⓔ	7 Ⓐ Ⓑ Ⓒ Ⓓ Ⓔ	12 Ⓐ Ⓑ Ⓒ Ⓓ Ⓔ	17 Ⓐ Ⓑ Ⓒ Ⓓ Ⓔ	22 Ⓐ Ⓑ Ⓒ Ⓓ Ⓔ
3 Ⓐ Ⓑ Ⓒ Ⓓ Ⓔ	8 Ⓐ Ⓑ Ⓒ Ⓓ Ⓔ	13 Ⓐ Ⓑ Ⓒ Ⓓ Ⓔ	18 Ⓐ Ⓑ Ⓒ Ⓓ Ⓔ	23 Ⓐ Ⓑ Ⓒ Ⓓ Ⓔ
4 Ⓐ Ⓑ Ⓒ Ⓓ Ⓔ	9 Ⓐ Ⓑ Ⓒ Ⓓ Ⓔ	14 Ⓐ Ⓑ Ⓒ Ⓓ Ⓔ	19 Ⓐ Ⓑ Ⓒ Ⓓ Ⓔ	24 Ⓐ Ⓑ Ⓒ Ⓓ Ⓔ
5 Ⓐ Ⓑ Ⓒ Ⓓ Ⓔ	10 Ⓐ Ⓑ Ⓒ Ⓓ Ⓔ	15 Ⓐ Ⓑ Ⓒ Ⓓ Ⓔ	20 Ⓐ Ⓑ Ⓒ Ⓓ Ⓔ	25 Ⓐ Ⓑ Ⓒ Ⓓ Ⓔ

SECTION 3

1 Ⓐ Ⓑ Ⓒ Ⓓ Ⓔ	9 Ⓐ Ⓑ Ⓒ Ⓓ Ⓔ	17 Ⓐ Ⓑ Ⓒ Ⓓ Ⓔ	25 Ⓐ Ⓑ Ⓒ Ⓓ Ⓔ	33 Ⓐ Ⓑ Ⓒ Ⓓ Ⓔ
2 Ⓐ Ⓑ Ⓒ Ⓓ Ⓔ	10 Ⓐ Ⓑ Ⓒ Ⓓ Ⓔ	18 Ⓐ Ⓑ Ⓒ Ⓓ Ⓔ	26 Ⓐ Ⓑ Ⓒ Ⓓ Ⓔ	34 Ⓐ Ⓑ Ⓒ Ⓓ Ⓔ
3 Ⓐ Ⓑ Ⓒ Ⓓ Ⓔ	11 Ⓐ Ⓑ Ⓒ Ⓓ Ⓔ	19 Ⓐ Ⓑ Ⓒ Ⓓ Ⓔ	27 Ⓐ Ⓑ Ⓒ Ⓓ Ⓔ	35 Ⓐ Ⓑ Ⓒ Ⓓ Ⓔ
4 Ⓐ Ⓑ Ⓒ Ⓓ Ⓔ	12 Ⓐ Ⓑ Ⓒ Ⓓ Ⓔ	20 Ⓐ Ⓑ Ⓒ Ⓓ Ⓔ	28 Ⓐ Ⓑ Ⓒ Ⓓ Ⓔ	36 Ⓐ Ⓑ Ⓒ Ⓓ Ⓔ
5 Ⓐ Ⓑ Ⓒ Ⓓ Ⓔ	13 Ⓐ Ⓑ Ⓒ Ⓓ Ⓔ	21 Ⓐ Ⓑ Ⓒ Ⓓ Ⓔ	29 Ⓐ Ⓑ Ⓒ Ⓓ Ⓔ	37 Ⓐ Ⓑ Ⓒ Ⓓ Ⓔ
6 Ⓐ Ⓑ Ⓒ Ⓓ Ⓔ	14 Ⓐ Ⓑ Ⓒ Ⓓ Ⓔ	22 Ⓐ Ⓑ Ⓒ Ⓓ Ⓔ	30 Ⓐ Ⓑ Ⓒ Ⓓ Ⓔ	38 Ⓐ Ⓑ Ⓒ Ⓓ Ⓔ
7 Ⓐ Ⓑ Ⓒ Ⓓ Ⓔ	15 Ⓐ Ⓑ Ⓒ Ⓓ Ⓔ	23 Ⓐ Ⓑ Ⓒ Ⓓ Ⓔ	31 Ⓐ Ⓑ Ⓒ Ⓓ Ⓔ	39 Ⓐ Ⓑ Ⓒ Ⓓ Ⓔ
8 Ⓐ Ⓑ Ⓒ Ⓓ Ⓔ	16 Ⓐ Ⓑ Ⓒ Ⓓ Ⓔ	24 Ⓐ Ⓑ Ⓒ Ⓓ Ⓔ	32 Ⓐ Ⓑ Ⓒ Ⓓ Ⓔ	40 Ⓐ Ⓑ Ⓒ Ⓓ Ⓔ

SECTION 4

1 Ⓐ Ⓑ Ⓒ Ⓓ Ⓔ	6 Ⓐ Ⓑ Ⓒ Ⓓ Ⓔ	11 Ⓐ Ⓑ Ⓒ Ⓓ Ⓔ	16 Ⓐ Ⓑ Ⓒ Ⓓ Ⓔ	21 Ⓐ Ⓑ Ⓒ Ⓓ Ⓔ
2 Ⓐ Ⓑ Ⓒ Ⓓ Ⓔ	7 Ⓐ Ⓑ Ⓒ Ⓓ Ⓔ	12 Ⓐ Ⓑ Ⓒ Ⓓ Ⓔ	17 Ⓐ Ⓑ Ⓒ Ⓓ Ⓔ	22 Ⓐ Ⓑ Ⓒ Ⓓ Ⓔ
3 Ⓐ Ⓑ Ⓒ Ⓓ Ⓔ	8 Ⓐ Ⓑ Ⓒ Ⓓ Ⓔ	13 Ⓐ Ⓑ Ⓒ Ⓓ Ⓔ	18 Ⓐ Ⓑ Ⓒ Ⓓ Ⓔ	23 Ⓐ Ⓑ Ⓒ Ⓓ Ⓔ
4 Ⓐ Ⓑ Ⓒ Ⓓ Ⓔ	9 Ⓐ Ⓑ Ⓒ Ⓓ Ⓔ	14 Ⓐ Ⓑ Ⓒ Ⓓ Ⓔ	19 Ⓐ Ⓑ Ⓒ Ⓓ Ⓔ	24 Ⓐ Ⓑ Ⓒ Ⓓ Ⓔ
5 Ⓐ Ⓑ Ⓒ Ⓓ Ⓔ	10 Ⓐ Ⓑ Ⓒ Ⓓ Ⓔ	15 Ⓐ Ⓑ Ⓒ Ⓓ Ⓔ	20 Ⓐ Ⓑ Ⓒ Ⓓ Ⓔ	25 Ⓐ Ⓑ Ⓒ Ⓓ Ⓔ

Middle Level Practice Test

Be sure each mark *completely* fills the answer space.
Start with number 1 for each new section of the test. You may find more answer spaces than you need.
If so, please leave them blank.

SECTION 1

1 Ⓐ Ⓑ Ⓒ Ⓓ Ⓔ	13 Ⓐ Ⓑ Ⓒ Ⓓ Ⓔ	25 Ⓐ Ⓑ Ⓒ Ⓓ Ⓔ	37 Ⓐ Ⓑ Ⓒ Ⓓ Ⓔ	49 Ⓐ Ⓑ Ⓒ Ⓓ Ⓔ
2 Ⓐ Ⓑ Ⓒ Ⓓ Ⓔ	14 Ⓐ Ⓑ Ⓒ Ⓓ Ⓔ	26 Ⓐ Ⓑ Ⓒ Ⓓ Ⓔ	38 Ⓐ Ⓑ Ⓒ Ⓓ Ⓔ	50 Ⓐ Ⓑ Ⓒ Ⓓ Ⓔ
3 Ⓐ Ⓑ Ⓒ Ⓓ Ⓔ	15 Ⓐ Ⓑ Ⓒ Ⓓ Ⓔ	27 Ⓐ Ⓑ Ⓒ Ⓓ Ⓔ	39 Ⓐ Ⓑ Ⓒ Ⓓ Ⓔ	51 Ⓐ Ⓑ Ⓒ Ⓓ Ⓔ
4 Ⓐ Ⓑ Ⓒ Ⓓ Ⓔ	16 Ⓐ Ⓑ Ⓒ Ⓓ Ⓔ	28 Ⓐ Ⓑ Ⓒ Ⓓ Ⓔ	40 Ⓐ Ⓑ Ⓒ Ⓓ Ⓔ	52 Ⓐ Ⓑ Ⓒ Ⓓ Ⓔ
5 Ⓐ Ⓑ Ⓒ Ⓓ Ⓔ	17 Ⓐ Ⓑ Ⓒ Ⓓ Ⓔ	29 Ⓐ Ⓑ Ⓒ Ⓓ Ⓔ	41 Ⓐ Ⓑ Ⓒ Ⓓ Ⓔ	53 Ⓐ Ⓑ Ⓒ Ⓓ Ⓔ
6 Ⓐ Ⓑ Ⓒ Ⓓ Ⓔ	18 Ⓐ Ⓑ Ⓒ Ⓓ Ⓔ	30 Ⓐ Ⓑ Ⓒ Ⓓ Ⓔ	42 Ⓐ Ⓑ Ⓒ Ⓓ Ⓔ	54 Ⓐ Ⓑ Ⓒ Ⓓ Ⓔ
7 Ⓐ Ⓑ Ⓒ Ⓓ Ⓔ	19 Ⓐ Ⓑ Ⓒ Ⓓ Ⓔ	31 Ⓐ Ⓑ Ⓒ Ⓓ Ⓔ	43 Ⓐ Ⓑ Ⓒ Ⓓ Ⓔ	55 Ⓐ Ⓑ Ⓒ Ⓓ Ⓔ
8 Ⓐ Ⓑ Ⓒ Ⓓ Ⓔ	20 Ⓐ Ⓑ Ⓒ Ⓓ Ⓔ	32 Ⓐ Ⓑ Ⓒ Ⓓ Ⓔ	44 Ⓐ Ⓑ Ⓒ Ⓓ Ⓔ	56 Ⓐ Ⓑ Ⓒ Ⓓ Ⓔ
9 Ⓐ Ⓑ Ⓒ Ⓓ Ⓔ	21 Ⓐ Ⓑ Ⓒ Ⓓ Ⓔ	33 Ⓐ Ⓑ Ⓒ Ⓓ Ⓔ	45 Ⓐ Ⓑ Ⓒ Ⓓ Ⓔ	57 Ⓐ Ⓑ Ⓒ Ⓓ Ⓔ
10 Ⓐ Ⓑ Ⓒ Ⓓ Ⓔ	22 Ⓐ Ⓑ Ⓒ Ⓓ Ⓔ	34 Ⓐ Ⓑ Ⓒ Ⓓ Ⓔ	46 Ⓐ Ⓑ Ⓒ Ⓓ Ⓔ	58 Ⓐ Ⓑ Ⓒ Ⓓ Ⓔ
11 Ⓐ Ⓑ Ⓒ Ⓓ Ⓔ	23 Ⓐ Ⓑ Ⓒ Ⓓ Ⓔ	35 Ⓐ Ⓑ Ⓒ Ⓓ Ⓔ	47 Ⓐ Ⓑ Ⓒ Ⓓ Ⓔ	59 Ⓐ Ⓑ Ⓒ Ⓓ Ⓔ
12 Ⓐ Ⓑ Ⓒ Ⓓ Ⓔ	24 Ⓐ Ⓑ Ⓒ Ⓓ Ⓔ	36 Ⓐ Ⓑ Ⓒ Ⓓ Ⓔ	48 Ⓐ Ⓑ Ⓒ Ⓓ Ⓔ	60 Ⓐ Ⓑ Ⓒ Ⓓ Ⓔ

SECTION 2

1 Ⓐ Ⓑ Ⓒ Ⓓ Ⓔ	6 Ⓐ Ⓑ Ⓒ Ⓓ Ⓔ	11 Ⓐ Ⓑ Ⓒ Ⓓ Ⓔ	16 Ⓐ Ⓑ Ⓒ Ⓓ Ⓔ	21 Ⓐ Ⓑ Ⓒ Ⓓ Ⓔ
2 Ⓐ Ⓑ Ⓒ Ⓓ Ⓔ	7 Ⓐ Ⓑ Ⓒ Ⓓ Ⓔ	12 Ⓐ Ⓑ Ⓒ Ⓓ Ⓔ	17 Ⓐ Ⓑ Ⓒ Ⓓ Ⓔ	22 Ⓐ Ⓑ Ⓒ Ⓓ Ⓔ
3 Ⓐ Ⓑ Ⓒ Ⓓ Ⓔ	8 Ⓐ Ⓑ Ⓒ Ⓓ Ⓔ	13 Ⓐ Ⓑ Ⓒ Ⓓ Ⓔ	18 Ⓐ Ⓑ Ⓒ Ⓓ Ⓔ	23 Ⓐ Ⓑ Ⓒ Ⓓ Ⓔ
4 Ⓐ Ⓑ Ⓒ Ⓓ Ⓔ	9 Ⓐ Ⓑ Ⓒ Ⓓ Ⓔ	14 Ⓐ Ⓑ Ⓒ Ⓓ Ⓔ	19 Ⓐ Ⓑ Ⓒ Ⓓ Ⓔ	24 Ⓐ Ⓑ Ⓒ Ⓓ Ⓔ
5 Ⓐ Ⓑ Ⓒ Ⓓ Ⓔ	10 Ⓐ Ⓑ Ⓒ Ⓓ Ⓔ	15 Ⓐ Ⓑ Ⓒ Ⓓ Ⓔ	20 Ⓐ Ⓑ Ⓒ Ⓓ Ⓔ	25 Ⓐ Ⓑ Ⓒ Ⓓ Ⓔ

SECTION 3

1 Ⓐ Ⓑ Ⓒ Ⓓ Ⓔ	9 Ⓐ Ⓑ Ⓒ Ⓓ Ⓔ	17 Ⓐ Ⓑ Ⓒ Ⓓ Ⓔ	25 Ⓐ Ⓑ Ⓒ Ⓓ Ⓔ	33 Ⓐ Ⓑ Ⓒ Ⓓ Ⓔ
2 Ⓐ Ⓑ Ⓒ Ⓓ Ⓔ	10 Ⓐ Ⓑ Ⓒ Ⓓ Ⓔ	18 Ⓐ Ⓑ Ⓒ Ⓓ Ⓔ	26 Ⓐ Ⓑ Ⓒ Ⓓ Ⓔ	34 Ⓐ Ⓑ Ⓒ Ⓓ Ⓔ
3 Ⓐ Ⓑ Ⓒ Ⓓ Ⓔ	11 Ⓐ Ⓑ Ⓒ Ⓓ Ⓔ	19 Ⓐ Ⓑ Ⓒ Ⓓ Ⓔ	27 Ⓐ Ⓑ Ⓒ Ⓓ Ⓔ	35 Ⓐ Ⓑ Ⓒ Ⓓ Ⓔ
4 Ⓐ Ⓑ Ⓒ Ⓓ Ⓔ	12 Ⓐ Ⓑ Ⓒ Ⓓ Ⓔ	20 Ⓐ Ⓑ Ⓒ Ⓓ Ⓔ	28 Ⓐ Ⓑ Ⓒ Ⓓ Ⓔ	36 Ⓐ Ⓑ Ⓒ Ⓓ Ⓔ
5 Ⓐ Ⓑ Ⓒ Ⓓ Ⓔ	13 Ⓐ Ⓑ Ⓒ Ⓓ Ⓔ	21 Ⓐ Ⓑ Ⓒ Ⓓ Ⓔ	29 Ⓐ Ⓑ Ⓒ Ⓓ Ⓔ	37 Ⓐ Ⓑ Ⓒ Ⓓ Ⓔ
6 Ⓐ Ⓑ Ⓒ Ⓓ Ⓔ	14 Ⓐ Ⓑ Ⓒ Ⓓ Ⓔ	22 Ⓐ Ⓑ Ⓒ Ⓓ Ⓔ	30 Ⓐ Ⓑ Ⓒ Ⓓ Ⓔ	38 Ⓐ Ⓑ Ⓒ Ⓓ Ⓔ
7 Ⓐ Ⓑ Ⓒ Ⓓ Ⓔ	15 Ⓐ Ⓑ Ⓒ Ⓓ Ⓔ	23 Ⓐ Ⓑ Ⓒ Ⓓ Ⓔ	31 Ⓐ Ⓑ Ⓒ Ⓓ Ⓔ	39 Ⓐ Ⓑ Ⓒ Ⓓ Ⓔ
8 Ⓐ Ⓑ Ⓒ Ⓓ Ⓔ	16 Ⓐ Ⓑ Ⓒ Ⓓ Ⓔ	24 Ⓐ Ⓑ Ⓒ Ⓓ Ⓔ	32 Ⓐ Ⓑ Ⓒ Ⓓ Ⓔ	40 Ⓐ Ⓑ Ⓒ Ⓓ Ⓔ

SECTION 4

1 Ⓐ Ⓑ Ⓒ Ⓓ Ⓔ	6 Ⓐ Ⓑ Ⓒ Ⓓ Ⓔ	11 Ⓐ Ⓑ Ⓒ Ⓓ Ⓔ	16 Ⓐ Ⓑ Ⓒ Ⓓ Ⓔ	21 Ⓐ Ⓑ Ⓒ Ⓓ Ⓔ
2 Ⓐ Ⓑ Ⓒ Ⓓ Ⓔ	7 Ⓐ Ⓑ Ⓒ Ⓓ Ⓔ	12 Ⓐ Ⓑ Ⓒ Ⓓ Ⓔ	17 Ⓐ Ⓑ Ⓒ Ⓓ Ⓔ	22 Ⓐ Ⓑ Ⓒ Ⓓ Ⓔ
3 Ⓐ Ⓑ Ⓒ Ⓓ Ⓔ	8 Ⓐ Ⓑ Ⓒ Ⓓ Ⓔ	13 Ⓐ Ⓑ Ⓒ Ⓓ Ⓔ	18 Ⓐ Ⓑ Ⓒ Ⓓ Ⓔ	23 Ⓐ Ⓑ Ⓒ Ⓓ Ⓔ
4 Ⓐ Ⓑ Ⓒ Ⓓ Ⓔ	9 Ⓐ Ⓑ Ⓒ Ⓓ Ⓔ	14 Ⓐ Ⓑ Ⓒ Ⓓ Ⓔ	19 Ⓐ Ⓑ Ⓒ Ⓓ Ⓔ	24 Ⓐ Ⓑ Ⓒ Ⓓ Ⓔ
5 Ⓐ Ⓑ Ⓒ Ⓓ Ⓔ	10 Ⓐ Ⓑ Ⓒ Ⓓ Ⓔ	15 Ⓐ Ⓑ Ⓒ Ⓓ Ⓔ	20 Ⓐ Ⓑ Ⓒ Ⓓ Ⓔ	25 Ⓐ Ⓑ Ⓒ Ⓓ Ⓔ

17

Answer Key to ISEE Practice Tests

ISEE UL VERBAL 1

1. C
2. A
3. A
4. D
5. C
6. C
7. B
8. D
9. C
10. A
11. C
12. B
13. B
14. C
15. B
16. A
17. A
18. D
19. D
20. D
21. B
22. B
23. D
24. A
25. D
26. C
27. B
28. A
29. C
30. B
31. C
32. B
33. B
34. B
35. A
36. C
37. B
38. B
39. D
40. A

ISEE UL MATH 2

1. A
2. C
3. D
4. D
5. B
6. D
7. A
8. C
9. B
10. D
11. C
12. D
13. A
14. B
15. A
16. A
17. D
18. B
19. D
20. C
21. C
22. A
23. A
24. D
25. A
26. C
27. D
28. A
29. C
30. C
31. B
32. B
33. B
34. C
35. B
36. A
37. A
38. D
39. C
40. C

ISEE UL READING 3

1. C
2. D
3. B
4. D
5. C
6. A
7. D
8. A
9. B
10. C
11. A
12. D
13. B
14. A
15. C
16. D
17. B
18. B
19. C
20. C
21. C
22. D
23. C
24. B
25. C
26. C
27. C
28. A
29. D
30. D
31. B
32. B
33. A
34. B
35. C
36. A
37. D
38. C
39. B
40. D

ISEE UL MATH 4

1. A
2. D
3. C
4. D
5. C
6. C
7. A
8. B
9. A
10. C
11. B
12. B
13. A
14. D
15. B
16. C
17. D
18. B
19. D
20. D
21. A
22. C
23. A
24. B
25. D
26. B
27. A
28. B
29. D
30. D
31. B
32. B
33. A
34. C
35. B
36. D
37. C
38. C
39. B
40. D
41. B
42. D
43. B
44. C
45. A

46. C
47. D
48. D
49. A
50. A

ISEE ML VERBAL 1

1. B
2. B
3. C
4. D
5. D
6. D
7. D
8. C
9. A
10. B
11. C
12. C
13. C
14. B
15. D
16. A
17. B
18. D
19. C
20. A
21. A
22. B
23. B
24. C
25. D
26. A
27. D
28. C
29. C
30. C
31. D
32. A
33. B
34. B
35. B
36. A
37. A
38. B
39. C
40. D

ISEE ML MATH 2

1. C
2. B
3. D
4. B
5. B
6. A
7. C
8. B
9. B
10. A
11. C
12. C
13. B
14. C
15. B
16. D
17. D
18. C
19. D
20. D
21. A
22. C
23. C
24. A
25. D
26. C
27. B
28. C
29. B
30. A
31. A
32. C
33. B
34. D
35. A
36. A
37. B
38. A
39. C
40. B

ISEE ML READING 3

1. D
2. B
3. D
4. B
5. A
6. A
7. C
8. B
9. C
10. C
11. A
12. B
13. D
14. C
15. C
16. A
17. B
18. A
19. B
20. C
21. B
22. A
23. A
24. D
25. C
26. C
27. A
28. C
29. B
30. D
31. B
32. C
33. C
34. D
35. A
36. B
37. D
38. B
39. A
40. A

ISEE ML MATH 4

1. B
2. D
3. A
4. D
5. C
6. A
7. D
8. C
9. C
10. B
11. D
12. C
13. A
14. B
15. B
16. C
17. C
18. D
19. A
20. C
21. C
22. B
23. B
24. D
25. C
26. D
27. B
28. A
29. C
30. B
31. D
32. B
33. A
34. D
35. C
36. C
37. D
38. D
39. B
40. C
41. A
42. A
43. D
44. A
45. A

46. C
47. B
48. D
49. A
50. D

18

Scoring Your Practice
ISEE

CHECK YOUR ANSWERS

Use the answer key to determine how many questions you answered correctly and how many you answered incorrectly. You should not have left any answers blank, even if you didn't get to work through the problem!

COUNT THE NUMBER OF QUESTIONS YOU ANSWERED CORRECTLY

There are no deductions for incorrect answers, so simply count up the number of questions you got right. Write those totals here:

Verbal _____

Quantitative _____ (total for both sections)

Reading _____

ARE THESE MY RAW OR SCALED SCORES?

Unfortunately, no. Unlike the Board that administers the SSAT, the organization that administers the ISEE (ERB) has not released scoring information. We do know that incorrect answers are not penalized, and that more difficult questions are worth more points. However, the little information we have been able to obtain from ERB does not allow us to give you an accurate raw or scaled score.

Further, we cannot provide the other types of scales you will find on an ISEE score report, either—the percentiles and stanine score. ISEE percentiles are compiled by comparing students in the same grade who have taken the test in the past 3 years, but no further information is available at the time of this printing.

We encourage you to contact ERB for more information on their scoring procedures, and to request any practice materials they can make available.

TO APPROXIMATE HOW YOU'VE DONE

Stanine scores are an ISEE score from 1 to 9, on a bell curve. That means that most students score a 4, 5, or 6. To give you some idea of how you've done, we've scaled the test in blocks of stanine scores, which are different for each grade. Be sure that you've done the correct level test (Middle Level for grades 5, 6, and 7, and Upper Level for grades 8, 9, 10, and 11). Skip down to your grade now. If you got significantly fewer questions right than are listed, you would probably receive a stanine score that is below average (1, 2, or 3). If you got significantly more questions right than are listed, you would probably receive a stanine score that is above average (7, 8, or 9).

Grade 5

Section Number of Questions Right for a Stanine of 4,5,6
Verbal   15
Quantitative   40
Reading   20

Grade 6

Section Number of Questions Right for a Stanine of 4,5,6
Verbal   19
Quantitative   45
Reading   25

Grade 7

Section Number of Questions Right for a Stanine of 4,5,6
Verbal   23
Quantitative   50
Reading   30

Grade 8

Section Number of Questions Right for a Stanine of 4,5,6
Verbal   19
Quantitative   40
Reading   25

Grade 9

Section Number of Questions Right for a Stanine of 4,5,6
Verbal   23
Quantitative   45
Reading   27

Grade 10

Section Number of Questions Right for a Stanine of 4,5,6
Verbal   25
Quantitative   50
Reading   30

Grade 11

Section Number of Questions Right for a Stanine of 4,5,6
Verbal   25
Quantitative   50
Reading   30

ABOUT THE AUTHORS

Elizabeth Silas graduated summa cum laude from Boston College's linguistics program. She teaches, tutors, and trains instructors for the Princeton Review in SSAT, PSAT, SAT, SAT II Writing, and GRE preparation.

Reed Talada began teaching for The Princeton Review in 1988 and has worked full-time in both New Jersey and Boston since 1991. He graduated cum laude from Drew University with a degree in Political Science.

NOTES:

NOTES:

NOTES:

NOTES:

FIND US...

International

Hong Kong
4/F Sun Hung Kai Centre
30 Harbour Road, Wan Chai,
Hong Kong
Tel: (011)85-2-517-3016

Japan
Fuji Building 40, 15-14
Sakuragaokacho, Shibuya Ku,
Tokyo 150, Japan
Tel: (011)81-3-3463-1343

Korea
Tae Young Bldg, 944-24,
Daechi- Dong, Kangnam-Ku
The Princeton Review- ANC
Seoul, Korea 135-280,
South Korea
Tel: (011)82-2-554-7763

Mexico City
PR Mex S De RL De Cv
Guanajuato 228 Col. Roma
06700 Mexico D.F., Mexico
Tel: 525-564-9468

Montreal
666 Sherbrooke St.
West, Suite 202
Montreal, QC H3A 1E7 Canada
Tel: (514) 499-0870

Pakistan
1 Bawa Park - 90 Upper Mall
Lahore, Pakistan
Tel: (011)92-42-571-2315

Spain
Pza. Castilla, 3 - 5° A, 28046
Madrid, Spain
Tel: (011)341-323-4212

Taiwan
155 Chung Hsiao East Road
Section 4 - 4th Floor,
Taipei R.O.C., Taiwan
Tel: (011)886-2-751-1243

Thailand
Building One, 99 Wireless Road
Bangkok, Thailand 10330
Tel: (662) 256-7080

Toronto
1240 Bay Street, Suite 300
Toronto M5R 2A7 Canada
Tel: (800) 495-7737
Tel: (716) 839-4391

Vancouver
4212 University Way NE,
Suite 204
Seattle, WA 98105
Tel: (206) 548-1100

National (U.S.)

We have over 60 offices around the U.S. and run courses in over 400 sites. For courses and locations within the U.S. call 1 (800) 2/Review and you will be routed to the nearest office.

www.review.com

Expert Advice

Counselor-O-Matic

Pop Surveys

www.review.com

Paying for It

www.review.com

THE
PRINCETON
REVIEW

Getting In

Word du Jour

www.review.com

www.review.com

College Talk

Find-O-Rama College Search

www.review.com

Best Schools

SAT Survival

www.review.com

We Help You Meet Your Primary Goals for a Secondary Education

Cracking The SSAT/ISEE

1999 Edition • 0-375-75168-8 • $18.00

The Secondary School Admission Test (SSAT) and Independent School Entrance Examination (ISEE) are required by over 500 independent, and Catholic schools nationwide. *Cracking the SSAT/ISEE* will help you prepare for the tests that will earn admission into the best secondary schools.

The book includes:

- practice drills
- four complete sample tests
- The Princeton Review's famous techniques for scoring high on standardized tests

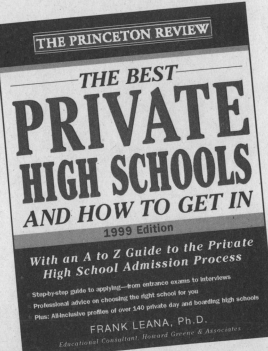

The Best Private High Schools and How to Get in

1999 Edition • 0-375-75208-0 • $20.00

Author Frank Leana, Ph.D., brings 20 years of experience as a nationally recognized expert in academic counseling for secondary school to this guide. He shares his knowledge of the private high school admissions process, telling you everything you need to know including:

- how to apply
- how to handle the interview
- taking the tests: what to expect
- financing
- how to select the right school with the help of detailed reviews of the best 140 private schools

 Visit Your Local Bookstore or Order Direct by Calling 1-800-733-3000